MW01114414

CD&I (C 116)

2 May 2016

ERRATUM

to

MCWP 3-16

FIRE SUPPORT COORDINATION IN THE GROUND COMBAT ELEMENT

1. Change all instances of MCWP 3-16, *Fire Support Coordination in the Ground Combat Element*, to MCTP 3-10F, *Fire Support Coordination in the Ground Combat Element*.

2. Change PCN 143 000059 00 to PCN 147 000041 00.

3. File this transmittal sheet in the front of this publication.

PCN 147 000041 80

To Our Readers

Changes: Readers of this publication are encouraged to submit suggestions and changes that will improve it. Recommendations may be sent directly to Commanding General, Marine Corps Combat Development Command, Doctrine Division (C 42), 3300 Russell Road, Suite 318A, Quantico, VA 22134-5021 or by fax to 703-784-2917 (DSN 278-2917) or by E-mail to **morgann@mccdc.usmc.mil**. Recommendations should include the following information:

- Location of change
  - Publication number and title
  - Current page number
  - Paragraph number (if applicable)
  - Line number
  - Figure or table number (if applicable)
- Nature of change
  - Add, delete
  - Proposed new text, preferably double-spaced and typewritten
- Justification and/or source of change

Additional copies: A printed copy of this publication may be obtained from Marine Corps Logistics Base, Albany, GA 31704-5001, by following the instructions in MCBul 5600, *Marine Corps Doctrinal Publications Status.* An electronic copy may be obtained from the Doctrine Division, MCCDC, world wide web home page which is found at the following universal reference locator: **http://www.doctrine.usmc.mil**.

Unless otherwise stated, whenever the masculine gender is used, both men and women are included.

DEPARTMENT OF THE NAVY
Headquarters United States Marine Corps
Washington, D.C. 20380-1775

28 November 2001

FOREWORD

Marine Corps Warfighting Publication (MCWP) 3-16, *Fire Support Coordination in the Ground Combat Element*, is a framework for coordinating and employing supporting arms in consonance with maneuver elements. While this publication covers many aspects of fire support, it focuses on fire support coordination in the infantry division, regiment, and battalion. The doctrine applies across the full range of military operations—from humanitarian assistance to a major theater war.

Fire support doctrine is based on a common understanding of the nature of war and on our warfighting philosophy as described in Marine Corps Doctrinal Publication (MCDP) 1, *Warfighting*. This doctrine provides for fast, flexible, and decisive action in a complex environment characterized by friction, uncertainty, fluidity, and rapid change.

This publication is a field reference guide for commanders, their staffs, and fire support coordination personnel. It forms the basis for specific fire support coordination tactics, techniques, and procedures.

This publication supersedes Fleet Marine Force Manual (FMFM) 6-18, *Techniques and Procedures for Fire Support Coordination*, dated 27 March 1992.

Reviewed and approved this date.

BY DIRECTION OF THE COMMANDANT OF THE MARINE CORPS

EDWARD HANLON, JR.
Lieutenant General, U.S. Marine Corps
Commanding General
Marine Corps Combat Development Command

DISTRIBUTION: 143 000059 00

FIRE SUPPORT COORDINATION IN THE GROUND COMBAT ELEMENT

TABLE OF CONTENTS

Chapter 3. Fire Support Planning

Section I. Principles

Section II. The Marine Corps Planning Process

Section III. The Fire Support Plan

Section IV. Supporting Arms Fire Plans

Section V. Quick Fire Support Planning

Section VI. Offensive Operations

Section VII. Defensive Operations

Section VIII. Retrograde Operations

Section IX. Other Tactical Operations

Section X. The Rehearsal

Chapter 4. Targeting

Section I. Organizations and Personnel

Section II. The Targeting Process

Chapter 5. Executing the Fire Support Plan

Section I. Fire Support Coordination Tasks

Section VI. DASC-FSCC Coordination

Section VII. Counterfire Collecting and Reporting

Section VIII. Family of Scatterable Mines

Section IX. Smoke

Section X. Illumination

CHAPTER 1. FUNDAMENTALS

Fire support is fires that directly support land, maritime, amphibious, and special operations forces to engage enemy forces, combat formations, and facilities in pursuit of tactical and operational objectives (JP 1-02). Fire support coordination is the planning and executing of fires so that targets are adequately covered by a suitable weapon or group of weapons (JP 1-02).

The Marine air-ground task force (MAGTF) is the Marine Corps' principal organization for all missions across the full spectrum of military operations. MAGTFs consist of a command element (CE), a ground combat element (GCE), an aviation combat element (ACE), and a combat service support element (CSSE). The MAGTF principally employs fire support provided by the GCE and the ACE, but may also receive external fire support from other joint, combined, and coalition forces.

MARINE CORPS WARFIGHTING PHILOSOPHY

The Marine Corps warfighting philosophy is based on rapid, flexible, and opportunistic maneuver capabilities. Maneuver warfare is a warfighting philosophy that seeks to shatter the enemy's cohesion through a series of rapid, violent, and unexpected actions which create a turbulent and rapidly deteriorating situation with which he cannot cope (MCDP 1). Fire support in maneuver warfare produces combat power and is applied through combined arms.

The MAGTF and GCE are combined arms teams by the nature of their organization. The GCE's ability to deliver fire is most effectively employed when it creates a combined arms effect. Combined arms is the full integration of arms in such a way that in order to counteract one, the enemy must make himself more vulnerable to another. It pairs firepower with mobility to produce a desired effect upon the enemy (MCDP 1). In addition to the typical example of combined arms where indirect fire suppresses an enemy, enabling

either maneuver or attack by direct fire, multiple supporting arms can create a combined arms effect. Artillery raids in the Gulf War intentionally attracted enemy counterfire to enable air attack of enemy radar and artillery units. The enemy had to suffer the effects of indirect fire or risk losing its own artillery assets. The 3d Marine air wing used a similar technique when conducting attacks against the Iraqi integrated air defense system (IADS). Suppression of enemy air defenses (SEAD) packages accompanied Marine aircraft conducting strikes against Iraqi positions and equipment. When Iraqi fire control radars were activated, the aircraft from the SEAD package attacked the radars with high-speed antiradiation missiles (HARMs). Once again, the Iraqis were placed in a dilemma. To defend against the air attacks, they placed their fire control radars in jeopardy.

Combat power is the total means of destructive and/or disruptive force which a unit can apply against the enemy at a given time. Combat power consists of tangible factors such as the destructive effect of available firepower. But, just as importantly, it consists of intangible factors such as surprise, tempo, and morale.

FIRE SUPPORT TASKS

Fire support functions are performed in relation to—

- Supporting forces in contact.
- Supporting the commander's concept of operation.
- Integrating fire support with the scheme of maneuver.
- Sustaining fire support.

Regardless of the unit supported, these tasks give the commander and his fire support representatives a frame of reference to evaluate the overall effectiveness of fires. They serve as unifying factors for supporting arms. The four tasks do not change or replace traditional missions, roles, and operations. They provide a common point of departure for all supporting arms. For example, naval surface fire support

(NSFS) in general support of a regiment does not consciously plan to perform the four tasks. It accomplishes its mission by furnishing a continuous volume of naval gunfire that supports forces in contact and the commander's concept of operation. It integrates its support with the scheme of maneuver through liaison officers who plan fire support areas (FSAs) to support the scheme of maneuver.

Supporting Forces in Contact

Prerequisite to this task is the ability to immediately respond to and meet the fire support needs of forces engaged with the enemy. This task enhances the friendly force's survivability and increases their freedom of maneuver. Individual fire support assets support forces in contact in many ways; e.g., artillery supports forces in contact by performing its traditional roles of close support and counterfire.

Supporting the Commander's Concept of Operation

This task enables the force commander to influence the battle with firepower. It gives him the means to create effects on enemy forces or functions that contribute to his mission accomplishment. Fires can shape the battlespace by attacking the enemy's center of gravity (COG) through enemy critical vulnerabilities and creating decisive combat power with a combined arms effect.

Integrating Fire Support with the Scheme of Maneuver

Integrating fire support with the scheme of maneuver requires precise arrangement of coordinated activities in time, space, and purpose to produce the most effective fires. It provides the right attack means delivered on the right target at the right time, creating a combined arms effect. Integration must occur within the supporting arms and the other warfighting functions (maneuver, intelligence, command and control, logistics, and force protection).

Sustaining Fire Support

This task ensures fire support endurance and continuity in providing fires. It involves the actions to achieve logistics sustainment and technical support for supporting arms available to the commander.

ROLE OF THE GROUND COMBAT ELEMENT

Each MAGTF element has specific roles in coordinating fire support. The CE implements the MAGTF commander's intent and normally focuses on deep operations to shape the battlespace for the major subordinate commands (MSCs). The ACE is a major provider of fire support through offensive air support (OAS), electronic warfare (EW), and unmanned aerial vehicle (UAV) support. The CSSE commander is normally assigned responsibility for the conduct of rear area operations. Since no formal supporting arms coordination agency exists within the CSSE's rear area operations center (RAOC), the CSSE may be augmented with fire support representatives. However, it is the GCE that receives the majority of fire support—its own—as well as fires provided by other MAGTF elements.

GCE fire support coordination centers (FSCCs) interact with the CE through the MAGTF force fires coordination center (FFCC). The FFCC coordinates those matters that cannot be coordinated by FSCCs within the GCE and those matters that affect the MAGTF as a whole. The MAGTF LF FFCC coordinates fires with higher, adjacent, and external commands. It is the element of the amphibious force (AF) that forms the supporting arms coordination center (SACC) with representatives from the amphibious task force (ATF). It maintains close coordination with the GCE for integrating fire support plans of the deep and close battle.

The GCE interfaces with the ACE through the Marine air command and control system (MACCS). Control and coordination of direct air support is achieved through tactical air control parties (TACPs) organic to GCE units, through the direct air support center (DASC), and through other MACCS agencies.

The GCE coordinates NSFS through naval gunfire (NGF) liaison sections including U.S. Navy personnel communicating to support ships.

The GCE plans, integrates, and coordinates all fire support within the GCE's area of operations. It plans fires, conducts targeting, and integrates fires with maneuver in close operations. The GCE plans and coordinates the delivery of its organic fire support; the delivery of fire support provided by other means (such as aviation or NSFS), or nonlethal means (such as electronic attack [EA] or electronic warfare support [ES]) that contribute to a combined arms effect. The GCE conducts fire support coordination for its own artillery and mortar fires in support of its maneuver elements. All artillery is normally organic or attached to the GCE. In MEF operations, a force artillery may be established to provide C2 for cannon and rocket artillery not attached to GCE assets; e.g., USMC Reserves, U.S. Army, U.S. Army Reserves, and Allied. The GCE coordinates with other elements, as required, and with adjacent external forces. The organization the GCE uses to perform these tasks is the FSCC.

FIRE SUPPORT
COORDINATION CENTERS

A fire support coordination center (FSCC) is a single location in which there are centralized communications facilities and personnel incident to the coordination of all forms of fire support. An FSCC exists from division to battalion levels. The fire support coordinator (FSC) organizes and supervises the FSCC under the staff cognizance of the G-3/S-3. The number of personnel and amount of equipment varies with the level of command and responsibility, the size and complexity of the forces involved, the degree of planning and coordination required, and the desires of the commander.

All echelons of the GCE establish an FSCC as an advisory and coordinating agency. The FSCC is located with the combat operations center (COC). Facilities, equipment, and material are provided by the parent headquarters. Supporting arms units provide representatives and equipment to conduct coordination, targeting, and communications functions for their respective supporting arms. Detailed listings of personnel by grade, military occupational specialty (MOS), and billet description are found in unit tables of organization (T/Os).

Division FSCC

This center plans, coordinates, and employs fire support. Supporting arms representatives identify requirements, estimates of supportability, and make recommendations to the division commander for allocating fire support. Its key role is targeting due to its assets and ability to collect and analyze target information.

Fire Support Coordinator

The division artillery officer/commanding officer, artillery regiment is the division FSC. The artillery regiment's assistant FSC performs the FSC duties when the artillery commander is absent from the division COC.

Fire Support Coordination Section

This section provides liaison to division forces for artillery control and coordination. It coordinates all supporting arms to support the concept of operations and is provided by the headquarters battery of the artillery regiment. The section consists of two assistant fire support coordinators (AFSC), a naval gunfire officer, a target information officer (TIO), a liaison chief, an observer/liaison man, and three artillery scout observers. The headquarters battery of the artillery regiment provides field radio operators and equipment to operate artillery nets.

Target Information Section

This section is normally formed upon activation of the FSCC during the initial planning phase. Duties include target acquisition, target dissemination, and attack recommendation and assessment. Target information section (TIS) personnel typically include the TIO and one to three enlisted personnel to work with the target intelligence officer (TGTINTELO) from the G-2 section. TIS personnel are provided by the artillery regiment. The TIO supervises TIS operations under the staff cognizance of the FSC. See chapter 4.

Air Section

This section of the operations section (G-3) is an organic component of HQ battalion. It consists of a division AirO and an assistant AirO. Although not a part of the division TACP in the FSCC, personnel from the division air section may augment the division TACP in the FSCC. The division AirO works closely with the FSC. Some functions of the air section are to—

- Advise the division commander, his staff, and commanders of those units not having TACPs on air support, including antiair warfare (AAW).
- Participate in forming operation plans and orders on air employment.
- Participate with the FSC in targeting and selecting appropriate means of attack.
- Prioritize and resolve conflicts in air support requests (ASRs).
- Prepare, forward, and coordinate ASRs.
- Relay pertinent information to other tactical air control elements.

Naval Gunfire Fire Section

This section establishes and maintains facilities for liaison and communications between supported units and appropriate control agencies. It informs and advises the GCE commander on employing, requesting, and controlling NGF. The section consists of a naval gunfire support officer (NGFO), an assistant NGFO (Navy), an NGF chief, and a shore fire control party (SFCP) man.

Regimental FSCC

The regimental FSCC plans, coordinates, and integrates supporting arms to support the regiment's scheme of maneuver for current and future operations. The regimental FSCC performs targeting and develops targets with its own target acquisition (TA) assets, in addition to those developed at higher headquarters. It allocates assets for the attack of targets in its area of operations. Assets include a direct support (DS) artillery battalion and available NGF and aviation. The FSCC develops the regiment's fire support plan, requests NGF and air support, and plans fires within the regiment's area of operations. The regimental FSCC allocates fire support assets to subordinate

battalions (CAS sorties, NGF ships, etc.) and assists and supervises subordinate FSCCs. The regimental FSCC coordinates—

- Clearance of fires that affect the regiment's area of operations. Normally, coordination will be conducted by subordinate battalions while the regiment monitors and effects coordination with higher, adjacent, and subordinate units, as required.
- Ingress and egress routes for all aviation missions including assault support, CAS, and reconnaissance.
- Employment of all supporting arms in support of the regiment.

Fire Support Coordinator

The DS artillery battalion commander is normally the regiment's FSC. The artillery battalion liaison officer performs FSC duties when the battalion commander is absent from the infantry regimental FSCC.

Liaison Section

This section is provided by the HQ battery of the supporting artillery battalion. It consists of an artillery battalion liaison officer, an assistant liaison officer, an observer liaison chief, two scout observer men, and four field radio operators. The section conducts artillery liaison and coordination functions for the regiment. It also operates the fire support coordination and artillery nets in the FSCC.

Tactical Air Control Party

Organic to the regiment, the tactical air control party (TACP) consists of one AirO and four field radio operators. The AirO is a special staff officer to the regiment commander on aviation matters. He is also the officer in charge (OIC) of the regiment's TACP where he functions as the air representative within the FSCC.

NGF Liaison Team

The regimental NGF liaison team is from the HQ battery of the supporting artillery battalion. It consists of a naval gunfire liaison officer (NGLO), an NGF chief, two SFCP men, and three field radio operators. They perform the same liaison and coordination functions as their NGF division counterparts.

Battalion FSCC

The battalion FSCC performs fire support coordination in terms of closely integrating multiple supporting arms with maneuver. It monitors and receives all fire support requests originating within the battalion. The battalion FSCC ensures that supporting arms are integrated with the scheme of maneuver and that friendly forces are not endangered. It may also coordinate missions for observers to attack targets outside the battalion's zone of action.

Fire Support Coordinator

The infantry battalion weapons company commander is the FSC.

Liaison Section

This section is organic to a firing battery of the supporting artillery battalion. It consists of four officers, an observer liaison chief, four observer liaison men, and nine field radio operators to support a battalion. The senior officer is the artillery liaison officer in the battalion FSCC. The remaining three officers are forward observers (FOs) and each heads an FO team to support a company. The FO team consists of the FO, a fire support man, and two field radio operators. When required, a FO team may be divided into two elements, each capable of independent operations for a limited period. More than simply calling for and adjusting artillery fires, the FO teams plan the company artillery fires and can coordinate all fire support at that level.

MCWP 3-16.6, *Supporting Arms Observer, Spotter, and Controller*, contains detailed discussions of responsibilities of the FO team, forward air control (FAC) party, NGF spot team, and mortar FO.

Tactical Air Control Party

The TACP is organic to the battalion. It consists of three aviators and twelve field radio operators. The senior aviator acts in a dual capacity as the battalion's AirO (a special staff officer to the battalion commander in regard to all aviation matters) and as the OIC of the battalion TACP. As the OIC, he works within the FSCC as the air representative. Each of the other two aviators is the leader of a forward air control (FAC) party with four communicators each. A FAC party requests and provides terminal control of CAS. More than simply calling for and directing CAS, the TACP provides input to the company fire plan.

Shore Fire Control Party

The battalion shore fire control party (SFCP) is from the HQ battery of the supporting artillery battalion. It includes a battalion NGF liaison team and an NGF spot team. The liaison team consists of an NGLO, an NGF chief, and three field radio operators. It performs liaison and coordination functions in the battalion FSCC. The spot team consists of an NGF spotter (Marine lieutenant), two SFCP men, and two field radio operators. The spot team is normally employed with a company of the battalion. However, it may be divided into two elements, each capable of independent operations for a limited period. Spot teams call for and adjust NGF.

81mm Mortar Platoon Representative

The battalion's organic 81mm mortar platoon provides a mortar liaison party to work in the battalion FSCC and four FO teams to support the companies and/or man observation posts. The mortar liaison party consists of a mortar representative, two field radio operators, and a wireman. An FO team consists of the FO, two field radio operators, and a wireman.

Separate Battalion FSCC

Separate battalions operating as maneuver elements; e.g., light armored reconnaissance or tank battalions, establish FSCCs. This FSCC functions the same way as an equivalent level infantry unit FSCC. The FSCC staff consists of personnel to provide fire support expertise; e.g., artillery, mortar, NGF or air. Personnel are organic to the separate battalion or are provided by the artillery regiment and Marine division. Tank and light armored reconnaissance battalions have a permanently assigned artillery officer as the FSC.

Company Fire Support Coordination

A company does not have an FSCC. The company commander is responsible for coordination of his fires and organizes his personnel accordingly. He is assisted by artillery and mortar observers, the FAC, and the

NGF spotter. The company commander may assign an officer as the company FSC to coordinate supporting arms with the company's scheme of maneuver.

Direct Air Support Center

The direct air support center (DASC) is normally collocated (electronically or physically) with the senior FSCC. The DASC can provide direct air support control functions to a division GCE. Support of multiple division GCEs requires assets beyond those normally found in a single Marine air support squadron (MASS). When there is more than one division in the GCE, the DASC may be augmented and collocated with the MAGTF FFCC while an air support element (ASE) is collocated with each division FSCC.

Functions of the Senior FSCC in the GCE

- Reporting pertinent information such as the location of friendly artillery units, fire support coordinating measures (FSCMs), and enemy antiaircraft weapons to other staff sections of the MAGTF FFCC for further dissemination as required.

- In amphibious operations, providing representation to the supporting arms coordination center (SACC).

- Conducting targeting functions to meet the GCE commander's intent.

- Serving on the MAGTF targeting committee.

- Establishing reporting requirements, FSCMs (for example, restricted fire areas [RFAs]), and fire support coordination procedures when existing procedures are inadequate.

FSCC ARRANGEMENT

Internal Organization

Internal organization should allow for rapid coordination and exchange of information between FSCC personnel and other staff sections. The FSCC is physically located within the COC. Its configuration may vary with the mode of operation and tactical situation; i.e., tent, HMMWV or AAVC-7A1 configuration.

The FSCC must be close enough to the G-3/S-3 and G-2/S-2 for easy information exchange. Positioning of automated information systems, maps, and status boards should facilitate sharing of information. The FSC should position himself to facilitate internal supervision of the FSCC and coordination with the G-2/S-2 and G-3/S-3.

Current automated information systems print messages and status information. However, an FSCC journal should be maintained to record significant events affecting the operation. Incoming and outgoing messages should be filed chronologically after routing. The FSCC journal provides necessary information for oncoming watch-standers. A separate fire mission log should also be maintained to keep the journal uncluttered, provide an ordered, chronological flow, and indicate mission clearance. See appendix A for a sample fire mission log. Further, FSCC personnel need easy access to all fire support nets and automated information systems. FSCC watch officers and staff noncommissioned officers must be able to closely supervise radio and automated information system operators to facilitate coordination. Fire support nets should be separate from the supported command's tactical and command radio nets. Because both types of nets are extremely busy, adjacent location can lead to increased noise in the COC and impede coordination among fire support personnel. See MCWP 6-22, *Communications and Information Systems.*

Graphics, Maps, and Overlays

As automated information systems can graphically represent information and incorporate information into individual cells, reliance on manually maintained maps is reduced but not eliminated. See FMFM 6-18.1, *MCFSS Techniques and Procedures.*

If possible, an FSCC should have three maps: two of a scale of 1:50,000 and one of a scale of 1:500,000 or 1:250,000. One of the 1:50,000 maps are used for current operations; the other for planning or when the FSCC displaces. Larger scale maps are used for aviation planning. Devices for mounting overlays and maps throughout the COC should be standardized so overlays can be interchanged quickly between the planning map, the G-2/S-2 map, the G-3/S-3 map, and the fire support coordination map. The use of colored pushpins, restrictive fire area (RFA) templates, airspace coordination area (ACA) templates, and maneuver symbols may save time and prevent critical information from being erased.

Laminate maps or cover them with acetate. Post information on overlays for unobstructed examination. The following arrangement of overlays is effective.

First, Closest to the Map

This overlay posts information that does not normally require frequent change; e.g., scheme of maneuver, FSCMs or checkpoints.

Second

Post information that normally requires frequent updating; e.g., location of friendly units including target acquisition assets or fire capability fans.

Third, Targets

This overlay is rolled down into position on the map board when required.

Fourth and Successive Overlays

Post special purpose information such as programs of fire. These overlays are removed from the map board when not used.

FSCC PERSONNEL DUTIES

Though fire support coordination roles of division, regiment, and battalion FSCCs differ, there are common sets of duties at each echelon.

Supporting Arms Representatives

Duties common to all supporting arms representatives are to—

- Advise the commander and FSC on capabilities of the supporting arm represented.
- Prepare estimates of supportability.
- Assist in preparing the fire support plan.

- Provide input to the FSC as he plans FSCMs.
- Coordinate and deconflict the delivery of fires in consonance with maneuver.

Watch Officers/Chiefs

All officers and staff NCOs assigned to an FSCC must be able to supervise the FSCC without assistance during routine operations. This requires familiarization with all supporting arms and duties of other supporting arms representatives. During critical operational periods, actual supporting arms representatives must be recalled to their positions. In establishing watch lists, duties include—

- Assignments to distribute expertise on each watch; e.g., artillery liaison officer (LNO) with NGF chief; NGLO with artillery liaison chief.
- Minimum assignment of personnel with multiple tasks; e.g., AirOs often have tasks other than fire support, such as arranging for assault support.
- Watch officers/chiefs have requisite knowledge to plan, coordinate, and execute fire missions with automated information systems.

Fire Support Coordinator

The FSC organizes, trains, and supervises FSCC personnel. Commanders delegate the authority to FSCs to control and supervise the FSCC. Duties of the FSC or AFSC are to—

- Advise the commander on fire support.
- Coordinate preparing estimates of supportability.
- Participate in the targeting process.
- Provide guidance for automated information systems; e.g., HPT, target delay time or firing asset preferences.
- Prepare the fire support plan with help from the supporting arms representatives.
- Ensure that the fire support plan can be implemented with assets available and, if necessary, coordinate with the operations officer (G-3/S-3) and the commander to request additional assets or to modify plans.
- Recommend FSCMs to the commander.
- Work with the operations officer as he plans maneuver control measures (will impact on FSCMS).

- Provide clearance on requests for fire missions and air strikes from subordinate units.

- Coordinate clearance of fires, when required, with senior and adjacent units. This may be delegated to the appropriate supporting arms representative.

- Disseminate target information received to other staff members, subordinate units, and commands requiring the information.

- Advise the commander on target selection and attack guidance.

- Maintain close liaison with the operations officer and the intelligence officer to ensure the most effective planning and application of fire support.

- Execute the attack of targets based on the commander's guidance and the targeting process.

Artillery Liaison Officer

The AFSCs provide artillery representation in the division FSCC. An artillery LNO and his liaison section is provided by an artillery battalion to regiment and battalion FSCCs. These liaison officers and sections remain with their respective supported units to allow continuity in planning and operations. Duties are to—

- Monitor the artillery conduct of fire (COF) net and provide clearance on requests for fire (battalion only). Regiment and division FSCCs monitor the artillery battalion and regiment fire direction net, respectively, to keep abreast of artillery fire planning and significant artillery missions.

- Pass requirements for fire support to the appropriate FDC for action.

- Coordinate artillery unit requirements (such as approval for displacement and resupply routes) with the supported commander and with the commander in whose area of operation the movement will occur, if outside the supported unit's area of operations.

- Remain abreast of current operations and logistics status of artillery units and keep the FSC informed.

- Keep the supported unit S-2 or TIO advised of all target information received through artillery nets.

- Keep the artillery unit advised on the plans and tactical situation of the supported unit. Examples of information passed to the artillery unit include target information, FSCMs, time checks, location of friendly units, routing of aircraft, location of minefields (friendly and enemy) and lanes through them, and other obstacles.

Air Officer

The AirO is a special staff officer at division headquarters. At regiment and battalion, the AirO is assigned to the S-3 section. At all levels, the AirO provides aviation representation in the respective FSCC. Duties are to—

- Provide aviation information and expertise.

- Pass the commander's air support requirements to the appropriate air support control agency.

- Coordinate ASRs and joint tactical air requests (JTARs) from subordinate units to ensure adequate attack of targets, avoid duplication in the attack of targets, and protect friendly units.

- Receive target information relayed through Marine air command and control system (MACCS) agencies.

- Monitor the tactical air request (TAR) net in the FSCC for information, or clearance if required, on immediate ASRs and JTARs.

- Supervise and coordinate TACP activities.

- Request SEAD fire in support of air strikes from other supporting arms representatives, as necessary.

- Maintain situational awareness on information pertaining to ASRs, prospective air support targets, assigned missions, and SEAD requirements.

- Provide necessary coordination with the DASC in support of GCE maneuvering units.

- Coordinate with the ACE when planning forward arming and refueling points (FARPs) within the maneuver unit's boundaries.

- Coordinate ingress and egress of aircraft through the unit's area of operation.

- Plan and disseminate air control measures; e.g., holding areas (HAs) or contact points.

Naval Gunfire Officer/ Naval Gunfire Liaison Officer

The NGFO is a special staff officer at the division headquarters. NGLOs are Navy officers provided by the supporting artillery battalion to the regiment and battalion FSCCs. Duties are to—

- Monitor the NGF spot nets and provide clearance on requests for fire (battalion only). The NGF support net is monitored at division and regiment FSCCs to keep abreast of NSFS information.
- Assist in transmitting requests for fire between other stations; e.g., artillery or other ground observers and NSFS ships.
- Request NGF ships to occupy specific fire support stations (FSSs) or areas for the attack of targets, mask clearance or troop safety.
- Remain abreast of ships' ammunition status and rotation schedules and keep the FSC informed.
- Supervise and coordinate SFCP activities at the battalion level.
- Keep the TIO or supported unit S-2 advised of all target information received through NGF channels.

Target Information Officer

The artillery regiment provides a TIO to work in the division FSCC TIS (when formed). The TIO is responsible for targeting. (See chap. 4.) His duties require him to work closely with the TGTINTELO in the G-2 section. Because there are no TIOs in the regiments or battalions, the FSC may have to perform some TIO duties or delegate to the supporting arms representatives. Duties are to—

- Receive reports on potential targets from the G-2/ S-2, subordinate elements, artillery units, and also from other FSCCs.

- Keep the FSC and other supporting arms representatives informed on the status of targets.
- Keep appropriate target files.
- Perform preliminary weaponeering.

81mm Mortar Platoon Representative

Each infantry battalion FSCC has a representative from the 81mm mortar platoon. Duties are to—

- Monitor the mortar conduct of fire net and clear requests to fire.
- Coordinate with the FSC on movements of the mortar platoon or any of its sections.
- Keep the FSC informed of the firing capacity of the mortar platoon, including ammunition status.
- Pass requirements for planned fires to the mortar platoon FDC.

Other Personnel

Personnel in other staff sections may be required to work closely with FSCC personnel. In addition to staff officers (G-2/S-2, G-3/S-3), personnel include special staff officers from engineer, tank, AAV, LAR, anti-tank, LAAD units, and the EWO. Input could be—

- An engineer's battlefield analysis. This input aids in terrain and route reconnaissance and gives guidance for targeting on bridges and structures.
- A nuclear, biological, and chemical defense (NBCD) officer's analysis of weather affects on smoke, chemical, and biological weapons. This input aids in targeting, particularly with regard to the hazardous effect of munitions on industrial chemicals.
- An ASE serving as a liaison for the DASC at the FSCC. Input could be to transfer requirements for air support and update the scheme of maneuver.

CHAPTER 2. FIRE SUPPORT COMMUNICATIONS NETS

Fire support communications nets are established to conduct fire support coordination as efficiently as possible with a minimum number of communications assets. Radio communications allow net monitoring by fire support agencies at each echelon. Planning considerations include available assets, number of nets required, number of stations per net, requirements for data and voice transmission, security requirements, and information flow. When the communications system incorporates data communications, planners must ensure equipment compatibility between fire support agencies at each echelon. Subscribers must configure their data terminals with the correct parameters as well as ensure messages and transmissions are addressed to appropriate agencies.

The commander is responsible for employing communications and information systems (CIS). The G-6/S-6 is responsible to the commander for all CIS planning and employment. The volume of information to be processed and analyzed to support decisionmaking is exploding and threatens to overwhelm the commander and his staff. Efficient CIS help the commander to overcome this challenge. CIS must satisfy command and control (C2) requirements of the expeditionary force. CIS must provide commanders and their staffs with the tools to rapidly collect, process, analyze, and exchange information to support planning and execution. Systems employment must not adversely affect freedom of action or mobility. Communications must be reliable, secure, flexible, and responsive.

The two original forms of communication (written and voice) have been augmented by automated information systems with a third form of communication; i.e., data. Data communications increase the speed of communicating by transmitting large amounts of information while reducing signature and enhancing survivability. Data communications require prior integration to succeed in information processing and dissemination.

SECURITY

Force protection entails communications security. Communications that can be intercepted are a lucrative source of intelligence to the enemy. However, speed and accuracy of communications are also critical to friendly operations, particularly in fire support. There may be situations when requirements conflict; e.g., insufficient encryption devices to cover all nets coupled with a requirement for rapid communications. A good rule of thumb is that *security* takes precedence on nets where targeting or fire planning information is passed (the enemy may intercept these communications and take appropriate counteraction). On the other hand, *speed* and accuracy take precedence on nets where immediate requests for fire are passed. If these communications are intercepted, there is seldom time for targeted personnel or units to react.

MAGTF TACTICAL COMMUNICATIONS NETWORK

The design of the communications network to support a MAGTF is based on the nature of the operation, the commander's intent, the concept of operations, and the composition and task organization of the MAGTF and attached and supporting forces.

In the early stages of an operation, single-channel radio (SCR) normally provides the principal means of communications. As the operation evolves, local area networks (LANs) and a switched backbone are established to meet the information transfer requirements of C2 at higher echelons and to connect to the Defense Information Systems Network (DISN). Maneuver battalions continue to depend on SCR throughout the operation with limited interface to the switched backbone. Special-purpose systems provide dedicated communications support for certain functions, such as position location and navigation and air defense.

The Marine Corps is currently fielding, or will soon field, equipment systems that will provide data transmission capability to fire support agencies at all echelons. These systems will decrease response times to requests for fire by speeding transmission time to affect necessary coordination.

Single Channel Radio

SCR is the principal means of communications support for maneuver units. SCR communications equipment is easy to operate. Networks are easily established, rapidly reconfigured, and, most importantly, easily maintained on the move.

SCR provides secure voice communications and supports limited data information exchange. VHF and UHF bands are normally limited to line of sight. Satellite communications (SATCOM) provide mobility, flexibility, and ease of operation with unlimited range. SCR limitations include susceptibility to enemy EW; cosite, footprint, terrain, and atmospheric interference; the requirement for close coordination and detailed planning; a need for common timing, frequency, and equipment; and limited spectrum availability. The latter is particularly critical in SATCOM.

MAGTF SCR equipment is fielded in many configurations and includes hand-held, manpack, vehicle-mounted, ground-mounted, and sheltered radios. These radios operate in simplex and half-duplex modes. The most widely employed tactical radios provide integrated COMSEC and jam resistance through frequency hopping.

SCR is used primarily for secure voice communications. However, SCR can also transmit and receive data by using terminal devices such as the digital message system (previously called and more commonly known as the digital communications terminal [DCT]) and the tactical communications interface module (TCIM). Tactical SCRs operate in HF, VHF, and UHF bands as shown in table 2-1.

HF Radio

HF radio equipment is capable of both long- and short-range secure voice and data communications. The primary Marine Corps HF radio is the AN/PRC-104.

VHF Radio

The primary Marine Corps VHF radio is the single channel ground and airborne system (SINCGARS). SINCGARS is a family of light-weight combat radios that serves as the primary means of communications for C2 and fire support.

UHF Radio

Military UHF radio equipment operates in the 116–150 megahertz upper VHF frequency range and the

Table 2-1. SCR.

Frequency Band	MAGTF SCR Equipment Used	Operating Frequency Range (MHz)	Typical Application
HF	AN/PRC-104 AN/PRC-138 AN/GRC-193 AN/MRC-138 AN/VRC-102	2–29.999	Radio line of sight and beyond/long range
VHF	AN/PRC-68 SINCGARS family	30–88	Radio line of sight and relay/retransmission
	AN/PRC-113 AN/VRC-83	116–150	Critical line of sight (ground to air)
UHF	AN/PRC-113 AN/VRC-83 AN/GRC-171	225–400	Critical line of sight (ground to air)
	AN/PSC-3 AN/PSC-5		SATCOM footprint

225–400 megahertz military UHF radio spectrum. UHF radios also include UHF-TACSAT radios capable of long-range communications. The primary Marine Corps UHF radios are the AN/PRC-113 and the AN/PSC-5.

Local Area Networks

Local area networks (LANs) are data communications networks that are designed to support information exchange, collaboration, and resource sharing in a particular unit, agency, facility, center, or cell in a confined geographic area. Because of the limited distances involved, LANs can support high data throughput up to 100 megabites per second, although 10 megabites is more common. LANs include terminal equipment connected to a transmission medium such as wire or fiber-optic cable. LAN media used in the MAGTF include both copper-based coaxial and twisted-pair cable used within local facilities, such as a regiment COC, and fiber-optic cable used as a higher speed backbone that connects multiple facilities in a large headquarters complex. Fiber-optic backbone LANs are also used aboard Navy ships with copper-based coaxial and twisted-pair LANs within an operational workspace such as the landing force operations center (LFOC). MCWP 6-22 contains extensive discussion on how specific LAN media, access methods, technologies, protocols, and equipment are employed to meet specific unit requirements.

Switched Backbone

The MAGTF switched backbone consists of switching, routing, and wideband transmission systems that provide a high-capacity communications backbone for the MAGTF as well as connectivity with the DISN. It is the tactical equivalent of commercial local and long-distance networks and sometimes interfaces with and uses those commercial networks. Switched backbone uses a mix of older equipment developed under the TRI-TAC program and newer equipment and technology. It is tailored to meet the requirements of a particular operation and can adapt to support the unfolding tactical situation and overall scheme of maneuver. Planning, redesign, and adaptation are continuous as switched backbone equipment and personnel arrive in theater and the MAGTF transitions to operations ashore. Larger headquarters, rear areas, expeditionary airfields, and C2 centers at higher echelons are princi-

pal subscribers. Maneuver battalions cannot be constrained by the switched backbone's inherent lack of mobility and normally link to it through an SCR interface. The MAGTF switched backbone includes switches, internet protocol routers, and wideband multichannel radio transmission systems.

The TRI-TAC family of equipment, developed in the 1970s under a joint program of the Marine Corps, Air Force, and Army and fielded in the mid-1980s, provides the major components of the MAGTF switched backbone. The Marine Corps and the Air Force employ the TRI-TAC-developed AN/TTC-42 and SB-3865 unit-level circuit switches (ULCSs). Computers play a key role in operation, maintenance, and control. Computer-controlled communications links and switching enable efficient, flexible use of limited resources. Computerized switches and routers route voice, data, and video information at various points or nodes in the network. Telephones TA-954 DNVT, TA-1042 DNVT, TSEC/KY-68/78 DSVT, and multimedia terminals (STU-III) are used to gain access. At divisions and regiments, the switching nodes that support fire support agencies are connected via tactical multi-channel radios AN/TRC-170 and AN/MRC-142.

Wire is most often used to connect cells within a COC and connect multiple automated terminals within a cell. Where the tactical situation permits, wire provides a redundancy for some radio nets. Often an FSC may want a direct wire link that does not pass through a switchboard (hotline) to the supporting artillery FDC or the TPC. Wire communications can be secured and used for voice and data communications.

Messenger

Using messengers must be planned because they provide a secure, reliable means of communications. When time permits, they may be the most effective means for sending fire support plans and overlays.

Special-Purpose Systems

Special-purpose system assets are designed to provide specific position location, navigation, information distribution, and cooperative identification services. They serve all MAGTF elements, often through externally managed satellite and aircraft relay systems, and provide real-time information to tactical users at the point of need.

Precision Lightweight Global Positioning System (GPS) Receiver (PLGR)

The AN/PSN-11 PLGR is a small, handheld, GPS receiver that weighs approximately 3 pounds. It provides precise positioning and timing solutions based on signals received from the GPS satellite constellation. Position can be displayed in virtually any format (latitude/longitude, military grid reference system, and universal transverse mercator). It contains 49 map datums. Users can program way-points for navigation with back azimuths and distances to the next way-point available with the push of a button. The PLGR is compatible with night vision goggles.

Enhanced Position Location Reporting System

The enhanced position location reporting system (EPLRS) shares many characteristics with PLRS, but provides a significant increase in data communications capability. Since various data rates supporting various broadcast and point-to-point modes are currently available, EPLRS provides a dedicated data communications capability between regiment and battalion tactical data networks (TDNs) within the GCE. This network will also be extended to lower echelons throughout the MAGTF. EPLRS serves as a source for automated friendly position location information (PLI), navigation information, and communications capability for automated systems.

Digital Communications Terminal (AN/PSC-2)

The DCT is a rugged, lightweight, microprocessor-controlled, handheld message processor. It provides Marine users at all echelons with point-to-point and netted data communications. It is compatible with most MAGTF radio, wire, and encryption equipment. It supports data transfer up to 2.4 kilobits per second in the analog frequency shift keying (FSK) mode and, depending on the transmission media, up to 16 kilobits per second in the digital baseband mode. The DCT allows the operator to enter and read data in both free text and fixed or variable message formats (VMFs). VMF is the tactical message standard adopted by

DOD for ground forces. All of the Services have agreed to use this standard.

Target Handoff System

The THS is still in the formative stages. It is designed to replace the digital messaging system (DMS). THS will provide personnel at the company level with a tactical input/output battlefield situational awareness and data communications capability. THS will be used to receive, store, retrieve, create, modify, transmit, and display fire support information and commander's critical information via tactical radios, networks, and wirelines. THS will assist the user to manage information such as positions of other units, coordinates of designated points, preformatted messages, and free text information.

Data Automated Communications Terminal

The DACT provides company fire support personnel with a tactical input/output battlefield situational awareness and data communications capability. DACT will be used to receive, store, retrieve, create, modify, transmit, and display map overlays and commander's critical information via tactical radios, networks, and wire lines. DACT will use an embedded global positioning system (GPS) receiver to display its own location, which can be automatically transmitted to other stations. DACT can assist the user to manage information such as positions of other units, coordinates of designated points, pre-formatted messages, and free-text information.

Advanced Field Artillery Tactical Data System

The AFATDS is a joint Army/Marine Corps system to replace the initial fire support automated system (IFSAS). It is a multi-Service, integrated, battlefield management and decision support system that incorporates automation into the fires warfighting function to assist the commander in planning, delivery, and coordination of supporting arms. Terminals are located in FSCCs, DASC, TACC, and artillery battalion and regiment FDCs.

Tactical Combat Operations

TCO will automate the commander's ability to receive, fuse, select, and display information from many sources and disseminate selected information throughout the battlespace. TCO attributes include automated message processing, mission planning development and dissemination of operations orders and overlays, displaying friendly and enemy situations, displaying tactical control measures, and interfacing with wide and local area networks. Terminals will be located in the MEF, DASC, TACC, and COCs of divisions, infantry battalions and regiments, artillery battalions and regiments, and LAR and tank battalions.

FIRE SUPPORT RADIO NETS

Radio nets are groups of designated stations connected to each other. They may be identified to carry either voice and/or data transmissions. Unit standing operating procedures (SOPs) should contain procedures for establishing communications and troubleshooting on voice or data nets. Data radio nets do not have the range capability of voice nets. Directional antennas help minimize this limitation. Figure 2-1 on page 2-6 shows fire support radio nets and designates control, guard, and monitor responsibilities.

The MAGTF force fires coordination (MAGTF FFC): VHF, voice/data net is activated by the MAGTF FFCC in operations that are not amphibious.

Examples of division fire support coordination (Div FSC): VHF, voice/data net traffic include fire plans, target information, and fire support coordinating measures (FSCMs). Regiment FSCCs also use this net for cross-boundary coordination of aircraft and fires.

At a lower level, the regiment fire support coordination (Regt FSC) VHF: voice/data net is similar to the division FSCC net with emphasis on traffic related to coordination and execution of fire plans. Battalion FSCs use this net to pass fire support requirements to the regiment FSC and to coordinate cross-boundary fires.

These nets will normally accommodate communications requirements for effective fire support. When used for their stated purpose, circuits do not become overloaded and remain free for necessary communications. However, if some nets become unavailable through heavy traffic, enemy interference, or equipment failure, FSCC personnel should not hesitate to use any available net to pass urgent traffic.

Nets may be used as alternate tactical or command nets by maneuver units in special situations. The number of nets plus the availability of wire provides flexible options for FSCC personnel to provide continuous communications.

MCWP 3-16 is the primary reference for fire support communications nets. See FMFM 6-18-1 for net configuring procedures for data transmission with automated fire support systems. See also MCWP 6-22.

ARTILLERY AND MORTAR RADIO NETS

Artillery Conduct of Fire (Arty COF): VHF, Voice/Data

This net provides a means for observers to request and adjust artillery fire. Artillery LNOs at regiment and battalion FSCCs monitor/receive net traffic to coordinate requests for fire. FOs and LNOs may use the net to exchange target and fire planning information. If conducting battalion-directed operations, the artillery battalion FDC establishes as many as three COF nets and acts as net control on each. The artillery battalion FDC may assign a COF net for each maneuver battalion for continuity of fire support during battery displacements. The supported unit's LNOs and FOs remain on the assigned COF net. The artillery battalion FDC receives all calls for fire (CFFs) and determines the firing battery that will provide fire support to the maneuver battalion. If conducting autonomous operations, each battery FDC maintains a COF net and acts as net control, each net is monitored by the battalion FDC when present. When observers are employing digital devices, one or more COF nets must be dedicated to data communication.

Division/GCE Artillery Air Spot: VHF, Voice

This net provides a means for aircrews to adjust artillery fire. When in use, artillery LNOs monitor for targets in their unit's designated area of operations just as they do with COF nets. FOs may use this net to coordinate with aircrews for attack of targets in their company's area of operation.

Legend:
C - Net Control
X - Guard
R - As required (When directed)

	LF FFC (VHF) (1)*	DIV FSC (VHF)*	REGT FSC (VHF)*	LF ARTY CMD	ARTY REGT CMD (HF)	ARTY REGT FD (VHF)*	ARTY REGT TAC (VHF)	DIV/GCE ARTY AIR SPOT (VHF)	ARTY BN CMD (VHF)	ARTY BN FD (VHF)*	D/S ARTY COF (VHF) (2)*	TAR (HF) (1)	TAD (UHF/VHF) (1)	TACP LOCAL (VHF)	DIV/GCE NGF SPT (HF)	NGF AIR SPOT (UHF/VHF)	NGF CONTROL (HF)	NGF GRND SPOT (HF)	SFCP LOCAL (VHF)	NGF CONTROL OVERLOAD (HF)	LF NGF SPT (HF)	BN MORTAR (VHF)
SACC (AFLOAT)	C			C												C	C			C	C	
TACC (AFLOAT)												X	X			R						
MAGTF FFCC	C			C								X				R	X				R	C
FAHQ	X																					
DIV FSCC	X	C			R	R	R	X	R			X		C	C	R					X	
DASC (ASHORE)												C	C									
INF REGT FSCC	R	X	C	R		R			R	R	X	R	X	X		C	R				R	
INF BN FSCC			X						R	R	X	X	X	C			R	C	C		R	X
SEP BN FSCC		X		R	R	R		R	R	R	R	X	X	C	R	R		C	C		R	X
ARTY REGT	R	X		R	C	C	C	C														
D/S ARTY BN	R		X	R	X	X	X	R	C	C	C											
ARTY BTRY								R	X	X	X											
RADAR BEACON TM																						
ARTY FO								R				X										
FAC												X	X	X								
MORTAR FO																						X
NGF SPOT TM																		X	X			
LAAD MISSILE TM (3)																						
FIRE SPT SHIP(S)																X	R	X	X	R	X	
MORTAR PLAT																						C

NOTES:
(1) Net control located in SACC until displaced ashore.
(2) Net control at battalion (battalion directed operations) or battery (autonomous operations).
(3) LAAD nets established as required.
* Data and/or voice nets.

Figure 2-1. Fire Support Radio Nets.

Artillery Regiment Fire Direction (Arty Regt FD): VHF, Voice/Data

This net provides a means for the artillery regiment to exercise tactical FD; e.g., transmitting orders, fire missions, fire plans, tactical information, and meteorological data to subordinate battalions. It also collects, exchanges, and passes combat and target information. Subordinate units may use it to request reinforcing fires. The artillery officer at the division FSCC may monitor this net to keep abreast of artillery fire planning and pass fire support coordination traffic if no other net is available.

Artillery Battalion Fire Direction (Arty Bn FD): VHF, Voice/Data

When transmitting voice traffic, this net provides a means for the artillery battalion FDC to exercise tactical FD of subordinate units. If tactical FD is decentralized, this net may be used by batteries to request reinforcing fires. The artillery LNO at the regiment FSCC (battalion FSCC as required) may monitor the Arty Bn FD net to keep abreast of artillery fire planning and significant artillery missions. When transmitting data traffic, tactical FD is incorporated into a COF net and the Arty Bn FD is used for coordinating reinforcing fires.

Artillery Regiment Tactical (Arty Regt Tac): VHF, Voice

This net provides a means for the artillery regiment commander to command and control subordinate units. Types of traffic include changes in tactical mission assignments and displacement or fire capability reports. It may also be used as an alternate net for FD and fire support coordination traffic.

Artillery Regiment Command (Arty Regt Cmd): HF, Voice

This net provides a means for the artillery regiment commander to command and coordinate administrative and logistical activities of subordinate units. It may be used as an alternate net for FD and tactical orders. The division FSCC may monitor this net, as required, principally as an alternate net for communicating with the artillery regiment should other nets become inoperative.

Artillery Battalion Command (Arty Bn Cmd): VHF, Voice

This net provides a means for the artillery battalion commander to command and control subordinate units. It is used principally for administrative, logistic,

and tactical traffic not related to FD. The supported infantry regiment or separate battalion FSCC may monitor this net, as required, principally as an alternate net for communicating with the DS battalion should other nets become inoperative.

MAGTF/LF Artillery Command/Fire Direction (Arty Cmd/FD): HF, Voice

This net is established in amphibious operations for rapid dissemination and coordination of fire support information. It is used for the artillery regiment and SACC to remain current on the status of artillery battalions. When the MAGTF consists of two GCEs or a force artillery, both artillery regiments and the force artillery monitor this net. The net remains active until the artillery regiment headquarters or both artillery regiment headquarters and the force artillery are ashore and have established their own command/FD nets. If only one GCE, this net normally transitions to the artillery regiment command net with the artillery regiment as net control. If two GCEs, the net normally terminates or becomes the command net of the force artillery.

Other Artillery Nets

Artillery units routinely use other radio nets for internal functions; e.g., survey, meteorology or radar telling. These nets are omitted from this publication since they do not pertain to fire support coordination and would not be required in an FSCC. They are discussed in FMFM 6-18-1.

Ground Combat Nets Monitored by Artillery

Artillery battalions and regiments monitor the supported unit's tactical and intelligence nets. Monitoring keeps them abreast of the tactical situation and able to anticipate and project fire support requirements.

Infantry Battalion Mortar Net: VHF, Voice

This net provides a means for mortar FOs to request and adjust fire on targets and for the 81mm mortar representative at the battalion FSCC to coordinate requests.

NAVAL GUNFIRE RADIO NETS

NGF ships may have limited communications terminals that can be used for fire support. When possible, the MAGTF LF should make prior coordination with the ATF to ensure that the proposed communications plan of the AF is workable by the assigned ships.

NGF Ground Spot: HF/VHF, Voice

This net provides a means for NGF spot teams to request and adjust NGF, normally between a spot team and the assigned DS ship. This net is also used to exchange vital information between stations. The battalion NGLO monitors the net to provide clearance or communications relay, if necessary.

NGF Air Spot: UHF/VHF (Depends on Aircraft), Voice

This net provides a means for aircrews to request and adjust NGF. The NGLO of the unit in whose area of operation the fires will impact monitors the net to provide clearance. NGF spot teams may use this net to coordinate with an aircrew for attack of targets in their respective company's area of operation.

Shore Fire Control Party Local (SFCP Local): VHF, Voice

The SFCP local net provides a means for the battalion NGLO to coordinate the activities of his SFCP. It is also used for the OIC of the spot team to communicate with the members of that team when dispersed.

Division/GCE NGF Support: HF, Voice

This net provides a means for NGF planning between the division/GCE NGFO officer and regiment NGLOs. It is used by divisions and regiments to assign missions to GS ships. This net can also be used by regiments to request additional NSFS and aircrews.

MAGTF/Landing Force NGF Support: HF, Voice

This net provides a means to request NSFS and coordinate employment of NSFS ships in GS of the LF.

NGF Control: NGF Control Overload: HF, Voice

This net provides the Navy amphibious commander with a means for requesting and assigning NSFS ships, making relief and emergency reports, and transmitting orders regarding the execution of scheduled fires. It is an NSFS-equivalent of the artillery command and FD nets. The SAC uses this net to coordinate NSFS ship employment. Depending on the volume of traffic or other criteria, the Navy amphibious commander may establish one or more NGF control overload nets. Examples of traffic are ammunition status and results of attack on targets. Composition is the same as the NGF control net.

AVIATION RADIO NETS

The DASC, when practical, normally collocates with the GCEs senior FSCC. Optimally, collocation is by physical proximity. However, an electronic link may be an acceptable alternative when DASC siting requirements differ from the FSCCs; i.e., necessity for line of sight (LOS) communications with aircraft, tactical or geographical considerations, and communications connectivity with other MACCS agencies. The following nets are normally found in the DASC and are monitored by the AirO in the FSCC.

Tactical Air Command (TAC)

This net connects the DASC to all other MACCS agencies.

Direct Air Support (DAS)

This net is a discreet net between the DASC and TACC used to transfer information on air support requests and mission/aircraft status.

Tactical Air Request/
Helicopter Request (TAR/HR): HF, Voice

This net connects the DASC to all potential direct air support aircraft requesters. It receives requests for immediate air support. FSCCs monitor and receive air requests and approve, deny or modify them. BDAs and emergency helicopter requests may also be passed over this net. Preplanned air support requests may be passed but should normally be passed by other means; e.g., wire or messenger. Multiple TAR nets may be required.

Helicopter Direction (HD)

This net is used by the DASC, airborne coordinators, and terminal controllers for helicopter control and coordination.

Tactical Air Direction (TAD): UHF/VHF, Voice

This net is used by the DASC, airborne coordinators, and terminal controllers to control and direct fixed-wing aircraft; e.g., FAC or FAC(A) and for an air control agency to brief support aircraft on target information and handoff to a FAC, FAC(A), or TAC(A).

Tactical Air Control Party
Local (TACP Local): VHF, Voice

This net provides a means for coordination between the AirO in the battalion FSCC and the FAC parties. Stations include the AirO in the battalion FSCC (net control) and the FAC parties.

CHAPTER 3. FIRE SUPPORT PLANNING

Planning is the act of preparing for future decisions in an uncertain and time-constrained environment. It should incorporate flexibility and, when required, enable intuitive or recognitional decisionmaking. The commander must recognize benefits and potential pitfalls of planning. He is responsible to ensure that planning is conducted properly to avoid these pitfalls. The commander disciplines the planning process and teaches the staff the relevance of product content (MCDP 5).

The goal of fire support planning is coordinating and integrating fires from armed aircraft, land-based and sea-based indirect fire systems, and electronic warfare systems that directly support land, maritime, amphibious, and special operation forces to engage enemy forces, combat formations, and facilities in pursuit of tactical and operational objectives. Fire support planning answers the question "How will fires support the scheme of maneuver?" To accomplish this, the staff determines—

- What types of targets to attack.
- How to acquire and track targets.
- When to attack targets.
- What fire support assets are available to attack targets.

- How to coordinate the attacks.
- What defines success.

The collection plan must be integrated with and supported by the fire support plan. Fire support planning provides crucial input for developing the collection plan. It links acquisition assets to finding specific enemy formations to attack or required information to answer the commander's CCIRs. NAIs and TAIs must support the requirements of the fire support plan.

The result of fire support planning must be an effective, integrated, executable, and flexible plan. An effective fire support plan clearly defines and focuses on achieving the effects required to support the scheme of maneuver, which together, form the overall concept of operation. An integrated fire support plan uses all available acquisition and attack assets and maximizes combat power to create a combined arms effect. An executable fire support plan has the time, space, and resources to achieve and assess the planned effects. A flexible plan is simple, understandable, and has the agility to support the commander's intent when the unforeseen arises through well-defined decision points. Finally, maneuver commanders and all fire support agencies must understand the plan.

SECTION I. PRINCIPLES

Fire support planning is a continuous, concurrent cycle of analyzing the enemy and friendly situation; conducting targeting; tasking and allocating fire support assets; scheduling fires; and coordinating execution to integrate fire support with the scheme of maneuver and maximize combat power. Its tangible result is a fire support plan. Effective fire support planning requires a continuous interaction between higher and lower echelons. The philosophy behind Marine Corps fire support planning is a top down, bottom up refine-

ment approach. The following principles provide guidance regardless of the tactical situation.

PLAN EARLY AND CONTINUOUSLY

To effectively integrate fire support with the scheme of maneuver, planning must begin when the commander states his mission and provides his planning guidance. The FSC should solicit that additional guidance from the commander whenever needed.

EXPLOIT ALL AVAILABLE TARGETING ASSETS

The FSC should ensure that target acquisition requirements are identified and incorporated as CCIRs in the collection plan and that target information from all available resources is rapidly evaluated. This includes information from all sources within the MAGTF.

CONSIDER ALL AVAILABLE FIRES

The FSC considers the use of available assets at both his echelon and higher. Available fires includes nonlethal means such as smoke, illumination, and EW resources. He also considers the commander's guidance for using supporting arms in current and future operations.

USE THE LOWEST ECHELON CAPABLE OF FURNISHING EFFECTIVE FIRE SUPPORT

The lowest echelon that has the means to accomplish the mission should furnish the fire support. The FSC decides what is needed and, if his own assets are inadequate, requests additional fire support from the echelon that controls the required asset.

USE THE MOST EFFECTIVE FIRE SUPPORT MEANS

Requests for fire support are sent to the supporting arm that can deliver the most effective fires within the required time. In making his decision, the FSC considers the nature and importance of the target, the engage-

ment time window, the availability of attack means, the results desired, and the number/type of assets required to achieve the desired effect.

FURNISH THE TYPE OF FIRE SUPPORT REQUESTED

The fire support requester is usually in the best position to determine his fire support requirements. However, the FSC is in a position to weigh the request against the commander's guidance and the current and future needs for fire support. If a request is disapproved, the FSC stops the request and notifies all concerned. When possible, he substitutes a new fire support means and alerts the agencies that are to provide the support and the requesting unit.

AVOID UNNECESSARY DUPLICATION

A key task for the FSC is to ensure that unnecessary duplication of fire support is resolved and that only the minimum force needed to achieve the desired effect is used. Eliminating unnecessary duplication conserves fire support assets, facilitates sustainment, and maintains tempo. This does not mean that only one asset is used. Taking advantage of the complementary characteristics of different types of assets and integrating their effects provides the synergy of combined arms.

COORDINATE AIRSPACE

Inherent in fire support coordination is the deconfliction of airspace by supporting arms. FSCMs and coordination procedures protect aircraft while incorporating CAS and DAS with indirect fires in support of close operations and deep operations. The extent of airspace coordination depends on available time. At lower levels, such coordination is performed by FACs, forward observers, and aircrews.

PROVIDE ADEQUATE SUPPORT

The mission and the commander's guidance determine the effects that fire support must achieve for the plan to succeed. The FSC must clearly inform the maneuver commander when he lacks adequate resources to support his plan.

PROVIDE RAPID COORDINATION

Procedures for rapid coordination ensure speed and flexibility in delivery of fires. Established channels for coordination facilitate rapid coordination. The FSC must know the characteristics of available fire support weapons and their status. The FSC must maintain situational awareness as the battle develops to attack planned targets and targets of opportunity.

PROVIDE SAFEGUARDS AND SURVIVABILITY

Force protection includes considerations of both friendly and enemy threats. The FSC must be aware of situations that increase the risk of fratricide. The primary mechanisms for limiting fratricide are close coordination at all levels and situational awareness. Use of FSCMs, coordination of position areas, and the locations of friendly forces during target analysis con-

tribute to safeguarding friendly units. Safety measures must minimize the potential for fratricide while not limiting boldness and audacity in combat. Fires that increase survivability include SEAD for aviation assets and proactive counter fire to ensure freedom of movement of maneuver forces.

ESTABLISH FIRE SUPPORT COORDINATING MEASURES

FSCMs facilitate the rapid engagement of targets throughout the battlespace and at the same time provide safeguards for friendly forces. They ensure that fire support will not jeopardize troop safety, interfere with the delivery of other fire support means, or disrupt adjacent unit operations. FSCMs are discussed in appendix B.

ESTABLISH COMMUNICATIONS SUPPORT

Timely and efficient exchange of information is a key requirement for all successful operations. Physical collocation of coordinating agencies provides the surest form of communication. If personal coordination is required but collocation is not possible or desired, liaison personnel are used and an electronic interface is established (voice and/or data).

SECTION II. THE MARINE CORPS PLANNING PROCESS

Fire support planning is a part of the Marine Corps Planning Process (MCPP) and is integrated with the other warfighting functions (command and control, intelligence, maneuver, logistics, and force protection). It applies the MCPP tenets of topdown guidance, the single battle concept, and integrated planning. Steps of the MCPP (figure 3-1 on page 3-4) support the Marine Corps warfighting philosophy of maneuver warfare. It helps organize the thought process of a commander and his staff

throughout the planning and execution of military operations. The MCPP applies across the range of military operations and is designed for use at any level of command. It can be as detailed or as abbreviated as time, staff resources, experience, and the tactical situation permit.

The process described is a means to an end; the final output for fire support planning must be an effective, integrated, flexible, and executable fire support plan.

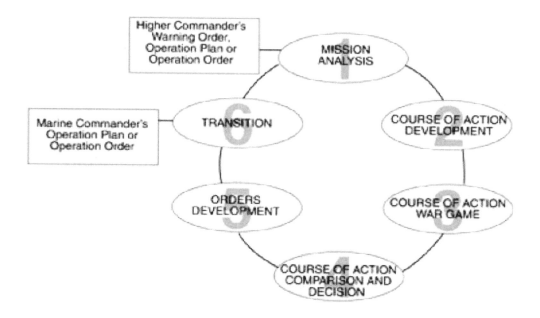

Figure 3-1. Steps of the Marine Corps Planning Process.

The process outlined here is intended to help FSCs to better understand their role in the overall planning process and the procedures to develop a thoroughly integrated and effective fire support plan. See MCWP 5-1, *Marine Corps Planning Process*.

DIVISION PLANNING

Higher echelons are generally organized with more planning capacity than lower echelons. Higher echelon planning should attempt to reduce the burden of lower echelon planning. The higher echelon's efforts are generally focused on influencing future operations while supporting current operations.

Planning includes disseminating guidance and information on targeting, anticipating requirements, allocating assets, and coordinating with higher and adjacent agencies. Planning should not impede nor substitute the planning efforts of lower echelons. Fire support planning by higher echelons seeks to—

● Support forces in contact by using fires to isolate the battlefield for current operations, and providing force protection; e.g., counterfire.

● Support the commander's plan by establishing guidance on fire support and by using fires to shape the battlespace for future operations.

● Combine the different supporting arms to shape the battlespace and set the stage or enable current operations.

● Sustain fire support by allocation and distribution of assets and by anticipating requirements and providing logistical support.

REGIMENT AND BATTALION PLANNING

Lower echelons plan concurrently with higher echelons (see appendix C). Close liaison facilitates concurrent planning. Lower echelons focus on providing close supporting fires and the coordination needed to integrate them with maneuver. Fire support planning at lower echelons seeks to—

● Support forces in contact by providing close supporting fires.

● Support the commander's scheme of maneuver.

● Integrate fire support with maneuver to create a combined arms effect.

- Sustain fire support by judiciously employing limited assets where they will have the greatest effect.

COMPANY PLANNING

Planning at the company level may use the troop leading steps commonly referred to as BAMCIS. Figure 3-2 lists the fire support actions during each step of BAMCIS. Actions may be done in any sequence or simultaneously. The company fire support planner must organize the efforts of his assets to meet all these requirements in a time-constrained environment. See MCRP 3-11.1A for more information.

MISSION ANALYSIS

Because fire support planning is a continuous process, the FSC must continually update his fire support estimate. Once a mission (or a probable mission) is identified, the efforts of the FSCC become focused. The mission statement received includes the task, together with the purpose, that clearly indicates the action to be taken and the reason. FSC's responsibilities during

TROOP LEADING STEP	FIRE SUPPORT ACTIONS
Begin Planning	Update friendly and enemy situations. Find out assets available, allocations, and FSCMs. Obtain battalion's target list worksheet, FSEM, and attack guidance. Understand the battalion fire support plan and how it affects your company. Identify fire support tasks for your company. Brief your commander on above. Receive the commander's mission. Receive the commander's fire support guidance. Participate in warning order. Issue warning order to fire support personnel and mortar section on fire support issues.
Arrange for Reconnaissance	Conduct map analysis. Plot obstacles and known enemy locations. Plot all battalion targets. List fire support tasks. Advise the commander if guidance can/cannot be met with available assets and allocations. Refine battalion targets, if necessary, and request additional assets as required. Determine if battalion targets support the commander's guidance. Plot targets necessary to support commander's guidance (within target allocation). Determine purpose, engagement criteria, trigger points, and primary and alternate executors. Develop target list worksheet. Develop FSEM. Brief commander on initial fire support plan.
Make Reconnaissance	Ensure battlefield observation is maintained. Accompany maneuver leaders on reconnaissance. Confirm or modify plan. Verify target locations, trigger points, and observation plan (primary and alternate).
Complete the Plan	Modify the plan as necessary after reconnaissance. Brief commander on the scheme of fires. Emphasize observer movement, OP requirements, and triggers. Receive approval for fire support plan. Transmit target list worksheet and coordination requirements to battalion FSCC and company mortars. Brief fire support personnel on fire support plan.
Issue the Order	Participate in company orders brief. Ensure fire support representatives and mortar section leader attend orders brief if possible.
Supervise	Conduct rehearsals. Conduct inspections as required. Continue to refine targets and triggers for actual location, ground reconnaissance or new enemy information. Continuously update and coordinate the plan as necessary.

Figure 3-2. BAMCIS.

mission analysis are primarily focused on gathering information and participating in the staff's analysis of the mission. This allows the FSC and the supporting arms representatives in the FSCC to begin developing the situational awareness crucial to building a fire support plan. Understanding the enemy situation; the intent of higher HQ; commander's initial planning guidance; identifying the unit's specified, implied, and essential tasks; determining restraints or constraints; and identifying information shortfalls provides fire support planners information and direction to continue planning.

The resulting mission statement, commander's planning guidance, and commander's intent to subordinate commands will drive planning during course of action development. During mission analysis, the staff may identify issues that will require additional guidance from the commander.

Commander's Initial Planning Guidance

Commander's guidance provides preliminary decisions required to focus planners on the commander's conceptual vision of the operation. The commander develops this guidance using his commander's battlespace area evaluation (CBAE), experience, and information on the mission from higher headquarters. The commander's initial planning guidance provides the staff and subordinate commanders additional insight on how he views the mission and the resources required to achieve the desired end state. Depending on the time available, he may provide general guidance, as well as specific points; e.g., a particular enemy capability or a certain task organization. From this guidance, the FSC begins to frame fire support's role in the plan.

This guidance is more proscriptive than commander's intent. It should address what he wants fires to accomplish (task and purpose), the focus of fire support, what he initially sees as high-payoff targets (HPTs), any force protection issues (such as radar zones), and constraints or restraints from higher headquarters. The key is to focus on the "effects" that the commander wants fires to achieve. See page 3-8. An example of commander's guidance for fire support in a deliberate attack in an urban operation follows.

1) I see our supporting arms assets accomplishing three tasks:

a) Starting with isolation, I want fires to limit the enemy's ability to reinforce and resupply forces in Obj A and Obj B through the use of complementary systems (artillery, UAV, FAC(A), and attack aviation). Position assets and integrate UAV and FAC(A) to limit the enemy's ability to move forces.

b) I see fires being used to destroy the enemy's ability to use strong-points and the upper stories of buildings through the use of field artillery and PGMs.

c) Finally, fires must deny the enemy's ability to mass a counterattack or reinforcing forces on the avenue of approach parallel to our axis of advance. We can use UAVs and FAC(A)s and positioning artillery units to fire along the long axis of the likely enemy avenues of approach.

2) The focus of fires initially is to the isolating force to aid in the isolation effort, then to scouts and reconnaissance assets along our axis of advance. In the remaining phases, the focus will be on Obj A and B to ensure the assault force has freedom to maneuver.

3) My HPTs are—

a) Initially C3, indirect fire assets, and armored vehicles operating in formation greater than a section.

b) Gaining a foothold—indirect fire assets, C3, and then strong-points.

c) Secure—counterattack/reinforcing forces, indirect fire assets, and C3.

4) My force protection priorities are on the lead forces of the assault force. Ensure that sensor zones are in place to support their movement and assault on Objs A and B. Ensure artillery units providing fire support have adequate security. Place NFAs on buildings or specific locations that may house industrial chemicals to avoid the release of hazardous material. Ensure that boundaries and FSCMs are easily discernable to ground forces and aviation assets. Ensure that positions/buildings that have been occupied by our forces are marked. (Marking must be seen by ground and air assets.) Ensure that fire support nets are supported with retransmission sites to communicate with supporting arms assets and higher HQ. Position mortars with the assault force to ensure quick response.

Within the guidance, the commander should focus much more on what he wants done to the enemy and how he sees that helping the operation to succeed. For example, "Disrupt the ability of enemy ADA to engage the lift helicopters from PZ BLUE to LZ X-RAY to allow the helo force to arrive at the LZ with its forces intact." Advantages of this guidance over "suppress ADA for the air assault" follow.

Suppress applies to artillery and mortars but does not apply to EW. By stating the affect in targeting terms, we also talk to the maneuver planner. He can support this task by planning air routes away from known or suspected ADA positions. He can choose to execute in visibility conditions that "disrupt" these systems.

The clear focus on a specific capability and when it is important helps focus the entire staff on *which* ADA is important and *when* it is important. ADA that is identified but can't affect the air route may not be high pay-off. This specificity can keep fires focused on the right target at the right time. The commander's guidance for fire support developed at this point is refined through the planning process and is later included with the above detail in the operations order.

Higher Headquarters Order

The FSC must fully understand the mission (task and intent) of the commanders two echelons above his unit. He must understand the concept of operations (scheme of maneuver and fire support plan) of his higher headquarters. Understanding the higher head-quarters plan and how his unit "fits" into the higher headquarters plan is essential to top down planning. The FSC must identify what his unit's responsibilities are to the higher headquarters' fire support plan as well as the fire support capabilities he has been allocated. These tasks may be found in the fires paragraph and the essential fire support tasks (EFSTs) developed by higher headquarters. See appendix D.

Appendix 19 and the R&S plan are also sources for tasks that the FSC and the unit must accomplish. Information from analyzing the higher headquarters order may include—

- The commander's intent two echelons up.
- Missions of higher and adjacent units.
- The future mission of the unit.
- If there are any contingency missions for the unit.
- External fire support assets made available.
- FSCMs.
- Fire support coordination procedures. An example of this requirement may exist in joint/combined operations for such procedures as cross-boundary fire support coordination, airspace management for the deep supporting fires, and targeting.

- Targeting tools (attack guidance matrix, HPT list, target list, etc.).
- Planned fires.
- Technical advice on fire support.
- Rules of engagement (ROE). ROE must be fully understood by all personnel and incorporated into the fire support plan as appropriate.
- Munitions restrictions.

See appendix E for Appendix 19 to Annex C.

Specified and Implied Tasks

Like other members of the staff, the FSC must identify specified and implied tasks. Input comes from the higher headquarter's order (fires paragraph, Appendix 19, FSEM or R&S plan) and from the unit commander's guidance. From these identified specified and implied tasks, the FSC will determine the EFSTs that must be accomplished to achieve the commander's guidance. During this portion of the planning process, the FSC should determine the task and purpose of the proposed EFSTs. EFSTs are different than the tasks normally associated with the mission or tasks paragraph. Normal tasks are directed to units to attack, defend or support to achieve a certain purpose. However, the task in an EFST is enemy oriented and uses a targeting objective to achieve a purpose that is friendly oriented. EFSTs are designed to ensure synchronization of all assets and that those involved understand their role in execution of the fire support plan and the desired effects.

Additional Constraints or Restraints

Additional constraints or restraints may be identified during mission analysis and should be reflected in the proposed fire support tasks. Topics are noted and carried forward for use in subsequent planning.

Effects of IPB on Fire Support

Intelligence preparation of the battlespace (IPB) is the primary analytical methodology used to produce intelligence in support of decisionmaking. It is a systematic, continuous, mission-focused process of analyzing the threat and the environment in the area where the operation is to take place. The IPB process is not exclusive to the S/G-2. It should include input from other special staff officers such as the engineer and NBCD officers. Avenues of approach (friendly and enemy), weather patterns and projections, time/space factors, and threat situation templates are reviewed and evaluated for their impact on operations. This analysis may identify additional information requirements. FSCs must understand and apply the affects that IPB has on fire support. See MCWP 2-3, *Intelligence Analysis and Production*. Information from IPB may include—

- Organization, capabilities, limitations, and methods of employment of the enemy. Particular emphasis is on fire support assets, direct fire weapons, aviation/air defense capabilities, and vehicle mobility.

- Likely enemy courses of action.

- Known, suspected, or likely enemy locations.

- Secure points that offer clear observation of the area of operation.

- Cover and concealment in the area of operation.

- Where obstacles are in the area of operation (manmade or natural).

- Location of key terrain.

- The weather forecast and how it will affect—
  - NVG or thermal site effectiveness.
  - Aircraft flying in a high threat environment.
  - Aircraft-identifying targets.
  - Lasers.

- Terrain's affect on mobility (friendly and enemy). Howitzers may get stuck. Mortars may take longer to move and emplace.

- Terrain's affect on communications equipment (life of batteries).

- The kinds of munitions best-suited for the terrain and weather (effects on smoke and illumination, submunitions effectiveness, and precision guided missiles [PGMs]).

- When the operation begins.

- Time available to plan.

- The expected duration of the operation.

Effects-Focused Fire Support

Effects are the results of actions—both lethal and nonlethal. The commander uses lethal and nonlethal means to obtain physical as well as psychological effects against the enemy commander. Approaching commander's guidance for fire support from an effects-focused standpoint

incorporates targeting into both the MCPP and the fire support planning process. Fire support representatives should have a clear understanding of the mission and the commander's planning guidance. Prior to the targeting effort, the FSC must thoroughly understand the commander's guidance and how it applies to fire support. It is critical that fires objectives are thoroughly integrated with the objectives of maneuver. The effects of fires should be articulated in terms of conditions and measures of effectiveness to facilitate assessment and should be included in the CCIRs. If the desired effect was not achieved, the action may need to be repeated or another method sought. At this stage, intelligence and objectives for fires should be formulated. This process must not focus on specific percentages normally associated with damage criteria, but must concentrate on the effects fires produce and what they can do to the enemy to shape the battlespace, set conditions for decisive action, and support maneuver forces. For example, not "destroy 40 percent of the enemy artillery," but "deny the enemy the ability to mass fires above the battery level for 48 hours to enable the battalion to conduct a heliborne assault."

Depending on the time available, the commander may provide general guidance and specific points he wants the FSC to consider (a particular enemy fire support capability or task organization,). Once the commander's guidance is understood, the FSC should analyze the enemy center(s) of gravity to determine the threat weaknesses that are critical vulnerabilities. (A critical vulnerability is something that a force needs to function effectively and is or can be made vulnerable to attack. Critical vulnerabilities provide an aiming point for applying friendly strengths against threat weaknesses.) The FSC identifies and plans fires against the enemy's critical vulnerabilities to hamper his ability to function, defend, attack, or sustain his forces or to command his forces. See MCDP 1-0, *Marine Corps Operations*, for more information on effects and commander's guidance.

Status of Supporting Arms

The FSC must translate data on supporting arms into meaningful capabilities. For example, artillery ammunition counts should be converted to a form that communicates capabilities to the commander; 300 M825 smoke rounds may translate to ten, 600 meter, 20 minute duration smoke screens; DPICM (600 rounds) can translate into ten, artillery battalion massed fire missions firing three volleys per mission; 200 rounds of 155 millimeter illumination can be translated into approximately 75 minutes of illumination for an area with a 1 kilometer radius (firing four gun illumination). A similar analysis can be made of any ships made available by higher headquarters for NGF. CAS sorties allocated by higher headquarters may be translated, based on type of aircraft, time on station, and ordnance load, into number of strikes available. This information will be necessary for the FSC during the planning process.

Participating in the mission analysis phase allows the FSC to develop a shared situational awareness with the rest of the staff that will help integrate the fire support plan with other functional plans to support particular COAs. From the analysis of supporting assets, effects of IPB, specified and implied tasks, and commander's guidance, the FSC will have determined proposed EFSTs. These EFSTs should be briefed to the commander during the mission analysis brief along with the refined mission statement, commander's intent, etc. It is important that the commander and the FSC have a common understanding of "what" fires will do for the unit before determining the "how." From mission analysis the FSC should have approved EFSTs and commander's guidance for fires. The FSC should issue a warning order to subordinate FSCs, observers, or supporting arms representatives. Included would be the mission of the supported unit, commander's intent and his guidance for fires, and proposed EFSTs.

COURSE OF ACTION DEVELOPMENT

The next step is developing COAs that accomplish the assigned mission. Normally, several COAs are developed for follow-on analysis, but time constraints may reduce that number. A COA must be suitable, feasible, acceptable, distinguishable (when multiple COAs are developed), and complete. The FSC must conceptualize how to integrate fires into each developing COA. As a minimum, the fire support portion of a COA should allocate target acquisition assets, attack assets, planned target areas, and create the sequence that targets will be attacked. Fire support planning is an integral portion of the concept of operations and, like other functional plans, shapes the battlespace and sets conditions that facilitate mission accomplishment. It

cannot be a separate plan developed in a vacuum. Depending on time available, the FSC may have to prioritize the one or two key fire support tasks and targeting objectives in enough detail to facilitate COA wargaming and selection.

Begin Targeting

The targeting process begins during mission analysis and provides initial input for fire support and collection planning. Targeting requires an assessment of the terrain and enemy, without regard to unit boundaries, and identifies those enemy formations, equipment, facilities, and terrain that the enemy commander requires to successfully complete his mission; i.e., high-value targets (HVTs). Attacking these targets would be expected to seriously degrade important enemy functions in the friendly commander's battlespace. After these HVTs are identified, the FSC begins to refine the list to identify those targets whose loss to the enemy will significantly contribute to the success of the proposed COA; i.e., HPTs. This refinement continues during COA wargaming and allows the FSC to develop specific tasks for fire support that affect these targets in the manner required by the COA. Initial plans may be made for acquiring, tracking, attacking, and assessing actions taken against HPTs.

At the highest level of command within the GCE, the targeting process begins with the IPB and target value analysis (TVA) for the entire area of operation. The commander, the G-2/S-2, the G-3/S-3, and the supporting arms representatives focus targeting efforts to support the scheme of maneuver. This interaction is the foundation of building collection and fire support plans. Targets are developed and disseminated to lower echelons with any tasks for the attack of specific targets (top down).

Lower echelons conduct targeting concurrently with higher echelons. Lower echelons plan targets to meet their commander's requirements. Targets are compared with those provided by the higher echelon. Requests for targets to be added to the target list are submitted to the higher echelon for action (bottom up refinement).

When the tactical situation permits, targets are disseminated as soon as possible. If using overlays, the receiving unit fastens the overlay to its map and identifies gaps or duplications in coverage without the need to plot individual targets (figure 3-3). Automated information systems (IFSAS and AFATDS) can rapidly share and update target lists. AFATDS can analyze targets (based on guidance) and determine target duplication without plotting any targets. See appendix F for AFATDS information.

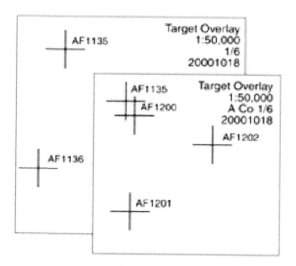

Figure 3-3. Target Overlay Technique.

The target list is a tool for recording planned targets. It must be kept current and as short as possible. Targets are deleted when they are destroyed or no longer of value. New targets are added as required. Targets essential to one operation, or phase of an operation, may not be essential to the next. For example, an offensive operation may not require the same targets as that for the defense. When transitioning from one operation or phase of an operation to the next, previously planned targets that remain valid should be retained with the same target number. This reduces the number of changes to the target list and makes record keeping easier.

Targets that can be planned and approved without coordination with another unit and those that have been coordinated are submitted directly to the appropriate supporting arm or FSCC. While a target list may be maintained at any echelon, the infantry, tank, or LAR battalion FSCC is usually the lowest echelon maintaining a list since it is responsive to the companies and has fire support representatives to disseminate changes. The target list worksheet is a useful tool to identify targets to be engaged by supporting arms along with scheduling requirements when digital communications are not available. Information contained in the target list worksheet can be disseminated via data or voice transmission from the lowest to highest echelons.

Quantify Desired Effects (Success)

As the FSC and the staff build the COA and determine how to accomplish each EFST, they must first try to quantify desired effects. It is a clear means of telling subordinate elements what they have to do. Supporting assets also use this quantification of effects to determine the ammunition or attack parameters to accomplish the EFST. The FSC and staff must focus on what must be done, not on what can be done. If it is determined that the desired effects cannot be achieved with the allocated assets, then the method must be reworked or additional assets requested. However, broad categorizations of the enemy are almost never achievable when associating a percentage to damage criteria (30% = destruction, etc.). Effects should be expressed as a measurable action of combat effectiveness that enables maneuver to accomplish a mission or task; e.g., limit the enemy's ability to mass indirect fires above the platoon level for 48 hours to enable the battalion to cross the river.

Table 3-1 on page 3-11 shows the differences between targeting objectives and effects of fires. Targeting objectives are tied directly to the maneuver commander's guidance and what must be done to the enemy to meet the commander's desired effects of fires.

Plan the Method for Each Fire Support Task

The FSC determines fire support and acquisition asset requirements to accomplish the fire support tasks assigned to each supporting arms agency. Requirements are expressed in amounts and types of fire support and acquisition assets. Initial requirements are prepared and then refined during COA analysis and wargaming. Formats for recording of requirements are contained in MCWP 3-24, *Assault Support*, MCWP 5-1, and MCWP 3-31.1/NWP 3-09.11M, *Supporting Arms in Amphibious Operations*. If requirements surface subsequent to allocating attack resources, requests for additional resources are forwarded to the next higher echelon. Requests for additional resources can take the form of radars, recon, JSTARs, radio bn, reinforcing fires, or identifying specific targets to higher headquarters for attack by their resources.

Table 3-1. Difference between Targeting Objectives and Effects of Fires.

TARGETING OBJECTIVES	EFFECTS OF FIRES
DISRUPT: To not let the enemy perform a specific function.	HARASSING FIRE: Fire designed to disturb the rest of the enemy troops, curtail movement, and, by threat of losses, lower morale.
DELAY: To not let the enemy perform a specific function when he wants to.	SUPPRESSING FIRE: To create a temporary or transient degradation by an opposing force of the performance of a weapons system below the level needed to fulfill its mission objectives. Normally associated with duration.
LIMIT: To reduce options or COAs available to the enemy.	NEUTRALIZING FIRE: Fire that is delivered to render a target ineffective or unusable. The unit has degraded capability of accomplishing its mission.
DESTROY: To ruin the structure, organic existence or condition of an enemy target that is essential to an enemy capability.	DESTRUCTION FIRE: Fire delivered for the sole purpose of destroying material objects to render a unit incapable of accomplishing its mission.
DIVERT: To force the enemy to tie up critical forces or resources from one area to another.	

Fire support capabilities must be allocated for each COA. Allocation establishes what capabilities all commanders have to employ. Allocation is essential for concurrent planning at lower echelons. The MAGTF apportions air and NSFS capabilities for a specific use; e.g., a certain percentage of air for CAS or a certain number of ships for support. These capabilities are then allocated to subordinate units; e.g., number of sorties for CAS or assignment of tactical missions to NSFS ships. Artillery is allocated by assigning tactical missions. See Appendix O.

Task Target Acquisition Assets

The S-2, S-3, and FSC must work together to build the R&S plan to identify which asset, based upon the COA's scheme of maneuver and priorities, can accomplish the task and a plan getting that asset into a position to execute the fire. Along with identifying the tasks fire support assets must achieve, acquisition assets must be allocated and tasked to observe the attack of the assigned EFSTs and provide feedback for assessment.

Priority of Fires

Fire support may be further allocated by assigning priority of fires. Priority of fires provides guidance to organize and employ fire support means in accordance with the relative importance of a unit's mission and establishes the priority in which calls for fire will be answered. Priority of fires may be given for all fire support assets or a specific supporting arm.

Positioning

Allocation of fire support will effect the positioning of fire support assets (artillery, mortars, and NSFS). For example, positioning an artillery battalion with a tactical mission of direct support in proximity to the area of operation of a supported regiment facilitates support to that unit. Positioning also includes the location of target acquisition assets (weapons locating radars, observers, etc.) to acquire targets and observe fires. Positioning requires close coordination with maneuver units' S-3s.

Ammunition

Ammunition is a major consideration for allocating fire support. Ammunition expenditures may be tightly controlled when ammunition supplies are restricted. If ammunition restrictions are such that one fire support means cannot provide adequate support, other fire support sources must be considered. It may be necessary for the ground commander to consider modifications to the scheme of maneuver to compensate for the ammunition shortage. Ammunition allocation can be expressed in terms usable to the commander such as a number of battalion or battery volleys, minutes of illumination for a specific sized area, number of targets, number of specific-sized mine fields of a specific density, or sorties of CAS available.

To provide close fire support or set the conditions for maneuver to exploit, timing of fires is crucial. The FSC must understand the tentative timing flow of the scheme of maneuver to establish triggers. These triggers should be refined during COA analysis, through subordinate refinement, and rehearsals.

Test Feasibility

As the FSC and staff develop COAs, they must apply doctrinal or accepted planning factors to ensure the plan is feasible. Factors can come from the Marine Corps Combat Readiness Evaluation System (MC-CRES), T&R manuals, other "book" answers, or educated guesses based on previous experiences.

Assist S-2 in Collection Plan Refinement

The FSC must coordinate with the S-2 to ensure there are adequate, redundant collection assets integrated with the detect phase of the targeting process. Observers, terminal controllers, counter-mortar/battery radars, and sensors should be incorporated in the FS plan and the collection plan.

During COA development, the FSC has functioned within the staff process. As a result, the tentative fire support plans for each COA should be incorporated and integrated with the schemes of maneuver. Outputs from this phase should be a tentative plan for each COA. These fire support plans should include the—

● Concept of fires, describing how fires will support the scheme of maneuver to accomplish the commander's intent. It is a sequencing of EFSTs.

● Draft fire support execution matrix (FSEM).

● Draft target list worksheet and overlay.

● Draft target synchronization matrix.

● Collection/reconnaissance and surveillance plan.

COURSE OF ACTION WAR GAME

This step examines friendly COAs against threat COAs. It allows the staff to adjust identified problems or weaknesses in the friendly COAs. Wargaming is a technique that aids COA analysis. It can be done formally or informally. Formal wargaming is a disciplined, interactive mechanism that examines the execution of friendly COAs in relation to threat reac-

tion. Informal wargaming may be as simple as a "what if" conversation between the commander and selected staff officers. Whether formal or informal, wargaming relies heavily on tactical judgment and experience. It allows the staff to gain a common vision of the operations and to test the plan against the array of possible enemy and friendly actions. Wargaming provides the FSC with the opportunity to validate or refine the fire support plan.

Continue Targeting

Refinement of HPTs continues. Wargaming may identify additional HPTs or invalidate previously identified HPTs from COA development. Changes in HPTs must be coordinated for inclusion in the refined collection plan for acquisition, tracking, and assessment. Other targeting tools, such as the attack guidance matrix (AGM), may require refinement after wargaming.

War Game Fire Support Tasks

Fire support tasks are wargamed with the scheme of maneuver for each friendly COA against possible enemy COAs. This provides a means to test the fire support plan's effectiveness and its integration with the scheme of maneuver. Wargaming can—

● Validate existing fire support tasks.

● Identify refinements to existing tasks (including assigning the task to another supporting arms agency).

● Identify additional fire support tasks.

Refine Fire Support Requirements

Wargaming assists the FSC in validating or refining the previously identified requirements that accomplish the fire support tasks. Identifying additional or reassigning specific fire support tasks to other supporting arms agencies can require the FSC to revise his fire support requirements for each COA analyzed.

Adjust Fire Support Allocation

Allocating fire support capabilities may require adjustment based on refinements to COAs made during wargaming.

Prepare Estimates of Supportability

For deliberate planning, each supporting arms commander or representative in the FSCC may prepare an estimate of supportability. The estimate of supportability analyzes the area of operations, enemy capabilities, and each COA proposed to the commander. It cites advantages and disadvantages of each COA from the viewpoint of a particular supporting arm. The estimate may be a written document and/or presented as a formal briefing. In detailed planning, a concept of operations and fire support tasks may be developed for each COA. If time is short, the estimate may be expedited and explained in as much detail as the tactical situation requires. This may take the form of the supporting arm commander, or his representative, providing a verbal estimate of that supporting arm's capability to support a contemplated COA. A formal estimate of supportability is normally only done during deliberate planning above the battalion level.

At the conclusion of wargaming, the FSC should have adjusted the fire support plans of each COA. As outputs to this step, the FSC should have final drafts of the fires paragraph and information required in appendix 19, such as FSEM, target overlay or TSM. See appendix G for sample estimates of supportability.

COURSE OF ACTION COMPARISON AND DECISION

This step evaluates, compares, and decides the COA that best accomplishes the mission. The FSC must be prepared to brief his estimate of supportability of each COA to the commander. The level of detail for his brief will vary depending on the commander's evaluation criteria and level of participation in the wargaming.

Course of Action Evaluation

Each COA is evaluated against the commander's evaluation criteria. The FSC should normally brief the method to accomplish each fire support task along with the advantages and disadvantages of each COA from the perspective of each supporting arm. The FSC may decide to have his supporting arms representatives brief the latter information. Advantages and disadvantages are then discussed and recorded. A comparison (figure 3-4) can assist the staff in making recommendations for a particular COA.

Course of Action Comparison

The staff ranks each COA with respect to advantages and disadvantages in addition to evaluation criteria such as mission accomplishment, EFSTs, and warfighting functions. These ranks are totaled and compared. This comparison gives the commander the information he needs to make a sound decision. However, these rankings may be more subjective than objective numbers indicate. For example, one COA may be determined to be the "best" but it may not be supportable by one of the warfighting functions. The commander must consider this and determine if additional support is required or if the COA must be adjusted or thrown out. Figure 3-5 on page 3-14 is an example of a comparison matrix.

Commander's Decision

The commander compares COAs and selects the COA that best accomplishes the mission. The commander may identify portions of the selected COA for further refinement by the staff. Once the commander selects a COA, warning orders may be issued to subordinate commanders and appropriate supporting arms agencies.

CRITERIA	COA 1	COA 2	COA 3
Advantages	RISK—Lowest risk.	COUNTERFIRE—Simplicity.	MSN/TASKS—Best means of accomplishing EFST.
Disadvantages	FIRES—EFSTs difficult to accomplish.	C2—Difficult to control due to mobile plan.	RISK—Accepts most risk.

Figure 3-4. COA Comparison: Advantages and Disadvantages.

CRITERIA	COA 1	COA 2	COA 3
Intelligence	3	2	1
Force protection	2	1	3
Maneuver	2	1	3
Decisive action	3	2	1
Simplicity	3	2	1
Movement—number and length	2	3	1
Mission/fires—accomplish EFSTs	3	2	1
Counterfire	1	3	2
Command and control	2	3	1
CSS supportability	3	2	1
Other	2	1	3
TOTAL	26	22	18

Figure 3-5. Comparison Matrix.

ORDERS DEVELOPMENT

Orders development articulates the commander's intent, guidance, and decisions into a clear, useful form that will be understood by subordinates and supporting arms agencies that must execute them. Orders may be written or verbal, depending on time available.

Finalize Targeting Decisions

Final refinements to targeting decisions are made based on additional guidance or modifications specified by the commander during the COA comparison and decision brief. Plans must be finalized for acquiring, tracking, attacking, and assessing actions taken against HPTs. It is crucial that plans for assessing the effectiveness of attacks provide feedback to the FSC in a timely manner to determine requirements for re-attack. Final targeting products should include, at a minimum, the HPT list, target selection standards, and attack guidance matrix.

Finalize Essential Fire Support Tasks

Final refinements to the fire support tasks identified by the commander during COA comparison should be incorporated into the concept of operations. Schedules of fire, FSCMs, and an FSEM are adjusted, as required, to reflect any modifications to the tasks.

Finalize Engagement Areas

An engagement area is an area where the commander intends to trap and destroy an enemy force with massed fires of all available weapons. The engagement area development process is vital to achieving the commander's intent. It compels the FSC to consider such factors as the number of indirect fire assets available, training proficiency of observer/firing unit, the enemy's direction/rate of march, trigger and intercept points, terrain analysis, anticipated enemy actions, and the amount of time the enemy can be expected to remain inside the area. The process requires forethought, analysis, and mathematical calculation. See table 3-2 on page 3-15.

Table 3-2. Engagement Area Development Process.

Step 1	Visualize how the enemy will/might attack.
Step 2	Select where and how to engage the enemy.
Step 3	Position forces to engage the enemy with direct fires.
Step 4	Position obstacles to support direct fires.
Step 5	Plan indirect fires to support direct fires and obstacles.
Step 6	Complete the plan, select/prepare final positions, site obstacles, and triggers.
Step 7	Rehearse.

Finalize Triggers

Triggers are a physical point on the ground or an action or event. During offensive operations a trigger is often a maneuver action or event. In the defense a trigger is more often a physical spot on the ground. Trigger development sequence determines the—

- Position on the ground that you want to engage the enemy or to silhouette the enemy with fires.

- Enemy rate of movement. This may be done by estimation, on the basis of past experience, from doctrinal literature, or from scout reports of enemy speed.

- Time of flight of the rounds from the weapon system firing the mission.

- Processing time; i.e., time required from the call for fire to rounds being fired from the weapon system.

- Total mission time; i.e., the time of flight plus processing time.

- Trigger point. Place the trigger point the required distance from a planned target location based on the total mission time x speed of enemy = distance.

Observation Plan

The observation plan is an integral portion of the fire support plan. It should provide the task and purpose for each phase of the operation. The observation plan should be synchronized with the scheme of maneuver during the MCPP. Construct an observation plan in concert with the S2 and S3. The FSC should plan to have observers/sensors in position to support the maneuver commander's intent and each EFST. The observation plan should address where the observer/sensor needs to be, security, communications, how the observer/sensor gets into and out of position, what the observer/sensor is to accomplish, and disengagement criteria if necessary.

Effect Coordination

Coordination promotes the development, understanding, and subsequent execution of the fire support plan. Proper coordination is key to responsive coordination during execution of operations. FSCC representatives should, at a minimum, conduct the following tasks.

The fire support plan provides the detailed, logical sequence of fire support events executed by each supporting arm to accomplish their tasks. It includes the individual fire support plans of each supporting arm. These plans explain how each supporting arm will accomplish its fire support tasks and execute the supported commander's fire support plan. The supported unit provides the necessary planning information; e.g., timing of fires or special instructions, for supporting arms to conduct their fire planning. See section IV.

The FSC coordinates preparing the fire support plan with other supporting plans for the operation; e.g., obstacle/barrier plan, surveillance and reconnaissance plan, and C2 warfare plan.

The level of detail in the fire support plan varies with the tactical situation and time available. When time is abundant, the plan may be recorded in a formal format such as Appendix 19 to Annex C of the Operations Order. When time is short, certain aspects may occur without a need for documentation; e.g., orders to reposition fire support units may be issued verbally and accomplished while the plan is finalized. Documentation in these situations should include information to execute the fire support plan. This information should include, at a minimum, the following:

- Concept of operation.
- Fire plan and tasks for each supporting arm.
- Target priorities and attack guidance.
- Priority of fires.
- Target list update.
- FSCMs.
- Fire support coordination procedures that are not covered in SOPs.
- Restrictions or changes in restrictions.
- Schedules of fire.

TRANSITION

The transition provides a successful shift from planning to execution. Successful transition ensures that those charged with executing the order have a full understanding of the plan. Transitions may include briefs and rehearsals to increase situational awareness of the subordinate commanders and the staff, and instill confidence and familiarity with the plan.

Rehearse the Fire Support Plan

The rehearsal is an effective transition drill. A combined arms rehearsal is key to synchronize all warfighting functions before execution. Key fire support points that should be highlighted during the rehearsal include synchronization of the fire support plan with the scheme of maneuver, target execution responsibilities (primary and alternate observers), artillery and mortar positioning and movement plans, and verification of target acquisition. Plan FSCMs, CAS employment, and verification of windows to mass battalion fires.

Adjust the Fire Support Plan

Refinements are adjustments to the fire support plan by subordinate elements. Refinements are crucial in top down fire support planning. These refinements would include changes to the observation plan and target locations based on the subordinate unit's analysis of the terrain and selected scheme of maneuver. The higher

FSCC receives changes and approves or denies them. Choices the FSC has for target refinement include—

- Numbering targets every five rather than sequentially; e.g., AD 1000, 1005, 1010. If this method is used, the FSC increases the regiment's target number by one (AD 1005 to AD 1006), determines the appropriate target location, and sends the refinement information to the regiment. Once the refined targets are plotted and approved, the regiment FSC then forwards the accepted refinements to other subordinate elements and fire support assets. By using this method, all involved will understand that the target has been refined but is executed in accordance with the original intent.
- Maintaining the original target number but adjusting the location. This does not clutter the target list but FSC's must ensure that all elements receive and incorporate the adjusted location.
- Using a battalion target number. Battalions can quickly target enemy locations but not all elements will have the refined location.

As the tactical situation dictates, the FSC recommends changes to the fire support plan to the commander. The FSC is responsible for effecting the changes the commander approves. The means for disseminating changes should be established in advance; e.g., messenger, wire, or radio (data or voice) transmission. If during fire planning, a supporting arm determines that certain support cannot be provided, they notify the appropriate FSC who then adjusts the fire support plan. The FSC may drop targets from the fire support plan or reassign them to another supporting arm. Figure 3-6 on page 3-17 shows fire planning using the MCPP.

MISCELLANEOUS

Message Routing Protocol and Clearance Procedures

Message routing protocol determines routing of a request for fire; i.e., whether it goes initially to the FSCC or supporting arm. Both decisions depend on communications net structure, type of transmission (data or voice), expected volume of traffic, and the training level of the FSCC. Routing requests for fire can be centralized and decentralized.

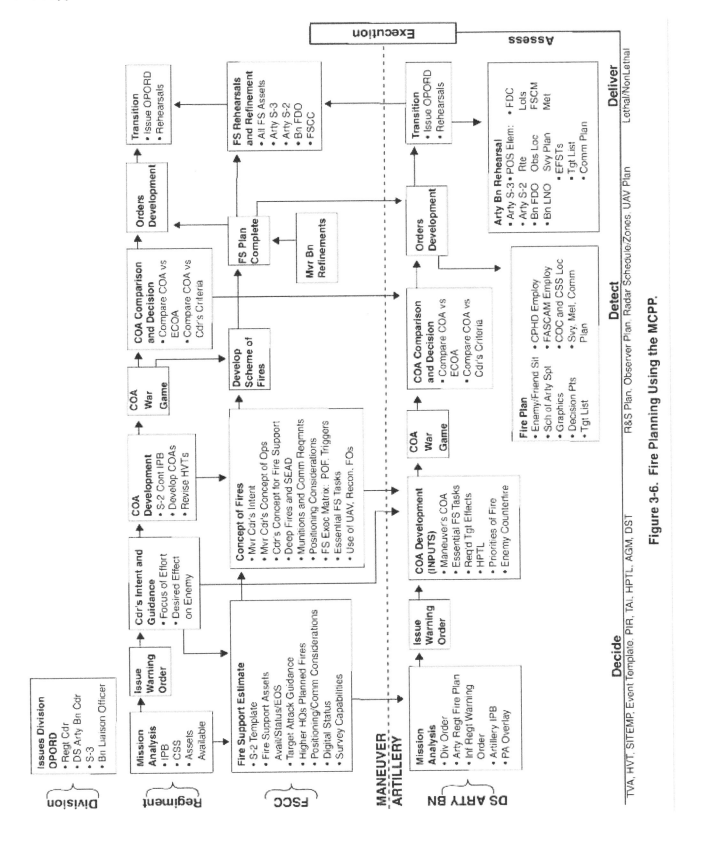

Figure 3-6. Fire Planning Using the MCPP.

In the centralized option, all requests for fire are sent to the FSCC for approval and then relayed to the appropriate supporting arm. The advantage of this option is the ability of the FSCC to modify, coordinate, and clear every mission. The FSCC may be the only unit in direct communication with observers when operating on a dispersed battlefield. The primary disadvantage is the delay caused when mission coordination/deconfliction occurs prior to forwarding the mission to the appropriate supporting arm. In amphibious operations, the higher echelon FSCC may be in the SACC.

In the decentralized option, requests for fire support are sent directly to the supporting arm (NSFS ship, artillery/mortar FDC, DASC). The supporting arm processes the mission while the FSCC concurrently coordinates and clears or denies the request for fire. Advantages to this option are the speed that concurrent processing and coordinating provides and the ability of the observer to communicate directly with the supporting arm for clarification or special missions (FPFs, Illumination, or Copperhead). Disadvantages to this option are the possibility of firing an uncoordinated mission when employing passive clearance and the requirement for the observer to maintain communications with the supporting arm.

Two options for clearing requests for fire are positive and passive approval. They specify the communication required between the FSCC and the supporting arm before firing or engaging a target.

Positive clearance requires a transmission from the FSCC to the supporting arm indicating clearance or denial. This includes NSFS requests. NSFS spotters and ships must wait for the FSCC to provide clearance before giving "Ready. Break. Fire." Voice transmissions indicating clearance or denial must be sufficiently different to avoid the chance of misunderstanding. For example, "Artillery on grid 123 456 cleared," for approval, and, "denied clearance on grid 123 456," are unmistakably different. Data transmissions use a plain text message stating the target number and cleared/denied. The supporting arms receipt of a call for fire from the FSCC can indicate mission clearance when utilizing centralized FSCC message routing.

Passive clearance (silence is consent) does not require a transmission from the FSCC to the supporting arm to clear the mission. The supporting arm assumes the mission is cleared unless the FSCC indicates the mission is denied. This requires the FSC to quickly determine conflicts that may necessitate cancellation of the mission and perform the required coordination. The FSC should acknowledge that the message/mission has been monitored to preclude conflicts resulting from loss of communications whether using voice or data transmission. Passive clearance can only be used in conjunction with decentralized FSCC message routing.

Acquire Clearance to Fire on Targets

Obtaining clearance to fire on targets is generally associated with fire support coordination during execution; however, during final planning, preliminary coordination can be effected. Preliminary coordination facilitates the execution of fire support plans and attack of targets outside the requesting unit's area of operation. The unit requesting fire support is responsible for obtaining approval for the attack from the unit in whose area of operations the target is located. The unit granting the approval for the fires notifies the requesting unit of changes which may negate the approval. Those requests for fire support which require special coordination through higher or adjacent headquarters, or where special restrictions apply, are passed to the next higher echelon FSCC as soon as possible. Clearance of targets within a unit's zone can also be coordinated to expedite the execution of targets and provide a scenario where passive clearance may be used.

Establish Fire Support Coordinating Measures

Fire support coordinating measures are tools that can facilitate the rapid attack of targets and provide safeguards to friendly forces. The type and number of fire support coordinating measures are dependent on the tactical situation. The early and prudent establishment of fire support coordinating measures can make planning and execution of fire support more efficient. Planning the establishment of fire support coordinating measures must be in conjunction with the establishing of maneuver control measures such as boundaries. FSCs should be careful not to use FSCMs as maneuver control measures and visa versa (i.e., the FSCL should not be used as a forward boundary).

Coordinate the Positioning of Fire Support Assets

The FSC must coordinate the positioning of fire support assets so they can respond to fire support requirements. Positioning of fire support assets and movement/displacement plans are coordinated to speed movement, ensure availability of support, and maintain tempo. Movement priorities and passage procedures must be coordinated to facilitate artillery units moving through the supported unit's area of operations. This may be the most critical function of fire support planning in terrain where movement is restricted to roads.

Coordinate Fire Support Delivery Procedures and Observation Coverage

Procedures for delivering fire to any unit in the supported units area of operations which do not have assigned observers must be coordinated. Plans to provide observation of the area of operations should be coordinated with the S-2, S-3, and company commanders. Examples include locating target acquisition assets to observe planned fires, determining how a reconnaissance team will fire a planned target, or disseminating PRF codes for observers and preset munitions.

Coordinate Fire Support Communications

The FSC must work closely with the operations and CIS officers to ensure that communications planned to coordinate fire support are adequate.

Establish Restrictions on Fires, As Required

A commander may wish to limit the use of certain types of ammunition in his area of operation or place restrictions on the attack of specific targets or target sets. These restrictions must be clearly articulated to both his subordinate commanders and the supporting arms agencies. Examples of these include restrictions on use of smoke, illumination, improved conventional munitions (ICM), and family of scatterable mines (FASCAM) or placing targets on a restricted target list or a no strike target list.

Coordinate the Delivery of Specialized Munitions

Certain munitions (improved conventional munitions, smoke, FASCAM, illumination, etc.) have the capability to produce unintended effects on operations of both the units employing them and those adjacent to the employing unit. Employment of these munitions must be coordinated to ensure effectiveness to the supported unit without hindering operations of others nearby. For example, the uncoordinated delivery of illumination could reveal another units location, restrict the use of night vision devices, and injure friendly personnel with empty carrier projectiles.

Effect Other Required Coordination

Additional coordination may be required depending on the situation, mission, and the type of operation being planned. Examples may include identification of LF representatives in amphibious operations, fire support for rear area operations, integration with aviation operations (air defense conditions, airspace control and coordination procedures, SEAD procedures, etc.), and integrating command and control warfare (electronic attack, electronic deception, etc.) with the fire support plan.

Disseminate the Fire Support Plan

The fire support plan is disseminated to those units that will use or provide fire support. It should be distributed as soon as it is prepared and should not be delayed to await preparing other documents. When the fire support plan is a complex document, it is often best to disseminate it in segments (such as tabs and enclosures) as soon as these are complete and approved by the commander.

SECTION III. THE FIRE SUPPORT PLAN

This tactical plan prepared by the FSC contains the information for employing fire support assets. It identifies specific maneuver units responsible for engaging targets with identified fire support assets at a specific time or event. It is the basis of how each supporting arms agency conducts its own fire planning. The fire support plan consists of essential information. Some information must be written and disseminated to subordinate and supporting units for execution. The extent of documentation depends on the quantity and type of data to be disseminated, time available, training of personnel, and the adequacy of SOPs. The FSC uses the format that best meets his needs.

AS PART OF THE BASIC ORDER

When the fire support plan is included in the basic order, the amount of detail depends on the echelon of command and the level of detail to be included.

At company and battalion levels, the concept of fires normally is part of the concept of operations paragraph. This paragraph is written to include both direct and indirect fire support assets. Depending on the level of detail necessary, the fires paragraph created during the planning process may be included as the indirect fire portion of the fire support paragraph to show the integration of direct and indirect fires in support of the concept of maneuver.

Should the operation order not include any annexes, then the remaining portions of the fire support plan, such as the FSEM, schedules of fire and observer plan, would be included as attachments to the order.

Within the concept of operations the concept of fires paragraph (3.b. (2)) shows the overarching requirements that fire support will achieve to meet the commander's intent. The concept of fires is the sequencing of the task, purpose, and identified asset from each essential fire support task (EFST) (see appendix D) in sequence with the concept of operations. The remaining detailed information can be found in appendix 19 to Annex C. See the following sample paragraphs.

3b. ( ) Concept of Operations.

   (1) ( ) Concept of Maneuver.

   (2) ( ) Concept of Fires. 1/1 will initially use artillery and NSFS to disrupt the enemy regiments reconnaissance ability to identify and report our battle positions and obstacle locations to allow 2/1 to remain undetected within its battle positions, prepared to maximize fires within engagement area (EA) Mack. R/W CAS and artillery will be used by 2/1 to delay the advanced guard main body of the enemy regiment west of phase line Iowa to enable 1/1 to conduct rearward passage of lines with 2/1.

AS APPENDIX TO ANNEX C

The operations annex provides substantive guidance for the planning of the concept of operations. Within the annex, fire support is included as subparagraph (t) of paragraph 3, Conduct of Operations. This will normally refer to Appendix 19, Fire Support, but may be used as another location for the fire support plan, which includes the concept of operations for fires, should a separate appendix not be required. See MCWP 5-1.

The fire support plan may be written as an appendix (appendix 19) to the operations annex (annex C) of an OPORD or OPLAN. The appendix contains information to convey the commander's plan for fire support. It restates the current situation and the fires paragraph. The execution paragraph includes the commander's intent and each supporting arm's tasks.

The appendix contains tabs that complement the basic fire support plan; e.g., air fire plan, artillery fire plan or fire support coordination plan. If individual fire plans are not tabbed, then separate paragraphs stating fire plans and each arm's concept of operations should be included. Fire support coordination guidance, if not tabbed, is stated as a separate paragraph. Tabs provide detailed information or products typically included with the fire support plan, such as:

● Individual fire plans.

● The fire support coordination plan.

- Targeting.
- The Marine Corps fire support system plan.
- Enclosures.

The fire support appendix provides complete and detailed information on the fire support plan. Administration and logistics states specific command guidance for ammunition management, but primarily references the logistics annex (annex D) and combat service support (annex P). The command and signal paragraph identifies the necessary command relationships and the communications support for the plan. However, adequate time must be available to prepare a detailed document.

FRAGMENTARY ORDER FIRE SUPPORT PLAN

A frag order fire support plan is a fire support plan prepared using a shortened format. See appendix H for an example frag order fire support plan with quick fire support planning.

Commander's Guidance

The commander spells out how fire support will support the scheme of maneuver. He establishes what, where, when, and why fire support must accomplish to support the overall plan. This may be graphically depicted as a fire support execution matrix (FSEM). The FSEM is a concise, simple tool that graphically shows the fire support events associated with particular events in the scheme of maneuver. It can show when certain fires occur, who controls them, and priorities of fire. The FSEM shows activities of all supporting arms. The commander provides instructions and critical information essential to executing the plan; e.g., ammunition allocation, changes to attack guidance, and new FSCMs.

Those targets closely tied to the scheme of maneuver and are critical to the success of the operation are disseminated with the frag order fire support plan. See appendix I for targeting and execution tools.

AS PART OF THE BASIC FRAGMENTARY ORDER

Another option for disseminating the frag fire support plan is to place it in the basic fragmentary order (FRAGO). Fire support information normally consists of changes to an existing fire support document (appendix or frag fire support plan). The fire support plan may be a new FSEM, commander's guidance, or a list of specific fire support tasks, depending on the tactical situation.

SECTION IV. SUPPORTING ARMS FIRE PLANS

Each supporting arm and its representatives in the FSCC conduct fire planning. Their fire planning consists of those activities necessary for them to coordinate employment of their weapons to support the concept of operations. Scheduling fires, determining provisions for attacking targets of opportunity, positioning of firing units and observers, coordinating communications and CSS, and computation of firing data (as applicable) are examples of fire planning information. Fire planning information required by the supported unit to employ a specific supporting arm is contained in applicable tabs to the fire support plan. Detailed procedures, instructions, and information for use by the supporting arm is recorded in applicable annexes to the operation order.

The desired effect is a major consideration in fire planning. It influences selecting the weapon, type and amount of munitions, and the required time of delivery. Availability and characteristics of the weapons and munitions, troop dispositions (unit locations and proximity to targets), and the scheme of maneuver are also considered. The goal is to use the best available weapon munition combination to achieve the desired effect on approved targets.

AIR FIRE PLAN

Aviation assets are made available through an apportionment process. Apportionment (air) is the determination and assignment of the total expected air effort by percentage and/or by priority that should be devoted to the various air operations and/or geographic areas for a given period of time (JP 1-02).

The MAGTF commander works closely with and may receive taskings from higher commanders in the apportionment process. The MAGTF commander, based on recommendations by the ACE commander, determines the allocation of aviation effort within the MAGTF. The ACE commander also makes recommendations to the MAGTF commander for distributing its allocated CAS sorties. Air control measures are established to allow aircraft maneuverability while minimizing interference with indirect fires. AirOs in the GCE identify/anticipate aviation requirements and pass tactical air requests up the chain of command. Requests are reviewed for approval or disapproval, prioritized, modified as required, coordination initiated, and (if approved) forwarded to the next higher echelon. Once all requirements have been identified, prioritized, and approved, they are passed to the TACC, where the MAGTF direct support portion of the ATO is prepared.

The AirO prepares the air fire plan to provide air support information to the supported unit. It is made in coordination with the supporting ACE and development of the air operations annex, which addresses aviation specific procedures and information. The air fire plan provides information on immediate and preplanned CAS (scheduled or on-call). With preplanned CAS, Marines from the GCE may track their JTAR request numbers on the ATO in any of the following ways:

- Review the given air day air support list (ASL) in AFATDS. Confirm mission status for each request submitted, and open the request to review mission data. If further information is needed, review the ATO in AFATDS.

- Submit a request to the DASC to review a given request status through the ATO/ACO tool (AAT Browser) in TBMCS using the "Re" field as the basis of query.

- Use the "find" feature of the Execution Management Control (EMC) of TBMCS to search for mission line comments containing GCE request numbers. Before operations start, MAGTFs should develop a numbering system for preplanned requests. Specific blocks of numbers are assigned to subordinate units. Predetermined numbers allow requesting units to follow their requests from initiation to execution. The request number stays with the request as it is processed through the FSCCs to the Marine TACC. The published ATO includes the request number. Examples of other information in the air fire plan include—

- Aircraft alert status.
- Coordination measures and procedures incident to air safety.
- An air target list annotated with necessary attack instructions.
- Applicable air delivery procedures; e.g., target marking or SEAD.
- Laser PRF codes.
- Air request procedures.
- Graphic illustration of all preplanned air strikes.

When possible, reference is made to other publications and parts of the OPORD; e.g., SOPs or the air operations annex. For more discussion on air fire planning, see MCWP 3-23, *Offensive Air Support*.

Planning not only directs and coordinates actions, but generates shared situational awareness. The more liaison between the supported unit and the ACE, the quicker the plan can be developed and effectively executed.

ARTILLERY FIRE PLAN

The fire plan of the artillery battalion in direct support of an infantry regiment or separate battalion is done by the artillery battalion S-3. He plans the fires of any reinforcing artillery. The S-3 receives target information, fire support requirements, and guidance/input from artillery LNOs, the artillery regimental S-3, and the artillery regimental S-2. Fire support tasks assigned to the artillery are the basis for his fire plan. The artillery battalion S-3 prepares the artillery battalion's fire plan and forwards applicable portions of it (schedules of fires, firing positions, movement plans, etc.) as early as possible to the supported unit for approval. A copy is also sent to the artillery regiment along with requests for additional fires. The completed fire plan is distributed to the firing batteries and reinforcing artillery.

Artillery LNOs also receive the plan and ensure that all FOs are notified and, if necessary, can observe fires planned in their sectors. The artillery unit continues its planning to ensure that the required support can be rendered (positioning of firing elements, ammunition availability, firing restrictions, etc.).

The artillery regiment S-3, in coordination with the AFSC and G-3, prepares the artillery fire plan for the division's fire support plan. The artillery fire plan incorporates the requirements of subordinate artillery units and fire support requirements of the division. The plans of the battalions assigned the direct support mission are reviewed, duplications eliminated and necessary additions/changes made, and integrated into the division artillery fire plan. The fires of artillery battalions in general support reinforcing (GS/GS-R) are planned by the artillery regiment. These fires are employed on targets requested by the artillery battalions in DS, targets identified by the artillery regiment, and targets designated by the division commander.

The artillery regiment may also plan counterfire. Based on the complexity of the counterfire plan, a separate tab may be required. The counterfire plan addresses how counterfire will be prosecuted and assigns unit counterfire responsibilities.

The artillery fire plan is normally done in FDCs. However, some planning tasks may occur in the supported unit's FSCC (division or regiment) when multiple supporting arms are being integrated into the fire support plan (counterfire procedures, scheduling of fires, etc.). Remaining artillery fire planning tasks are then performed at the appropriate FDC (fire direction, resupply, and positioning to meet the fire support requirements, etc.).

81MM MORTAR FIRE PLAN

Fire planning for the infantry battalion mortar platoon is normally done by the platoon commander or platoon sergeant. They receive target information, fire support

requirements, and guidance/input from the FSC. Fire support tasks assigned to mortars are the basis for the mortar fire plan.

Fire planning for the company mortar section is normally done by the company commander or his designated representative. As with the 81mm mortars, fire support tasks assigned to company mortars are the basis for the company mortar fire plan.

NAVAL SURFACE FIRE SUPPORT PLAN

The MAGTF's NSFS requirements are submitted to the appropriate naval component commander. He examines overall Navy and MAGTF requirements and subsequently allocates NSFS assets to support the MAGTF. In amphibious operations, an NSFS plan is prepared by the MAGTF NGLO who coordinates closely with the AF FFC/FSC in planning NSFS. The MAGTF NGLO provides information on the MAGTF concept of operations; e.g., scheme of maneuver, that allows the AF to plan NSFS employment to meet MAGTF requirements; e.g., positioning of fire support areas and stations. The use of NSFS depends to a large degree on hydrography, number, and type of ships available, and on the commander's priorities and guidance.

The MAGTF NSFS plan contains pertinent information and instructions taken from the AF NSFS plan. Subordinate echelons may simply refer to higher echelon plans and not issue a separate plan. NSFS plans normally include specific instructions on the tactical use of NSFS. The NSFS plan contains an NSFS operations overlay, a schedule of fires, and instructions on communications and reports. Upon deployment, much of the planning between the supported unit and the supporting ship may occur via radio or teletype. See MCWP 3-31.1/NWP 3-09.11M, *Supporting Arms in Amphibious Operations*, for more information on NSFS fire planning.

COUNTERFIRE PLAN

Enemy fire support systems can potentially inflict serious damage on friendly maneuver forces, fire support systems, and supporting infrastructure. Therefore, the enemy's fire support system, which includes the cannons, rockets, mortars, target acquisition, C2, and logistics elements, must be eliminated as a viable threat. Proactive counterfire is a vital consideration for both maneuver and fire support planning. Proactive counterfire should be integrated into the MAGTF and GCE commanders' battle plans and not fought as a separate battle. The fire support coordinator is responsible for establishing a proactive counterfire plan based on the commander's priorities and guidance. Location of target sets, capabilities of sensor platforms, and ranges of available weapon systems dictate counterfire responsibilities. Usually, the MAGTF is responsible for proactive, deep counterfire, establishing overall priorities, and allocating resources. The presence of a force artillery, when augmented with USA Q-37 radar and rockets, provides a deep, reactive counterfire capability as well. The artillery regiment, in support of the division, provides organic radar assets to the GCE for reactive counterfire, and can serve as a counterfire headquarters.

Counterfire is either proactive or reactive. Mid- to high-intensity conflicts demand an aggressive, proactive counterfire effort to limit or damage hostile fire support systems. This requires allocating proportionate target acquisition and delivery assets at the MEF and division level. In reactive counterfire, designated fire support assets respond to enemy mortar and artillery fires during or immediately following enemy engagement of friendly forces.

In the offense, friendly counterfire should initially focus on enemy long-range weapon systems used to conduct hostile counterfire missions. It is a critical element for friendly forces to generate the necessary momentum and to counteract enemy artillery.

In the defense, counterfire should focus on artillery formations supporting ground attacks and on the enemy's counterfire systems. Attack systems must be positioned to meet the enemy's main effort with counterfire target acquisition elements focused on the most likely avenues of approach where the enemy is expected to concentrate his indirect fire weapons.

Available assets should be emplaced for maximum lateral and in-depth coverage.

Two primary concerns of the FSC when creating a counterfire plan are radar zone management and establishing quick fire channels.

In radar zone management, the maneuver commander's guidance should include top-down planning and bottom-up refinement guidelines, priorities within the unit's sector for radar zones and most importantly, assigned responsibility to facilitate the plan's execution. Timely information quickly shared with the artillery battalion S2 will ensure accurate critical friendly zones (CFZs) are emplaced to provide responsive counterfire and force protection when the maneuver elements are most vulnerable to enemy indirect fires.

To clarify radar zone management and incorporate the maneuver commander's guidance, a proper planning sequence must be followed. Radar zone planning must be structured around a simple sequential process. See appendix J for radar zone management.

In quick fire channels, the headquarters responsible for counterfire planning can establish a direct link to the supporting arm to attack the target (quick fire channel). This is particularly effective for reactive counterfire.

SUPPORTING ARMS IN AMPHIBIOUS OPERATIONS

Amphibious operations are the most complex of all military operations. They are often conducted by forces who have been brought together shortly before the operation begins. Success of the operation requires a common understanding of standard fire support coordination procedures between all joint forces. MCWP 3-31.1/NWP 3-09.11, *Supporting Arms in Amphibious Operations* contains detailed information on supporting arms TTPs for amphibious operations.

SECTION V. QUICK FIRE SUPPORT PLANNING

Quick fire support planning responds to immediate problems using fire support assets available. Authority has already been given for a supported unit to plan fires of one or more supporting arms. Normally, time does not permit detailed evaluation of targets and fire planning by fire support agencies. The FSC, assisted by supporting arms representatives in the FSCC, identifies targets to be engaged, allocates available fire support assets to engage the targets, schedules associated fires, and determines other pertinent information. He then disseminates the plan to all appropriate supporting arms agencies for execution. General preparation steps follow.

RECEIVE THE OPERATION ORDER AND COMMANDER'S GUIDANCE

Determine the—

- Concept of operation.

- Targets to be engaged.

- Desired effects on targets.

- Order and timing of target engagement.

- Duration of fires.

- H-hour.

- Priority of fires.

- Estimated rate of movement.

- Time check with commander and supporting arms elements.

DETERMINE AVAILABLE ASSETS AND ISSUE WARNING ORDERS

Determine the—

- Firing units from the artillery battalion in DS that will be designated to execute the plan.

- Availability of the mortar platoon.

- Availability of NSFS.

- Availability of OAS (i.e., the number of sorties, aircraft type and ordnance, time on station, and method of control).

SCHEDULE TARGETS

Schedule targets in accordance with the scheme of maneuver, commander's guidance, and allocated assets. The quick fire support plan may be disseminated using voice or data transmissions. Figure 3-7 on page 3-26 is used for either method. The schedule includes designation of asset to be used; shell/fuze combination or ordnance mix; duration of fire for each target; and time to fire.

DISSEMINATE

Disseminate the plan to the fire support agencies, higher headquarters FSCC, and subordinates, as required. The plan may also be transmitted by radio or wire.

FIRE PLAN _ _ APPLE _ _ _ SUPPORTING _ _ 2/4 _ _ _ _ ORIGINATOR _ _ _ _ _ _ _ _ MODIFICATIONS BY _ _ _ _ _ _ _ _ _ _ _

_ _ _ _ _ _ _ _ 1240 _ H-HOUR _ _ _ _ _ _ _ _ _ _ _ _ _ _ SHEET _ _ _ OF _ _ _ _ _ DATE/TIME GROUP _ _ _ _ _ _ _ _ _ _ _ _ _ _ _ _

	(a)	(b)	(c)	(d)	(e)
LINE	TARGET NO.	DESCRIPTION	LOCATION	ALT	REMARKS
1	AD 5011	BUNKER	420267	160	
2	AD 3001	AT GUN	416268	220	
3	AD 0421	AT ROCKET	412260	210	
4	AD 3092	OP	409271	170	
5	AD 3093	OP	421261	180	
6					
7					
8					
9					
10					

			SCHEDULE		
	(f)	(g)	(h)		(i)
LINE	ORG	FIRE UNITS	TIMINGS -5 H -5 -10 -15		REMARKS
1	1/12	A	AD 3092 / 36 (a) AD 5011 / 36 (b)		
2		B	AD 3093 / 36 (a) AD 3001 / 42 (b)		
3		C	AD 3093 / 42 (b)		
4					a. 95% BMK 50% VT
5					b. VT
6					
7					
8					

Figure 3-7. Quick Fire Support Plan Form.

SECTION VI.   OFFENSIVE OPERATIONS

The FSC should focus on tasks, command and control (C2), and planning.

TASKS

The following examples of fire support tasks may be required during offensive operations based on the tactical situation and the mission.

Provide Fire Support in the Preparation Phase

Attack targets as part of a deception effort. Use smoke to screen the movement of friendly forces preparing for the attack. Disrupt enemy defenses before the attack by engaging enemy indirect fire weapons and OPs, reserves or second echelon forces, C2 centers, logistic and assembly areas, and front-line defenses.

Support the Movement to Contact and Potential Meeting Engagements

Provide immediately responsive fires to leading elements. Attack deep targets with massed indirect fires and air support. Implement an aggressive counterfire plan to prevent enemy indirect fires from unnecessarily delaying the advance. (This requires rapid artillery radar cueing.) Make maximum use of preliminary coordination.

Provide Support During the Attack

Use all available fire support means to destroy, neutralize or suppress targets that could impede or react to the attack.

Plan Fires During Consolidation

Protect friendly units during reorganization. Break up enemy counterattack. Prevent enemy reinforcement, disengagement or resupply.

Provide Support for Exploitation

Provide mobile, flexible fire support for maneuvering units. Place fires on bypassed enemy pockets of resistance to fix them for attack by a more suitable means of fire or by follow-up forces. Provide fires to slow enemy retreat.

COMMAND AND CONTROL

In the offense, the attacker has the initiative and can concentrate maneuver forces and firepower at the time and place of his choosing. A balance between centralized and decentralized control of fire support assets should be maintained to allow responsive fires, massing of fires, and shifting of fires as the main effort shifts.

PLANNING

Make plans as detailed as time allows before the attack. Make maximum use of the FSEM and the attack guidance matrix. SOPs should be well understood.

Make fire support planning and coordination flexible for execution at lower echelons. Allocating fire support to subordinates and simple coordination procedures will facilitate this.

Make speed in execution easier by planning priority targets, on-call targets, and schedules of fires; e.g., groups or series.

Anticipate CAS requirements. Coordinating the assignment of alert status; i.e., ground or airborne can increase responsiveness. Attack helicopters may be positioned forward in designated holding areas. Plan for airspace coordination.

Plan only essential targets. Cancel targets no longer needed and update targets; e.g., descriptions and locations, as the supported unit moves forward.

Use permissive FSCMs well-forward to accommodate speed of advance and preclude endangering friendly forces. Use on call FSCMs and to the maximum extent possible, key their activation to existing maneuver control measures; e.g., phase lines.

Provide continuous adequate fire support coverage within the zone of action.

Position indirect fire weapons well-forward.

Consider the assignment of route precedence to indirect fire units.

Consider replenishment of units.

Plan for continuous communications. Make use of radio relays, brevity codes, and signals. Use wire and messengers during preparation and shift to radio when the attack has begun.

Maintain close and continuous coordination with the FSC of the designated reserve unit to facilitate fire support if the reserve is committed.

Plan observation, including target acquisition, adjustment of fires, surveillance of prearranged fires, and battlefield surveillance. Observers must be positioned where they can see the battlefield. Remember reconnaissance teams, aircrews, and artillery weapons locating radars.

The rest of this section identifies other considerations appropriate to specific offensive operations. They should be used as a guide. They are not all-inclusive nor do they always apply.

MOVEMENT TO CONTACT

Assign priority of fires to the main effort.

Plan fires on critical points along the route of march.

Plan priority targets.

Plan fires to support the momentum of the supported unit; e.g., screens, suppressive fires on bypassed enemy defenses or obstacle clearing.

Consider laser designators positioning. Some may be positioned with the lead units. (See appendix K for employing lasers.)

Ensure communications for calling for fire.

Ensure FSCs in trailing and adjacent units coordinate and pass information continually.

Consider positioning FOs, FACs or spot teams in overwatch positions.

Plan for hasty attack contingencies.

Plan for SEAD and counterfire.

HASTY ATTACK

Give priority of fires to the main effort.

Plan fires on known and/or suspected enemy direct fire positions.

Plan electronic attack of critical targets when assets are available.

Plan priority targets.

Plan fires on likely assembly areas.

Plan fires on the objective, on gaps, and beyond the objective to exploit success.

Use smoke to obscure line of sight of enemy observers and to screen friendly movement.

DELIBERATE ATTACK

Plan fires to—

- Support the maneuver's attack on the objective.

- Prevent the enemy's withdrawal from the objective.

- Create a gap in the enemy's defenses or to cause him to react where he becomes vulnerable; e.g., fires to disrupt his direct fire weapons to facilitate maneuver of the supported unit.

- Attack enemy indirect fire assets to keep them from firing on friendly forces as they advance.

Consider using preparation fires on the objective coordinated with maneuver.

Attack targets beyond the objective to prevent reinforcements and resupply.

Plan smoke on flanks and crossings of exposed areas.

Plan fires on flanks of supported unit's advance to prevent counterattack or reinforcement; e.g., FASCAM.

Plan electronic attack on critical targets when assets are available.

Ensure fire support is positioned and supplied to provide continuous support during the attack.

RAIDS

Prepare detailed fire support plans to cover all phases of the operation and foreseeable emergency contingencies; e.g., aborting mission before reaching objective.

Fires may be directed against the objective immediately before the attack.

Plan fires to prevent reinforcements, screen the raid force, and support a withdrawal.

EXPLOITATION AND PURSUIT

Use supporting fires to maintain momentum.

Plan fires to suppress bypassed pockets of resistance.

Consider FASCAM on bypassed units to immobilize them but use caution for the safety of follow on forces.

Consider the use of CAS and attack helicopters to attack fleeting targets.

Restrictive fire lines (RFL) may be required between exploiting and converging forces.

Plan to shift FSCMs in advance of the supported unit.

SECTION VII. DEFENSIVE OPERATIONS

In the defense, the battlefield is organized into the security area, the main battle area (MBA), and the rear area. See MCWP 3-1, *Ground Combat Operations* and MCWP 3-15.1, *Antiarmor Operations*, for a detailed discussion on the conduct of the defense.

SECURITY AREA

Tasks

Engage the enemy with fires beyond the security area to create confusion and cause him to deploy early.

Provide adequate and continuous close support for committed units of the security force.

Maintain close liaison and communications with the MBA for withdrawal of the security force.

Command and Control

Assign on-order tactical missions to artillery units in the covering force to facilitate egress to the MBA.

Organize the covering force, including its own artillery, to operate independently.

Centralize control of fire support during battle handover.

Support the covering force in the division fire support plan. Regiment and battalion FSCs perform most fire support coordination in the covering force.

Clearly delineate the procedure for transfer of C2 for fire support responsibilities between security forces and forces in the MBA.

Planning

Centralize planning and coordination as much as possible to facilitate withdrawals, battle handoff, etc.

Plan fires to neutralize enemy reconnaissance elements and to slow, stop or canalize enemy movement.

Plan and coordinate routes, positions, communications, and control of fires with the MBA for the supported maneuver units.

Plan, coordinate, and disseminate permissive FSCMs to facilitate rapid engagement of enemy forces.

Plan FASCAM (air or artillery) to canalize and slow enemy forces.

Plan fires to cover obstacles.

Plan CAS on known concentrated enemy positions, but retain on-call CAS for immediate reaction when the enemy's main attack is discovered.

Plan screening or obscuring smoke in front of friendly positions to reduce enemy observation and to facilitate withdrawal to subsequent battle positions.

Establish communications procedures and radio nets for calls for fire and coordination/clearance during the rearward passage of lines.

Plan fires on enemy C2 elements and key enemy vehicles to cause confusion, force early deployment, break up formations, separate tanks from infantry, and force tanks to button up.

Plan fires to cover disengagement and repositioning of supported maneuver elements.

Plan fires to complement direct fire weapons.

Position lasers forward to overwatch the likely avenues of approach.

Plan target acquisition to detect targets for deep attack; e.g., reconnaissance, UAVs, and sensors.

Coordinate any electronic attacks to protect friendly communications required during withdrawal to subsequent battle positions.

MAIN BATTLE AREA

Tasks

Mass fires to canalize and slow enemy forces. Plan fires/FASCAM on obstacles to disrupt enemy breaching efforts and to fix enemy units. Use fire support to isolate enemy forward echelons. Use smoke and other fires to assist supported units in disengaging and moving. Plan fires to separate infantry from armor.

Command and Control

Make contingency plans and implement based on the enemy main effort.

Maximize use of wire communications including laying wire in advance to planned alternate positions.

Centralize control of fire support.

Planning

Plan massed fires on enemy avenues of approach. Plan engagement areas within the battle area using all fire support means available.

Plan fires on potential enemy overwatch positions and observation posts.

At battalion level, coordinate supporting arms fires with direct fire weapons, including antitank guided missiles (ATGM). Integrate fires with obstacles to slow and canalize the enemy for better shots from direct fire weapons or other supporting arms.

Establish final protective fires (FPFs) and allocate them to units with the main defensive effort. Artillery and mortar FPFs should be planned and closely tied to direct fire final protective lines (FPLs). Ensure that everyone understands who is to order firing the FPF, under what conditions, and when; i.e., the signal or code word.

Plan on-call CAS for lucrative targets such as armored formations.

Develop a fire support plan for the counterattack.

Reinforce obstacles with fire. Consider FASCAM to augment the existing obstacles and/or re-seed breached minefields.

Use smoke screens behind forward enemy elements to isolate them and break up their formations. Smoke can be fired behind the enemy during daylight to silhouette.

Plan CAS employment; e.g., responsive airspace coordination or alert status. Air support is planned on deep targets and those targets that can be attacked as the situation develops using on-call missions and search and attack methods.

Plan fires to support disengagement and repositioning maneuver forces.

Plan for counterfire. Consider a counterpreparation to disrupt enemy preparation fires. Use all available assets. Air support can be employed on-call and in search and attack missions against deep counterfire targets.

Plan fires to bring the enemy under fire early or to withhold fires until the enemy reaches designated positions or trigger points to effect surprise. Figure 3-8 shows a trigger point.

The FSC must work closely with the G-2/S-2 to synchronize fires with the enemy's movement. The time distance table in appendix L may make this easier.

See appendix L for more information on targeting, symbology, and scheduling.

REAR AREA

Fire support planning and coordination in the rear area is complex. The rear area may contain a large number of combat support and combat service support (CSS) units. This density and the challenge of timely exchange of information between fire support agencies and the CSS unit's parallel chain of command can increase the chance of fratricide. Commanders may choose to require positive clearance for missions requested in the rear area. See MCWP 3-4.2, *Rear Area Operations*.

Establish liaison with the force controlling the rear area.

Allocate or designate fire support to support a rear area contingency plan.

Identify fire support request procedures, means of observation, and communications links for fire support for a rear area contingency.

Determine the ammunition requirements for any rear area contingency.

Designate fire support elements by on-order missions.

Make liaison early between the GCE unit with the on-order rear area mission and the rear area operations center (RAOC).

Rear area units fire support plans must be incorporated into the MAGTF's fire support plan.

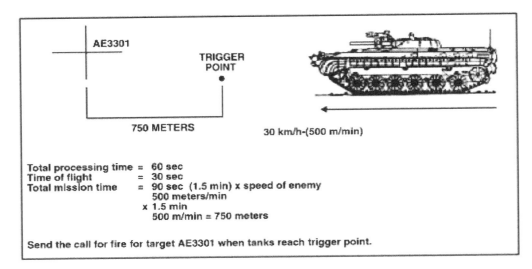

Figure 3-8. Trigger Point.

SECTION VIII.   RETROGRADE OPERATIONS

The three types of retrograde operations are delay, withdrawal, and retirement. Since retirement is conducted by forces not in contact with the enemy, there are few fire support tasks other than positioning fire support in the retirement column so they can readily respond if needed.

DELAY OPERATIONS

Tasks

Attack the enemy forces far forward. Assist combat units with disengagement fires. Cover obstacles, gaps, and flanks with fire. Provide maximum continuous fire for forces as they displace to the rear. Mass fires to slow the enemy as he deploys to concentrate for attack of blocking positions.

Command and Control

Greater decentralization is required than in position defense. Allocate assets to lowest possible levels.

Planning

Initially, position fire support to exploit range. Later, echelon in depth for maximum continuous fire. Ensure indirect fire assets have priority on routes.

Plan fires on natural obstacles and create obstacles with fires, e.g., FASCAM.

Maximize use of special munitions.

Integrate with scheduled fires to support disengagement actions.

Ensure that observers are positioned in overwatch positions.

Plan SEAD and counterfire.

Plan suppression of enemy overwatch positions.

Plan to support a counterattack.

WITHDRAWALS

There are two types of withdrawal operations that are distinguished by the enemy's reaction to the withdrawal: withdrawal under enemy pressure and withdrawal not under enemy pressure. Planning considerations for both are the same as a prudent commander always plans to execute a withdrawal under enemy pressure. To disengage a force from enemy contact, procedures for relieving fire support units must be clearly established and coordinated. Concurrent planning is performed by each unit involved. The biggest challenges are coordination and communications.

Tasks

Tasks are the same as delays but with greater emphasis on close fires to support disengaging forces. Provide the security force and detachment left in contact (if employed) adequate supporting arms for continual fires.

Command and Control

Maximum decentralization is required. Responsibility for fire support is passed from the force in contact to the security force. There must be a plan of events mutually agreed upon. The responsibility may be passed before, during or after the movement. Artillery units will often change missions from GS to DS and vice versa.

Planning

Plan fires on withdrawal routes.

Conduct detailed planning for scatterable mines to slow pursuit.

Mass fires to help disengagement and discourage enemy pursuit.

Plan fires on obstacles and barriers. Create obstacles with FASCAM and by cratering roads.

Displace artillery as late as possible without being overrun. Coordinate the timing and routes of withdrawal of the outgoing artillery with the responsible maneuver command. Keep the artillery unit in position until forward ground defense units have been relieved. The DS artillery units must coordinate with the supported unit and any relieving or reinforcing artillery on how continuous artillery support will be provided.

Use CAS to interdict enemy reinforcement routes.

During rearward passage of lines, provide targets, fire plans, and order of battle information to the force being passed through. Arrange for an exchange of outgoing and incoming FSCC liaison personnel.

Plan smoke to screen movement, actual unit locations, and passage points.

Plan electronic attack on critical nodes if the necessary assets are available.

Concentrate combat power in the areas of the passage of lines.

Plan for secrecy. In a withdrawal not under pressure, stealth and security are sought. Fire support is on-call and used only when the operation is compromised.

Position aircrew or spot teams in overwatch positions.

SECTION IX. OTHER TACTICAL OPERATIONS

Other tactical operations are routinely conducted during offensive, defensive, and retrograde operations. Each usually requires fire support and may involve special considerations for the FSC.

ENCIRCLED FORCES

An encircled force is a force that has lost its freedom of maneuver as a result of enemy control of all ground routes of evacuation and reinforcement. Two operational options are possible: defense by an encircled force and breakout from encirclement. Counterfire is paramount because encircled forces are particularly vulnerable to enemy massed indirect fire (the enemy knows their exact location).

Tasks

Reorganize available fire support. Determine with the force commander the most critical areas in the defense, future breakout plans of the force, and the amount of outside help available. Prepare for the breakout. Obtaining all available outside support, particularly air.

Command and Control

Centralized control of fire support assets is required.

Planning

Plan fires for the defense and the subsequent breakout.

Effect coordination with outside fire support elements.

Use fire support for deception, if necessary.

Establish FSCMs. RFLs between converging friendly forces may be needed.

Coordinate counterbattery radar search sectors.

Position encircled indirect fire weapons where they can best support the breakout operation.

Use CAS and precision guided munitions extensively during the breakout.

LINKUPS

Linkups are the joining of two friendly forces. The two may be moving toward each other or one may be stationary. The controlling higher headquarters of both forces establishes the command relationship between the two forces and the responsibilities of each. The FSCM most commonly used to support a linkup is an RFL. Forces that link up exchange as much information as practical before the operation. Consider fire support needed before, during, and after linkup; recognition signals and communications needs for both forces; and future operations following the linkup.

Tasks

Ensure fire support personnel know the FSCMs and recognition signals. They must be continuously aware of the progress of linkup forces.

Command and Control

Centralized control of fire support is desired. Communications nets must be adequate for the control of fire support at all levels.

Planning

Most planned fires are short of the RFL. Targets beyond the RFL must be cleared for attack by the controlling higher headquarters.

Smoke and illumination fires must not cause adverse effects on the other friendly forces.

Plan fires to ensure that the enemy force between two friendly forces cannot escape. Use of scatterable mines should be considered to block enemy withdrawal.

Position indirect fire weapons to allow them to mass fires at linkup points.

Firing positions should afford easy access to routes to be used after the linkup.

Permissive FSCMs should allow the moving force maximum freedom of movement.

RELIEF IN PLACE AND PASSAGE OF LINES

Procedures and timing for shifting responsibility for fire support coordination from the stationary force or force being relieved to the passing force or relief force must be clearly established and coordinated. Concurrent planning is performed by each unit involved. The biggest challenges, as with linkups, are coordination and communications.

Tasks

Ensure all fire support personnel know the FSCMs and recognition signals for the linkup. They must be continuously aware of the progress of linkup forces.

Command and Control

Maximum centralization is required. Responsibility is passed from the FSC of the force in contact to the relieving/passing unit. There must be a plan of events that has been mutually agreed upon. The responsibility may be passed before, during or after the movement occurs.

Planning

Use smoke to screen movement and passage points as required. Use electronic attack on critical enemy nodes if assets are available. Concentrate combat power in areas of passage of lines.

RIVER CROSSINGS

Offensive river crossings may be hasty, deliberate or crossings of opportunity. Hasty and deliberate crossings are extremely complex operations. Maintaining momentum is paramount. If our forces are delayed at the crossing site, they are extremely vulnerable. The role of fire support is to assist in protecting the crossing force and sustaining momentum. In a hasty crossing, fire support must be provided from means immediately available. In a deliberate crossing, additional fire support means should be considered; e.g., repositioning GS artillery.

Tasks

Make fire support immediately available to the crossing forces.

If necessary, task GS units to provide fire support while DS artillery moves with the supported unit.

Plan smoke and suppressive fires on likely enemy OPs and direct fire positions within range and line of sight of the crossing site or area.

Request electronic attack of enemy listening posts and indirect fire direction nets within range of the crossing site or area when assets are available.

Command and Control

Centralized control is desired. Provide continuous fire support when DS units cross the river.

Planning

Plan fire support based on the type of crossing.

Consider the visibility conditions and the width of the crossing areas.

Plan fires to reduce enemy defenses at crossing sites and to seal off far bank positions.

Use aircrews as overwatch for approaching forces.

Position indirect fire weapons close to the river obstacle in the offense to extend their fires on the far side.

Echelon occupation of far bank positions when these positions are out of range of enemy small arms fires.

Plan smoke to obscure actual and decoy crossing sites and to screen friendly movements.

Integrate electronic attack to support the operations when assets are available.

Use CAS to assist in establishing a bridgehead on the far side of the river.

Plan FASCAM that will isolate and then deny enemy's reinforcement.

HELICOPTERBORNE OPERATIONS

Fires must be planned for the helicopter approach and retirement lane and to protect helicopters during landing and takeoff and while in the landing zone (LZ). These fires must be coordinated closely with the infantry S-2, S-3, and AirO. Enemy antiaircraft and indirect fire weapons are the priority targets. Consider LZ preparation fires, screening fires to provide protection to troops arriving/departing the LZ/pickup zone (PZ), and deception fires. Maximum use of EW and SEAD should be planned to safeguard friendly aircraft.

NIGHT OPERATIONS

Night operations are used to achieve surprise, continue day operations, and exploit technological superiority; e.g., night vision devices; compensate for enemy capabilities; e.g., CAS or counter enemy night attacks. Intentional use of illumination in offensive or defensive operations is employed when the possibility of achieving surprise is remote, the enemy has night vision capability, and where control of units requires the use of daylight control measures. Initial plans not to employ illumination during offensive or defensive operations are made using stealth to achieve surprise in closing with the enemy before he discovers the attack. Even if initial plans call for the operation to be nonilluminated, illumination may be planned and executed on-call.

Tasks

Developing the illumination plan is the primary additional task. Illumination may enhance target acquisition for night observation devices, CAS, or the naked eye. It is also employed to degrade enemy night vision capabilities. Because illumination can affect the entire battlefield, the authority for approving illumination plans should be retained at the battalion level or higher. This prevents accidental illumination of night activities.

Command and Control

Night operations require greater centralized control than day operations. Control lessens the risk of fratricide and prevents compromising friendly actions or positions by premature fires.

Planning

Coordinate illumination fires with adjacent units and formations.

Employ smoke to degrade enemy night vision devices. Smoke may be used to assist friendly forces in bypassing enemy units.

Employ laser designation and IR pointers, in addition to illumination, for CAS marking.

Employ EW to isolate certain elements and degrade C2.

Consider visual signals to initiate shifting/lifting fires.

Marking rounds for purposes of orientation if required.

Place FSCMs on identifiable terrain.

Use radars (weapons locating radar operating in the friendly mode), laser designators, night vision devices, or illumination to adjust supporting fires at night.

Plan fires beyond the limit of advance to stop enemy retreat or reinforcement.

Plan the use of counterbattery fires against illumination delivery units.

Adjust FPFs and illumination height of burst during daylight hours for safety.

Employ ground radars, counterbattery radars, remote sensors, and night vision equipped FOs for target acquisition.

Plan defensive fires in detail based on nighttime direct fire capabilities.

Consider FASCAM to separate attack echelons from follow on forces, disrupt the enemy reserve, and fill gaps in the defense.

Use illumination projectiles to blind enemy reconnaissance and forward elements.

Coordinate night CAS and illumination placement for pilots who are aided or unaided with goggles.

JOINT AIR ATTACK TEAM OPERATIONS

A joint air attack team operation (JAAT) is a combat operation involving a combination of attack helicopters and tactical fixed-wing aircraft normally supported by field artillery or naval surface fire support, operating together to attack surface targets. MCRP 3-23A, *Multi-Service for Joint Air Attack Team (JAAT) Operations*, provides the concept, responsibilities, planning considerations, and procedures for JAAT operations.

SECTION X. THE REHEARSAL

The rehearsal is one of the most overlooked aspects of fire support planning. It provides attendees the opportunity to visualize the battle, improve total comprehension of the plan, promote responsiveness, and identify areas of confusion, friction or conflict that may have been overlooked. Its purpose is to validate that the fire support plan supports the scheme of maneuver.

The extent of the rehearsal is limited by imagination, the tactical situation, time, and resources available. It should use the maneuver OPLAN and the fire support plan. The rehearsal should rehearse maneuver and fire support *together*. The rehearsal should include sufficient fire support agencies to ensure all tasks and the timing of their execution is clearly understood by all; e.g., timing of delivery of fires on targets; execution of the artillery displacement plan; procedures for switching frequencies; observation; triggers; and reconnaissance team reporting requirements and procedures. Sufficient time should be allowed to prepare, conduct, and critique; modify the original plan as a result of the rehearsal; and prepare for battle.

ATTENDEES

Attendees should include commanders, key representatives, FSCs (two levels down), and all supporting arms representatives. When appropriate, include EW,

engineer, LAAD, target acquisition, and reconnaissance representatives.

TYPES

Types of rehearsals vary from the echelon (senior through subordinate), to warfighting function, to medium (map, model or radio). Organization and conduct varies depending on available time. A rehearsal SOP increases speed and efficiency on how a rehearsal can be conducted. The FSC's rehearsal prepares supporting arms for fire support plan execution. The maneuver rehearsal is conducted by the XO or S-3 and incorporates the fire support plan.

The type of rehearsal depends on the nature of operations and time and assets available. Preparing the rehearsal should ensure access for attendees and adequate representation of events to occur.

Models

Models may be constructed showing buildings, compounds, or built up areas. Model rehearsals require good intelligence information on the area of operation and more time to construct. Model rehearsals are normally used for special operations.

Map Rehearsal

The rehearsal may be conducted on any map with appropriate overlays. Map rehearsals may be used when time and rehearsal space is limited. This limits the number of participants to those who can gather around a single map unless projected onto a large screen (C2PC). Actions to be taken are discussed through verbal recitation by attendees.

Sand Table

The sand table expands the area around where rehearsal attendees may gather around a single graphical representation of the operation. Maneuver graphics may be depicted using engineer tape, string, spray paint, or simply carving out lines in the ground. Key terrain, topography, and objectives may be depicted by using rocks, items of equipment or piling up dirt. Preparing this rehearsal allows for an increased number of attendees and a better visual aid. Larger sand tables allow attendees to occupy unit positions on the model.

Radio Rehearsal

Radio rehearsals can be conducted for schedules of fire, timing with maneuver, and other events. They are conducted on fire support nets when time and the tactical situation do not allow assembly of key personnel.

CRITICAL EVENTS

If time is limited, critical events identified by the FSC (fire support events, contingencies or transitions of the fire support plan from one phase to another) may be all that are rehearsed. The FSC should prioritize events if time is limited.

SUBORDINATE REHEARSALS

The fire support plan should be rehearsed before the maneuver rehearsal. This provides the opportunity to resolve fire support plan issues for more efficient integration into the maneuver plan. Subordinate elements and supporting arms should be allowed to perform their rehearsals.

CLOSURE

When the rehearsal is completed, issues of concern must be addressed and any changes to the plan made immediately. Before adjourning, attendees must acknowledge changes and inform agencies that did not participate.

CHAPTER 4. TARGETING

Targeting is the process of selecting targets and matching the appropriate response to them, taking account of operational requirements and capabilities. (JP 1-02) It is conducted once the commander's intent, enemy centers of gravity, and enemy critical vulnerabilities are identified. The FSC and the targeting team select enemy units, facilities, or capabilities that he can least afford to lose or that provide him with the greatest advantage. Target subsets that must be acquired and attacked to meet the commander's intent and accomplish the mission are further identified.

SECTION I. ORGANIZATIONS AND PERSONNEL

The division has the only formally structured targeting section with personnel specifically designated for targeting duties in the GCE. At regiment and below, personnel can be dedicated exclusively to targeting tasks only if the commander requests additional personnel or shifts individuals from their normal duties. Targeting at lower levels is usually done by FSCC and S-2 section personnel without augmentation, but lower intelligence sections may be reinforced from division G-2 direct support teams. All fire support and intelligence personnel play a role in the targeting process.

AMPHIBIOUS FORCE

Amphibious Force Intelligence Center

The amphibious force intelligence center (AFIC) is the focal point for all intelligence collection, analysis, production, and reporting. It is manned by ground, air, and naval intelligence personnel from the ATF and MAGTF staffs. The MAGTF representative is the target intelligence officer (TGTINTELO). He handles target intelligence and passes it to the SACC. The principal MAGTF intelligence elements are the surveillance and reconnaissance cell (SARC) and the production and analysis (P&A) cell. Both are part of the intelligence battalion's intelligence operations center (IOC).

The SARC is the primary element for supervising MAGTF collection operations. It directs, coordinates, and monitors intelligence collection operations and reporting conducted by organic, attached, and direct support collection assets. It provides timely intelligence reports to designated MAGTF elements IAW specified intelligence reporting criteria.

The P&A cell is the primary production and analysis element of the MAGTF. It processes collected information and other intelligence and produces all-source intelligence products in response to requirements of the MAGTF. The P&A cell's target analysis/BDA teams focus on detailed analysis of targets identified by the MAGTF commander, his staff, and the MSCs' commanders which are not destined for the air tasking order (ATO). Target and BDA analysis and intelligence support for ATO-nominated targets are generally managed by the MAW G-2 section. The target analysis/BDA teams provide the full range of target development and analysis to support deliberate and reactive targeting efforts of the MAGTF. BDA elements also maintain the comprehensive picture of battle damage caused to targets and prepare BDA reports and assessments that support the MAGTF combat assessment effort. Most intelligence personnel assigned to target information center (TIC) operations will be sourced from the P&A cell's target analysis/BDA teams.

See MCWP 3-31.1/ NWP 3-09.11M, *Supporting Arms in Amphibious Operations*, MCWP 2-1, *Intelligence Operations*, and MCWP 2-12, *MAGTF Intelligence Analysis and Production*.

Target Information Center

The TIC is located in the SACC. The primary functions of the TIC are to keep the SACC informed of the status of high-value targets (HVTs), high-payoff targets (HPTs), and high priority targets, maintain liaison between the SACC and the AFIC, and prepare and maintain the AF target list and target bulletins. Personnel in the TIC are the AF TGTINTELO, MAGTF target information officer (TIO), and assistants as required. The TIC maintains coordination and liaison with the air intelligence officer in the tactical air control center (TACC [afloat]) and the MAGTF FFC. The AF TGTINTELO is under the staff cognizance of the N-2, but works in the TIC coordinating intelligence support to targeting. The MAGTF TIO comes from the MAGTF FFCC. He processes target data in the SACC and passes it to MAGTF fire support agencies ashore. See MCWP 3-31.1/NWP 3-09.11M, *Supporting Arms in Amphibious Operations*, for information on the TIC.

Figure 4-1. Joint Targeting Cycle and D3A.

MAGTF COMMAND ELEMENT

Normally, targeting within the MAGTF CE is performed by the FFCC targeting cell. The focus is on the deep operation and the necessary transition to the close operation. The MAGTF must integrate D3A with the air targeting cycle since the MAGTF commander's primary tool for deep operations is aviation.

Under direction of the TIO, the targeting cell, in close coordination with TGTINTELO, helps plan future operations by incorporating the tactical targeting methodology of D3A with the six-step, joint targeting cycle. (See figure 4-1.) It executes in current operations by integrating the time-driven ATO of the ACE with event-driven needs for fires in the operation. During operations ashore, the MAGTF CE supports the targeting activities of the GCE and the mission planning of the ACE by rapidly passing target data to the GCE and ACE and by responding to their requests for target data.

The MAGTF CE's targeting focus is on targets in the MAGTF commander's area of influence. Targeting is one way for the MAGTF commander to shape the battlespace.

DIVISION TARGETING

In the division, the target information section (TIS) serves as the division FSCC's primary source of target information for planning and coordinating the delivery of fire support. Functions are oriented to the tactical support requirements of the division and to the target information requirements of the division FSCC. The TIS uses intelligence provided by the TGTINTELO (G-2 section/intelligence battalion) and the intelligence officers of artillery units. The targeting process is discussed in section II. The TIS is normally established at the division level but may be formed at the regimental level as required by the tactical situation.

If a TIS is not established at the regimental level, the supporting arms representatives in the FSCC perform the necessary target information functions. The division TIS focuses primarily within the division's area of influence. Specific TIS functions are to—

● Maintain required target and situation maps.

● Maintain target data using automated methods; e.g. target files.

- Consolidate, evaluate, and display target information and intelligence.

- Recommend target classification and attack priorities to the FSC as required.

- Obtain information and intelligence on the results of attack on targets by the supporting arms from all elements and sources.

- Coordinate all matters with MAGTF TGTINTELO and artillery unit S-2 for target and counterfire intelligence support.

- Maintain current lists of targets. These include countermortar, counterbattery, and SEAD lists and providing this information to the supporting arms representatives and to the LF as a whole.

- Prepare and ensure dissemination of target bulletins (TARBULs) after control of the AF target list has been passed ashore.

TARGETING COMMITTEE

The commander needs advice from experts in many areas. A targeting committee brings these experts together as a matter of standard procedure. The committee performs duties similar to those in MCRP 3-16A, *TTP for Targeting Process*, for the targeting team. The chairman is the decisionmaker who is the commander or his designated representative. The targeting committee may include members of the GCE, ACE, CSSE, intelligence support,

MAGTF CE, and, during amphibious operations, ATF personnel.

INTELLIGENCE COLLECTION AND PRODUCTION ASSETS

To support targeting efforts, the collection plan must use all available assets. Division assets are limited (ground and light armored reconnaissance units, combat patrols, weapons locating radars, etc.). The MAGTF CE controls additional collection assets that may support division and MAW targeting efforts (force reconnaissance, radio battalion, UAVs, etc.). The MAGTF CE exercises staff cognizance of the majority of the MAGTF's intelligence production capabilities. The MAGTF CE can also access external MAGTF collection and production assets that can provide intelligence support. METT-T considerations and the overall MAGTF concept of operations may result in significant intelligence resources being either attached to or placed in direct support of the division. For example, for a mid-intensity conventional combat operation where the division is the MAGTF's main effort, the division will almost certainly get either attachments or direct support from the MAGTF's direct support teams (DSTs), radio battalion, CI/HUMINT company, UAV squadron's remote receive station, and ground sensor platoon (GSP). See MCWP 2-2, *Intelligence Collection*, and the MCWP 2-15 *Intelligence Support Operations* series for more information on collection assets.

SECTION II. THE TARGETING PROCESS

Targeting is a continual, decisionmaking process. Commanders and key personnel (fire support, intelligence, operations and planning) must understand the functions associated with the process, be knowledgeable of the capabilities and limitations of acquisition, target intelligence development, and attack systems, and be able to integrate them. The entire targeting process must be fully integrated into the tactical decisionmaking process.

Targeting is an integral part of the planning process that begins with receipt of the mission and continues through

the development and execution of the plan. It is based on the friendly scheme of maneuver and/or tactical plan. It includes an assessment of the weather, terrain, and the enemy situation. This assessment then identifies those enemy units, equipment, facilities, and terrain which must be attacked or influenced to support the concept of operation. Targeting and intelligence support to targeting include determining/deciding which targets are to be acquired and attacked, when and how they are to be acquired and attacked, and what is required to achieve the desired effects on target. Selected HVTs and HPTs are also identified for deliberate follow up action and analysis (combat assessment [CA]).

The targeting methodology for the GCE is *decide, detect, deliver, assess (D3A)*. Targeting must be completely integrated into the fire support planning process. For example, the priorities established by the commander in the *decide* phase are not for targeting alone, but include his guidance for intelligence operations, fire support planning, and execution of fires. The four phases of D3A are inherently intertwined and overlapping. Simply put, the D3A methodology should determine—

- What enemy capabilities, functions, formations should be targeted whose loss to the enemy will set conditions that contribute to the success of the friendly course of action?

- What must we do to these targets to deny them to the enemy?

- Have these targets been located with enough accuracy to successfully attack them? If not, where should we look for them? With what collection asset? What level of production effort is required to develop the needed target intelligence?

- When will we attack these targets? Will they be attacked as detected? At a specific time in the operation? Or, in a particular sequence?

- What fire support assets will we utilize to attack these targets?

- Once attacked, how will we assess the success of the attack to determine if we have deprived the enemy the use of the target?

- If we do not achieve the desired effect, what is the impact on the friendly COA? If necessary, how will we reattack the target and evaluate effectiveness of the reattack?

DECIDE

Intent

This phase translates commander's intent into priorities and attack guidance. As the first step in the targeting process, it provides the overall focus and sets priorities for intelligence collection, production and dissemination, and attack planning. Targeting priorities must be established for each stage or critical event of an operation. For targeting to succeed, all must understand the unit mission, commander's intent, and the commander's planning guidance. The commander bases his initial guidance on the intelligence preparation of the battlespace (IPB). IPB is the foundation for the rest of the targeting process. It is a continuous and systematic method for analyzing the enemy, weather, and terrain in a geographical area. (See MCRP 2-12A, *Intelligence Preparation of the Battlefield*.)

Target Value Analysis

The target information officer or G-2/S-2 performs TVA, a detailed analysis of the enemy in selected COAs. TVA provides a relative ranking of target sets (or categories) based on enemy characteristics: doctrine, tactics, equipment, organizations, and expected behavior. It begins when the target analyst in the G-2/S-2 places himself in the position of the enemy commander. The target analyst, in coordination with other staff members, wargames friendly COAs and analyzes their impact on enemy operations and likely responses. Wargaming finalizes individual staff estimates. It identifies HVTs in priority of assets that the enemy commander needs to successfully complete a specific COA. It also identifies HPTs (derived from HVTs), whose loss to the enemy will contribute to the success of the friendly COA. See MCRP 3-16A/FM 6-20-10, chapter 2.

Products

Products from the decide function are incorporated into the fire support annex of the OPORD.

Target Acquisition Taskings

Target acquisition (TA) assets that belong to fire support agencies; e.g., radar or FOs are incorporated into the collection plan to contribute to target information.

High-Payoff Target List

A high-payoff target list (HPTL) is the prioritized list of HPTs established and used by targeting personnel and FSCCs to develop the attack guidance matrix (AGM).

Attack Guidance Matrix

The AGM is a document that tells how, when, and to what effect an HPT will be engaged. The AGM is incorporated into the maneuver and fire support plans. It is the commander's attack guidance and is designed to support his plan. An AGM that supports the division commander's plan may not support a regiment or battalion commander's plan. One AGM rarely supports the needs of an entire force and may differ between the various levels of command.

Targeting Selection Standards

TSS establishes criteria to distinguish between known targets and suspected targets based on the attack system's target location error (TLE) requirements, size and status of enemy activity, and timeliness of information. TSSs and TLEs are used by FSCCs and attack assets to help plan and direct supporting intelligence requirements/operations and to quickly identify targets for attack and confirmation.

Requirements for Battle Damage Assessment

The commander may specify targets of a critical nature that require immediate BDA to determine effects and support rapid CA. Requirements will be incorporated into the collection plan and may be classified as commander's priority intelligence requirements (PIR). When possible, fire support organizations provide initial BDA to the FSC and the supporting intelligence officer on targets attacked.

DETECT

This phase is designed to validate known and suspected HPTs based on guidance from the decide phase, as well as locate and identify new targets that meet HPT criteria. Detecting is accomplished by executing the intelligence operation plan. Target acquisition assets are tasked to collect information for target analysis and production. Intelligence collectors focus on the relevant characteristics of the intelligence operation plan and FSC-provided targeting information requirements (IRs) and TSS. Target priorities from the decide

phase expedite processing of information and the rapid production of tailored, pertinent intelligence products to support targeting. Products are actual targets and suspected targets.

The G-2/S-2 is the primary staff officer who executes the intelligence operation plan and validates the overall effectiveness of intelligence support to targeting. The commander's priority intelligence requirements (PIRs) drive intelligence collection, production, and dissemination plans and should incorporate fire support targeting requirements. The G-2/S-2 must work closely with the FSC to determine target location error (TLE) and dwell time requirements for collection systems to produce valid targets. This should result in clear, concise taskings to target acquisition assets. As information is collected and intelligence produced, it is disseminated by intelligence personnel to the TIS in accordance with current intelligence reporting criteria. Targets acquired or developed that are specified for attack are passed to the FSCC to engage under the attack guidance matrix. Suspected targets are forwarded to the FSCC for tracking and correlation with other information for target development.

A MAGTF has a wide variety of assets available to detect and identify targets; e.g., national intelligence collection assets like satellite photography or a squad leader's shelling report (SHELREP).

In order to access multiple assets, the FSC works closely with the G-2/S-2. The G-2/S-2 requests support from collection resources at higher levels of command. Following the guidance in the decide phase, the G-2/S-2 will exercise staff cognizance from MAGTF and supporting units with intelligence collection and production capabilities that normally employ in general support. C2 management is executed via the intelligence battalion commander in his role as the G-2/S-2's intelligence support coordinator (ISC). Sources of information include—

- Communications collection and direction finding (radio battalion and the VMAQ squadrons).

- Visual reconnaissance (ground reconnaissance elements and LAR elements).

- Videotape and handheld imagery (primarily UAV squadrons, but also the HML/A squadrons, ground reconnaissance units, and LAR battalion).

- Multi-sensor imagery (UAV squadron and F/A-18D squadron).
- Electronic reconnaissance (EA-6B squadrons).
- Ground remote sensors (intelligence battalion's ground sensor platoon).
- Visual ground reconnaissance (division and force reconnaissance units).
- Prisoner of war interrogation (interrogation platoon, intelligence battalion).
- Pilot debriefs (conducted by the ACE G-2).

Other MAGTF target acquisition assets are found at battalion level and below (LAR battalion, artillery FOs, NGF spot teams, and the scout/sniper platoon). The primary mission of these assets is to support their parent units. The bulk of their effort is with planned targets or targets of opportunity. Essential target information for reporting acquired targets consists of the reporting unit; time of acquisition; target location, size, and activity; TLE; dwell time; and stationary or moving status. The FSCC can develop targets in zone by monitoring calls for fire, CAS requests, and counter battery radar reports.

DELIVER

The objective of this phase is executing attack guidance on targets in support of the commander's plan. The key to the deliver phase is well-established procedures for execution, prior coordination, and rehearsals.

The deliver phase is comprised of a set of tactical and technical engagement solutions. The MAGTF relies on a decisionmaker, i.e., the staff/watch officer at the detecting fire support agency, to exercise his authority in attacking targets. His tactical decision is based on the AGM and the current situation. If he decides not to attack but to *track* a target, it is passed back to the TIS.

After targets are identified by the FSCC, determining when and how to attack a target is made considering attack resources available, their capabilities, desired effects, and rules of engagement (ROE). This refined analysis produces the following tactical decisions: time of attack, desired effect, and the attack system to use. Another important decision is

employing combined arms to attack certain targets, including lethal and nonlethal fires. Any remaining coordination with higher, lower, adjacent units, or other Services is done at this time.

Once tactical decisions are made, the target is passed to the selected supporting arm for technical attack decisions; e.g., the unit to conduct the attack, number and type of munitions, and response time. The supporting arm's ability to respond based on range, time on station, available munitions, and reaction time cannot be assumed but are functions of the prior coordination and the current tactical situation.

The extent of the deliver phase depends on time available, the type of target, and attack guidance. Targets attacked immediately are prioritized in accordance with attack guidance. A time sensitive target (moving or short dwell time) may need tracking if it is not attacked within the appropriate response time. Planned targets may be attacked individually or incorporated into the appropriate asset fire plan; e.g., ATO or schedule of fires. When time is available, a thorough analysis is conducted for detailed consideration of targets. In targeting for amphibious operations, particularly pre D-day, the final decision on the attack of targets may be made at the AF level. At lower levels, the authority to decide to attack is normally decentralized because of the need for responsiveness. When time is limited, the process may be greatly abbreviated.

ASSESS

The CA reveals if the commander's guidance is met and determines the overall effectiveness of force employment. In the decide phase, the commander designated critical targets that required immediate BDA and the type of surveillance desired. G-2/S-2 and fire support planners identified how damage assessment was collected, considering limited assets and continued requirements for the detect phase. The degree of reliability and credibility of BDA depends largely on enemy targets and their operations, MAGTF collection resources, and the scope of intelligence analysis and production needed to produce the required intelligence. BDA, when analyzed with an assessment of the effectiveness of the attack tactics, weapon systems, munitions, fusing and delivery systems—munitions effects assessment (MEA)—leads to recommendations for reattack, further target selection or modifying commander's guidance. Collectively, BDA, MEA, and reattack recommendations (RR) comprise CA. (See figure 4-2.) Also see MCWP 2-12, *MAGTF Intelligence Production and Analysis*, for more information on BDA capabilities and operations.

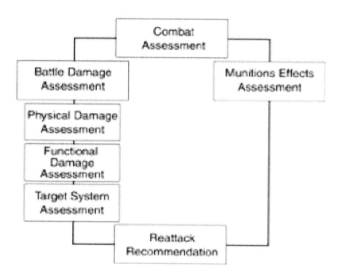

Figure 4-2. Combat Assessment Process.

Employment of fire support assets for reattack is coordinated the same way as employment of TA assets for detection. This is most easily done when assessment is planned, coordinated, and, when possible, executed concurrently with the attack. At lower levels, specific targets may be designated for assessment. When the attack of a target is controlled and observed by an FO, FAC, NGF spotter, or any other observer, separate tasking for assessment is usually not necessary. When active assessment is not possible, other measures can be used to assess effects on a target. For example, if an artillery battery were to be attacked, the appropriate measure of a successful attack might be terminating firing by the target. If a target is so important that destroying or neutralizing it must be confirmed before a planned course of action can be initiated or continued, then positive assessment must be made.

Battle Damage Assessment

BDA is the timely and accurate estimate of damage resulting from the application of military force, lethal or nonlethal, against a target. It is primarily an intelligence responsibility, however, at the tactical level, BDA provides commanders a snapshot of targeting effectiveness and enemy status. In the targeting process, BDA helps to determine the effects of our attacks and other force employment on the enemy and if reattack of a target is necessary. It may take many forms, including number of casualties, damage to equipment, target reaction to the attack or deception efforts. BDA consists of three elements: physical damage assessment, functional damage assessment, and target system assessment.

Phase I - Physical Damage

Phase I is the quantitative extent of physical damage through munitions blast, fragmentation, and/or fire damage effects to a target. This assessment is based on the most immediately available data. Typically, data originates from operational forces that cannot conduct detailed observation of weapons effects because they are engaged with enemy forces. Thus, initial phase I analysis may consist of nothing more than a "hit" or "no-hit" call provided by the shooter.

Phase II - Functional Damage

A functional damage assessment (FDA) is built on phase I reports as well as all-source intelligence collected and developed from assets at all levels. FDA at a minimum will describe the estimated effect of attacks and other force employment on the target's ability to perform its intended mission. It may also include an estimate of the time required for the enemy to reconstitute or replace the target functions destroyed or degraded. Tactical units provide input to their intelligence sections to support phase II analysis, which is usually conducted at the MAGTF, component or theater level.

Phase III - Target System

Target system assessment is a broad assessment of the impact and effectiveness of all types of attacks and other employment of forces against an entire target system's capability; e.g., an enemy's integrated air defense system (IADS). Target system assessment is conducted by theater and national level intelligence agencies.

Munitions Effects Assessment

Conducted concurrently and interactively with BDA, this is an assessment of the weapon system and the munitions employed to determine and recommend any required changes to the methods, tactics, weapon system, munitions, fusing or delivery parameters to increase effectiveness. At the tactical level, fire support planners make this assessment by comparing expected results from tactical and technical decisions made during the deliver phase with BDA.

Reattack Recommendations

Based on BDA and MEA, the FSC and G-2/S-2 advise the commander on reattack of targets and further target selection to achieve his objectives. Reattack recommendations consider objective achievement, target and aim point selection, attack timing, tactics, and weapon system and munitions selection.

SECTION III. RECORDING TARGET DATA

Automated information systems have had a significant impact on recording target data. Recording target data consists of recording potential targets, developing targets, sharing target information, graphically representing targets on overlays, and maintaining target files.

TARGET NUMBERING

All FSCs are involved in target numbering. A target numbering system provides a common reference, avoids duplication in assigning numbers, and identifies the target originator. Target numbers are assigned by the planner on planned targets or targets of opportunity that retain tactical significance even after they have been attacked. A good indication that a target of opportunity has tactical significance is if the FO or spotter controlling the mission requests that the target be recorded when he ends the mission.

MAGTF units use the Marine Corps target numbering system. It incorporates the NATO and ABCA armies' standardization agreements AArty P-1, *Artillery Procedures*, and QSTAG 221, *Target Numbering System*. The intent of the Marine Corps target numbering system is to eliminate the need to revise the target numbering system during mobilization or when working with non-USMC units. The system provides the maximum target number availability for allocation to units to minimize the frequency for reuse of numbers. Any

changes to the numbering scheme will come from the senior commander of the MAGTF or joint task force (JTF). See appendix L.

Another target numbering system used in joint targeting that FSC's should be aware of is the basic encyclopedia (BE) number and unit identification number system. This compendium of installation and unit intelligence taken from the modernized integrated data base (MIDB) is the most inclusive of all lists. BE numbers describe every identified installation with an active function or of valid interest to intelligence agencies, particularly to the operational staffs of the Unified Commands. The BE contains data on the identification, location, and function of each installation. It is used to select potential fixed targets for employing ground, sea or air weapons or to identify installations to be withheld from attack, such as public utilities and hospitals. The BE lists installations in Eurasia, Western Europe, Latin America and the Atlantic, Middle East and Africa, and Southeast Asia and the Western Pacific. Numbers are assigned primarily by the Defense Intelligence Agency (DIA). The unit identification number is the only unique identifier of a mobile unit or target. Once established, it is never changed or reused, even if a unit in a national force changes its subordination or location.

The unit identification number is a list of mobile targets and fielded forces and is comprised of ten alphanumeric characters that include the code of the originating agency (who created the record), the order of battle type, the allegiance of the unit, and an accession number. Unit identification numbers help intelligence analysts keep track of the enemy order of battle. The discrete reference number used to record targets depends on the level of command within the MAGTF, automated information system being used, and local theater procedures. For more information on MIDB, see MCWP 2-12.

TARGET LIST

A target list consists of targets maintained and promulgated by the senior echelon of command; it contains those targets that are to be engaged by supporting arms, as distinguished from a "list of targets" that may be maintained by any echelon as confirmed, suspected, or possible targets for informational and planning purposes (JP 1-02). The target list is maintained in the automated target file or printed form. There should be only one target list in an operation.

MAGTF Target List

When an ATF target list or JTL is not published, the MAGTF CE may establish a MAGTF target list. The published list contains those targets that supporting arms of the ACE, GCE, and other assets available to the MAGTF are to engage as well as those submitted to higher joint headquarters for attack.

Target Bulletins

The commander who maintains the ATF target list keeps other interested commanders informed of all list changes by information messages called target bulletins (TARBULs). As new targets are discovered and BDA on known targets is produced, this information and intelligence is disseminated.

The TARBUL is promulgated over the most expeditious means of communications using a standard message format. TARBULs are numbered consecutively during an operation. The first TARBUL issued by the responsible commander is labeled as "TARBUL Number One;" the last TARBUL issued by that commander

is annotated as "Final Bulletin." The same procedure is used each time the target list is transferred from one commander to another. The format is as follows:

- Serial Number of Bulletin.
- New Targets.
- Targets Destroyed.
- Targets Damaged/Percentage.
- Canceled Targets.
- Reactivated Targets.

TARBUL distribution depends on task force size and composition. It is normally distributed to all interested commanders of higher, adjacent, and lower echelons of the AF by the commander responsible for the AF target list. It is distributed to AF elements as designated. They use the TARBUL to update *their* lists of targets and target files.

LF elements must report to the MAGTF the location and description of newly acquired targets appropriate for inclusion on the AF target list, the results of attacks on targets listed on the AF target list, and those listed targets that have been overrun. The target report (TAREP) is used to pass target data. The TIO, in cooperation with the TGTINTELO, evaluates and consolidates reports of target information and intelligence and prepares TARBULs for approval and release.

Joint Target List

The joint force commander (JFC), usually through the joint targeting coordination board (JTCB), prepares a joint target list (JTL) and a joint integrated prioritized target list (JIPTL). The JTL is the master target list that supports the JFC's objectives, guidance, intent, and courses of action. In wartime, the operation plan (OPLAN) JTL annex is updated and serves as an initial list of campaign targets. See JP 3-60, *Joint Targeting*, for further explanation.

The JTL is not a prioritized list of targets. It lists prioritized target *categories* like C2, airfields, or lines of communications. When directed by the JFC, the JTL is updated daily or as required via target information report (TGTINFOREP) messages from components.

Joint doctrine employs a JIPTL for prioritizing specific targets from the JTL. Prioritization refers to a target's relative importance and significance within a specific target system and to other targets. Prioritization does not necessarily denote operational sequencing.

TARGETING BOARDS

The highest echelon of command is responsible for maintaining the target list. At that level, the targeting committee hosts a targeting board. The board assesses targeting effectiveness and updates priorities and the target list. Its basic process inputs subordinates' recommendations from target lists. It considers them with the commander's guidance and priorities, and produces a prioritized target list.

Lower echelons, although without a dedicated targeting staff, should hold targeting meetings. Meetings are informally held by the XO with the S-2, S-3, and FSC to ensure targets address the commander's desires and have been incorporated into the fire support and R&S collection plans. It is not a separate function and should be in conjunction with the planning process.

If time permits, conducting a targeting board should include an intelligence update on the enemy situation, collection and productions plans, and expected enemy courses of action. Operation updates include requirements from higher echelons, changes to commander's guidance, and review of current operations and available assets. The FSC reviews current attack guidance and recommends changes. The target list itself is maintained by assessing targets that have been attacked, canceling targets, reactivating targets, and nominating new ones. Targets planned by subordinate echelons may be nominated for inclusion on the target list. Such targets must be considered as significant to the MAGTF, AF or JTF. The MAGTF targeting board evaluates these targets for inclusion on the target list. In amphibious or joint operations, the MAGTF makes appropriate recommendations to the AF or JTF.

TARGET FILES

A target file consists of the target list, confirmed and suspected targets, targets planned to support maneu-ver, and target information. Automated information systems enable target files to be maintained at different echelons and share appropriate common information with subordinate, adjacent, and higher levels. The target file is not the target list nor a single list of targets. It is a unit's data base that performs two functions: it uses the target file to make nominations to the targeting board that controls the target list, and it maintains its own lists of targets. The division target processing center (TPC), or highest level S-2, is the clearing house for all target information gathered at lower levels.

File Production

The initial target file may consist only of targets gathered from national assets or a DIA data base. The target file increases as fire support planners at battalion and company levels nominate targets to support maneuver. As intelligence collection and production plans are executed at different levels, target acquisition assets contribute target information, which builds the file.

Target information includes target descriptions and sizes, target locations in grid coordinates or polar direction, date-time groups, and report values (RV), the radial error associated with the type of observer (similar to TLE). Criteria for processing target information and intelligence are established based on the HPTL, TSS, and targeted areas of interest (TAIs), named areas of interest (NAIs), and current intelligence reporting criteria. Target information and intelligence that meet established standards becomes a target while other information and intelligence may be used to develop a target based on the similarities, proximity, differences in report time, and tactical significance when correlated with other reports.

File Maintenance

Although automated information systems have expansive memory for maintaining information, they can be degraded when inundated with excessive information. Maintaining target files according to the following principles keeps information current, common, and responsive to the using units.

Targets are maintained by their originating organization; e.g.; a regiment target that is in a subordinate battalions' target files is only updated/canceled by the originator (regiment) of the target. The regiment is responsible for notifying all users of any change in the target's status.

Units with targets in their area of operations but originating elsewhere should make recommendations on the maintenance of those targets.

Units with targets in their area of interest but originating elsewhere may make recommendations on the maintenance of those targets.

Considerations for file maintenance include—

- Targets destroyed by friendly forces.
- Targets overrun by advancing elements.
- Targets that have a high mobility factor and are not attacked within a set time period.
- Targets attacked that show no activity within a set period of time.
- Target information files combined into a target.
- Changes in requirements for target information.

Specific criteria for file maintenance are as established in unit SOPs and may be modified depending on the current tactical situation and tempo of operations.

LIST OF TARGETS

A list of targets may be maintained at any echelon as confirmed, suspected or likely targets that are of particular concern to their operations. The list contains targets for planning and informational purposes. Targets on the list may or may not be engaged. An informal company list may even contain essential target reference points (TRPs). A list may be maintained for a specific target type; e.g., counterfire, SEAD. The list of targets is independent from the target list, but both may be contained in the same target file.

Format

There is no standard format for such lists, but normally they are constructed based on search criteria entered in the automated information system. At company levels they are often maintained on a target list worksheet.

The information recorded normally contains, at a minimum, the target number, target location, description, and any amplifying remarks. An example of a target list worksheet is in appendix L.

Processing

A list of targets may be prepared and maintained at any echelon. Targets included may be derived from several sources; e.g., the GCE target file, fire planning, battlefield intelligence, etc. Each FSCC should maintain a named target list, which is actually a list of targets that can be used for various purposes. Subordinate FSCC's should send their list of targets to the senior FSCC anytime it changes. Senior FSCC's should merge their subordinate's lists of targets, resolve duplication, and republish the target list to their subordinates based on unit SOP or commander's guidance.

The originating unit maintains a copy of the list of targets for its use, forwards a copy to the supporting arms units, and submits a copy to the next higher echelon. This may be done electronically. Because the same target may have been planned by more than one unit, the possibility exists for a target to be assigned two target numbers. A fire mission on a target with two target numbers will cause confusion and must be avoided. Thus, the higher echelon compares the list with lists submitted by other units and eliminates duplications. Duplications are remedied by the higher echelon deciding on a single target number for the target, and making appropriate notifications to affected units; e.g., originating units, supporting arms units.

As each step up the ladder is completed, it should eventually reach the MAGTF CE. The MAGTF FFCC should merge all subordinate FSCC's lists of targets into one MAGTF target list for a given 24-hour period if the MAGTF is not engaged in amphibious operations. If the MAGTF is engaged in amphibious operations then the SACC will develop this list. This will give all supporting commands a common target list in the form of the AF target list.

Maintenance

Lists of targets must be kept current to be useful. Targets that have been attacked and meet the commander's guidance are no longer viable and should be removed to decrease the amount of targets that must be tracked by operators and staffs. The same principles for file maintenance apply to lists of targets. Additions are made as new targets are identified or planned. Fielding of automated information systems and the quick passage of information through the LAN, EPLRS, and SCR can aid in rapidly modifying and disseminating lists of targets to higher and lower elements.

The headquarters that designated and planned the target to be attacked is responsible for determining if a target is to be deleted or maintained. During the planning process, certain criteria need to be developed as to when a target should be deleted. Since targets may be mobile, target location may only be viable for a short time. Should this time be exceeded, modify or delete the target.

Target location is a large determination as to its relevance. Is it behind the FLOT? Do we expect to need it? Is it on terrain that is no longer key terrain?

The nature of the target needs to be determined. Has the target been attacked? Have the attacks met the commander's guidance? Is the target still of value to the commander?

Using AFATDS, a mission-fired report (MFR) is generated by the first AFATDS that receives the information when a mission ends. This MFR contains the BDA data and who fired the mission. Depending on the automatic message routing parameters set-up, it is then sent to subordinate and higher units to provide the status of the target.

Currently AFATDS cannot delete or change a target and automatically update the list of targets in higher and subordinate units' databases. There are several methods to disseminate changes to lists of targets.

Plain Text Message

The headquarters responsible for the target sends a plain text message (PTM) listing all deleted and added targets. This is similar to an electronic TARBUL. The units receive this message and make adjustments to the list of targets in question.

Named Target List

The headquarters develops a new named target list with deletions, additions, and changes incorporated. This list is distributed to higher and subordinate elements along with a PTM to delete the old target list and institute the new one.

TARGET MAP OVERLAY

The target map is maintained to provide a visual display of targets appropriate for attack by supporting arms. FSCMs should be readily accessible for use with the target map. Some targets posted on the target map are targets—

● In the unit's zone of action that can interfere with the concept of operations.

● That are not in the unit's area of operation but can interfere with the concept of operations.

● That are not immediately important but may become important to the concept of operations.

Maintenance

FSCCs and FDCs maintain targets on an overlay. The overlay is a supplement to the target file. Planned targets, such as known or suspected targets, capable of interfering with the commander's scheme of maneuver are plotted. These targets are derived from the fire support plan, the target list, and the unit's list of targets. The target overlay is used as a tool to resolve duplication of targets, to integrate the scheme of maneuver with the plan of supporting fires, and to determine the most appropriate unit to engage the target. Target overlays are maintained by FOs and spotters with only essential information for rapid referral for the attack of planned targets.

Standard Procedures for Annotating Maps and Overlays

Known or suspected targets are plotted using standard map symbols, indicating the date-time group of the initial sighting. See appendix L.

Targets reported as destroyed are so indicated by placing an X through the target symbol. Those targets partially destroyed are indicated by a single line through the target and the percentage of damage, if reportable, along the side. Significant enemy contact is noted by the use of a red circle at the location of the contact. Amplifying remarks are recorded. Friendly and enemy symbology used on these products and displays will be in accordance with MIL-STD-2525B, *Common Warfighting Symbology*, and MCRP 5-12A, *Operational Terms and Graphics*.

TARGET/OBJECTIVE STUDIES

IPB affects the targeting process through the evaluation of terrain, weather, and the association of threat forces at specific times and locations within the battlespace. NAIs and TAIs are identified. HVTs and HPTs are derived and a list of targets is submitted for consideration. Once the commander has approved a target, intelligence sections develop target/objective studies to support mission planning. Target/objective studies are focused, detailed intelligence products that aid in applying fires or the maneuver of forces against a specific target set or area. These studies can also be used by smaller MAGTFs and units, such as a MEU(SOC), for mission preparation and execution.

Target/objective studies are graphically oriented and may use many of the graphics derived during the IPB process. One such product is a target folder or file described on page 4-10. The folder may contain the following information depending on the specific mission:

- Orientation graphic.
- Time-distance graphic.
- Weather forecast.
- Hydrographic forecast and astronomical data.
- Intelligence briefing notes for mission.
- Graphic INTSUM.
- Objective area graphic enhancements:
  - Orientation graphic (10 to 20 kilometers around objective or as specified in unit SOP).
  - Mission planning graphic (5 kilometers around objective or as specified in unit SOP).
  - Objective area graphics.
- Objective area imagery.
- Imagery and graphics of insertion points and targets.
- SERE plan.
- Challenge and reply passwords.
- Mission-specific data as required.

SECTION IV. TARGETING CHECKLIST

Specific considerations for the FSC during the targeting process help the fire support planning process by identifying concerns within the framework of the D3A targeting methodology.

The commander's planning guidance and intent are critical to facilitate effective targeting.

DECIDE

What HVTs have been nominated as HPTs?

What are the desired effects for each HPT?

When do we attack each HPT?

How do we attack each HPT?

Are there any restrictions or constraints from higher authority or under international law?

Which HPTs require BDA?

What are the applicable rules of engagement (ROE)? Are streamlined clearance procedures present to ensure responsive fires and force protection?

What targeting assets (organic, attached, and supporting) are available to detect and attack HPTs?

What detect, deliver, and assess support is needed from higher headquarters?

When must requests to higher headquarters be submitted to obtain the support?

What detect, deliver, and assess support is required from subordinate units? When is reinforcing required?

What detect, deliver, and assess support requests have been received from subordinate units and what has been done with them?

Has the AGM been synchronized with the decision support template and maneuver and fire support plans?

Is a common datum in use among all concerned units? If not, are procedures in place to correct differences?

DETECT

Are HPTs incorporated in CCIRs?

What accuracy, timeliness, and validity standards; i.e., TSS are in effect for detection and delivery systems?

Are all target acquisition assets fully used?

Have responsibilities been assigned to the appropriate unit for detecting each HPT?

Have verification procedures using backup systems been established where necessary?

Are target acquisition and BDA requirements distributed properly among systems that can accomplish both?

DELIVER

Have communications links and any necessary procedures been established among the detection systems, the decisionmaker, and the delivery systems?

Have responsibilities been assigned to the appropriate unit for the attack of each HPT?

Has a backup attack system been identified for critical HPTs should the primary system be unavailable at the time the HPT is verified?

Have FSCMs and clearance procedures been established for firing across boundaries?

Have coordination procedures been established with other components for firing beyond the FSCL?

Have potential fratricide situations been identified and procedures established to positively control each potential situation?

Have responsibilities been assigned to the appropriate unit for providing BDA on specified HPTs?

What are the procedures to update the HPT list and synchronize the AGM and decision support template if it becomes necessary to change the scheme of maneuver and fire support as the tactical situation changes?

ASSESS

Are the assessment assets linked to specific HPTs? Are they still available?

Have assessment asset operators been notified of the attack of a target requiring assessment?

Have assessment asset operators been updated as to the actual target location?

Has all coordination for the assessment mission, particularly airborne assets, been accomplished?

Is the mission underway?

Has information from the mission been delivered to the appropriate unit for evaluation?

Has the targeting team reviewed the results of the attack to determine reattack requirements?

CHAPTER 5. EXECUTING THE FIRE SUPPORT PLAN

Execution implements the fire support plan and manages fire support available to combat units. It also applies fires to shape the battlespace, coordinate attacks, protect the force, and reduce duplication of effort.

SECTION I. FIRE SUPPORT COORDINATION TASKS

Basic tasks are—

- Advise the commander of changes in the status of fire support.
- Recommend changes in fire support employment based on the current tactical situation.
- Deliver fires on targets detected in the targeting process by executing attack guidance.
- Select the best supporting arm to attack a target considering availability, weaponeering, and coordination requirements.
- Clear requests for fire using an established approval mode.
- Integrate fires to support the scheme of maneuver.
- Coordinate fires between lower, adjacent, and higher units.
- Coordinate fires between the observer and supporting arm and/or multiple firing units.
- Request additional fire support when needed.
- Establish and maintain FSCMs to aid the rapid engagement of targets and provide safeguards for friendly forces/installations.
- Resolve fire support conflicts at lowest possible level.
- Disseminate information within the FSCC, to other COC staff sections, and to adjacent battalions, supporting artillery units, and higher headquarters; e.g., unit locations, FSCMs, target information, and fire support status reports.

COMPANY FIRE SUPPORT COORDINATION

When no adjacent units are affected, the coordination required for fire support is best accomplished by the company commanders and the supporting arms representatives assigned to their units. Battalion FSCCs have no need to intervene unless a requested fire support asset has to be diverted to a higher priority mission. Artillery batteries and NSFS ships can normally handle simultaneous missions. FSCs should not intervene to cancel requests for higher priority missions unless the artillery fire direction center (FDC) or ships report that they cannot handle any more missions. Simultaneous missions should not be approved if fire support effectiveness will be degraded. Coordination between companies is essential for effective battalion fire support coordination. Coordination among the supporting arms representatives within a company can be facilitated by assigning an individual the task of coordinating the company's supporting fires. Such coordination reduces the frequency with which FSCC personnel must intervene to cancel or modify requests for supporting arms and frees battalion FSCC personnel for tasks that companies cannot accomplish (e.g., coordination with higher headquarters, requesting additional fire support assets). Battalion SOPs should establish procedures for coordination between companies; e.g., cross boundary fires, target hand-offs or requests for observation support.

BATTALION FIRE SUPPORT COORDINATION

A large portion of the coordination tasks required to execute the fire support plan are accomplished at the battalion level. Battalion FSCCs monitor/receive calls for fire and air requests from the companies. This is normally performed by the appropriate supporting arms representatives (artillery LNO, AirO, NGLO, or mortar representative). Supporting arms representatives assist the FSC in performing the tasks required to coordinate and clear the missions (see section III for detailed procedures). Fires, such as a counter mechanized program, may also be initiated by the battalion FSCC. Established message routing (centralized or decentralized) and clearance procedures (positive or passive) will specify mission flow for clearance of fires.

REGIMENT FIRE SUPPORT COORDINATION

Regiment FSCCs play a key role in planning and using fire support. Regiment FSCCs assist battalion FSCCs in fire support coordination by granting clearance for fires delivered in the regiment's area of operation beyond the battalion's area of operation and coordinating the routing of aircraft with adjacent forces The attack of targets in the regiment's area of operations detected during the targeting process is coordinated at the regiment FSCC.

Artillery

The artillery LNO at the infantry regiment FSCC provides information and expertise on all artillery matters. He represents the direct support artillery battalion commander. The artillery LNO does not normally monitor artillery COF nets. The artillery LNO in each battalion FSCC and the DS artillery battalion FDC monitor those nets and forward significant information to the regiment LNO. He monitors the artillery battalion fire direction (FD) net to keep abreast of significant artillery missions. He assists the artillery LNO in battalion FSCCs in obtaining additional artillery support, if required. In the automated FSCC, he is able to automatically retrieve data from the battalion FSCCs and FDC, process artillery target information, clear artillery fires, and quickly disseminate critical fire support information to subordinate units.

Coordination of artillery fire by adjacent maneuver battalions is normally effected by direct coordination between the units involved. However, if direct coordination cannot be effected or conflicts arise which cannot be resolved, the artillery LNO or FSC at the regiment will assist by effecting the required coordination or resolving the conflict.

The artillery LNO may request fires on targets within the regiment's area of operation. These fires may be provided by the DS battalion or the fires from other artillery (GS, GS-R) units. These fires are coordinated with higher, lower, or adjacent units, as required.

Air

The AirO at the regiment FSCC provides information and expertise on all aviation matters. He monitors immediate air requests and may approve, cancel, amend or recommend that another fire support agency provide the fire support requested. He consolidates preplanned air requests forwarded from the battalions. The AirO makes recommendations to the FSC who determines, based on the commander's guidance, the best way to satisfy competing demands for air support. The regiment AirO coordinates air support missions with the regiment FSC and makes recommendations for incorporating SEAD. Approved requests for air support are forwarded to the division.

Naval Surface Fire Support

The NGLO at the infantry regiment has information and expertise on all NSFS matters. If the regiment is allocated a ship in GS, the regiment NGLO coordinates the fires of the GS ship based on the guidance from the regiment commander. These fires may also be used to reinforce the fires provided to subordinate battalions.

DIVISION FIRE SUPPORT COORDINATION

The division FSCC has the key role in conducting targeting, as well as attacking targets to support the division commander's concept of operation. It plans and coordinates fires on targets of interest to the division. The division FSCC assists the regimental FSCCs in fire support coordination. If the division generates a target to be fired, the FSC may use any of the means available to the division (lethal and nonlethal). Coordination with adjacent or higher fire support coordination agencies is required prior to firing on targets outside the division boundary.

Artillery

The AFSC in the division FSCC is also the artillery LNO. He employs the division's GS and GSR artillery in counterfire, planned fires, and the attack of detected targets in the division area of operation. He assists the artillery LNO at the infantry regiments in obtaining additional artillery support. The AFSC resolves conflicts that arise concerning artillery support that cannot be resolved at a lower level. He assists regimental artillery LNOs in effecting coordination when direct coordination cannot be accomplished.

Air

The AirO functions generally in the same manner as the regimental AirOs. He monitors immediate air requests and compiles preplanned air requests forwarded from the regiments to the division FSCC. The division AirO provides close liaison with the DASC agency to assist in coordination of requirements and routing of air support.

Naval Surface Fire Support

The division NGFO performs functions generally in the same manner as the regimental NGLOs. If a request for additional NSFS is received from any regiment, the FSC directs the NGFO to coordinate the mission with a GS ship and the regimental NGLOs. He then ensures that the requesting agency is properly linked with the appropriate ship. The NGFO plans targets to be fired by the division's GS ships.

MAGTF FORCE FIRES COORDINATION

The MAGTF FFCC plans, coordinates, and executes lethal and nonlethal fires in support of the MAGTF commander's concept of operations. The FFCC is the senior fire support coordination agency. The force fires coordinator (FFC) is responsible to the MAGTF commander for planning, coordination, and conduct of fire support operations in the MAGTF deep operation and for coordinating MSC fire support operations in the close and rear operations. The FFCC works closely and in concert with the MAGTF air section and the

G-2 target intelligence section. The FFCC is organized into four functional sections.

Plans/Target Information Section

This section conducts all planned fire support coordination functions including support for OPLAN/CONPLAN/FRAGO development and deliberate targeting. In coordination with future operations and future plans, the plans section develops the MAGTF commander's concept of fire support. This section works closely with MAGTF representatives at JFACC/HHQ fire support agencies; e.g., the deep operations coordination center (DOCC). The target information officer (TIO) organizes and conducts the MAGTF targeting board. It recommends targeting guidance, priorities, and asset allocation, to the MAGTF commander for approval or modification. Fire support planning and targeting products are handed off to current fires in the COC for execution.

Current Fires Section

Current fires executes the deep operation and coordinates fires for the close and rear operations as required. This section receives the fire support plan from target information and ATO from the air center in the TACC; monitors execution of the fire support plan; revises and adjusts the plan in keeping with the developing situation; and engages reactive targets per the MAGTF commander's guidance. Although current fires is primarily focused on the deep operations area, it is also responsible for coordinating rear area fires, conducting/coordinating deep fires, and when required, assisting the MSCs with their close fires. Within the COC, current fires coordinates closely with current operations, intelligence, the C3 analysis cell, and liaison officers (LNOs). Current fires maintains close contact with the ACE TACC and force artillery (FA). Current fires must maintain close contact with the adjacent U.S. Army DOCC in addition to the other organizations described. Current fires conducts reactive targeting with current operations and intel, and directs the attack of targets with the appropriate assets.

Force Fires Liaison Section

Force fires includes those LNOs sent from the FFCC to external (higher and adjacent) commands and those fire support LNOs sent to the MAGTF. It provides a coordinated MAGTF view of the battlespace to all external MAGTF fire support LNOs, and receives and consolidates LNO reports and requests. Force fires also provides a central location for external fires LNOs provided to the MAGTF. For more information on MAGTF fires, refer to MCWP 3-42.1, *Fire Support in MAGTF Operations*.

Air Section

The air section assists the current fires section and is directly responsible for all matters pertaining to the use of aviation assets in the current battle. It maintains close contact with the TACC, monitors the ATO, and focuses on reactive targeting in the MAGTF deep battle per targeting principles. The air section assists in validating the targets scheduled for air attack by informing the TACC of all significant target information and intelligence on the location and nature of those targets. The air section also monitors the status and readiness of ACE assets.

REAR OPERATIONS

Fire support coordination in the rear area is accomplished in the RAOC. The FSC in the RAOC, augmented by fire support representatives, coordinates and clears fire missions in the rear area. He coordinates with the senior GCE FSCC and the MAGTF FFCC for fulfilling fire support requests. The MAGTF FFCC resolves conflicts that arise in fire support coordination involving the rear area. FSCMs may be established within the rear area and should be coordinated closely with the MAGTF and GCE FSCCs.

The RAOC uses the MAGTF fire support coordination net and the MAGTF tactical net for external fire support coordination traffic. The RAOC AirO must be able to communicate on the TAR net. Internal fire support coordination traffic will be primarily on the combat service support security net.

For information on fire support coordination in the rear area, see MCWP 3-41.1, *Rear Area Operations*.

SECTION II. GAINING AND MAINTAINING SITUATIONAL AWARENESS

Rapid and effective fire support coordination requires situational awareness. An established SOP for information flow in the FSCC is essential to tracking operations. Information requirements are graphical and quantitative in nature and usually represented on situation maps, status boards, and reports.

SITUATIONAL MAPS

Situational (sit) maps provide a graphic representation of the battlespace that is only as accurate as the information reported and recorded. The following information should be kept current.

FSCMs

FSCMs must be activated and canceled relative to the tempo of the operation. They are one of the primary tools used to clear fires. FSCs at each echelon are responsible for maintaining a firm grasp of active and canceled FSCMs. The sit map must reflect the current FSCMs in effect at all echelons.

Unit Locations

Units and personnel invariably move as the operation progresses making if difficult to maintain a trace of the forward line of own troops (FLOT). This is especially true in maneuver warfare. It is only through the plotting of units both friendly and enemy (via reporting) that the fire support coordinator can maintain an accurate representation of the battlefield. This is an essential factor in preventing fratricide and creating a picture of enemy disposition.

The FSC, S-3, and S-2 should work in proximity to each other (physically or virtually). This allows unit reporting for fire support coordination purposes and allows the supporting arms representatives to provide redundancy in reporting unit locations to the FSCC.

Global positioning system (GPS) is a space-based radio navigation system that provides position, velocity, and time. It uses devices such as the precision lightweight GPS receiver (PLGR) to provide a means for units to accurately locate their positions. Accuracy of these reported positions allows for faster coordination of fires. Observers can fix their own location, enhancing their ability to locate targets accurately. The enhanced position location reporting system (EPLRS) provides a position and navigation service to users and makes position location information available to C2 systems. The service is provided in all surface environments during both day and night operations and all conditions of visibility. EPLRS is a medium for data communications, enabling users to send/receive messages. This capability is advantageous for disseminating targets, fire plans or FSCMs even if automated fire support devices are unavailable.

Targets

Active, planned, and inactive targets are plotted to graphically show the fire support plan and aid in coordinating fires. As missions are processed, a buildup of targets creates a picture of the enemy disposition.

Other Information

Fire support personnel need to maintain other pertinent data (obstacles, primary and alternate positions or engagement areas).

STATUS BOARDS AND SHEETS

Status boards and sheets reflect pertinent information for quick reference. Examples of information may include the available assets (e.g., air on station or unit FIRECAPs), ammunition status, priority targets in effect, and active mission information. See appendix N for sample FSCC status board and sheet formats. See appendix O for fire support reference data.

REPORTS

Reports vary in format from simple verbal acknowledgments to printed data search from an automated command and control system. Reports commonly used inside the FSCC reflect the status of a given fire support asset, ammunition on hand, or the status of a fire request. The basic tenets of reporting are "What do I know? Who needs to know? How do I tell them?"

INFORMATION REQUIREMENTS BY ECHELON

It is important to determine what information is essential for FSCCs at each echelon. Lower echelon FSCCs generally require greater detail on the current tactical situation in their area of operations. Higher echelon FSCCs require more general information on trends and capabilities that can affect current and future operations. Figure 5-1 on page 5-6 gives examples of the level of detail and area of emphasis most appropriate for FSCCs at each echelon for each significant category of information. It is only a guide. The tactical situation dictates specific information requirements

INFORMATION EXCHANGE

Information is of little use when not efficiently disseminated to the individual or agency that requires it. Information is exchanged over various tactical and fire support nets. Members of the FSCC and COC should not assume that information received over a fire support net is only of interest to fire support personnel or agencies. Effective communication systems must share information laterally as well as up and down the chain of command.

Automated information systems enhance our ability to share information. Parameters may be established within the system that allow it to automatically disseminate information, such as messages of interest (MOI), while search criteria for gathering information can automatically retrieve information from other databases. For example, the essential elements of a SHELREP transmitted by a company over an artillery COF net informs the battalion FSCC of the tactical situation and promptly notifies the artillery FDC so counterfire actions can be initiated (cueing of weapons-locating radars). See FMFM 6-18-1.

CATEGORY OF INFORMATION	BATTALION	REGIMENT	DIVISION
Location of Friendly Units	All organic and attached companies. Any small units or patrols in battalion's zone or sector not located with parent company; e.g., recon or security elements.	Front line trace of organic or attached battalions and locations of boundaries between battalions. Any separate units under control of regiment or in regiment's sector but outside zones or sectors of battalions.	Front line trace of organic or attached regiments and location of boundaries between regiments. Any separate units under control of division or in division's zone or sector but outside zones or sectors of regiments.
Disposition of Supporting Arms Units	Location of all sections of 81mm mortar platoon. Location of any artillery battery in the battalion's zone or sector. Firing capabilities of all DS and reinforcing artillery which can range that battalion's zone or sector. Location of any NSFS ships in DS of the battalion or in GS of the regiment or division which can range the battalion's sector. Times, routes, destinations of all artillery batteries conducting displacements in that battalion's zone or sector.	Location and firing capabilities of all units of DS artillery battalion. Location of all GS or reinforcing artillery that can range that regiment's zone or sector. DS artillery battalion's plans for displacing batteries. Location of any NSFS ship in GS of the regiment or division that can range the regiment's zone or sector.	Firing capabilities of all artillery (cannon and rocket).* Location of all NSFS ships in DS of battalions or GS to regiments or the division.* Displacement plans of artillery units to support *division* operations; e.g., attacks or withdrawals. Army/joint/coalition fire support assets. *** This information is passed to the air control agency.**
Status of Aviation	Status of assigned aircraft for air requests (preplanned and immediate; fixed and rotary wing). Information pertaining to friendly and enemy air defense.	Status of assigned aircraft for air requests for battalions and the regiment (preplanned and immediate; fixed-and rotary-wing including aircraft conducting air observation mission). Information pertaining to friendly and enemy air defense.	Status of aircraft allocation to division. Status of assigned aircraft for air requests for regiments and the division (preplanned and immediate: fixed and rotary wing including aircraft conducting air observation missions). Information pertaining to friendly and enemy air defense.
Plans of Units	Scheme of maneuver. Designation of main and supporting attacks. Any special plans that require plans of supporting fires; e.g., counter-mechanized.	Scheme of maneuver. Designation of main and supporting attacks. Designation, location, and likely employment of the reserve. Any special plans that require plans of supporting fires; e.g., counter-mechanized.	Same as regiment.
Ammunition Status	Accurate and current count of 81mm ammunition. Shortages of any type of ammunition that could affect fire support planning. Forecast of when the DS ships will leave the fire support area/station to resupply ammunition.	Count of artillery ammunition in the DS and reinforcing battalion (regiment FSCC should receive the count as often as the artillery unit calculates it - normally twice daily). Forecast of when the GS ship will leave the FSA/station to resupply ammunition. Shortages of any type of aviation ordnance that could affect fire planning.	Any changes in the available supply rate for the force of any type of ammunition. Any changes in the available supply rate for the force of any type of aviation ordnance. Count of artillery ammunition in the GS battalion(s). Forecast of when the GS ships will leave the fire support area/station to resupply ammunition.
Fire Support Coordination	FSCMs planned and in effect. Updates to targets.	Same as battalion.	Same as battalion.

Figure 5-1. Information Needed at FSCCs.

SECTION III. TACTICAL FIRE DIRECTION PROCEDURES

Tactical fire direction is the "if" and "how" to attack a target. Mission processing procedures described in this section can be used for scheduled and immediate requests for fire.

Additional considerations for offensive and defensive operations are also listed.

PROCESSING FIRE SUPPORT

The following procedures are recommended for coordinating planned and immediate fire support at all echelons. The actual order of procedures is based on message routing and approval procedures.

Plot the Target

Plot on the map all fire missions originating, impacting in, or crossing through the unit's area of operations. Verify if target attack affects friendly units, violates or requires additional FSCMs. The fire mission reference card (figure 5-2) is a useful tool for recording fire missions and keeping all FSCC, S-3, and S-2 representatives informed of on-going fire missions. Appropriate data is recorded on a preformatted (by unit SOP), laminated card or printed from an automated system and then routed to the appropriate personnel where the pertinent information is recorded.

Consult the Attack Guidance Matrix

Based on the nature of the target, extract the appropriate attack guidance to determine required effects and recommended munitions for attack. Additional considerations should include, at a minimum, ROE, priority of the mission, assets currently available, weaponeering for the chosen asset, responsiveness of the asset, coordination requirements, and commander's guidance.

Conduct Necessary Coordination

Coordinate internally with supporting arms representatives to time the delivery of fires, coordinate gun target

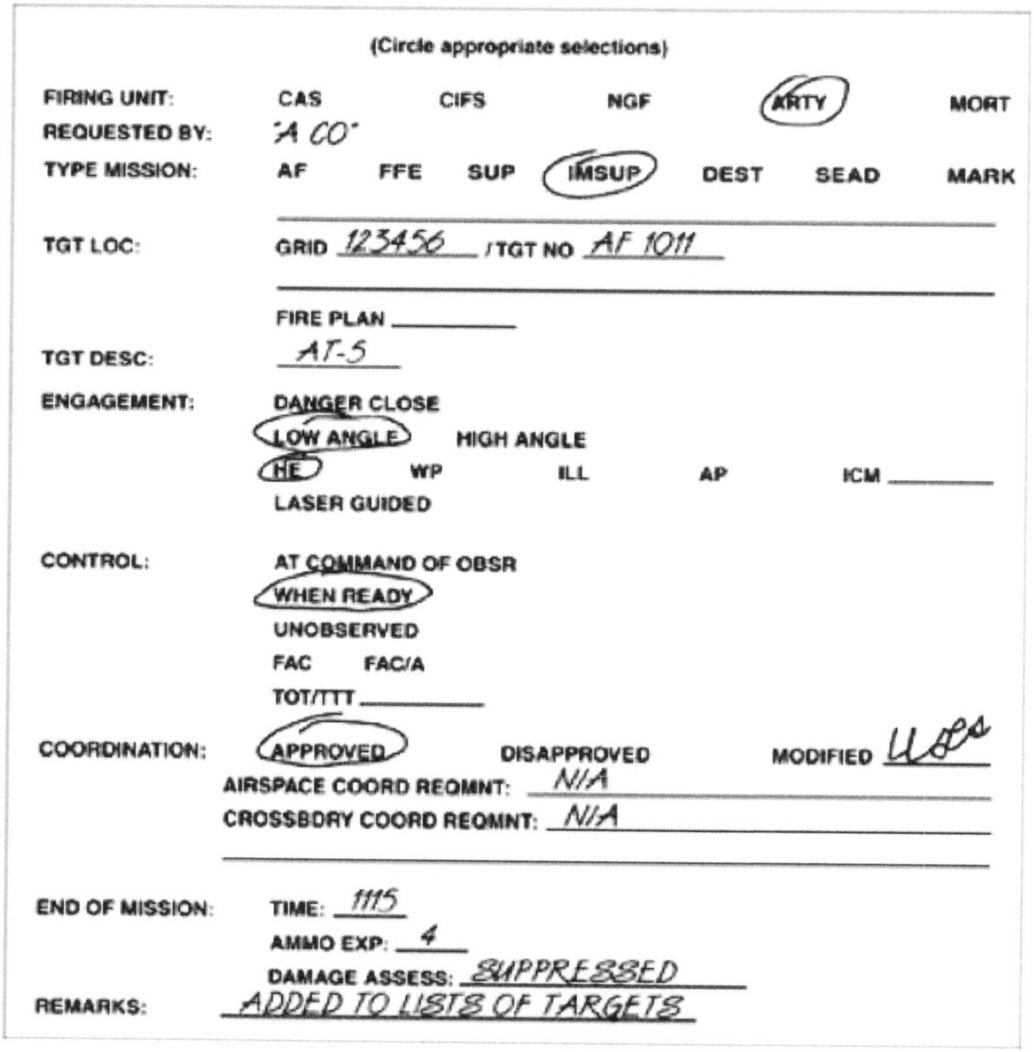
(Circle appropriate selections)

FIRING UNIT: CAS CIFS NGF ARTY MORT
REQUESTED BY: "A CO"
TYPE MISSION: AF FFE SUP IMSUP DEST SEAD MARK

TGT LOC: GRID 123456 /TGT NO AF 1011

FIRE PLAN

TGT DESC: AT-5

ENGAGEMENT: DANGER CLOSE
LOW ANGLE HIGH ANGLE
HE WP ILL AP ICM
LASER GUIDED

CONTROL: AT COMMAND OF OBSR
WHEN READY
UNOBSERVED
FAC FAC/A
TOT/TTT

COORDINATION: APPROVED DISAPPROVED MODIFIED
AIRSPACE COORD REQMNT: N/A
CROSSBDRY COORD REQMNT: N/A

END OF MISSION: TIME: 1115
AMMO EXP: 4
DAMAGE ASSESS: SUPPRESSED
REMARKS: ADDED TO LISTS OF TARGETS

Figure 5-2. Example of a Fire Mission Reference Card.

lines/airspace, etc. When appropriate, contact lower, adjacent, and higher FSCCs to coordinate fires in or across their area of operation and to request reinforcing fires or special munitions approval.

Clear Fires

The FSC and supporting arms personnel ensure that fires will not adversely affect friendly forces. There are two methods of control: positive and passive. If using positive control, a verbal or automated response will be sent to the acquisition asset and firing unit whether the mission is clear. When using passive approval procedures and decentralized message routing, missions on voice nets should at least be acknowledged.

Complete the Mission

Continue to monitor the mission (progress of the aircraft in ACAs, subsequent corrections or shifts, etc.) through completion. Record BDA or surveillance, update sit maps, cancel temporary FSCMs, priority targets, etc., and disseminate information, as appropriate.

PLANNED FIRE CONSIDERATIONS

Scheduling the attack of a target is often the most effective way to provide fire support. However, when the time of attack approaches, the FSC must verify whether or not the current situation warrants a change in the scheduled air strike or fire mission. This also applies to timing of individual targets in a schedule of fire. The FSC should specifically—

- Verify target and refinements with requesting unit and controlling agency; i.e., can designated controller still observe target, is it accurately located and still viable?

- Verify ability of supporting arm to deliver fires.

- Consider the nature of the target. Priorities and attack guidance may have changed since the air strike or fire mission was scheduled.

- Cancel mission if no longer required or if previously granted clearance has been canceled.

- Ensure that the delivery of fires does not pose unnecessary danger to friendly units and that the

fires will not cause unnecessary interference with active missions; e.g., aircraft crossing artillery GTLs.

- Determine if any additional FSCMs are needed.

OFFENSIVE OPERATIONS

To effectively coordinate fire support for an attack, the fire support plan must be established and SOPs understood by all personnel concerned with fire support. The plan must be flexible; it is usually easier to modify a plan or deviate from it than to develop a new one.

All fire support personnel must keep abreast of the developing friendly and enemy situations including dispositions, capabilities and weaknesses, and their tactics. Supporting arms commanders and their representatives must know, understand, and anticipate the supported commander's actions and requirements. Once the attack starts, the FSCC should—

- Track targets fired on, the damage assessments received, and the targets not fired on in scheduled fires. Also, know the supporting arms assets that will be switched from scheduled fires if a higher priority target is reported unexpectedly.

- Track the execution of fires during different phases of the attack. These will usually be fired when assault elements reach a certain point or request fires.

- Make use of priority targets. Shift priority targets with the maneuver unit's movement and with changes in priorities of fire. Cancel priority targets when not used or bypassed.

- Clear artillery displacements to the crossing of phase lines or objectives by supported maneuver unit. Report this movement to artillery unit immediately.

- Shift fires when lead elements cross appropriate control measures; e.g., phase line or coordinated fire line (CFL). Ensure that communications are maintained with whoever directs those fires.

- Track the location of the lead elements. This facilitates rapid clearance of fire missions.

DEFENSIVE OPERATIONS

Prompt action by FSCCs can be critical to defeating an enemy attack. Although the enemy seeks surprise in the attack, there are usually some warnings. When these indicators appear, the S-2 should rapidly notify the FSCC watch officer who should—

● Recall the principals; e.g., FSC, artillery LNO, AirO.

● Alert the supporting artillery, NSFS ships, mortars, DASC, and next higher FSCC.

● Alert forward elements responsible for observing target triggers.

● Correlate the S-2's track of the enemy's advance with critical targets/killing zones in the fire support plan. Modify planned fires as required to ensure fires are on the probable locations of the enemy's front line positions (the area he will be in when he starts exchanging fire with our front line units), his command post, his reserves, the logistical supply area for his attack units, and routes he will move his reserves over.

● Pass target data to supporting arms.

● Ensure the barrier and observation plan is coordinated with indirect and direct fires.

During the attack, the FSC should keep the big picture in focus and use his supporting arms representatives to attend to details associated with employing those assets. There are often more targets than can be handled immediately. One of the keys to success is to use the supporting arms where they most influence the action; e.g., engagement areas that contain restrictive terrain.

TIMING THE DELIVERY OF FIRES

Methods for timing the delivery of fires must be well-understood by all units involved in fire support.

Synchronized Clock

Synchronization places all units on a common time. The synchronized clock uses a specific hour and minute based on local or universal time (as dictated by operation order or unit SOP). This method makes coordination easier and is simple to establish. But, it requires all units to be placed on this established time and periodic time checks. The synchronized clock is established by the senior headquarters and disseminated to all maneuver and supporting arms units.

A local time zone may be used to establish the synchronized clock. The use of local time requires periodic, coordinated transmissions of time checks by the senior headquarters.

Universal time is based on the Zulu Time Zone. Universal time facilitates establishment because supported units/fire support agencies can independently access an automated, continuous broadcast of time, by use of HF radio on frequencies 10.000, 15.000, or 25.000 or by telephoning DSN 762-1401. Universal time is particularly advantageous when operations involve joint forces and/or aircraft are operating from remote airfields.

Elapsed Time

Delivery of fires may be timed by specifying a number of minutes (and seconds, as required) to elapse from a stated countdown reference. Elapsed time is best used in immediate or time critical situations, when a synchronized clock has not been established or its accuracy is doubtful. It is often difficult to coordinate elapsed time when several units/fire support agencies are involved; e.g., a coordinated attack of a target by air, artillery, and NSFS.

Elapsed time may be expressed using the signal MARK. A MARK is transmitted as follows: "TOT 5 minutes from my MARK . . . Standby, MARK." The fires are timed to impact exactly when the specified time has elapsed from the transmission of the "MARK." The term, "MARK," is used when transmitting to artillery, NSFS, and mortar units.

Elapsed time may also be expressed using the signal HACK. HACK is used to transmit the time-to-target (TTT) for immediate or on call CAS. The term "HACK" is used when transmitting to an aircraft/air control agency. A HACK is transmitted by specifying the number of minutes and seconds to elapse before ordnance is to impact on the target. For example "8 (minutes understood) plus 00 (seconds understood) . . . HACK." The countdown commences precisely at the transmission of "HACK."

Event-Oriented

Timing of fires may be in relation to a specific event; e.g., H-hour or H-5, crossing of phase lines, etc.

SECTION IV. CLEARANCE OF IMMEDIATE FIRE SUPPORT REQUESTS

Although fire support planning tries to identify and co-ordinate all required targets and fire support tasks, there will always be previously unlocated enemy formations or lucrative targets identified during the execution of a plan. Rapid clearance of these targets is crucial in a battalion FSCC to provide responsive fires. The FSCC must understand current friendly locations and their tactical situation, fire support capabilities, and maintain communications connectivity. The FSCC's goal should be to verify, and if necessary, approve the request in less time than it takes for the supporting arms unit to be ready to fire, thereby causing no delay, if processed concurrently. The FSCC must quickly assess the following factors to determine the "best capable" asset to furnish the required support.

OBSERVER'S REQUEST

The observer is generally in the best position to observe the target and determine the required asset and munitions. If possible, the requested asset should be used to attack the target. But because the observer is only concerned with a small portion of the battlespace, he may not understand the overall situation with fire support assets; e.g., an artillery FO sends a call for fire to the battalion FSCC requesting artillery. The artillery battalion, supporting the regiment, is massing for a

higher priority mission and is unavailable. The FSC knows that he has a NGF ship in DS of the battalion. The FSC directs the NGLO to transfer the mission to the NGF ship and coordinate observation of fires with the FO through the artillery LNO.

COORDINATION

During top-down planning, fires are planned and integrated to optimize their effects. Due to the time-sensitivity of an immediate request, the FSCC must quickly conduct the coordination with higher and adjacent units, normally done during the fire support planning process, to coordinate the fires.

FSCMs Method

FSCMs facilitate timely and safe use of fire support. When properly used, FSCMs enhance the accomplishment of the mission. For example, a properly placed coordinated fire line makes reactive counterfire more responsive since there are less coordination requirements. Effective counterfire allows the supported unit to maneuver freely and use its supporting indirect fires proactively. The application of FSCMs varies with the operation and target density. FSCMs can assist in reducing the level of coordination/clearance for various mission scenarios. Figure 5-3 illustrates a series of coordination situations.

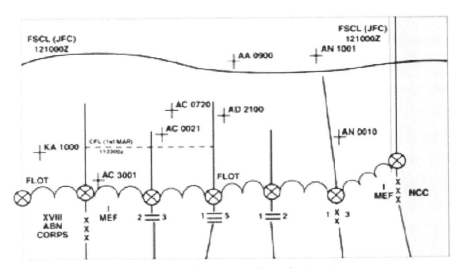

Figure 5-3. Clearance Requirements.

For 2d Bn, 1st Mar to fire on AC 3001, only internal clearance is needed (internal communications nets).

For 3d Bn, 1st Mar to fire on AC 3001, clearance from 2d Bn, 1st Mar is needed since the target plots in 2/1's zone of action and is below the CFL established by 1st Mar (1st Mar FS coordination net).

For 2d Bn, 1st Mar to conduct an airstrike on AC 0720, clearance must be obtained from 1st Mar. 2d Bn should inform and if necessary coordinate with 3d Bn on the 1st Mar FSC net. If necessary, 1st Marines should also coordinate with 5th Marines on Division FS Coordination Net concerning the routing of the aircraft into and out of 1st Marines zone.

All adjacent units desiring to fire on AD 2100 must get clearance from 5th Mar via the Division FS Coordination Net. No CFL is established and the target is in 5th Marines' zone.

For 2d Bn, 1st Mar to fire on AC 0021, clearance is not required since target is beyond CFL; however, 3/1 should be informed via the Regimental FS Coordination net as to the nature of the target and its effects.

All 1st MarDiv units desiring to fire on AN 0010 must coordinate with 3d MarDiv before firing. The target is in 3d MarDiv's zone of action. If 2/5 wants to fire on AN 0010, they may be able to coordinate directly with the adjacent battalion in 3d Mar Div.

AA 0900 is inside I MEF's forward boundary and beyond the FSCL. Fires beyond the FSCL do not require coordination but do require units or assets in the MEF's zone of action (reconnaissance teams or aviation assets) to inform the MEF of the fires against the target. To affect this, units desiring to attack targets beyond the FSCL must inform higher, adjacent, and supporting units.

For 2d Bn, 1st Mar to fire on KA 1000, 2/1 must coordinate through 1st Mar. 1st Mar would coordinate through 1st MARDIV with I MEF, who would contact the XVIII ABN Corps for approval. 2/1 may be able to coordinate directly with the adjacent battalion within XVIII ABN Corps.

For the naval component commander (NCC) to fire on AN 1001, the NCC must coordinate with I MEF for approval. The target is in the MEF's zone short of

the MEF forward boundary, but beyond the FSCL. If resolution cannot be achieved, then the JFC would effect coordination.

Attached Army multiple launched rocket system (MLRS) units are capable of delivering two types of fires: rocket and ATACMS. Rocket fires are cleared the same as cannon artillery fires. However, ATACMS fires include activation/deactivation of platoon airspace hazards (PAHs) and target air hazards (TAHs) since they normally engage targets well beyond the FSCL.

Gun-Target Line Method

GTLs are used in conjunction with coordinating air and indirect fires. It is an imaginary straight line from the guns to and through the target. Often selecting the unit to fire based on the GTL line can make the difference in the effects of fires on a target and when fires are lifted due to the proximity of friendly troops. The regular exchange of information between an FSCC and the FDC; e.g., locations of artillery positions or locations of maneuver units to FDC enhances selecting units to fire based on GTL geometry. The importance of GTLs in fire support coordination is illustrated in examples 1 and 2, page 5-12.

In example 1 on page 5-12, the artillery is to support an infantry company's attack on an enemy position. Dispersion of points of impact of mortar and artillery shells is greater along the GTL than on either side of the line. Selecting Battery A rather than Battery B to fire on the objective allows the infantry to advance closer before lifting fires due to the GTL. The artillery battalion FDC normally selects the battery to fire. Therefore, the FSC may be required to request a specific unit to fire, if possible.

In example 2 on page 5-12, NGF and artillery can range the target. The target is a suitable type for both artillery and NGF. However, the target is parallel to the GTL of the ship positioned at FSS 2. Dispersion of point of impact of NGF is greater along the GTL than on either side of the line and is more pronounced than the dispersion of artillery and mortars. Therefore, the FSCC selects NGF to conduct the engagement.

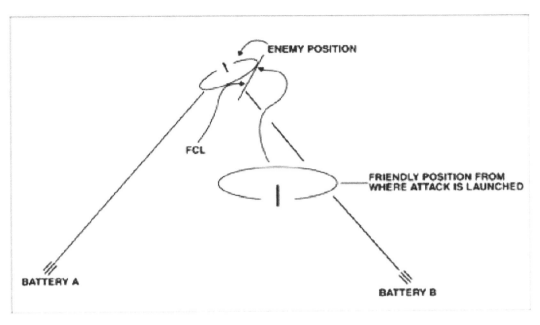

EXAMPLE 1
Selection of a Particular Gun-Target Line

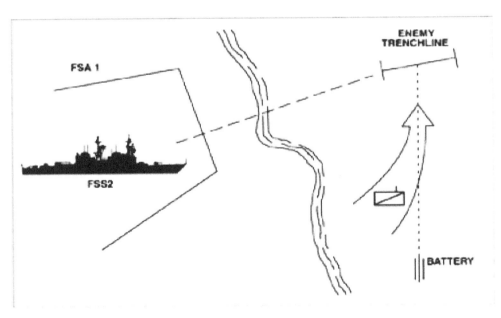

EXAMPLE 2
Selection of a Supporting Arm Based on Gun-Target Line

WEAPONEERING

Weaponeering is selecting the appropriate weapon and munitions based on the desired effects and the lethality or nonlethality of a specific munition.

For example, the battalion FSCC has POF of an artillery battalion, which is not currently being used, and a section of AV-8Bs are holding at a contact point. A commander wishes to neutralize an enemy mechanized company to delay the enemy's ability to support its breaching operations. The FSC may choose artillery fires to meet the task because of its ability to maintain fires for a period of time and the lethality of DPICM against mechanized armor. Should the commander wish to destroy the enemy's breaching vehicles, the FSCC may choose the section of AV-8Bs since they are more precision-capable to strike individual vehicles than artillery. Or, the FSC may choose to use artillery and EW aviation for a combined arms effect.

WEAPONS RESPONSIVENESS AND RANGE

The FSCC must consider the amount of time that a weapon system requires to respond and its ability to operate under the current weather or illumination conditions. The requested system must have the range to engage the target.

ACCURACY

Target location error (TLE) is the major contributor to ineffective fires. The FSCC must consider the observers ability to accurately determine the target's location. Does the observer have a GPS receiver or a laser range finder? While not using these tools should not preclude the FSCC from clearing fires, all participants must understand the ramification of TLE against munitions effectiveness. Another consideration is the weapon's ability to locate the target and achieve the desired effects. Laser spot trackers, forward looking infrared (FLIR), naval telecommunications system (NTS), target location designation hands-off system (TLDHS), and modular universal laser equipment (MULE) increase the chances to effect the target.

THE THREAT

The FSCC must visualize the current enemy situation and capabilities. The enemy's ability must be assessed against the use of a particular fire support asset. The existence of a threat may be prohibitive to a fire support asset and cause the FSCC to either react to the threat or find another asset that is not affected in order to complete the mission. For example, a company requests 15 minutes of artillery suppression on an objective. The enemy is known to have counterbattery radar and an active counterfire ability. The FSCC must decide if this threat precludes the firing of the mission with indirect fire or determine the means to mitigate the enemy's ability to acquire by requesting jamming or aviation to locate and destroy the counterbattery radar.

SECTION V. INTEGRATING AND COORDINATING AIR SUPPORT

One of the most challenging tasks performed by an FSCC is integrating and coordinating air support with surface fires. The overarching goal is integrating fire support assets and maneuver to achieve the desired effects from the air attack without suspending the use of the other supporting arms or unnecessarily delaying the scheme of maneuver. An additional goal is to offer a reasonable measure of protection to the aircraft from the unintended effects of our own surface fires and enemy fires.

INFORM SUPPORTING ARMS UNITS

When an air attack is requested, the FSC of the originating unit (battalion, regiment, or division) informs other concerned FSCCs and supporting arms units on the details of the mission as quickly as possible. The FSC will pass the aircrafts' time of arrival on station and tentative CAS TOT or CAS TTT. All timing for SEAD fires is based on a specific aircraft event time; e.g., CAS TOT/TTT on assault support L-hour. In immediate SEAD fire missions, the aircraft event time becomes the zero hour or H-hour for scheduling. The preferred method for coordinating timing is the use of a previously established synchronized clock. If a synchronized clock has not been established or is not universally available, an elapsed time may be used to coordinate timing. The FSC must also coordinate the route of the aircraft into and out of the units zone and ensure that the aircraft route does not adversely impact adjacent units.

DETERMINE SURFACE FIRES TO SUPPORT AIR ATTACK

The two primary forms of support are target marking and SEAD. They are often used together.

Target Marking

Whenever possible, a mark, with a back-up planned, should be provided to CAS aircraft. Targets can be marked by various means, including laser, artillery, mortars, NSFS, direct fire, another aircraft, or IR pointer. If none of these methods are available then the target should be identified by narrative description given by the terminal controller.

The mark is best coordinated directly by the FO and FAC working together, with the FO relaying instructions directly to the firing unit. Usually it is desirable to have the marking round burst 20-30 seconds before the aircraft's bombs impact on the target. WP usually provides an adequate mark although in high winds it quickly dissipates. Illumination is also usable as a mark. Illumination can be set to function and burn on the ground, or it can be set to function slightly above ground level for certain conditions; e.g., marking in snow. The M825 fired as a graze burst provides a large, long duration mark but is usually a limited commodity.

SEAD

The need for SEAD is assessed after evaluating options for routing aircraft away from known antiair threats. SEAD is that activity that neutralizes, destroys, or temporarily degrades enemy air defenses in a specific area by physical attack and/or EW. It may be accomplished through destructive means (indirect fire, direct fire, air attack or raids), disruptive means (EW, deception or flight tactics), or a combination of both.

The primary objective of SEAD is to destroy or degrade enemy surface-to-air defense capabilities, thereby increasing freedom of action and survivability of aircraft. Specific SEAD objectives will vary with the MAGTF's mission. SEAD involves planning and coordination from the company level up through the senior FSCC.

Localized and immediate SEAD are two types of planned SEAD; opportune SEAD is against targets of opportunity. Localized SEAD is usually done at the highest levels to ensure an area is clear of enemy air defense assets. Immediate SEAD is also planned and is similar to an on call mission. Opportune SEAD is generally used with immediate CAS requests. It requires terminal controllers to perform the immediate coordination of aircraft and indirect fires. (This is usually when the SEAD CFF is used.)

SEAD is most frequently delivered in support of a specific air attack. This involves attacking air defense weapons that can threaten friendly aircraft in the immediate vicinity of the target and on the aircrafts' ingress and egress routes. SEAD is normally planned in a schedule of fires or as a specific program. However, during an immediate CAS mission fire support personnel at the battalions and companies may have to perform opportune SEAD missions against air defense assets that had not been previously identified. See MCWP 3-16.6, *Supporting Arms Observer, Spotter, and Controller Handbook*, chapter 8.

Conducting SEAD with other supporting arms; e.g., mortars or artillery normally requires firing at the sustained rate of fire for a short period. SEAD effectiveness depends on accurate target location. The FSC, working with the FAC and FO, usually coordinates SEAD with target marking. For detailed information on SEAD, see MCWP 3-22.2, *Suppression of Enemy Air Defenses*.

Figure 5-4 on page 5-15 is an example of the steps and radio transmissions during a CAS mission with SEAD. As necessary information becomes available, some steps are completed simultaneously. The example illustrates coordination requirements. Specific aircraft tactics may differ. The FSC is assisting in immediate airspace coordination based on his situational awareness.

Step 1: CAS requested. Information FSCCs need to establish airspace coordination is included in the request; e.g., target location, IP, egress instructions, desired time of air strike, and special instructions such as offset. Standard request is in tactical air support request format.

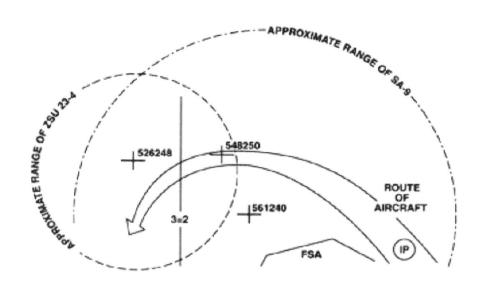

Figure 5-4. Sample CAS Mission with Opportune SEAD and Marking Support.

Step 2: FO requests SEAD fires on known AAA weapon in zone and a marking of target with artillery. FSCC monitors.

"Artillery Battalion, this is FO, SEAD, OVER. Grid to suppress—561240, grid to mark—548250, over. SA-9 in open, DPICM, continuous, standby for CAS TOT, over."

Step 3: 2d Bn, 1st Mar FSCC plots CAS mission on map using appropriate flight profile. FSC determines additional threat at 526248. The FSC instructs NGLO to initiate a SEAD mission on grid 526248. The spotter monitors and informs FO.

"Ship, this is NGLO, SEAD fire mission, target number AA2335, OVER. Grid to suppress—526248, altitude 120, direction 5110, ZSU 23-4, HE/CVT, 1 gun, 30 Salvos, continuous, standby for CAS TOT, over."

Step 4: The FSC determines what airspace coordination is needed. He selects lateral separation for the artillery fires on grid 561240. He selects altitude separation for the NGF on grid 526248 (NGLO determines maximum trajectory from FSA/FSS at the point where aircraft will cross to be 2,500 feet MSL). The FAC and FO are notified of the actions.

"FO, this is Artillery LNO. CAS will stay north of artillery fires." (Arty FDC monitors).

"FAC, this is AirO. Keep CAS north of artillery fires at grid 561240, stay above 2,500 feet MSL on egress to clear NGF on grid 526248."

Step 5: The FSC requests clearance from adjacent Bn FSCC for attack of target outside Bn's zone and for use if airspace (Regiment FSCC monitors and takes action as required).

"3d Battalion FSCC, this is 2d Battalion FSCC. Request clearance on NGF SEAD on grid 526248 at approximately 1019 through 1021. Egress south your airspace at approximately 1020."

Step 6: FAC briefs pilot. (Normal brief.)

Step 7: 3d Bn FSCC grants clearance. If the situation changes, appropriate notification will be made.

"2d Battalion FSCC, this is 3d Battalion FSCC, NGF on grid 526248 cleared."

Step 8: FAC sets CAS TOT (AirO monitors, informs FSC). Final coordination commences.

"Artillery Battalion, this is FO, CAS TOT 1020, over."

[**NOTE:** Artillery marking round will impact at 1019:30; SEAD fires will impact from 1019 through 1021.]

"Ship, this is NGLO, CAS TOT 1020, over."

DETERMINE REQUIRED AIRSPACE COORDINATION

A function of fire support coordination is to coordinate airspace usage when required. Indirect fire weapons and aircraft require the use of airspace to perform their missions. The ingress normally expressed as a final attack heading or final attack cone, egress routing of CAS aircraft, and gun-target lines are the largest factors in identifying coordination requirements. Several techniques may be employed. The method selected depends on the time available, tactical situation, unit SOP, and state of training.

Airspace Coordination Areas

A formal ACA requires detailed planning. It is not always needed but should always be considered. Upper and lower limits should be designed to allow freedom of action for air and surface FS for the greatest number of foreseeable targets. The artillery liaison officer and the FDC can determine the trajectory for a specific battery firing at a specific target to determine if it is safe to fire while an ACA is in effect. The FSC should consult the artillery liaison officer when deciding the altitude of an ACA. The objective is to determine if that altitude will allow the majority of targets to be attacked without interference problems.

Helicopter Operations

Helicopters require further coordination measures including helicopters employed to provide CAS, combat assault transport, aerial observation, and medical evacuation (MEDEVAC). Helicopter flights, fixed-wing aircraft flights, and indirect fires must be coordinated.

Helicopter routes are used as approach and retirement lanes for safe transit across the battlespace. They may also be designated as ACAs when they are actually in use by in-flight helicopters.

A holding area (HA) may be established for helicopters awaiting targets or missions. HAs serve as infor-mal ACAs while in use. They provide the helicopter an area and altitude in which to operate. HAs may be established during planning or operations, are referred to by name or number and effective time, and are activated when in use. For example—

Activation of Planned HA—HA Cobra, surface to 1,200 feet mean sea level or above ground level, effective (time) to (time).

Establish HA—HA Rattler, grid squares 0577 and 0677, surface to 500 feet mean sea level or above ground level, effective (time) to (time).

The battle position (BP) is a maneuvering area that contains firing points for attack helicopters. Like HAs, BPs serve as informal ACAs while they are in use. The planning and methods of establishment are also similar to those used for HAs. For more information on HA/BPs, see MCWP 3-23.1, *Close Air Support.*

Separation Plans

Separation plans are another means of coordinating airspace. There are four separation techniques to achieve airspace coordination for CAS or other aircraft in the area of operations.

Lateral Separation (Adjacent Targets)

Lateral separation plans are for coordinating attacks against two targets that are close together. The coordinator must know the GTL so the FAC/AO can restrict any aircraft crossing this line. Establishing a temporary, informal ACA is one way to do this. The aircraft (and/or airborne controller) are kept away from indirect supporting fires by lateral separation. For example, "Aircraft stay north of artillery fires at grid 561240." Or, "Aircraft stay north of the 24 grid line from easting 50 to 60." The ACA should be large enough so that aircraft can operate over the target, yet small enough so that supporting fires are not too restricted. The ACA can be defined by grid coordinates, grid lines, geographical features, or time. Figure 5-5 on page 5-17 illustrates lateral separation.

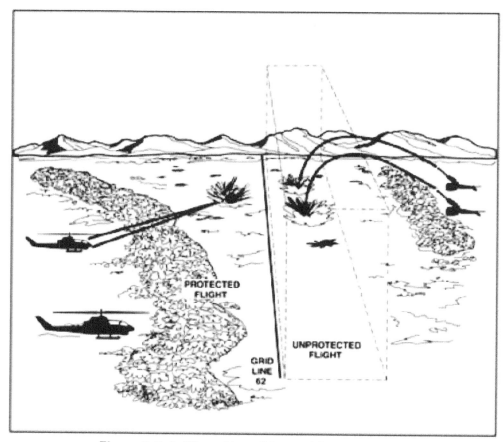

Figure 5-5. Artillery-Aircraft Lateral Separation.

Altitude Separation (Same Target)

Altitude separation plans can be used when CAS and indirect supporting fires are employed on the same target. The altitude restriction ensures clearance from both direct and indirect fire weapon's fragmentation pattern. For aircraft attacking the same target that is being suppressed, the altitude separation can be computed using the appropriate altitude in figure 5-6. See also figure 5-7 on page 5-18.

Supporting Arm	Method of Fire	Altitude Restriction (in feet AGL)
Artillery	Low Angle	2,000
Naval Gunfire	All Charges	2,000
Mortars		MAX ORD
Tank Main Gun		2,000
LAV 25mm Gun		3,000
M2 .50 caliber		3,000

Figure 5-6. Recommended Altitude Separation for Weapon System Effects.

Altitude and Lateral Separation (Different Targets)

When CAS engages a target that requires crossing a GTL, altitude restrictions can be computed based on where the indirect fires trajectory intersects the final attack cone. It can also be used for support aircraft crossing GTLs (see figure 5-8 on page 5-19). Required information for computations includes—

- Aircraft final attack cone.
- Firing unit location, munition type and charge to be fired.
- Firing unit range to target and vertical interval (target altitude - battery altitude = VI).

Computations for altitude and lateral separation lend to coordinating preplanned CAS. With adequate training they can be used with immediate CAS (see figure 5-9 on page 5-20). Computations require trajectory charts from the appropriate tabular firing tables (HE and DPICM) and a final attack cone template. When altitudes are passed, specify as above ground level or mean sea level.

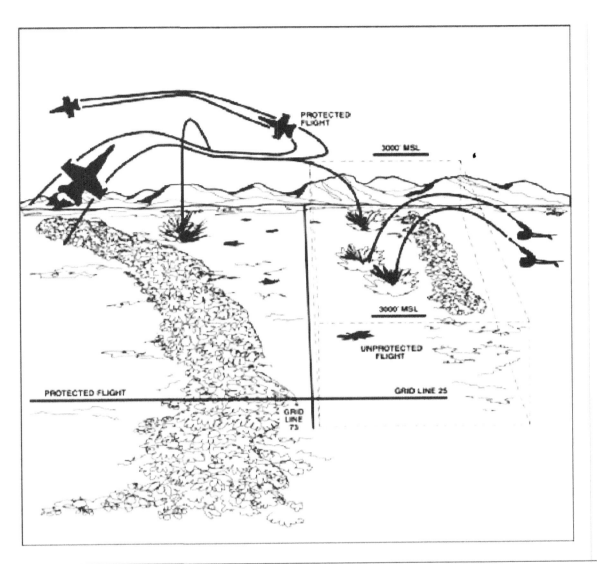

Determining the Ordinate at a Point Along the Trajectory
Determine the GTL and the firing unit range to target.
Determine the munition type and charge being fired.
Determine vertical interval (VI=Tgt Altitude - Firing Unit Altitude in meters).
Determine where the final attack heading or cone crosses the GTL and the gun target range at those points.
Refer to the appropriate trajectory chart by munition/charge and determine the arc corresponding to range to target.
Determine the altitude (in meters) corresponding to the ranges where the final attack cone crosses the gun target line by tracing the arc to those ranges.
Highest altitude + VI = ALT 1. Multiply by 33 to covert to feet (Note: if the final attack cone straddles the summit of the trajectory, use Max Ord for ALT 1.)
Lowest altitude + VI = ALT 2. Multiply by 33 to convert to feet.
Incorporate a 1000 foot buffer for nonstandard conditions.
ALT 1 + 1000=STAY ABOVE (expressed to the next highest 100 feet AGL). ALT 2 - 1000=STAY BELOW (expressed to the next lowest 100 feet AGL).

Figure 5-7. Artillery-Aircraft Altitude and Lateral Separation.

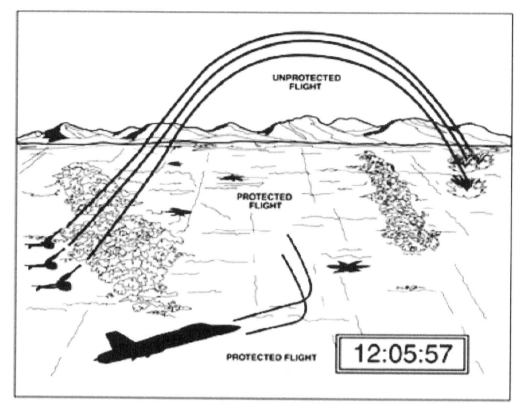

Figure 5-8. Altitude Restriction Computations.

Time Separation (Same or Different Target)

Time separation may be required when aircraft cannot be routed away from indirect-fire trajectories. This technique requires the timing of fires to be coordinated with the routing of aircraft so that even though aircraft and indirect fires may occupy the same space, they do not do so at the same time. For low-level CAS attacks, time separation can be used when aircraft are attacking targets just short of indirect fires along the GTL. See figure 5-10 on page 5-21.

NIGHT CLOSE AIR SUPPORT

Attacking moving targets or providing CAS at night is limited to low threat situations. In a night high threat scenario, current capability is very limited. The most important advantage of night CAS is the limitation it imposes on all enemy optically-sighted antiaircraft artillery (AAA) and infrared (IR) surface-to-air missiles

(SAMs). This is particularly true if operators do not have night vision devices. Airborne and ground illumination may degrade enemy night vision capabilities. Darkness imposes limitations on using CAS. During night and twilight, pilots have more difficulty visually locating targets and accurately distinguishing enemy and friendly forces.

Night CAS missions require extensive planning. TACPs must emphasize target and friendly force identification and the availability of target designation/illumination assets.

Target Identifiers

Although executing CAS missions at night has many advantages, darkness and unfavorable weather exasperates the problem for aviators to identify targets. To increase aviation assets effectiveness and strive for first pass hits, fire support planners

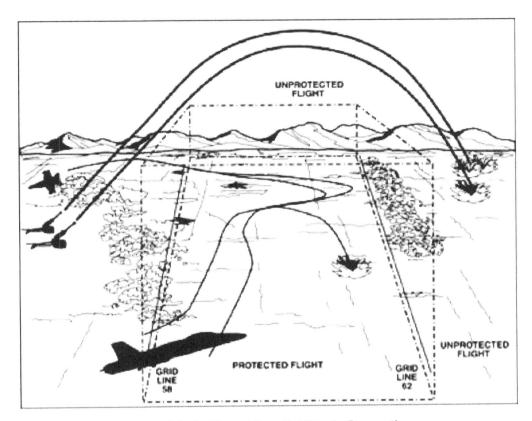

Figure 5-9. Artillery-Aircraft Altitude Separation.

must consider multiple and redundant means to aid aviators in identifying targets.

Airborne Illumination

Most USMC aircraft capable of providing CAS can employ flares that provide illumination for up to 3 minutes. See MCWP 3-23, *Offensive Air Support.*

Surface Delivered Illumination

Illumination can be delivered by artillery, mortars, and NSFS to illuminate the target area. If more than one illumination round is employed, pilots must be briefed. Illumination on the deck has a tendency to degrade NVG performance and disorient pilots. Use of 81mm mortar red phosphorous may also be considered for night CAS MARKS.

Enemy Ground Fire

Enemy ground fire, AAA, tracer rounds, and SAM firings can disclose target locations.

Laser Designators and IR Pointers

These tools can enhance night target acquisition. CAS aircraft with laser spot trackers can acquire targets marked by a designator without using conventional illumination. FACs and terminal controllers armed with IR pointers can identify targets to pilots using NVGs quicker than by "talking-on." Coordination is paramount between the ground unit, FAC, and CAS aircraft. Controllers and aviators must be wary of the number of pointers used by adjacent friendly units and the enemy. If there are a number of IR beams in the area, it will be difficult for CAS aircraft to identify the correct target area. All USMC aircraft can acquire laser or IR illuminated targets.

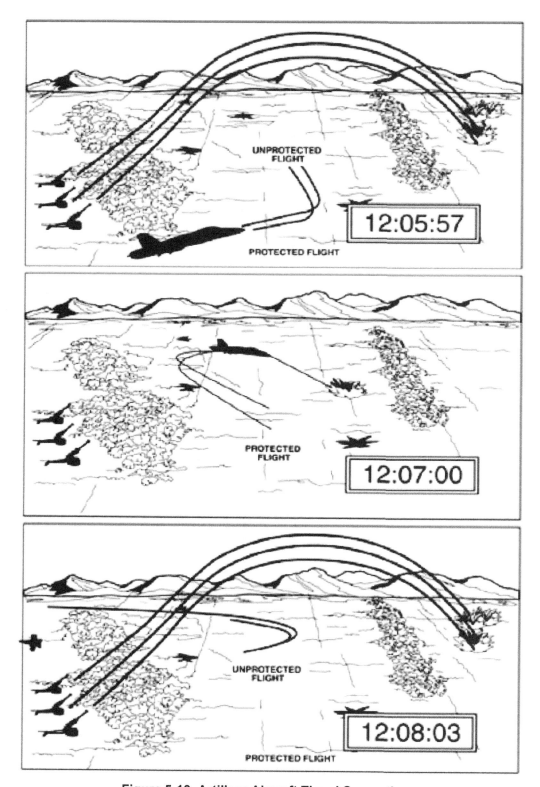

Figure 5-10. Artillery-Aircraft Timed Separation.

Friendly Positions

Marking friendly positions improves CAS safety and can provide target area references. Whenever possible, friendly positions should be marked if safe separation is a factor.

Flares in the air, such as pyrotechnics and 40mm illumination grenades, are effective marks but are usually visible to the enemy. Wind and cloud cover are important factors in using flares successfully at night.

Strobe lights, if available, can be used for night marking. Infrared filters can be installed when using NVGs and FLIR-equipped aircraft.

Any light source that can be readily covered and uncovered can be used for coded signaling. Vehicle headlights are useful nighttime marks, but for security, cover headlights and use tail or brake lights.

SECTION VI. DASC-FSCC COORDINATION

Upon phasing control ashore, the DASC directs OAS and assault support functions under the operational control of the TACC. The DASC is the principal air control agency responsible for directing aviation operations that support ground forces. The DASC processes requests for OAS, assault support, and reconnaissance. It provides procedural control for aircraft transiting its area of operations and coordinates with the ground force on routes, FARPs, frequencies, and airspace control measures.

The DASC or a DASC liaison team collocates with the GCE FSCC for the most effective integration of direct air support missions. This ensures the most economical use of resources for a timely, flexible response to requests from the MAGTF. When collocation is not possible; e.g., with a GCE FSCC in a fast moving mobile operation or during displacements, reliable communications must be established between the two agencies. See MCWP 3-25.5, *Direct Air Support Center Handbook*.

DASC RESPONSIBILITIES

The DASC is responsible to provide timely information to the FSCC on—

- Aircraft routing plans.

- BDAs reported by air crews.

- The status of outstanding requests.

- Pertinent intelligence data.

- Recommended FSCMs as they relate to air support.

- Changes to the ATO.

- UAV operations to preclude interference with surface fires.

- Air defense weapons status.

- Aircraft availability to satisfy joint tactical air strike requests (JTARs)/assault support requests (ASRs).

- Validation on requirements if requests were not received over TAR/HR.

- Diverts aircraft from preplanned missions if required.

- Recommendations on air allocation.

- Recommended alert status of aircraft (alert 15, 30, 60, etc.).

- FARP status.

FSCC RESPONSIBILITIES

The FSCC continuously provides the DASC with pertinent information. The point to remember is that the DASC pictures the battlefield based on the information it is provided by the FSCC, other MACCS agencies, and reports received from pilots. Information passed by the FSCC to the DASC includes—

- Boundaries, FSCMs, and maneuver checkpoints.

- Positions of indirect fire weapons.

- Pertinent intelligence data, especially antiair threats.

- Friendly unit locations.

- Scheme of maneuver, objectives, and the commander's intent.

- Air targets that require terminal control that exceeds the GCE's organic TACP capability; e.g., FAC(A).

- Status of terminal controllers with the GCE.

- Schedules of fire (and changes).

- LAAD locations (if LAAD is in DS of the GCE).

SECTION VII. COUNTERFIRE COLLECTING AND REPORTING

Counterfire is fire intended to destroy or neutralize the enemy indirect fire capability. It provides freedom of maneuver and unrestricted use of friendly indirect fire support. Units must be prepared to determine and report counterfire information.

Counterfire information produces intelligence on the location, number, disposition, zones of fire, caliber, and type of enemy artillery, mortar, and rocket weapons. It has great value in estimating enemy tactical capabilities. Counterfire information may also disclose new types of enemy ammunition and weapons, a knowledge that may permit early development of effective countermeasures.

COLLECTION MEANS

Some means used to collect information are crater and shell fragment analysis, SHELREPs, and detection by target acquisition devices; e.g., radars, air and ground observation, electronic signatures, and target prediction. Counterfire information is forwarded by observers to the FSCC in the most direct manner for processing. The SHELREP usually provides the medium for this reporting. The SHELREP allows for cueing of artillery radars in the appropriate search sector to locate the weapon. The FSCC will use this information to locate the enemy firing agency. Based on commander's guidance, several sources of information, intelligence or reports may be required to confirm target location. Once the target meets the criteria, the FSCC will task an agency to perform counterfire. Chapter 3, section IV discusses the planning sequence for counterfire.

REACTIVE COUNTERFIRE

Proactive counterfire based on IPB is the preferred counterfire method. However, not all enemy indirect fire can be destroyed prior to commencing an attack.

Reactive counterfire normally requires quick response capabilities for optimum effectiveness. MCRP 3-16B, *Targeting and Procedures for Time Critical Targeting*, has an indepth discussion of attacking time-sensitive targets. Aviation assets provide an excellent source to provide reactive counterfire, particularly outside the GCE's area of influence. An air quick fire channel, TAD-UHF net can be established between the counterfire section in the FDC, FSCC, or a FAC(A). Upon target acquisition, the AirO hands off the mission to the FAC(A), who executes with available CAS. Prior coordination with the DASC and coordination techniques for maneuver and indirect fires must be incorporated into the fire support plan.

SECTION VIII. FAMILY OF SCATTERABLE MINES

Artillery and air delivered mines provide the maneuver commander with a rapid, flexible means of delaying, canalizing, or attriting enemy forces in offensive and defensive operations. Family of scatterable mines (FASCAM) can also augment conventional minefield capability. The engineer officer and the G-3/S-3 at each level of command share the primary staff responsibility for the planning and employment of mines. The engineer advises the G-3 on the use of all minefield systems, including FASCAM. The G-3/S-3 recommends priorities, delegation of employment to subordinates, restrictions on usage, and positioning of minefields. The FSC has two responsibilities in incorporating FASCAM into the unit's minefield program: advising the supported unit on the capabilities and limitations of FASCAM and keeping the supporting arms notified as far in advance as possible of the supported unit's intentions to use FASCAM. The delivery of FASCAM may require approval from higher headquarters.

AIR DELIVERED MINES

Air delivered FASCAM has the same advantages of artillery FASCAM but can be employed anywhere aviation flies. The major difference between the two is that air delivered FASCAM has three selectable times: 4 hours, 48 hours or 15 days. Artillery has two options discussed below. Both types of mines are found in one piece of ordnance: the GATOR, CBU 78. It consists of 60 submunitions: 45 BLU-91B antitank and 15 BLU-92B antipersonnel mines. The mines arm themselves within two minutes of deployment. The BLU-91B employs the same warhead and functions as remote antiarmor mine system (RAAMS). The BLU-92B employs an omni-directional warhead and a fragmentation case to create its antipersonnel effect. It employs four 40 feet tripwires for detection. GATOR is best suited for preplanned missions. They are requested using the JTAR via normal air request channels. Regardless of the location of air delivered mines in relation to the FSCL, the use of air delivered mines is coordinated because of their obvious effect on future operations.

ARTILLERY DELIVERED MINES

RAAMS and area denial artillery munition (ADAM) each come in two preset self-destruct times: short duration (4 hours) and long duration (48 hours). Mines begin self-destructing at 80 percent of the stated time. Both munitions have an approximate 4.5 percent dud rate. When both munitions are employed together, fire ADAM *last*.

RAAMS (M718-L and M741-S)

RAAMS are used to achieve tactical kills on tanks and other armored vehicles. Each projectile contains nine mechanically fuzed, antitank mines. Upon arming (approximately 45 seconds after impact), the mine uses electromagnetic signature to detonate a shaped charge at the vehicle when it passes over the top of the mine. Mines function right side up or down, but only achieve mobility kills at cants of greater than 30 degrees. Some mines have an anti-disturbance feature.

ADAM (M692-L and M731-S)

ADAM projectiles are used against personnel. Each projectile contains 36 antipersonnel mines. Upon fuze function of the projectile, individual mines are dispersed over the target area. While arming (complete by 2 minutes after impact), each mine deploys 7 anti-disturbance, tripwire sensors. When disturbed, the mine propels its munition 3-8 feet into the air, detonating into 600 1.5 grain steel fragments. When employed in combination with other projectiles, ADAM rounds are always the last rounds fired.

MINEFIELD TARGET CATEGORIES

Two types of minefield target categories may be employed using FASCAM: planned and targets of opportunity. The type used depends on the amount of planning and coordination time available and the desired density of the minefield. The primary reference for minefield employment is MCWP 3-16.4/FM 6-40, *Manual Cannon Gunnery*.

Planned minefields are normally initiated and coordinated at higher echelons. They are planned as scheduled or on call to support barrier/obstacle plans. Planned minefields can consist of either short or long duration mines.

Targets of opportunity are immediate minefields initiated by calls for fire or unplanned operational changes. They consist of short duration mines delivered in preplanned or standard planning modules. Normally, a standard target of opportunity minefield is an adjusted, low angle, short duration, 200 x 400 RAAMS, 400 x 400 ADAM, medium density field. Depending on variables, this consists of approximately 36 to 48 RAAMS and 12 ADAM projectiles. Authorization to employ FASCAM and the number of howitzers immediately available to fire is a large factor in responsiveness.

Firing Unit Considerations

Three factors must be considered when employing artillery delivered FASCAM: the counterfire threat, availability of the desired munition, and how long the artillery unit will be occupied firing. The FSC must coordinate with the firing agency prior to execution to ensure responsiveness.

Minefield Density and Size

Standard minefield modules are 400 by 400 meters for ADAM and high angle RAAMS. Low angle RAAMS use a 200 x 200 meter module. The width of the field is always applied as a multiple of the module planning size. Lengths determine the number of aim points and are always the longest axis.

There are three basic minefield types *categorized by required density*: low, medium, and high density. Density depends on the mission of the minefield. A low density minefield harasses an enemy but is quickly breached. A medium density field will provide an effective obstacle if the minefield is covered with direct fire and enemy vehicles are buttoned up. High density fields require considerable clearing and are useful for forces that are heavily outnumbered and cannot provide adequate covering fires for the obstacle or need time to withdraw to subsequent positions.

Ammunition availability, unit positioning, and delivery capabilities provide an estimate of how many meters of minefield are available. The basic allowance for FAS-

CAM for a unit is low and normally restricted to short duration mines. To use significant quantities of FASCAM requires added logistical planning and a decision to use ammunition transport assets to move FASCAM at the expense of other, more widely used munitions. Minefields should be emplaced using all available units rather than firing one unit for a long duration.

SAFETY ZONE DETERMINATION

The safety zone represents the effective obstacle for friendly forces as it contains spillover mines from the targeted area (99 percent within the safety zone). No friendly forces should be located within the safety zones prior to emplacement nor maneuver through them before destruction. The FSC is responsible for obtaining safety zones. Safety zones for preplanned minefields are computed by the FSC for incorporation by the engineer and distribution by the G-3. Safety zones for short duration minefields are computed by the artillery FDC and forwarded to higher headquarters via the FSC after the mission is completed. The engineer officer coordinates the field artillery planning sheet with the FSC. Automated fire support systems (like AFATDS) can determine safety zones for FASCAM minefields. See figure 5-11.

Fired Minefield Data

See table 5-1. Use the following fired minefield data:

- Type of projectile fired (ADAM or RAAMS).

- Trajectory (high or low angle).

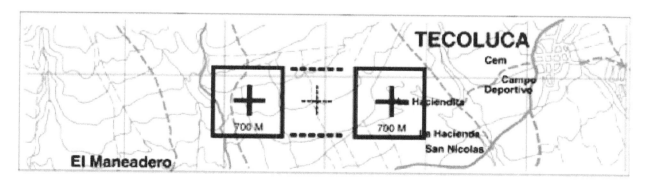

Figure 5-11. Safety Zone Example.

Table 5-1. Minefield Safety Zone.

Projectile & Trajectory	Range (KM)	MET & VE/Transfer Technique	Observer Adjust Technique
RAAMS Low-Angle	4	500 x 500	500 x 500
	7	550 x 550	500 x 500
	10	700 x 700	550 x 550
	12	850 x 850	550 x 550
	14	1000 x 1000	650 x 650
	16	1050 x 1050	650 x 650
	17.5	1200 x 1200	650 x 650
ADAM Low-Angle	4	700 x 700	700 x 700
	7	750 x 750	700 x 700
	10	900 x 900	750 x 750
	12	1050 x 1050	750 x 750
	14	1200 x 1200	850 x 850
	16	1250 x 1250	850 x 850
	17.5	1400 x 1400	850 x 850
RAAMS or ADAM High-Angle	4	750 x 750	700 x 700
	7	900 x 900	700 x 700
	10	1050 x 1050	750 x 750
	12	1200 x 1200	750 x 750
	14	1400 x 1400	850 x 850
	16	1500 x 1500	850 x 850
	17.5	1400 x 1400	850 x 850

- Range to minefield center.
- Technique (met + velocity error [VE]/transfer or observer adjust).
- Aimpoint coordinates (single or left and right).

Enter the table at the nearest range for the projectile type and trajectory and use the correct employment technique column to determine the size of the safety zone. Draw the determined safety zone centered over each aimpoint to establish the minefield safety zone.

Minefield Safety Template

- Enter the template with the fired minefield data.
- Technique (met + VE/transfer or observer adjust).
- Trajectory (high or low angle).
- Type projectile fired (RAMMS or ADAM).

- Range (to minefield center).
- Aimpoint coordinates (center or left and right).

Center the selected template safety zone square over the aim points. Draw a square to establish the minefield safety zone. See figure 5-12 on page 5-27.

DA FORM 5032-R, FIELD ARTILLERY DELIVERED MINEFIELD PLANNING SHEET

The delivery unit initiates the scatterable minefield report. For the artillery, the battalion receiving the call for fire designates the firing units. After the minefield is emplaced, the fired data is forwarded to the division, regiment, or battalion FSCC. The fired data is recorded on DA Form 5032-R, *Field Artillery Delivered Minefield Planning Sheet*, Section D. (See FM 6-40/MCWP 3-16.4). The FSCC computes the safety zone according to the fired data and passes it to the engineer for dissemination to higher, lower, and adjacent units as appropriate.

Interdiction or Area Denial

Artillery-delivered scatterable mines are not well-suited for interdiction or area denial. Because artillery-delivered minefields tend to be small and of low density (low ammunition availability), they are easily bypassed and/or breached. FA-delivered mines are poorly suited for interdicting roads because—

- Mines tend to break up or malfunction when they land on a hard surface road.
- Mines are easy to see against the uniform background of a road.
- Units on roads are already moving in column and columns are the best formations for breaching scatterable minefields.

If RAAMS and ADAM are used for interdiction or area denial, employ them—

- Only at choke points to keep the enemy from easily bypassing the minefield.
- In high-density fields to prevent breaching.
- When and where they are hard to detect; e.g., in limited visibility (at night or in fog) or where the enemy will be buttoned up (as in a chemically contaminated area).

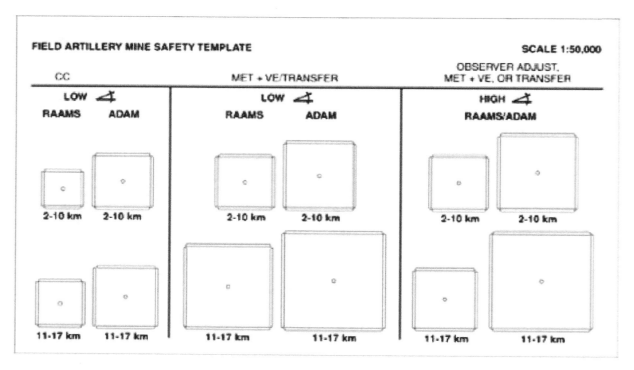

Figure 5-12. Mine Safety Template.

EMPLOYMENT AS AN OBSTACLE

Any type of FASCAM should be employed according to the basic principles of minefield employment.

Employ mines at a choke point.

Cover mines with effective direct fire and indirect fire by using HE-VT or DPICM.

Keep minefields under continuous observation. Use night observation devices and planned illumination targets at night.

Emplace minefields in belts if possible. It is better to force the enemy to breach three narrow minefields than to have him breach one wide one.

Plan to defeat enemy breaching efforts. Coordinate with the S2 and engineer to anticipate how and where the enemy will try to breach the minefield. Plan direct and indirect fires to defeat enemy breaching parties.

SPECIAL CONSIDERATIONS

FASCAM in general presents a unique planning challenge for fire support personnel because it is visible and vulnerable on the surface of the terrain. This leads to—

● Reducing the enemy's ability to see; use indirect fire to make him button up.

● Minimizing indirect fires on top of the FASCAM. This represents a judgment call. Firing on the minefield destroys breaching parties, but it also makes the minefield easier to breach by destroying the exposed mines.

One compromise is to concentrate indirect fires on targets immediately beyond the minefield and direct fires on targets in the minefield. If a mine plow or other mine-clearing vehicle enters the minefield and clears a lane, following vehicles will have to bunch up to enter the lane and may present a good target.

If the enemy has cleared a lane and is on the verge of breaching the minefield, consider firing a heavy concentration of smoke and/or DPICM directly on top of the minefield. Smoke should obscure the remaining mines as well as the clear lane markers that the vehicles are trying to follow. Using smoke will have to be carefully coordinated, since it will inhibit friendly direct fire weapons. However, a fire mission of this type should be on call in case the enemy places smoke in between your maneuver force and the minefield to screen his breaching efforts. If the enemy fires smoke first, it is to your advantage to shoot the minefield with smoke and/or DPICM to disrupt his crossing efforts.

TIMING

Artillery-delivered scatterable mines introduce another planning problem—timing. Firing mines too early gives the enemy time to avoid them, limits friendly freedom to maneuver, and can result in the mines self-destructing too early. Firing mines too late can result in their landing behind attacking enemy forces. This is why the trigger point for firing RAAMS and/or ADAM must be very carefully coordinated between the S2, S3, and FSC. The trigger point for firing artillery-delivered mines must meet two criteria:

● When the enemy reaches the trigger point, he must be committed to the avenue of approach where the mines will be delivered.

● It must be far enough forward of the proposed minefield that the minefield can be emplaced before the enemy reaches it.

The trigger point should be a targeted area of interest (TAI) in the S2's IPB. The TAI should be under surveillance at all times. The element observing the TAI should have the authority to fire the on call minefield or a direct communications link to whoever is going to call for the mines. The TAI must be far enough beyond the minefield that the minefield will be in place in time in a worst-case scenario. The FSC should allow for the time it takes to send the call for fire, process the call for fire, execute the mission, and arm the mines.

EMPLOYMENT TO AUGMENT AN OBSTACLE

FA-delivered scatterable mines are optional weapons for closing lanes in existing obstacles or reseeding breached minefields.

RAAMS and/or ADAM used to close a lane in an obstacle should be planned with the same considerations as RAAMS and/or ADAM planned as an obstacle. Another consideration in using RAAMS and/or ADAM to close a lane is how wide the artillery minefield should be. A rule of thumb is to use the width of the lane plus the expected delivery error when mines are fired. To minimize the amount of ammunition used, get the best possible grid to the center of the lane. Use survey if possible, intersection or resection if necessary. If possible and depending on the tactical situation, adjust the mission in advance onto the center point of the lane and record it as a target.

Planning for using artillery-delivered mines to close breached obstacles should involve the S2, S3, artillery LNO, engineer representative, and FSC. This group should identify the most likely points where the enemy will try to breach the obstacle and how wide the breach will probably be. As with using mines to close a lane, these points should be identified by the most accurate grid attainable, fired in, and recorded as targets. Even if the enemy does not breach at these exact locations, targets should provide accurate points to shift in firing mines.

The FSC must identify which observer is to fire RAAMS and/or ADAM to close a breach and under what conditions the obstacle is considered breached. The FSC should identify an alternate observer to fire the minefield in case smoke screens, communications problems or enemy fire prevent the primary observer from reseeding the obstacle at the proper time. This will probably require a voice call for fire over a command net.

SECTION IX. SMOKE

Smoke must be used in sufficient quantities to be effective. Factors affecting smoke's use are atmospheric conditions, type of smoke required, size of the area to be smoked, and length of time needed. Excessive amounts of ammunition may be required to meet the commander's guidance based on these conditions. The exact number of rounds is not known until the time of firing because it depends on weather conditions such as wind speed and direction. The FSC must also be wary of the hazardous gas that white phosphorus (WP) produces. It can pass through current issue protective masks and cause adverse effects on personnel that inhale the gas. Smoke may adversely affect others on the battlefield if not properly coordinated with adjacent units.

EMPLOYMENT METHODS

Smoke used to obscure is placed on or near the enemy position to interfere with his observation and ability to deliver fires.

Smoke used to screen is placed within the areas of friendly operation or in areas between friendly and enemy forces to degrade enemy observation. It is primarily intended to conceal friendly forces.

Smoke communicates actions on the battlefield (signal) or to mark locations.

Smoke used with other actions to confuse or mislead the enemy (deception) is generally used with other deceptive measures.

MORTARS

Mortars deliver a high volume of smoke at short ranges and are a rapid, effective means of obscuration depending on the available combat load. The 81mm mortar delivers WP and red phosphorous smoke. For more information, see MCWP 3-15.2, *Tactical Employment of Mortars.*

ARTILLERY

Artillery delivers large quantities of smoke at long ranges. It can deliver WP smoke in two forms. M110 WP is a bursting-tube projectile filled with WP and is used for marking and immediate smoke missions. The M825 (felt wedge or improved smoke) round is a replacement for the M116 series of HC rounds. It provides a faster, larger, and longer duration of smoke than the HC round. WP impregnated wedges may not be completely consumed as the smoke screen is produced. Unburned wedges may crust over and reignite when disturbed. It does not present a lethal threat to maneuvering troops. Smoke is available in limited quantities and should be planned for critical targets that support maneuver.

NSFS

NSFS can deliver limited quantities of WP. The firing unit should be forewarned of its intended use to allow for loading ammunition in the gun turrets for storage.

CONTROLLING SMOKE

Because smoke's effectiveness is greatly determined by weather and terrain, the observer controlling the mission is the key individual. However, the FSC should be knowledgeable in smoke employment so that he may judiciously plan its use. The NBCD officer can provide information on the effects of weather on the use of smoke and help determine smoke placement and effectiveness.

TIMING

Allow time for delivery and any buildup. All rounds are fired as standard missions with parallel sheafs under favorable conditions. See table 5-2 on page 5-30.

Table 5-2. Planning Data for Smoke.

DELIVERY SYSTEM	TYPE ROUND	TIME TO BUILD EFFECTIVE SMOKE	AVERAGE BURNING TIME	AVERAGE OBSCURATION LENGTH (METERS) PER ROUND WIND DIRECTION CROSS	HEAD/TAIL
5 in/54	WP	1/2 min	1 min	150	40
155mm	WP	1/2 min	1-1/2 min	150	50
	M825	1/2 min	5-15 min	400	100
120mm	WP	TBD	TBD	TBD	TBD
81mm	WP	1/2 min	1 min	100	40
	RP	1/2 min	3-10 min	200	50
60mm	WP	1/2 min	1 min	75	40

DELIVERY TECHNIQUES

Immediate smoke is applied to point targets to obscure and suppress enemy fires. By unit SOP it may be incorporated into immediate suppression calls for fire as a mix of WP and M825 smoke. Quick smoke is placed in between units to screen friendly movement from enemy observation or fires. Smoke can be used to obscure, screen, signal and mark, and deceive. See table 5-3.

Table 5-3. Smoke Delivery Techniques.

DELIVERY TECHNIQUE	TYPE OF TARGET	NUMBER OF GUNS	TYPE OF AMMUNITION	SHEAF	OBSCURATION TIME	C2
Immediate smoke (point/ suppression)	Point or small area 150 meters or less	2 guns	1st round WP/smoke	BCS	1/2 to 5 min	By SOP and/or maneuver company commander's approval
Immediate smoke/ (mortar)	150 meters or less	2 guns	2 rounds each WP	Parallel	1-3 min	By SOP and commander's approval
Quick smoke (mortar)	150-600 meters	4 81mm	WP	Parallel or open/special (as required)	4-15 min depending on ammunition availability	Battalion

SECTION X. ILLUMINATION

Employment of illumination requires considerable planning and coordination. Its ability to turn night into day has both positive and negative aspects that must be integrated into the overall fire support plan. Specific guidance on its use should always be sought from and consistent with higher headquarters.

CAPABILITIES

All fire support assets have illumination capabilities. See table 5-4.

The most important consideration for illumination employment is its effect on the entire battlefield. For example, a battalion that conducts an illuminated attack adjacent to a battalion conducting a nonilluminated attack may not be feasible. Every asset,

element, and weapon system that employs a night vision capability must be considered before employing illumination. Illumination employed correctly can improve friendly NVG performance as well as degrade enemy night vision. Illumination is also an incendiary on the deck.

Illumination employed at its intended height of burst is designed to provide light to see with the naked eye. Illuminants tend to burn all the way to the ground. When illumination is too close or actually enters the field of view of NVGs, it "washes out" or eliminates the effectiveness of the goggles. When natural illumination (such as from the moon) is inadequate, illumination 2 to 5 kilometers away from or behind the operating area enhances NVG performance. Thermal sights such as on tanks and LAVs are only affected by illuminants in close proximity to acquired targets, however, tank and LAV drivers use NVGs.

Table 5-4. Illumination Data.

HOWITZER MORTAR	PROJECTILE	INITIAL HEIGHT OF BURST	EFFECTIVE AREA (radius)	BURN TIME (minutes)	RATE OF DESCENT (meters per second)
81mm	M301A2	400 M	250 M	1	6
81mm	M301A3	600 M	250 M	1	6
155mm	M485A2	600 M	500 M	1	5
5"/54	MK 91	500 M	250 M	1	10
5"/54	MK 48	500 M	250 M	1	10
CAS	LUU-2A/B	600 M	750 M	4.5	5
CAS	M257	750	500 M	1.5	5
CAS	LUU-1/B	GROUND	TARGET MARK	30	-

NIGHT CAS

Illumination can be employed with night CAS. It is important to consider pilots usage of NVGs. One technique is to offset two artillery illumination rounds parallel to the final attack heading to orient the pilot as well as illuminate the target (see figure 5-13). The height of burst is increased to 900 meters and offset 600 meters beyond the target. Aviation illumination (LUU-2) uses a 900 meter height of burst and offsets 900 meters. Both techniques allow illu-

mination burnout at 300 meters. This provides the pilot who is aided with goggles sufficient ambient light to acquire the target.

AS PART OF A DECEPTION PLAN

Illumination can be employed as part of a deception plan due to its large battlefield signature. This is usually coordinated at regiment or higher levels. It is also effective at harassing enemy movement and degrading enemy night vision capability.

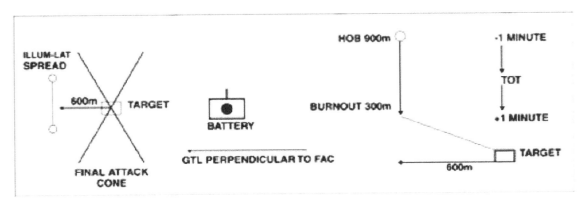

Figure 5-13. CAS Illumination Technique.

SECTION XI. PRECISION-GUIDED MUNITIONS

Precision-guided munitions (PGMs) can destroy mobile hard targets such as tanks. PGMs greatly enhance combat power. Primary PGMs in use are direct fire weapons such as the TOW and the Dragon.

The FSC's role in employing these weapons is to plan indirect fires and air strikes to complement and augment the effects of these weapons; e.g., the use of FASCAM to canalize tanks into a TOW's sector of fire. However, the FSC also has indirect fire and air-delivered, laser-guided munitions that can aid in the antiarmor/antimechanized effort. These include artillery (Copperhead) and air-delivered munitions. Most aviation PGMs are guided by laser energy, wires, or low-light TV. Undergoing experiments are aviation PGMs with global positioning system (GPS) guidance systems that strike directly on the grid input into the GPS warhead.

JOINT DIRECT ATTACK MUNITIONS

Joint direct attack munitions (JDAM) are designed as a low cost, autonomously controlled tail kit for the GBV-31(V)2B (MK-84) and the GBV-32(V)2B/ GBU-32(V)4B (BLU-109) 2,000 pound warheads and MK-83/BLU-110 1,000 pound warheads. Design requirements include accurate performance in adverse weather, less than 13 meter circular error probable (CEP), in-flight retargeting, and a launch-and-leave capability.

The tail kit contains a guidance control unit (GCU) consisting of a 3-axis inertial maneuvering unit, a GPS receiver and guidance processor. This GCU flies the weapon via 3 electro-mechanical fin assemblies.

JDAM is a bomb-on-coordinates weapon. Accuracy will directly relate to the quality of the coordinate input to the system.

JOINT STAND-OFF WEAPONS

A bomb-on-coordinates weapon, joint stand-off weapons (JSOW) is designed to provide an accurate stand-off delivery capability to U.S. forces. It consists of a winged, all-weather, glide vehicle, a GPS-aided IMU (same as JDAM). JSOW will provide up to 40 nautical miles stand-off from the intended target.

Current plans call for three variants:

- Submunition dispenser: AGM 154A-145 BLV 97 bomblets.

- Antiarmor: AGM 154B-24 BLV 108 sensor fused munitions.

- Unitary warhead: AGM 154C-BLV 111 (500 pound unitary bomb).

The unitary version will incorporate an imaging IR seeker in the nose and data link to increase accuracy over the JDAM. The warhead will not have a hard target penetration capability.

SECTION XII. IMPROVED CONVENTIONAL MUNITIONS

Improved conventional munitions (ICMs) are base ejection projectiles containing a number of submunitions. Submunitions are ejected through the base of the projectile and scattered in the target area.

ANTIPERSONNEL IMPROVED CONVENTIONAL MUNITIONS

The APICM is no longer in production but is still held in war reserves. The AP round is effective against exposed personnel. When the fuse functions, an expelling charge disperses 60 grenades out through the base of the projectile. When the submunition's striker plate located on the base of the grenade makes contact with the ground (see figure 5-14), the grenade is hurled 4 to 6 feet in the air and detonates.

DUAL PURPOSE IMPROVED CONVENTIONAL MUNITIONS

The dual purpose improved conventional munition (DPICM) is found in the M483A1 (referred to as ICM) and the new M864 base burn DPICM (BBDPICM).

DPICM is effective against lightly armored vehicles and very effective against personnel. On impact, each submunition detonates a shaped charge that can pierce 2.75 inches of rolled steel. Steel casing fragments create an antipersonnel effect (see figure 5-15 on page 5-34). M483A1 contains 88 grenades, the M864 contains 72 grenades.

Effects of cannon DPICM bomblet dispersion on the ground vary depending on range and charge. At minimum range, dispersion is elliptical in shape. At maximum ranges it is almost circular. Simply put, the M483A1 typically has a 50 meter radius bomblet dispersion, the M864 has a 75 meter radius bomblet dispersion. The default BCS circular sheaf is typically 200 x 200 meters; M864 is 250 x 250

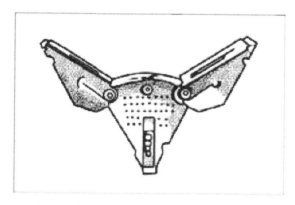

Figure 5-14. 155mm APICM Grenade.

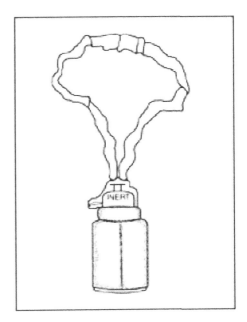

Figure 5-15. 155mm DPICM Grenade.

meters. DPICM projectiles should not need a height of burst correction unless there is an error in target location or data.

When the actual bomblet dispersion pattern is needed, refer to JMEMS publications. A simplified one dimensional pattern radius can be computed using the following formula: *M483A1 (.70 x Rng[km])+38 = pattern radius in meters.* M864 pattern radius is consistently 75 meters.

A small percentage (2 to 2.5 percent) of DPICM's submunitions may not detonate and may pose a hazard to friendly maneuver forces. ICMs should not be fired into wooded areas. Submunitions may become suspended in tree branches and later pose a threat to friendly forces. Firing DPICMs into mountainous

areas where the slope is greater than 60 percent increases the dud rate. Snow, mud, and water do not increase the dud rate, but they do make it difficult to locate and dispose of duds, thereby increasing the risk to friendly forces.

MULTIPLE LAUNCH ROCKET SYSTEM/HIGH MOBILITY ARTILLERY ROCKET SYSTEM

Marines should be familiar with the munition capabilities of both systems when Multiple Launch Rocket System (MLRS)/high mobility artillery rocket system (HIMARS) support is provided. MLRS/HIMARS projectiles originally consisted of the M26 rocket and Army tactical missile system (ATACMS) Block I. The M26 carries DPICMs; ATACMS carry antipersonnel antimateriel (APAM) submunitions. Current inventories are now expanding to include longer range versions of the projectiles with less submunitions.

A larger form of a cannon DPICM is used in the M26 rocket fired by MLRS/HIMARS. Each rocket carries 644 DPICM submunitions that can pierce 4 inches of rolled steel and create an antipersonnel effect. Other characteristics are the same as a cannon DPICM. The ER-MLRS rocket carries 444 submunitions.

APAM is the submunition used in MLRS/HIMARS ATACMS. A 1.3-pound ball-shaped grenade of composition B and a steel case, on impact, its fragmentation is effective against thin-skinned vehicles, materiel, and personnel. It is not effective against armored vehicles. Each ATACMS Block I carries 950 APAM grenades. ATACMS Block IA carries 300 APAM.

SECTION XIII. EMERGING MUNITIONS

Current weapons technology is increasingly capable— better now than ever before. But weapons must continue to improve to meet 21st century challenges and seize opportunities and technologies. To succeed on future battlefields, the Marine Corps and the Navy are posturing to purchase modern precision/near precision weapons for surface, air, and naval surface fire support.

ARTILLERY

Guided MLRS Rocket

This rocket is an improvement in accuracy to reduce rocket expenditure to 1/6th the current quantity at maximum ranges. With the addition of low-cost jam proof guidance and control, a 2 to 3 mil delivery accuracy is achieved. Maximum range is out to 60 kilometers. The improved accuracy reduces a units' logistics burden, increases crew survivability, and reduces collateral damage by increasing the capability to engage point targets.

MLRS/HIMARS Smart Tactical Rocket

This rocket will be a guided MLRS/HIMARS rocket carrying smart submunitions out to a range of approximately 60 kilometers. Submunitions will use onboard sensors to detect, classify, and engage stationary or moving targets.

Army Tactical Missile System Block II

Army tactical missile system (ATACMS) Block II is a semiballistic, surface-to-surface guided missile that carries 13 brilliant antitank (BAT) or BAT P3I submunitions to ranges out to 140 kilometers. Block II is an adaptation of the Block I missile fielded with modifications to accommodate the BAT submunition. The primary target set for the missile is large battalion-size concentrations of moving armor. Once dispensed, the BAT submunition can autonomously seek and destroy moving armored targets through acoustic and infrared sensors. BAT P3I submunitions will expand the target set to include hot or cold, stationary or moving, hard or soft targets including surface-to-surface missile transporter erector launchers.

Army Tactical Missile System Block IIA

Block IIA is a semiballistic, surface-to-surface guided missile that carries six BAT P3I submunitions to ranges from 100-300 kilometers. It will have GPS-augmented inertial guidance and off-axis launch capability. Once dispensed, the BAT P3I submunition can autonomously seek and destroy moving or stationary targets through acoustic, millimeter wave, and infrared sensors. The BAT P3I submunitions target set includes hot or cold, stationary or moving, hard or soft targets including surface-to-surface missile transporter erector launchers. The submunition has increased performance over the basic BAT submunition in adverse weather and countermeasure environments.

Sense and Destroy Armor Munition (SADARM)

The M898 sense and destroy armor cannon projectile contains two submunitions that are deployed over the target area via parachute. Each submunition searches a 75 meter radius footprint using infrared and active and passive millimeter wave sensors. Upon detection of a hard target, it fires an explosive formed penetrator into the top of the target vehicle.

M795 HE Projectile

The M795 is a 155 HE projectile. It will be employed against the same target array as the M107 HE projectile and achieve a range of 22.5 kilometers.

Extended Range M795

This projectile has similar ballistic characteristics as the M864 BBDPICM projectile. The extended range M795 will have a greater lethality at extended ranges than the M549 HE rocket-assisted (HERA) projectile. When fired with zone 5 modular artillery charge system (MACS), it can achieve a range of 37 kilometers (threshold) to 40 kilometers (objective).

XM982 Extended Range Munitions

This projectile will replace the M864 BBDPICM projectile and will provide 155 millimeter howitzers with an extended range, fratricide reducing, accuracy-enhancing capability to the Marine Corps. The XM982 concept combines both drag reductions from the M864 BBDPICM projectile and glide technology from the M712 Copperhead projectile. Currently, there are three variants of the XM982: DPICM, SADARM, and unitary warhead. Each has a GPS/inertial navigation system (INS) self-location system, is compatible with the multi-option fuze for artillery (MOFA), and will be inductively set via the portable inductive artillery fuze setter (PIFAS). A significant reduction in the fratricide probability for cannon DPICM firings will be reduced using DPICM submunitions with self-destruct/sterilization features. Hazardous DPICM duds will be reduced from the current M42/46 2-3 percent rate to equal to or less than 0.2 percent (1 in 500) when DPICM is the lethal cargo for the XM982 projectile.

NAVAL SURFACE FIRE SUPPORT

Mk 172 Cargo Projectile

The Navy is developing this projectile. It currently will carry 49 Mk 2 ICM bomblets, which are comparable to the US Army M80 bomblet, and may carry other submunitions such as BAT, SADARM, and smoke, in the future. The submunition dispersion pattern is circular with approximately a 50 meter radius. The XM 172 has an objective range of 26 kilometers with the 5 inch/54 and 40 kilometers with the 5 inch/62 caliber.

NSFS PGMs

The Navy is developing extended range munitions that will give commanders the ability to influence and shape the battlespace while staying over-the-horizon, during early phases of an amphibious assault when artillery has not been established ashore and during sustained operations ashore.

XM171 Extended Range Guided Munition (ERGM)

The ERGM is a 5 inch, 127 millimeter projectile that is fired from the 5 inch/62 caliber Mk 45 Mod 4 gun. It will carry 72 submunitions, which are adapted from the Army's M-80, containing a primary impact fuze and a self-destruct backup fuze to reduce the hazard of duds on the battlefield. It will be guided by a GPS guidance system with an INS for backup giving it a CEP of 20 meters. ERGM can achieve ranges in excess of 41 nautical miles with an objective range of 63 nautical miles. In contrast to conventional NGF munitions' flat trajectory, the ERGM has a much higher trajectory and near-vertical attack angle. It makes it well-suited for attacking targets in defilade which, due to terrain features, would cause conventional munitions to be ineffective. Due to the steep trajectory, a restricted operations zone may be required around the firing ships and target area similar to the use of PAH/TAH with ATACMs.

Autonomous Naval Support Round (ANSR)

The autonomous naval support round (ANSR) is being developed to achieve a long-range, fast response, low cost, volume fire projectile. The design incorporates the improvements in guidance electronics, warhead, and rocket motor design. ANSR has a small nose-mounted guidance section, moderate-sized warhead, large rocket motor, and improved tail assembly. ANSR is based on mature projectile design and has been gun-launch flight demonstrated to 23 nautical miles. The preliminary conclusion from the demonstration is that the aeronautical and airframe data directly supports over 60 nautical miles 5-inch range and 100 nautical miles 155 milimeters range for a tactical ANSR projectile.

Land Attack Standard Missile

Land Attack Standard Missile (LASM) is a modification of the Navy's primary surface-launched, AAW weapon, the Standard Missile-2 (SM-2). LASM will have a threshold range of 300 kilometers with a CEP of 20 meters. Missiles in the current inventory will be retrofitted with a new forward body section to make it suitable for land attack. The forward section will have a GPS/INS, a modified warhead, and height of burst fuzing. The warhead is the 76.5 pound, Mk 125 blast/fragmentation warhead currently in production.

Tactical Tomahawk

The Navy is acquiring a new generation GPS-navigated Tactical Tomahawk cruise missile capable of attacking strategic, operational, and tactical targets. Along with a 50 percent cost reduction over the Block III TLAM, additional system improvements include—

● In-flight retargeting.

● Real time BDA with a missile-mounted camera that provides a snapshot photograph for battle damage indications, BDA, and target identification.

● GPS mission planning onboard the firing unit.

● Battlefield loiter capability for responsiveness.

● Flexible architecture for future advances and alternative payloads (such as hardened target penetrator or brilliant antitank munitions).

AVIATION

Standoff Land Attack Missile Extended Range

Standoff Land Attack Missile Extended Range (SLAM-ER) is a precision strike standoff weapon designed for employment against heavily defended high value targets. The system is employed by F/A-18 strike fighters. It uses a combination of GPS/INS guidance and imaging, streaming video data-link for precision targeting. SLAM-ER can be employed at ranges in excess of 150 nautical miles.

Modernized Hellfire

The Modernized Hellfire is planned to replace the BGM-71 series TOW missile, AGM-114 series Hellfire missile, and the AGM-65 series Maverick missile in a single weapon for the Marine Corps and Navy. The Modernized Hellfire is envisioned as a rotary and fixed-wing weapon that will be designed to provide precision standoff in the engagement of tactical moving targets. The requirement for this weapon includes multiple seeker capabilities (semiactive laser, imaging infrared and possible millimeter wave radar) enhanced lethality and longer range than the weapons it will replace. The Marine Corps is currently pursuing a joint program with the Army designated the Common Missile System as a possible solution for this weapon.

Advanced Precision Kill Weapon System

This system is a low cost precision-guided rocket that uses semiactive laser guidance to destroy a wide variety of targets. The current weapon is being designed for the 2.75 inch rocket system, but will have functionality on the 5.00 inch rocket system as well. This weapon will provide a cost effective means of engaging point and area targets that do not warrant the expenditure of more costly precision-guided weapons.

APPENDIX A. SAMPLE FIRE MISSION LOG

The FSCC may use this log to track fire missions received. It should enable the FSC and staff to quickly identify missions fired for later analysis. Figure A-1 is a sample log. Figure A-2 on page A-2 is blank and may be reproduced. Enter information as follows.

Unit, OPORD, and DTG: applicable unit of the log.

Page Numbers: number consecutively.

Observer: observer ID number (automated information systems) or call sign.

Target Number: target number requested, one assigned by FDC (mortar or artillery), or JTAR number.

Target Location: target location as sent by the observer. May be any of the three methods of target location. Include datum if different from WGS-84. Include grid zone designator (SM 435675) for aviation assets.

Other Information: target description, method of fire, and method of control.

Clear: if the unit cleared the mission, enter "C." Enter "D" for denied. Include time of decision.

Fire Support Asset Assigned: the fire support asset used for the mission; e.g., "ARTY," "NGF," "R/W," "F/W," and "MORT."

Agency: agency that provided additional coordination.

Sent: time the request for coordination was sent to the agency that needed coordination.

Received: time coordination was received and if it was approved/cleared ("C") or denied ("D").

Refine: refinements sent in by the observer (usually to identify firing/effects trends).

Time: time end of mission (EOM) was received.

Disposition: enter if the target should be forwarded to higher headquarters. Include BDA (what was killed and how many remain and their current status).

| Unit:
OPORD:
DTG: | | | **Fire Mission Log** | | | | | | | | | Page ___ of ___ |

						Additional Coord			EOM		
Observer	Target Number	Target Location	Other Information	Clear	Fire Support Asset Assigned	Agency	Time Sent	Time Rcvd	Refine	Time	Disposition
Z3C	AC 1234	MS 345786	Troops in trenchline HE/VT, 5 min Supp, AMC	C	MORT					1035	10 men escaped NW–not organized

Figure A-1. Sample.

Unit: OPORD: DTG:			**Fire Mission Log**									Page ___ of ___

						Additional Coord			EOM		
Observer	Target Number	Target Loca-tion	Other Information	Clear	Fire Support Asset Assigned	Agency	Time		Refine	Time	Disposition
							Sent	Rcvd			

Figure A-2. Fire Mission Log.

APPENDIX B. FIRE SUPPORT COORDINATING MEASURES

Fire support coordinating measures (FSCMs) enhance the expeditious attack of targets and provide safeguards for friendly forces. Their use is governed by the tactical situation. FSCMs fall into two broad categories: permissive and restrictive. Some maneuver control measures also affect fire support coordination. FSCMs are recommended by the FSC and established by the commander. FSCMs are graphically shown as a black line or lines (solid or dashed). All measures are labeled with the title or abbreviated title of the measure followed by the establishing headquarters (in parentheses). The significance of identifying the establishing headquarters is that it designates the area where the FSCM applies. For example, a coordinated fire line (CFL) established by a battalion is effective within that battalion's zone of action. The effects do not extend beyond the battalion's zone. When a date-time group is used, the time zone must be shown. FSCMs can be effective immediately, at a scheduled time or on-call.

PERMISSIVE FSCMS

These measures authorize the attack of targets without clearance from the ground commander if certain circumstances are met.

Coordinated Fire Line

The CFL is a line beyond which conventional surface fire support means; e.g., mortars, field artillery, and NSFS ships may fire at any time within the zone of the establishing headquarters without additional coordination. See figure B-1.

The CFL expedites the attack of targets beyond the CFL without coordination with the ground commander in whose zone of action targets are located. It also provides the ground commander with an area within his zone

Figure B-1. Coordinated Fire Line.

where his forces can operate in safety from uncoordinated friendly surface delivered indirect fires.

Maneuver battalion commanders are responsible for selecting or approving a recommended CFL location for their zone of action or sector of defense, while supporting artillery commanders and artillery liaison officers at every echelon should make appropriate recommendations concerning its location. The location of the battalion's CFL is forwarded to the infantry regiment through both infantry and artillery fire support coordination channels, where it is approved, consolidated, and forwarded to division level as appropriate. A consolidated CFL may be established for the GCE as a whole, but this is not always practical.

The selected location of the CFL at all echelons is based on such factors as the scheme of maneuver, patrol plans, locations of security forces, and the troop safety desires of the ground commander. There is no requirement for the CFL to be placed on identifiable terrain. However, additional considerations are the limits of ground observation, the location of the initial objectives in the offense, and the requirement for maximum flexibility in both maneuver and the delivery of supporting fires.

Graphic portrayal of the location of the CFL is shown on maps, charts, and overlays by a dashed black line with the letters CFL followed by the establishing headquarters in parentheses above the line and the effective date-time group below the line. The FSCC of the establishing commander disseminates the location of the CFL to the fire support coordination agencies of subordinate, adjacent, and higher headquarters, as required. It is further disseminated to each level of command, to include the establishing command, and all concerned fire support agencies.

Fire Support Coordination Line

The fire support coordination line (FSCL) is an FSCM that delineates the coordination requirements for the attack of surface targets. It is established by the appropriate land or amphibious commander within his boundaries in consultation with superior, subordinate, supporting, and affected commanders. An FSCL is not a boundary and does not divide an AO. The FSCL applies to all fires of air, land, and sea-based weapon systems using any type of ammunition against surface targets. Forces attacking targets beyond an FSCL must inform all affected commanders in sufficient time to allow necessary reaction to avoid fratricide, both in the air and on the ground. See figure B-2.

Figure B-2. Fire Support Coordination Line.

In exceptional circumstances, the inability to conduct this coordination will not preclude the attack of targets beyond the FSCL. However, failure to do so may increase the risk of fratricide and could waste limited resources. When targets are attacked beyond the FSCL, supporting elements must ensure that these attacks do not produce adverse effects on, or to the rear of the line. Short of the FSCL, all air-to-ground and surface-to-surface attack operations are controlled by the appropriate land or amphibious force commander. Establishment of the FSCL must be coordinated with all affected commanders in order to avoid fratricide.

The primary purpose of the FSCL is to facilitate the expeditious attack of targets of opportunity beyond the coordinating measure. It provides a measure for coordination between ground elements and supporting forces without endangering friendly troops in the air or on the ground or requiring additional coordination with the establishing headquarters. The FSCL—

● Facilitates attack of surface targets beyond it.

● Provides ground commanders with sufficient control of aircraft short of it to ensure troop safety.

● Maximizes employment of weapons where they are most efficient, and provides aviation commanders, air control agencies, and pilots with enough information to identify where control or coordination is required before aircraft can attack ground targets.

In amphibious operations, the FSCL is normally established by the MAGTF commander after coordination with the navy amphibious commander. When air forces external to the ATF are supporting the amphibious operation, the MAGTF commander coordinates with the supporting forces in conjunction with the navy amphibious commander. When Marine Corps forces operate independently on land, the FSCL is established by the MAGTF commander. In joint or combined operations, the FSCL may be established by headquarters above the MAGTF. Before establishment, consultation should be made with appropriate ground and aviation elements.

The FSCL should follow well defined terrain features easily identifiable from the air. Positioning of the FSCL must consider the tactical situation. This should include the scheme of maneuver or plan of defense, weather, terrain, type and source of aircraft, and overall flexibility of maneuver and fire support. A key factor is the range of the land or amphibious com-mander's organic weapon systems.

The FSCL is disseminated by the establishing MAGTF commander to the FSCCs of subordinate, adjacent, and higher headquarters, as required. It is further disseminated at each level of command, including the establishing command, to all concerned fire support agencies, such as the DASC, TACC, FDC, SACC, and NSFS ships. Changes to the FSCL require notification of all affected forces within the AO and must allow sufficient time for these elements to incorporate the FSCL change. Generally, 6 hours is adequate to coordinate a change.

FSCL location is graphically portrayed on fire support maps, charts, and overlays by a solid black line with the letters FSCL followed by the establishing headquarters in parentheses above the line and effective date-time group below the line. See figure B-3 on page B-3.

Battlefield Coordination Line

A battlefield coordination line (BCL) is a fire support coordinating measure, established based on METT-T, which facilitates the expeditious attack of surface targets

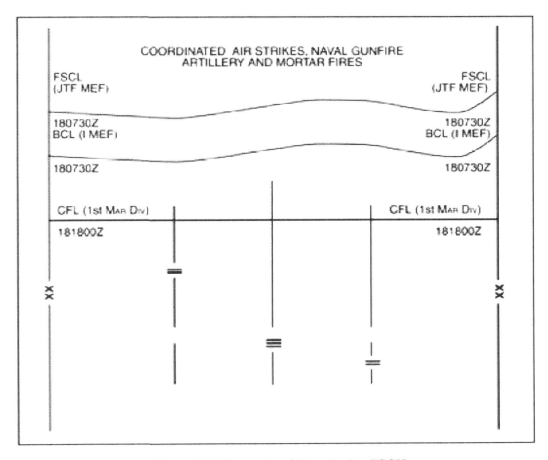

Figure B-3. Example of Permissive FSCM.

of opportunity between the measure and the FSCL. When established, the primary purpose is to allow MAGTF aviation to attack surface targets without approval of a GCE commander in whose area the targets may be located. To facilitate air-delivered fires and deconflict air and surface fires, an airspace coordination area (ACA) will always overlie the area between the BCL and the FSCL. Ground commanders may strike any targets beyond the BCL and short of the FSCL with artillery and/or rockets without coordination as long as those fires deconflict with the established ACA overhead. This includes targets in an adjacent ground commander's zone that falls within the BCL-FSCL area.

The BCL is an exclusive Marine Corps FSCM, similar to an FSCL, which facilitates the expeditious attack of targets with surface indirect fires and aviation fires between this measure and the FSCL. See figure B-4. Normally, Marine units prefer placing the FSCL close to the FEBA so that organic indirect fires can range most targets short

of the FSCL and organic air assets have maximum freedom to engage targets beyond the FSCL.

However, since in many operations the FSCL is controlled by the CINC or JTF commander, the FSCL may be placed at a significantly greater distance than the maximum range of Marine Corps indirect fire assets. This gives the enemy a sanctuary, between the maximum range of indirect fire supporting arms and the FSCL, in which aviation assets cannot freely engage without coordination and GCE assets are unable to influence. The BCL was thus developed as a supplemental measure that

Figure B-4. Battlefield Coordination Line.

may or may not be used. A key factor is the range and positioning of GCE organic weapon systems and the positioning of the FSCL. If the FSCL is placed such that a sanctuary exists between the range of Marine artillery and the FSCL, the MAGTF commander can use this internal coordinating measure to facilitate the attack of targets within this area.

The BCL allows MAGTF fire support assets to attack surface targets without further coordination with the GCE commander in whose area the targets may be located. Marine aviation may strike any target beyond the BCL and short of the FSCL without further coordination, including targets in an adjacent Marine commander's zone between the BCL and FSCL. Before firing, the ground commander should coordinate with the ACE (DASC) if surface delivered fires will violate ACAs associated with the BCL.

The MAGTF commander establishes the BCL. The BCL should follow well defined terrain features easily identifiable from the air. The positioning of the BCL must consider the tactical situation. This should include the scheme of maneuver or plan of defense, weather, terrain, type and source of aircraft, and overall flexibility of maneuver and fire support.

The BCL is disseminated by the establishing MAGTF commander to the FSCCs of subordinate, adjacent, and higher headquarters, as required. It is further disseminated at each level of command, including the establishing command, to all concerned fire support agencies such as the DASC, TACC, FDC, SACC, and NSFS ships.

BCL location is graphically portrayed on fire support maps, charts, and overlays by a solid black line with the letters "BCL" followed by the establishing headquarters in parentheses above the line and effective date-time group below the line. BCL is not currently supported by automated systems for depiction.

Free-Fire Area

The free-fire area (FFA) is a specific designated area into which any weapon system may fire without additional coordination with the establishing headquarters.

FFAs expedite fire and facilitate jettisoning of CAS munitions if an aircraft is unable to drop on a target.

FFAs may be established only by the military or civilian commander with jurisdiction over the area (usually division or higher). An FFA request must be forwarded to the appropriate approving official through the MAGTF commander.

Preferably, the FFA should be easily identifiable from the air, but it may be designated by grid coordinates, GPS coordinates or latitude and longitude.

The force commander disseminates the FFA including the effective dates and times of the FFA to all subordinate units.

The FFA is enclosed by a black line with the words Free-Fire Area or the letters FFA written inside the circumscribed area. The establishing headquarters may be identified as part of the graphic portrayal. See figure B-5.

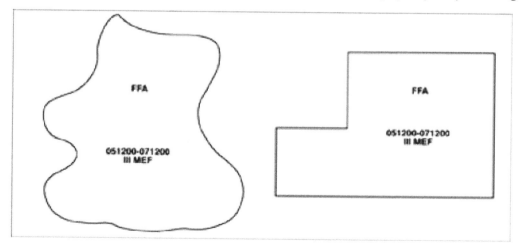

Figure B-5. Free-Fire Area.

RESTRICTIVE FSCMS

Restrictive FSCMs restrict the use of supporting arms.

Restrictive Fire Line

An RFL is a line established between converging friendly forces (one or both may be moving) that prohibits fires, or effects from fires, across the line without coordination with the affected force. It prevents fratricide between converging friendly forces.

The common commander of the converging forces establishes the RFL. He may delegate establishing authority to the senior commander of the two converging forces or to the commander of the maneuvering force in a linkup operation between a moving and a stationary force.

To provide for recognition, the RFL should be located on identifiable terrain. In linkup operations, the RFL is moved as close as possible to the stationary force to allow maximum freedom of action for the maneuver and fire support of the linkup force.

The FSCC of the establishing commander disseminates the location of the RFL to the fire support coordination agencies of subordinate, adjacent, and higher headquarters, as required. It is further disseminated to each level of command, to include the establishing command and all concerned fire support agencies.

The location of the RFL is graphically portrayed by a solid black line with the letters RFL followed by the name of the establishing headquarters above the line. The effective date-time group is written below the line. See figure B-6.

No-Fire Area

An NFA is an area where no fires or effects of fires are allowed. Two exceptions are when establishing headquarters approves fires temporarily within the NFA on a mission basis, and when the enemy force within the NFA engages a friendly force, the commander may engage the enemy to defend his force.

See figure B-7 on page B-6 for an example of an NFA.

The NFA prohibits fires or their effects in the area, normally to protect civilians or cultural areas.

Typically, the Navy amphibious commander/MAGTF commander or MEF establishes an NFA. On arrival of military forces, the force commander coordinates the location of an NFA with local authorities.

Normally an NFA is on recognizable terrain, but its location may also be expressed by grid coordinates or by radius in meters from a center point.

The establishing commander disseminates the NFA to all units of the force.

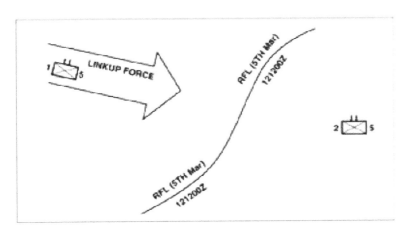

Figure B-6. Restrictive Fire Line.

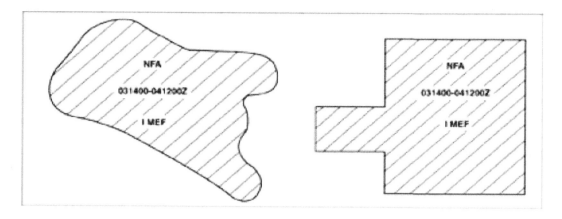

Figure B-7. No-Fire Area.

An NFA is graphically portrayed as an area outlined with a solid black line with black diagonal lines inside. The letters NFA are written inside the circumscribed area, along with the effective date-time group for commencement and termination. The area should also be identified by the designation of the headquarters that established the area.

Restrictive Fire Area

An RFA is an area in which specific restrictions are imposed and into which fires that exceed those restrictions will not be delivered without prior coordination with the establishing headquarters.

The RFA regulates fires into an area according to the stated restrictions. This means that fires or certain types of ordnance; e.g., ICM or WP, can be controlled where friendly forces are or will be located.

An RFA may be established by any ground unit commander within his own zone; however, it is not normally established below battalion level. When RFAs are used to protect a forward unit from friendly fires; e.g., reconnaissance team, the RFA size should be large enough to allow the maneuver of the unit but not so large as to needlessly restrict fire support in other areas. To facilitate rapidly changing maneuver areas, on-call RFAs may be used. Dimensions, location, and restrictions of the on-call RFA are prearranged. The RFA is activated and deactivated when requested by the maneuvering unit or scheduled by time or event.

An RFA may be on recognizable terrain, expressed by grid coordinates or by radius from a point.

An RFA is disseminated by the establishing commander to the fire support coordination agencies of subordinate, adjacent, and higher headquarters, as required. It is further disseminated to each level of command, including the establishing command, and to all concerned fire support agencies.

An RFA is portrayed by a solid black line defining the area with the letters RFA, the designation of the unit establishing the area, any special instructions, and the effective date-time group written inside the area. See figure B-8.

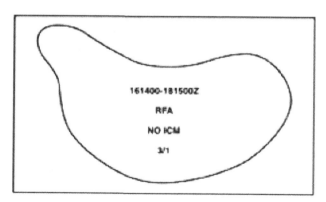

Figure B-8. Restrictive Fire Area.

Airspace Coordination Area

An ACA is a three-dimensional block of airspace in a target area, established by the appropriate ground commander, in which friendly aircraft are reasonably safe from friendly surface fires. The airspace coordination area may be formal or informal (JP 1-02).

Formal ACAs require detailed planning. More often, informal ACAs are established using time, lateral or altitude separation between surface- and air-delivered weapon effects. ACAs can vary from physically defined areas to the various methods of separation. Physical areas can include routes (control point to IP, HA to BP) or areas (over the target, IP, BP). See figure B-9.

The ACA ensures aircrew safety and effective use of indirect supporting surface fires by deconfliction of time and space.

The commander of the unit requesting air support also requests ACAs based on the recommendations of his FSC. Formal ACAs are established by the airspace control authority and can be scheduled, on-call (on order) or immediate. Scheduled ACAs will state the time they are to be effective; e.g., 181400Z to 181405Z.

The ACA may be referred to by a code name; e.g., BO-ZO or it may take some other form such as the MCFSS identification; e.g., AC15MR (ACA 1, 5th Mar), or the target number or grid coordinates of the target. A code name is the easiest to use, particularly for scheduled and on-call ACAs. An immediate ACA may or may not have a code name. The target number or a set of grid coordinates associated with the air support mission facilitates the dissemination of an immediate ACA.

A control point is a position marked by a buoy, boat, aircraft, electronic device, conspicuous terrain feature, or other identifiable object which is given a name or number and used as an aid to navigation or control of ships, boats, or aircraft. (excerpt from JP 1-02) During planning, control points are selected and named throughout the area. As necessary, these control points are designated as initial points (IPs), contact points, exit points (EPs) penetration control points (PCPs), etc. Control points can be used in the establishment and promulgation of ACAs. When this is done, the names of the control points are substituted for grid coordinates. For example, ACA BO-ZO, altitude 50 to 400 feet, Rose to Jones, width 500 meters, effective 281400Z to 281410Z. If all units do not have the aviation control points, they must be transcribed into grids. See figure B-10 on page B-8.

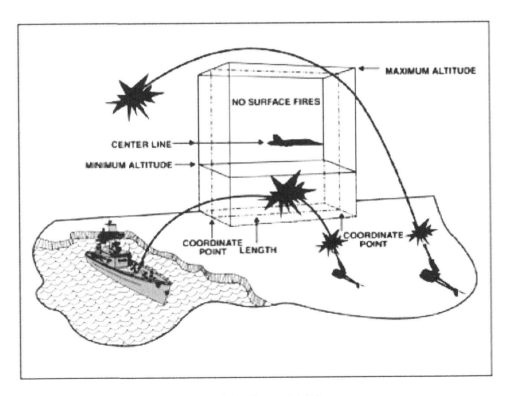

Figure B-9. Formal ACA.

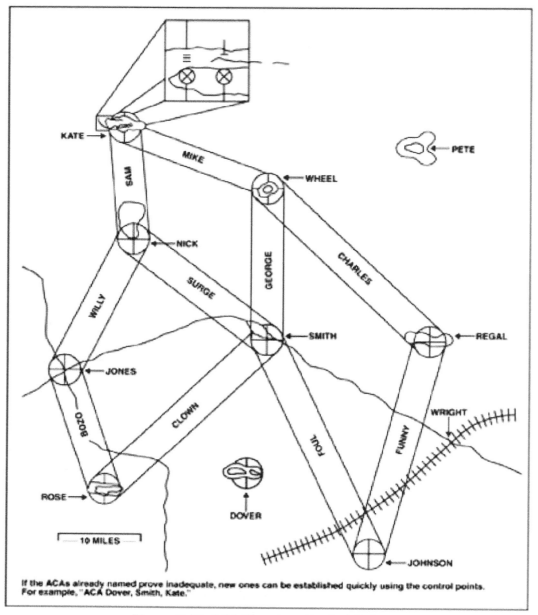

Figure B-10. ACA Based on Control Points.

Control points are often used to facilitate the establishment of ACAs for aircraft operating in those rear areas where their flight paths can conflict with artillery and naval gunfire rounds. Routes used frequently can be left in effect. Routes used occasionally (on-call) can be given code names and activated as required; e.g., activate ACA CLOWN 281400Z to 281410Z. When aircraft must follow unanticipated routes, they can be directed to proceed by a series of control points. These control points can be promulgated as the ACA; i.e., an immediate ACA.

Helicopter approach and retirement lanes may also be designated as ACAs for the period they are actually in use by helicopters. Likewise, holding areas and attack positions for rotary wing CAS may be designated as ACAs.

ACAs for aircraft operating within the envelope of enemy antiaircraft weapons present special problems. While the aircraft are operating outside of these envelopes, they can follow straight, predictable paths.

However, when they are within the envelopes, aircraft usually need freedom to maneuver. Thus, ACAs for aircraft operating in the vicinity of enemy antiaircraft weapons will usually contain long narrow boxes of airspace which avoids these envelopes or large volumes of airspace within these envelopes.

Figure B-11 shows what the ACA in a high threat area might look like. In this case, the ACA near the target is a large cylinder. Within the cylinder, the attacking aircraft has the space required to evade enemy antiaircraft weapons. It is important to note that the shape and size of that ACA within the antiaircraft envelope changes with threat and tactics. The size and shape will depend on the maneuvers of the aircraft, and that will depend on the type of aircraft and the required tactics to counter the threat. The air officer in the FSCC must keep abreast of evolving aviation tactics so the size and shape of ACAs can be determined to complement these tactics.

The ACA may be located above the target area; e.g., a rectangular box or cylinder, along the route of the aircraft; e.g., a corridor, or a combination.

The ACA's shape is determined by the path of the aircraft and the need to provide protection from friendly fires. Some ACAs are rectangular cubes; i.e., boxes of airspace. Other shapes may be required. Dimensions of an ACA can be published in any form

that provides the supporting arms agencies with enough information to plan their fires around the aircraft's flight path. For a rectangular ACA, the description may include the ACA's name, minimum and maximum altitudes, length (by grid coordinate points), width (total, bi-sected by the centerline), and the effective DTG. Altitude is feet above mean sea level unless otherwise stated. Altitude may be above ground level when the desire is to restrict the aircraft to relatively low altitudes above the ground; i.e., 500 feet and below. Above ground level may be particularly useful for helicopters. The vertical space between the ground and the top (or base) of an ACA based on mean sea level or above ground level differs significantly. See figure B-12 on page B-10.

ACA dimensions can also be established as SOP or according to a particular threat so that only the points where the ACA are based, effective time, and name need be published. ACA size and shape are dictated by the following:

- Type of aircraft. Generally, the higher the speed of the aircraft, the more room it needs to maneuver.

- Type of ordnance. Certain types of ordnance affect both route to target and turning radius of the attack aircraft. This in turn would affect the ACA. The FSC must work closely with the AirO in this regard.

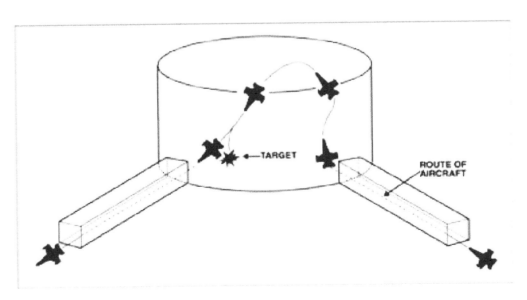

Figure B-11. ACA Based on Route of Aircraft.

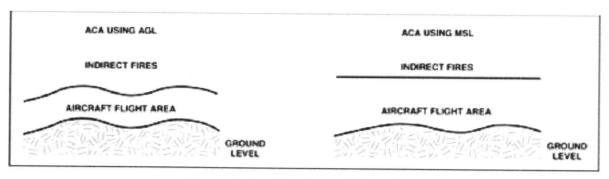

Figure B-12. ACAs Using MSL and AGL.

● Air defense threat. The threat often dictates the type of ACA employed in an operation. Within the enemy air defense envelope, aircraft need room for evasive maneuver. The most dangerous threat is an in-tegrated air defense system (IADS) with long range radars and missiles, which force aircraft to approach the target area at low altitude, integrated with mobile weapons; e.g., ZSU 23-4, in the immediate proximity of the target. To meet this threat, the attack aircraft use a low level pop-up technique. A simpler situation exists when either the enemy has no long range threat or that threat has been neutralized. In that case, the preferred attack aircraft tactics may be to remain at high altitude throughout the attack profile.

● Degrees of restriction. ACAs can vary in their degree of restriction on aircraft maneuver or surface-to-surface fires. Guidance for how restrictive immediate or informal ACAs should be is part of the fire support planning and coordination process. Examples include establishing—

■ ACAs that allow aircraft maximum freedom of movement. Such large ACAs are the most re-strictive of surface-to-surface fires. They should be kept in effect for the shortest period possible.

■ ACAs that encompass the aircraft's possible route and restrict aircraft by directions on the JTAR or 9-line brief such as offsets. Such in-structions can result in a much smaller ACA than would otherwise be possible. However, when fixed-wing aircraft maneuver in such a manner as they do when executing low level, pop-up de-livery, they cannot follow a precise track. Air-craft doing such maneuvers can easily move a quarter mile left or right of the intended path. Again, the effectiveness of such ACAs can be in-creased by keeping them in effect for the shortest possible time.

■ All ACAs 1,000 meters above the max ordinate for current low angle surface-to-surface fires.

■ ACAs above or below surface trajectories when aircraft routes or final attack cones cross gun tar-get lines. (Use firing table charts and add VI. Specify charge and method [angle of fire].) In this way, CAS and surface-to-surface fires can attack different targets simultaneously.

Scheduled and on-call ACAs are usually disseminated by the GCE and/or MAGTF FFCC as appropriate in a writ-ten document such as an overlay. Immediate ACAs are usually disseminated by the FSCC of the organization re-questing the air mission. Scheduled and on-call air sup-port requests are usually submitted 18 to 24 hours before the mission. During this period the ACAs associated with these missions are collected by the GCE or MAGTF FFCC, reviewed, adjusted, and disseminated to the re-quired agencies. ACA dimensions can also be established as SOP or according to a particular threat so that only the points on which the ACA are based, effective time, and name need be published.

A formal ACA is shown as an area enclosed by a solid black line. Data includes the letters ACA, the name, the originating headquarters, minimum and maximum alti-tude, and effective times. See figure B-13.

ACA BOZO, 1st MarDiv
Min Alt: 300 feet (MSL)   Max Alt: 1,500 feet (MSL)
Effective: 031000-131015 OCT 00

Figure B-13. Map Symbol for Formal ACA.

Restricted Operations Zone

A ROZ is not an FSCM. It is an airspace coordination measure and an area of defined dimensions within which the operation of one or more airspace users is restricted. See figure B-14. Examples are the platoon air hazard (PAH) and target air hazard (TAH) used with ATACMS units and in the future NGF ships firing extended range guided munitions (ERGMs) and land attack standard missiles (LASMs).

The ROZ restricts aircraft from defined areas to prevent fratricide. PAHs and TAHs aid in the deconfliction of airspace for ATACMS units by restricting aircraft from the airspace directly surrounding both the launch and impact area.

Since they are airspace coordination measures, ROZs are established by the airspace control authority. A PAH or TAH has no implications for indirect fires, but is submitted by the FSCC, or in the future the SACC, through the DASC to the TACC, or TACC-afloat. ROZs can be preplanned with stated DTG duration or on-call activation/deactivation, or impromptu with temporary (mission) duration.

A PAH or TAH ROZ can be located anywhere an ATACMS unit or target exists. The ROZ is identified as a radius from a point with an associated altitude. The PAH is computed by the ATACMS fire direction system based on trajectory and exit altitude. Radii vary from 3 kilometers to 5 kilometers. The TAH is also computed by the fire direction system but is based on entry altitude and missile trajectory, typically 1 to 10 kilometers. Altitudes for both ROZs vary from 5,000 to 15,000 meters.

ROZs are disseminated by the airspace control authority to aircraft and MACCS. Recommended PAHs and TAHs are computed by the firing unit and forwarded to the TACC via the FSCC and DASC.

ROZs are not portrayed on fire support coordination maps. PAHs and TAHs can be portrayed by a solid black line defining the area with the letters PAH or TAH, the altitude, the firing unit, and effective DTG.

Zone of Fire

A zone of fire is an area into which a designated ground unit or fire support ship delivers, or is prepared to deliver, fire support. Fire may or may not be observed (JP 1-02). Units and ships assigned zones of fire are responsible for attacking known targets and targets of opportunity according to their mission and the guidance of the supported commander.

Zones of fire in amphibious operations divide land into zones of fire. These zones are assigned to fire support ships and units as a means to coordinate their efforts with each other and with the scheme of maneuver of the supported ground unit. The unit or ship should be located so that it can best support the actions of the supported unit.

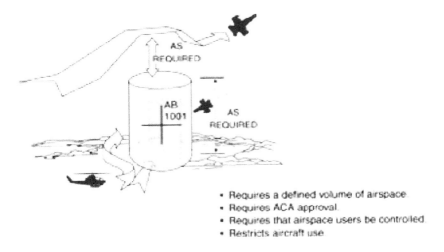

* Requires a defined volume of airspace.
* Requires ACA approval.
* Requires that airspace users be controlled.
* Restricts aircraft use.

Figure B-14. Restricted Operations Zone.

The commander of the naval task force providing naval surface support establishes and assigns zones of fire for the forces. The zone of fire for the artillery battalion or a ship assigned a mission of direct support normally corresponds to the AO of the supported unit. The zone of fire for an artillery unit or a ship assigned a mission of general support should be within the boundaries of the supported unit. When used in conjunction with naval surface fires, the size and shape of the zone of fire will depend on the terrain, the visibility, and boundaries of the supported unit.

Zones of fire are disseminated in the MAGTF OPORD. NSFS and artillery units incorporate their appropriate zones of fire into their fire plans.

Zones of fire are depicted as an area bounded by a solid black line and labeled ZF-1, ZF-2, or by MCFSS naming convention; e.g., ZO12MD (Zone 1, 2d MarDiv).

OTHER CONTROL MEASURES

Some control measures, although not fire support coordinating measures, play a role in fire support planning and coordination.

Boundaries

A boundary is a maneuver control measure. Boundaries designate the geographical limits of the AO of a unit. Within their own boundaries, unless otherwise restricted, units may execute fire and maneuver without close coordination with neighboring units unless otherwise restricted. Normally units do not fire across boundaries unless the fires are coordinated with the adjacent unit or the fires are beyond a fire support coordinating measure; e.g., CFL. These restrictions apply to all types of ammunition and to their effects. When such fires as smoke and illumination affect an adjacent unit, coordination with that unit is required. This does not preclude a commander from deciding, in certain situations, that his subordinate units may fire across boundaries at positively identified enemy units without coordinating for that specific target. This will only apply to direct fires and observed fires delivered by supporting arms. It also can only be applied to boundaries which that commander has established; e.g., a battalion commander can only apply this exception to his own companies' boundaries.

The area affected by a certain fire support coordinating measure, such as the CFL or FSCL, depends on the zone of action of the headquarters establishing the measure. For instance, as depicted in figure B-15, if

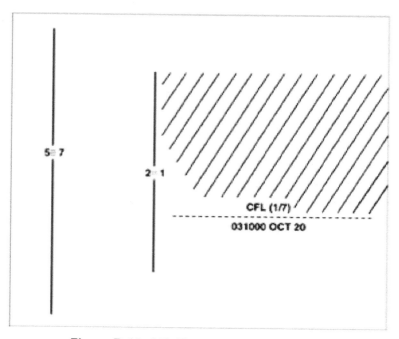

Figure B-15. CFL Established by Battalion.

the establishing headquarters is 1/7, the zone affected by the CFL is that of 1/7 (indicated by single diagonal lines). If the CFL was established by the 7th Mar (see fig. B-16), the affected area would include the zones of the subordinate battalions (consolidated by the regiment) as well as that of the regiment.

Phase Lines

A phase line is a maneuver control measure used by land forces for control and coordination of military operations. It is usually on recognizable terrain extending across the zone of action. Units normally report crossing phase lines and they can be used to identify limits of advance, control fires, or define an AO. The purpose of each phase line and any actions required by forces affected by the phase line is specified by the using unit.

Amphibious Objective Area

The AOA is a geographical area (delineated for command and control purposes in the order initiating the amphibious operation) within which is located the objective(s) to be secured by the amphibious force. This area must be of sufficient size to ensure accomplishment of the amphibious force's mission and must provide sufficient area for conducting necessary sea, air, and land operations. (JP 3-02)

Fire Support Area and/or Fire Support Station

A fire support area (FSA) is an appropriate maneuver area assigned to fire support ships from which to deliver gunfire support of an amphibious operation. A fire support station (FSS) is an exact location at sea within a FSA from which a fire support ship delivers fire. (JP 1-02). This designation stations ships within boat lanes of the assaulting force or where maneuvering room is restricted by other considerations.

Radar Zones

Search zones prioritize the search pattern and provide the reaction posture of the radars to best meet the maneuver commander's intent. Each Firefinder radar can store up to nine different zones. There are four different types of zones used with the radar: the critical friendly zone (CFZ), the call-for-fire zone (CFFZ), the artillery target intelligence zone (ATIZ), and the censor zone (CZ).

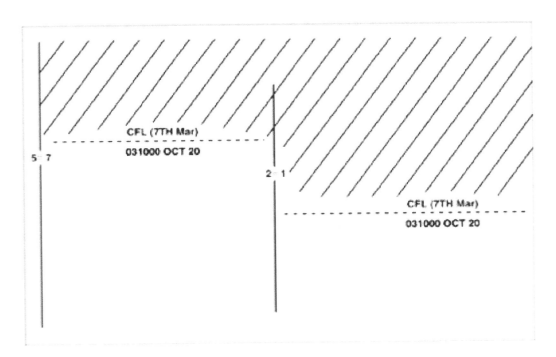

Figure B-16. CFL Established by Regiment.

Critical Friendly Zone

The CFZ designates the highest priority friendly locations of the maneuver commander and provides the most responsive priority of fires from the radars. Cued radars detecting incoming rounds into this zone immediately generate a priority request for fire. FSCs recommend to maneuver commanders positioning of CFZs and their size for best responsiveness. Typical CFZs include maneuver assembly areas, headquarters, FARPs, and other troop concentrations.

Call for Fire Zone

The call-for-fire zone (CFFZ) designates a search area beyond the FLOT that the maneuver commander wants suppressed or neutralized. The CFFZ designation is closely tied to the IPB process. A CFFZ would likely be a suspected enemy artillery position. The CFFZ provides the second most responsive priority for fires from the radar.

Artillery Target Intelligence Zone

The artillery target intelligence zone (ATIZ) enables a maneuver commander to watch an area closely while assigning higher priority to more important areas. Targets identified in this zone will be evaluated for attack as they are received but will not automatically generate a fire mission.

Censor Zone

A censor zone (CZ) designates areas from where the commander does not want to attack targets. The CZ is often used to avoid overlap and duplication.

Common Sensor Boundary

Target duplication between Firefinder radars is likely during combat operations. In addition, the sheer volume of targets being passed from the radars will overwhelm the targeting element, especially if the radars are under centralized control. An effective method of reducing the duplication of these targets for attack is to establish a common sensor boundary (CSB) for call-for-fire zones. The CSB is a line established by the artillery regimental HQ or force artillery that divides target acquisition (TA) areas of search into close and deep areas for the Q-46 and Q-37, if attached.

The CSB is established by designating a line beyond which no CFFZs for the Q-46 would be established. The Q-37 would not establish any CFFZs short of this line. All radars could process targets generated for attack from their CFFZs through the same or different headquarters. Some targets may still be duplicated. When the radars are used in this way, the maximum range capabilities of the radars are not restricted. The CSB is not a fire support coordinating measure, although the CSB may coincide with a CFL. The CSB is only a tool used by the target acquisition controlling headquarters to maximize effectiveness of radars. In determining CSB placement, consider—

- Range of the attack systems.
- Available attack assets.
- Effective ranges of TA assets.
- The likely enemy indirect fire weapon deployment areas developed through thorough IPB.
- Availability of ammunition or aviation assets.
- When a radar is required to move for survivability, that the CSB may have to be adjusted to ensure optimum radar coverage; e.g., if the Q-46 moves, the Q-37 will have to cover the Q-46 area of responsibility until the Q-46 is in position.

FSCMs AND OTHER CONTROL MEASURES IN AFATDS

Within automated information systems, FSCMs and control measures are referred to as geometries. Figure B-17 shows an example of how those systems depict fire support geometries.

Geometry	Situation: Friendly (F) Enemy (E)	Border Color: Friendly (F) Enemy (E)	Symbol	
			Current	Planned
Air Corridor (must be irregular)	F	F - Blue	Name #	Name #
Airspace Coordination Area	F	F - Red	ACA Name	ACA Name
ATI Zone	F	F - Blue	ATI ZONE Name	ATI ZONE Name
Call for Fire Zone	F	F - Blue	CCF ZONE Name	CCF ZONE Name
Censor Zone	F	F - Blue	CENSOR ZONE Name	CENSOR ZONE Name
Critical Friendly Zone	F	F - Blue	CF Zone Name	CF Zone Name
Fire Support Area	F or E	F - Blue E - Red	FSA Name	FSA Name
Fire Support Station	F	F - Blue	Name	
Forward Arming and Refueling Point	F	F - Blue	FARP Name	FARP Name
Free-Fire Area	F	F - Blue	FFA Name	FFA Name
No-Fire Area	F	Black with Red Fill	NFA Name	NFA Name
Restrictive Fire Area	F	F - Red	RFA Name	RFA Name
Zone of Responsibility	F	F - Blue		
Boundary Line	F or E	F - Blue E - Red	Second unit name / First unit name	Second unit name / First unit name
Coordinated Fire Line	F	F - Blue	CFL	CFL
Fire Support Coordination Line	F	F - Blue	FSCL	FSCL unit name
Restrictive Fire Line	F	F - Red	RFL	RFL

Figure B-17. AFTADS Geometries.

Appendix C. Battalion and Above Fire Support Planning

Table C-1. Mission Analysis.

INPUTS	PROCESS	OUTPUTS
Higher warning order or OPORD. Status of supporting arms. Info from higher, adjacent, and lower FSCCs. IPB products. Enemy COAs from S-2. HVTs by phase or critical event.	Understand higher maneuver and fire support plans. Organize and analyze facts. Identify specified and implied fire support tasks. Translate status of fire support assets into capabilities. Analyze effects of IPB on fire support. Use above to develop draft EFSTs.	Fire support mission analysis brief: Higher fire support plan. Fire support status (capabilities and limitations). Fire support IPB analysis. Fire support time line. Recommended fire support tasks. Commander approves or modifies fire support tasks and issues additional fire support guidance.

Table C-2. Course of Action Development.

INPUTS	PROCESS	OUTPUTS
Fire support mission analysis brief. Approved EFSTs. Commanders additional fire support guidance.	Determine where to find and attack the enemy to accomplish EFST. Identify HPTs in those formations (TVA). Quantify desired effects for EFSTs. Plan methods for EFSTs: Allocate assets to acquire and attack. Integrate triggers with maneuver COA. Use battle calculus. Assist S-2 in collection plan development to support target acquisition CCIRs.	For each COA developed: Concept of fires. Draft FSEM. Draft target list work-sheet and overlay. Draft TSM or modified TSM. Collection plan.

Table C-3. Course of Action War Game.

INPUTS	PROCESS	OUTPUTS
Draft fires paragraph. Draft FSEM. Draft target list worksheet and overlay. Draft TSM or modified TSM. Collection plan.	Targeting decisions: finalize HPTL. War game fire support plan against enemy COAs. Test and refine fire support plan. Modify draft fire support plans for each COA.	Final draft for each COA: Fires paragraph. Fire support appendix: FSEM. Target list worksheet and overlay. TSM. Refined HPTL, AGM, and TSS.

Table C-4. Course of Action Comparison and Decision.

INPUTS	PROCESS	OUTPUTS

Final drafts for each COA of:
    Fires paragraph
    Fire support appendix: FSEM.
    Target list worksheet and overlay.
    TSM or modified TSM.
    Refined HPTL, AGM, and TSS.
	Understand higher maneuver and fire support plans.
	Organize and analyze facts.
	Identify specified and implied fire support tasks.
	Translate status of fire support assets into capabilities.
	Analyze effects of IPB on fire support.
	Use above to develop draft EFSTs.
		Commander-approved COA.
		FSC identifies refinements to templates and tools for selected COA.
		Fire support warning order.

Table C-5. Orders Development.

INPUTS	PROCESS	OUTPUTS

Commander's selected COA.
Identified refinements to fire support templates and tools for the selected COA.
	Refine any changes to COA made during the decision process.
	Finalize and reproduce written products.
	Prepare orders brief.
		Final fire support plan:
		    Fires paragraph.
		    Fire support appendix:
		        FSEM.
		        Target list worksheet and overlay.
		        Target synchronization matrix.
		        HPTL, AGM, and TSS.

Table C-6. Transition.

INPUTS	PROCESS	OUTPUTS
OPORD.	Disseminate order.	Rehearsals. Backbrief.

APPENDIX D. ESSENTIAL FIRE SUPPORT TASKS METHODOLOGY

Based on lessons learned from previous fire support coordination exercises, the Marine Corps now uses a methodology called essential fire support tasks (EFSTs). The purpose of EFST is to translate the maneuver commander's intent into usable information for the fire support coordinator (FSC). The FSC uses EFSTs to focus supporting arms agencies on critical or essential tasks that must be accomplished to meet the maneuver commander's intent.

CONCEPT OF FIRES PARAGRAPH

As a subparagraph to the concept of operations, the concept of fires paragraph contains EFSTs and describes the commander's guidance for fires and the concept of fires to support the scheme of maneuver. The concept of fires must clearly describe the logical sequence of EFSTs and how they contribute to the concept of operations. The FSC uses the specified and implied tasks identified during mission analysis and from the commander's guidance for fire support to identify specific fire support tasks. The FSC must then determine the methodology to accomplish each task.

The methods frame the role of supporting arms agencies in the overall plan and serve to focus their efforts in supporting the scheme of maneuver. The concept of fires along with the concept of maneuver communicates how the force as a whole will achieve the commander's intent. For the FSC to meet the commander's intent, EFSTs must be closely integrated with maneuver.

EFSTs can also help focus the targeting effort by concentrating on enemy critical vulnerabilities and necessary targets that will facilitate maneuver. The primary audience for the concept of fires is the subordinate maneuver commanders and their fire support personnel. At each level of command (division, regiment, battalion) there are different levels of experience working with various fire support products and tools. This technique applies to all levels of FSCCs and staffs.

FORMAT

Overall paragraph organization should mirror that of the scheme of maneuver paragraph. If the maneuver paragraph is phased or otherwise organized, the concept of fires paragraph will take on the same organization. Just as maneuver tasks use task and purpose, fire support tasks are defined by the task, purpose, method, and effects (TPME) thought process. TPME may be used by the FSC to develop the concept of fires that is concise but specific enough to clearly state what fires are to accomplish in the operation. Within each phase of an operation, each EFST will be described in sequence of planned execution. This can be done using TPME in step action form or as subparagraphs. The information required in each subcategory is outlined below.

Task

Describes the targeting objective fires must achieve against a specific enemy formation's function or capability. Formations are HPTs or contain one or more HPTs.

Task = Objective, Formation, and Function.

Objective

MCRP 3-16A/FM 6-20-10, *Targeting*, outlines several terms to describe targeting objectives that can be used, however disrupt, delay or limit are most commonly used. Targeting objectives should not be mistaken for effects of fire such as: *harass, suppress, neutralize,* or *destroy* used to determine the degree of damage or duration of effects on a specific target. Targeting objectives entail the analysis of enemy situations relative to the objectives, mission, and the capabilities at the commander's disposal, in order to identify and nominate specific vulnerabilities that, if exploited, will accomplish the commander's intent through disrupting, delaying, limiting, or diverting enemy forces or critical resources. See chapter 3 for information on targeting objectives and effects of fire.

Disrupt. Means to preclude efficient interaction of enemy combat or combat support systems. Simplified, it means to not let an enemy formation perform a specific function: not to do what it is supposed to do.

> Example: Disrupt the AT battery long range fires against the TF flank companies.

Delay. Means to alter the time of arrival of a specific enemy formation or capability. It focuses on not letting the enemy do some function when it wants/needs to.

> Example: Delay the ability of the advance unit to support the security element with direct fires.

Limit. Applies to reducing the options or courses of action available to the enemy commander. For example, the commander may direct the use of air interdiction and fire support to limit the use of one or more avenues of approach available to the enemy. Also, he may direct the use of interdiction to limit enemy use of fire support. To limit capabilities implies we also disrupt enemy plans by precluding effective interaction or the cohesion of enemy combat and combat support systems.

> Example: Limit the ability of the enemy air assault company to establish an LZ in the high ground west of the firebase.

Divert. Addresses the commander's desire to tie up critical enemy resources. Attack of certain interdiction targets may result in the enemy commander's diverting capabilities or assets from one area or activity to another. Divert indirectly reduces the enemy commander's capability to continue his plans.

Formation

A specific element or subelement of the enemy. Can specify a specific vehicle type or target category as long as the element or subelement is clear.

> Example: The enemy platoon at the point of penetration.

Function

An ability of the formation to achieve its primary task and purpose. What is the formation doing that is unacceptable? What do we want the formation to do/not do? Helping words: "the ability to . . . ."

> Example: The ability to effectively direct fire against the breach force.

Purpose

Describes maneuver or operational purpose for the task. Identify as specifically as possible the maneuver formation that will leverage the targeting objective; describe in space and time what the objective accomplishes.

Purpose = Maneuver Purpose.

> Example: To allow Bravo Mech to occupy the support by fire position without becoming decisively engaged by the center enemy platoon.

Method

Describes how the task and purpose will be achieved. It ties the detect function or "lookers" (executor/observer/TA sensor) with the deliver function or "shooters" (lethal and nonlethal assets) in time and space and describes how to achieve the task. The following should be considered under method:

Method = Priority, Allocation, Restriction.

- Priority of fires (POF).
- Final protective fires (FPFs).
- Observers (pri/alt).
- Restrictions.
- Triggers.
- Special munitions.
- Target allocation.
- Target.
- Priority targets.
- EW.
- CAS/attack aviation.
- Any other instructions.

Priority

Describes the "how" of the EFST. For the looker, it can assign POF to execute the task outlined. It assigns observers in maneuver units or other acquisition means. Assignment of the looker requires the consideration of Target Selection Standards. When a specific asset; e.g., CAS, is to focus exclusively on a task, that information can be communicated here.

> Example: Priority of CAS is to destroy the enemy's Combined Arms Reserve tanks. This part of the method can also provide focus by using NAIs, TAIs, targets, or EAs to describe where attacks will occur.

Allocation

For the shooter, it describes allocating fire support assets to accomplish the EFSTs. Assets may include projected or mechanical smoke, indirect fires (suppress, neutralize, destroy, obscure, screen), FASCAM, CPHD, F/W and R/W CAS, and EW. In method, fire support assets identify their part of accomplishing the EFST. It is from the method of an EFST that the artillery and other FS/TA assets get their essential tasks.

Restriction

The method can also outline any limitations or restrictions on accomplishing the tasks; e.g., ammunition (no ICM on the OBJ), FSCM (ACA Blue) or other restrictions that may effect accomplishing the EFST. See bullet format and paragraph format examples below.

Effects

Attempts to quantify successful accomplishment of the task. It provides the looker with a measure of effectiveness (MOE) for the task. If multiple shooters are involved it helps delineate what each must accomplish. Effects provide a measure of when we are done with the task. It also provides the basis for the assess function in D3A and the decision to reattack or not. See appendix I, table I-7.

> Example: AGMB delayed for 20 minutes. 1 T80/4 BMPs destroyed by FASCAM. CAS destroys 4 T80s and 2 BMPs behind FASCAM. Enemy ADA jammed by EW during CAS attack.

Concept of fires and EFST information is placed in the Concept of Fires paragraph as shown below. An example of the information required for the concept of fires and EFSTs is shown on pages D-4 through D-5.

    3b. ( ) <u>Concept of Operations</u>

        (1) ( ) <u>Concept of Maneuver</u>

        (2) ( ) <u>Concept of Fires.</u> Task and purpose for each EFST from the base order.

Example: Method (Bullet Format)

- Priority: Arty POF to Alpha Co, Mortar POF to Charlie Co. Team Mech. Arty and Mortar POF when committed.
- Allocation: Alpha fires Arty Pri Tgt AB1000, Bn 3 DPICM when security element goes to ground. Charlie fires mortar Pri Tgt AB 2001 Plt 10 HE at AT-5 platoon when they set their firing line. Back up observer for both targets is Recon Tm 2 vic. OP1. Send suppression missions to Bn FSCC, expect mortar Plt 3 HE. CAS maintained at Bn level.
- Restrictions: RFA 200 meters radius over Recon Tm 2. No DPICM within 500 meters NP123456. ACA Joe in effect when CAS at IP, no fires south of 58 North/South gridline.

Example: Method (Paragraph Format)

Arty POF to Alpha Co, Mortar POF to Team Charlie. Team Mech gets Arty and Mortar POF when committed. Recon Tm 2 occupies OP 1 prior to LD. Upon contact, Alpha (P), Recon Tm 2 (A) fires Arty Pri Tgt AB 1000 Bn 3 DPICM at security element when it goes to ground. Charlie (P), Recon Tm 2 (A) fires mortar Pri Tgt AB2001 Plt 10 HE at AT-5 firing line when they set. Adjust and repeat as necessary. Send all suppression missions to Bn FSCC, expect mortar Plt 3 HE. CAS, if available, maintained by Bn. All RFAs 200 meters radius, Recon Tm 2. No DPICM within 500 meters NP 123456. ACA Joe i/e when CAS at IP, no fires south of 58 N/S gridline.

PHASE ONE, RECCE MOVEMENT FORWARD

TASK

Destroy the 2 x Forward Security Combat Outposts of the 127th battalion's main defensive positions to prevent identification of FO and scout forward movement and initial movement of 1/6 from AAHOTBED.

PURPOSE

To allow FOs and scouts to occupy forward OP locations and safeguard initial movement of 1/6 from AA HOTBED to LD (PL JIMMY).

METHOD

Priority: Artillery POF to FO TM 1, mortar POF to scouts.

Allocation: AB 1001 CPHD PRI TGT identified observation post (1 x BMP + Inf section) FO tm 1 (P), scouts(A) at H-180 backup Bn 3 DPICM. AB1002 CPHD PRI TGT identified observation post (1x T80 + Inf section) FO tm 2 (P), FO tm 1 (A) at H-120 backup Bn 3 DPICM. AB1005 templated OP scouts (P), FO tm 2 (A) when TM B Crosses PL BILL. AB1003 mortar SMK Deception 10 minutes 300 x 60 scouts (P) FO tm 2 (A) at H-10.

Restrictions: Clear Illum through regiment, no DPICM on MSR MARS, regiment release Authority for SD FASCAM. CFL PL TOM o/o PL DICK. RFAs 300 meters radius on all FO tm and scout locations. FFA 67599977-67009710-65009675.

EFFECTS

2 x observation posts destroyed (1 x Bmp, 1x T80, 2 x sections) 1 x OP destroyed FO tms and scouts in forward OP positions able to observe BPs and TF1-69 crosses LD unhindered from direct or indirect fires.

PHASE TWO, SUPPORT BY FIRE AND BREACH OPERATION

TASK

Disrupt the ability of the 127th regiments 2 X Plt BP from effectively engaging Breach Force with Direct and Indirect Fires.

PURPOSE

To allow TM B to occupy support by fire position and TM C to establish 2 x Breach lanes prior to assault on to OBJ GOLD South.

METHOD

Priority: Artillery POF TM A, mortar POF TM C.

Allocation: A1B (AB1003 and AB1004 2 x MIP BPs)1x Bty per TGT Continuos Fire 20 minutes TM B (P), FO tm 1 (A) as TM B crosses 34 Northing. AB1009 20 minutes FA SMK 300 x 60 TM B (P) TM C (A) as TM B crosses 34 Northing.

Restrictions: Clear illum through regiment, no DPICM on MSR MARS, regiment release authority for SD FASCAM. CFL PL DICK o/o PL HARRY. RFAs 300 meters radius on all FO tm and scout locations. FFA 67599977-67009710-65009675.

EFFECTS

TM B occupies SBF position, TM C establishes 2 breach lanes and retains 85% combat power. 2 x Plt BPs unable to effectively engage 1/6.

PHASE THREE, SEIZE OBJECTIVE GOLD

TASK

Disrupt the ability of the 127th regiments 2xPlt BPs and enemy regiment from effectively engaging TM C and TM Mech with direct and indirect fires.

PURPOSE

To allow 1/6 to seize objective GOLD.

METHOD

Priority: Artillery POF TM C o/o TM Mech, mortar POF TM C o/o TM Mech.

Allocation: AB1100 FA PRI TGT continuous fire 15 minutes East Plt Pos TM C (P) scouts (A) as TM C exits breach lane. AB1200 mortar Smk 60 x 300 15 minutes TM C (P), FO tm1 (P) as TM C clears breach lane. If the enemy is observed moving vicinity ELGIN FO tm 1(P), scout (A) initiates 2xCAS when CAS is 5 minutes off IP AB1010 1 x bty 6rds templated SA13 SEAD FO tm 1 (P)TM C (A) when CAS 3 minutes off IP AB1201 (1 Tube) mortar red phosphorus (RP) CAS marker. Once TMC seizes Objective GOLD East, artillery and mortar POF to TM Mech. AB1101artillery PRI TGT Continuous fire 10 minutes West TM Mech (P) scouts (A) when TM Mech moves through TM C. If the enemy is observed moving vicinity ELGINFO tm 1(P), scout (A) initiates 2xCAS when CAS is 5 minutes off IP AB1010 1 x bty 6rds templated SA13 SEAD FO tm 1 (P)TM C (A) when CAS 3 minutes off IP AB1201 (1 Tube) mortar RP CAS marker.

Restrictions: Clear illum through regiment, no DPICM on MSR, regiment release authority for SD FASCAM. CFL PL DICK o/o PL HARRY. O/O ACA ORANGE. RFAs 300 meters radius on all FO tm and scout locations. FFA Grids 67599977-67009710-65009675.

EFFECTS

1/6 seizes OBJ GOLD, SA13 unable to engage CAS.   CAS destroys enemy formation (3 x AT5s 12 x T80s).

PHASE 4, CONSOLIDATION

TASK

Limit the ability of the 127th regiment's remaining forces from penetrating PL KEN.

PURPOSE

To allow 1/6 to establish a hasty defensive position along PL HARRY before the FPOL with 2/6.

METHOD

Priority: Artillery POF TM Mech, mortar POF TM A.

Allocation: AB8000 FASCAM SD, MD, 400 X 200 TM C (P) TM B (A) when Plt or greater size of BMPs or T80s seen passing South PL KING along Peters Pass. TMB (P) TM Mech (A).   TM Mech to plan 1 x FA FPF. AB1020 mortar FPF TM C (P) as required.

Restrictions: Clear illum through regiment, No DPICM on MSR, regiment release authority for SD FASCAM. CFL PL HARRY. RFAs 300 meters radius on all FO tm and Scout locations. FFA Grids 67599977-67009710-65009675

EFFECTS

No remaining 127 MIRB forces able to penetrate PL KEN.

1/1 will initially use artillery and NSFS to disrupt the reconnaissance element's, from 132nd MRR, ability to identify and report our battle positions and obstacle locations to allow 2/1 to remain unde-tected within its BPs, prepared to maximize fires within EA Mack. Then R/W CAS and artillery will be used by 2/1 to delay the advanced guard, main body, of 132nd MRR west of PL Iowa to enable 1/1 to conduct rearward passage of lines with 2/1.

APPENDIX E. APPENDIX 19 TO ANNEX C

The following formats for the fire support annex are associated with a formal operation order. Refer to FMFM 1-7, *Supporting Arms in Amphibious Operations*, FMFM 6-9, *Marine Artillery Support*, FMFRP 5-71, *MAGTF Aviation Planning*, and MCWP 5-1, *Marine Corps Planning Process*, for specific formats and information required for the individual supporting arm tab/fire plan.

CLASSIFICATION

Copy no. _ of _copies
ISSUING HEADQUARTERS
PLACE OF ISSUE
Date/time group

APPENDIX 19 (Fire Support) to ANNEX C (Operations) to Operation Order (Number) (U)

(U) REFERENCE: List applicable references; e.g., maps, operation plans, doctrinal publications, SOPs, etc.

(U) Time Zone:

1. (U)   Situation

    a. (U)   Enemy Forces. Refer to Annex B (Intelligence). Identify any particular enemy capability which may have a definite impact on fire support.

    b. (U)   Friendly Forces. Reference may be made to annex.

        (1) (U) Provide a statement on the plan of the higher headquarters sufficient to ensure coordinated action by recipients of the fire support plan.

        (2) (U) Provide statement on the plan of adjacent forces that affect the operation.

        (3) (U) Identify additional supporting elements. Include task designators; e.g., TG 38.1. List artillery first (if any), followed by others in alphabetical order.

    c. (U)   Attachments and Detachments. List fire support units now attached or detached by the operation order, together with the effective time and date. Reference may be made to Annex A (Task Organization).

2. (U)   Mission

    See basic order.

3. (U)   Execution

        In separate lettered subparagraphs, give a brief concept of operations and state the concept of fires. This can be accomplished by referring to the concept of ops and providing a summary of the essential fire support tasks throughout all phases of the operation. Depending on the detail of attachments, a listing of each task, its purpose, method, and effect, may be included.

CLASSIFICATION

For each supporting arm, provide a general statement about what support is to be provided. Record allocation/tactical mission assignments in this paragraph if fire plan tabs are not used. If a tab is not included, state specific tasks associated with an essential fire support task; e.g., essential artillery tasks.

Depending on what information is provided in the individual tabs, miscellaneous information is provided for each paragraph. Priority of fires, priority of position areas for artillery units, reliance on particular supporting arms, zones of fire, instructions for fire planning, guidance on priority targets and the delivery of special fires, counterfire, and SEAD are examples of information that may be contained in this paragraph. Liaison officer and observer employment may also be addressed. Additional paragraphs may precede the coordinating instructions paragraph to further establish the fire support plan; e.g., SEAD, counterfire, counter-mech plans.

a. (U) <u>Commander's Guidance for Fires</u>. Commander's description of what he wants fire support to be able to do in order to support his intent.

b. (U) <u>Concept of Operations</u>. Make reference to paragraph 3b of the basic order or to Appendix 11 (Concept of Operations).

c. (U) <u>Concept of Fires</u>. Restated from paragraph 3.b. (2) and may be expanded to include detailed essential fire support tasks. Essential Fire Support Tasks (EFSTs) may be expressed in the form of Task, Purpose, Method, Effects. **EFST examples using TPME:**

(1) (U) <u>Task</u>. Disrupt reconnaissance element's, from 132nd regiments ability to identify and report our battle positions and obstacle locations.

(2) (U) <u>Purpose</u>. To allow 2/1 to remain undetected within its battle positions (BPs) prepared to maximize fires within engagement area (EA) Mack.

(3) (U) <u>Method</u>. Priority: Arty POF to 1/1. NSFS to 2/1. Allocation: 2 Recon Tms attached to 1/1. Recon Tm 3 located at OP B. 1/1 (P) and Recon 3 (A) fire AA 1001 to destroy ID'd recon C3 vehicles with CPHD or BN 2 DPICM when in vicinity of checkpoint 56. EW ID recon nets/locations and JAM. 1/1 plans two arty pri tgts (btry size). HPT ACRV, BRDM. Restrictions: RFA on OP B. Illum requires Regt approval. CFZ 1 is in effect over BPs. CFL 1 (PL Florida) is in effect.

(4) (U) <u>Effects</u>. 2 ACRV and 3 BRDMs destroyed west of PL Alabama. Recon nets jammed, and friendly BPs not ID'd.

(5) (U) <u>Task</u>. Delay AGMB of 132nd MRR west of PL Iowa.

(6) (U) <u>Purpose</u>. Allow 1/1 to do rearward passage of lines with 2/1.

Page number

CLASSIFICATION

CLASSIFICATION

(7) (U) <u>Method</u>. Priority: Arty POF to 1/1, NSFS to 2/1, CAS held at Regt. Allocation: Recon 3 TACON to 1/1. 1/1 (p) and Recon 3 (a) fire group A2A, Btry 4 ICM per target and NGF 50 salvos, when lead elements of AGMB cross PL Arizona. Upon completion, 1/1 (p) and Recon 3 (a) fire AA 2105, Arty Smk 500m, 20min. to allow 1/1 to begin passage. As final elements of 1/1 cross PL Virginia, 1/1 (p) and 2/1 (a) fires AA 2106, Arty FASCAM 400X400 SD RAAMs/ADAMs, medium density. 1/1 (p) and 2/1(a) controls section of AH-1s from BP Rattler to engage tanks and C3 vehicles behind FASCAM minefield. When 2 Sections of AV-8B arrive at CP Ford, 1/1 (p) or Cobra Sect (a) fires Program' Charlie" (SEAD) to allow AV-8Bs freedom to attack targets behind the FASCAM minefield from IP Chevy. Mark provided by 1/1, artillery (a). EW identify ADA and COF nets and jam. 1/1 gets 4 arty pri tgt (three guns each). 2/1 has one NSFS pri tgt. HPTs are C3, AD, and artillery. Restrictions: 200m RFA (NO ICM) over Recon 3 position. ACA Mongo in effect over IP Chevy when AV-8Bs check-in.

(8) (U) <u>Effects</u>. AGMB delayed west of PL Iowa for 30 min. 3 of 6 artillery tubes destroyed, 10 tanks destroyed, AD neutralized, and 6 ACRVs destroyed.

d. (U) <u>Air Support</u>

    (1) (U) <u>General</u>

    (2) (U) <u>Allocation</u>. Tab A (Air Fire Plan).

    (3) (U) <u>Miscellaneous</u>

e. (U) <u>Artillery Support</u>

    (1) (U) <u>General</u>

    (2) (U) <u>Organization for Combat</u>. Tab B (Artillery Fire Plan).

    (3) (U) <u>Miscellaneous</u>

f. (U) <u>Naval Surface Fire Support</u>

    (1) (U) <u>General</u>

    (2) (U) <u>Allocation</u>. Tab C (Naval Surface Fires Plan).

    (3) (U) <u>Miscellaneous</u>

g. (U) <u>Chemical Fires Plan</u>. (Omitted. Not used by USMC.)

h. (U) <u>Targeting</u>. Make reference to Tab E (Targeting).

i. (U) <u>Fire Support Coordination</u>. Make reference to Tab F (Fire Support Coordination Plan).

CLASSIFICATION

CLASSIFICATION

j. (U)   MCFSS. Make reference to Tab G (MCFSS Plan).

k. (U). Coordinating Instructions. Provide information that applies to more than one supporting arm. Examples: fire support coordination measures, H/L Hour, method of timing the delivery of fires (e.g., synchronized clock), target number allocations, observation/target acquisition employment, firing restrictions, attack guidance, target precedence, high-payoff targets, damage criteria, fire support coordination reporting requirements, route precedence, fire plan submission requirements, procedures/signals for shifting of fires. Reference may be made to applicable tabs; e.g., targeting, fire support coordination.

4. (U)   Administration and Logistics

Make reference to Annex D (Logistics/Combat Service Support, and/or administrative/logistic orders. Identify ammunition availability, allocations, and ammunition management measures; e.g., controlled supply rate (CSR).

5. (U)   Command and Signal

Provide instructions necessary for establishment and maintenance of command and signal procedures. Identify command relationships as required, signal information (e.g., instructions or restrictions pertaining to radio and pyrotechnics), and information pertaining to command posts; e.g., location of CPs afloat, initial positions ashore, designation of alternate CPs. Reference Tab F for automated systems communications parameters.

a. (U)   Command Relationships (as required)

b. (U)   Signal

c. (U)   Command Posts

ACKNOWLEDGE RECEIPT

/s/

TABS:
A Air Fire Plan
B Artillery Fire Plan
C Naval Surface Fire Support Plan
D Chemical Fire Plan (Omitted. Not used by USMC.)
E Targeting
F Fire Support Coordination Plan
G MCFSS Plan (refer to FMFM 6-18.1)
* Other plans may be included as required to complete the fire support plan; e.g., counter-mechanized fire plan, counterfire plan, SEAD plan.

Page number

CLASSIFICATION

Sample Format For Tab A to Fire Support Appendix

CLASSIFICATION

Copy no. _ of _copies
ISSUING HEADQUARTERS
PLACE OF ISSUE
Date/time group

TAB A (Air Fire Plan) to APPENDIX 19 (Fire Support) to ANNEX C (Operations) to Operation Order (Number) (U)

(U) REFERENCE:

(U) TIME ZONE:

1. (U)   Situation

   Provide appropriate details of the general situation, particularly on air support.

2. (U)   Execution

   This paragraph contains air support procedural information needed by the supported unit for the employment of close air support. Examples: allocation of sorties for planning purposes, aircraft alert status, air delivery procedures (e.g., target marking, SEAD, etc.), codes (e.g., to lift air attack, to designate MEDEVAC, to designate downed aircraft), air request procedures (e.g., cut-off times for submission of requests). The information is listed in separate lettered subparagraphs. Make reference to Annex—(Air Operations) for concept of air support.

3. (U)   Miscellaneous

   a. (U)   Coordinating Instructions

      This subparagraph provides information needed for the coordination of air support. Examples: fire support coordinating measures, instructions for TACPs, FAC(A)s, TAC(A), NAOs, UAVs, routing procedures. The information is listed in separate lettered subparagraphs.

   b. (U)   Air Safety

      This subparagraph provides information incident to aircraft safety. Examples: guidance on ACAs and SEAD, strike warning broadcasts. The information is listed in separate lettered subparagraphs.

4. (U)   Command and Signal

   a. (U)   Signal. Refer to Annex K (Communications)
                                   Page number

CLASSIFICATION

CLASSIFICATION

b. (U) <u>Command Posts</u>. Identify air control agency (e.g., DASC, TACC) locations.

ACKNOWLEDGE RECEIPT

/s/

ENCLOSURES:
1   Preplanned Air Support
2   Air Targets
3   Air Target Overlay

Copy no.__ of __ copies
ISSUING HEADQUARTERS
PLACE OF ISSUE
Date/time group

ENCLOSURE 1 (Preplanned Air Support) to TAB A (Air Fire Plan) to APPENDIX 19 (Fire Support) to ANNEX C (Operations) to Operation Order (Number)

LN #	TGT #	TYPE MSN	AIRCRAFT ORDNANCE	TOT/TIME ON STATION	ATK DIR	PULL OFF DIRECTION	TGT MARKING	CONTROL AGENCY	REMARKS

ENCLOSURE 2 (Air Targets) to TAB A (Air Fire Plan) to APPENDIX 19 (Fire Support) to ANNEX C (Operations) to Operation Order (Number)

LN #	TGT #	TGT DESC	TGT COOR-DUM	SIZE (METERS)	DIRECTION/ DISTANCE FRIENDLY UNITS	SOURCE	REMARKS

ENCLOSURE 3 (Air Target Overlay) to TAB A (Air Fire Plan) to APPENDIX 19 (Fire Support) to ANNEX C (Operations) to Operation Order (Number)

REFERENCE: Map

(The overlay contains air targets, fire support coordinating measures applicable to air support, and unit boundaries.)

Page number

CLASSIFICATION

Sample Format of Tab B to Fire Support Appendix

CLASSIFICATION

Copy no. _ of _copies
ISSUING HEADQUARTERS
PLACE OF ISSUE
Date/time group

TAB B (Artillery Fire Plan) to APPENDIX 19 (Fire Support) to ANNEX C (Operations) to Operation Order (Number) (U)

(U) REFERENCE:

(U) TIME ZONE:

1. (U)   Situation

    Provide appropriate details of the general situation bearing particularly on artillery support.

2. (U)   Mission

    (Example–Attack in Zone: 1/10 (DS) and 5/10 (R) provide close fires in support of the 2d Marines attack in zone NLT 100400NOV00 to destroy the enemy forces in order to reestablish the FLOT along PL Blue.)

    (Example–Movement to Contact: 1/10 (DS) and 5/10 (R) provide close fires in support of the 2d Marines movement to contact in zone NLT 100400NOV00 to destroy the 49th Tank Brigade's stay behind forces. On order, 2d Marines will establish crossing sites for the passage of 8th Marines along PL Red.)

3. (U)   Execution

    a. (U)   Commander's Intent (artillery battalion commander)

    b. (U)   Concept of Artillery Support. This is a detailed statement of the artillery commander's visualization of artillery support. It details what the artillery is going to do to support maneuver elements and meet the maneuver commander's intent.

    c. (U)   Organization for Combat. Details the organization and tactical missions by phase (include organic and reinforcing artillery).

Page number

CLASSIFICATION

CLASSIFICATION

d. (U) <u>Coordinating Instructions</u>. Includes instructions and details for coordination applicable to two or more subordinate elements. These instructions may be included as enclosures to the order. If enclosures are used then include only those items of generic interest. The following is a list of coordinating instructions that should be addressed:

- Target acquisition.
- Survey/MET.
- Automated fire control (AFATDS/IFSAS/ BCS).
- HPTL.
- Attack guidance matrix (AGM).
- NBC defense.
- Liaison requirements.
- Priority intelligence requirements (PIRs).
- Ammunition restrictions.
- Anti-fratricide measures.
- Rehearsals.

4. (U) <u>Administration and Logistics</u>

Make reference to Annex D (Logistics), Annex P (Combat Service Support), and/or administrative/logistic orders. Identify ammunition availability, allocations, and ammunition management measures.

5. (U) <u>Command and Signal</u>

Identify command relationships as required, signal information, and information pertaining to command posts; e.g., location of artillery headquarters afloat and initial positions ashore.

a. (U) <u>Command Relationships</u>. (As required.)

b. (U) <u>Signal</u>

c. (U) <u>Command Posts</u>

ACKNOWLEDGE RECEIPT

/s/

ENCLOSURES:
1 Artillery Target List
2 Artillery Synchronization Matrix
3 Artillery Target Overlay
4 Schedules of Fires
5 Observation/Target Acquisition Plan
6 Survey/Metro Plan

Page number

CLASSIFICATION

CLASSIFICATION

Copy no. _ of _copies
ISSUING HEADQUARTERS
PLACE OF ISSUE
Date/time group

ENCLOSURE 1 (Artillery Target List) to TAB B (Artillery Fire Plan) to APPENDIX 19 (Fire Support) to ANNEX C (Operations) to Operation Order (Number) (U)

* A target list worksheet may be used.

ENCLOSURE 2 (Artillery Synch Matrix) to TAB B (Artillery Fire Plan) to APPENDIX 19 (Fire Support) to ANNEX C (Operations) to Operation Order (Number) (U)

(U) REFERENCE: Map

		Phase 1		Phase 2		Phase 3		Phase 4	
Phases		LD to Obj Penny		Obj Nickel		Obj Dime		Obj Quarter	
Enemy		Cntr-Btry threat-Med		Cntr-Btry threat-Med		Cntr-Btry threat-High			
MVR	1/7	(SE) Rte April to clear Obj Sixpence		Mvmt to Contact along Rte April to PL Quiver		Atk to seize Obj Ring		Defend Obj Ring	
	2/7	(ME) Mvmt to Contact Rte Julie to clear Obj Penny		Along Rte Julie, Atk to seize Obj Nickel		1st LAR Fwd Pass. of lines. Helo Co to SBF 1 Become Regt reserve			
FSCMs	CFL	PL Quiver % PL Archer		PL Diamond ——————————————————————————————————————→					
	FSCL	PL Ruby ——→							
		Event	Trigger	Event	Trigger	Event	Trigger	Event	Trigger
Btry 1	Move	1. PA 9 AoF 1600 2. PA 32 AoF 100	1. N/A 2. %			2. R3P vic CP 56	2. EOM AD2003	1. PA 33 AoF	1. R3P complete
	Essential Task	1. Mass Bn (AID): Btry 2 - AD 2001	1. 1/7 at PL Orange			1. Fire Smoke - AD 2003	1. 2/7 clears Obj Dime	1. Mass Bn (A3D): Btry 2 - AD 2007	1. En. Crosses PL Arrow
Btry K	Move	1. PA 10 AoF 1600	1. N/A	3. PA 28 AoF 1500	3. EOM AD0014				
	Essential Task	1. Mass Bn (AID): Btry 3 - AD 2002	1. 1/7 at PL Orange	1. Fire CPHD AD0003,2 Rds 2. Fire Smk 20 min - AD0014	1. A/1/7 acquires 2. 1/7 crosses PL Quiver			1. Mass Bn (A3D): Btry 2 - AD 2007	1. En. crosses PL Arrow
COC		Move to PA 32 when K FIRECAP ——————————————————————————————————→							
Survey		Pri: L, K		Pri to A/1/7/ OP, Vic 435427, K, L		Pri: K, L			
Radar		N/A ——→							
Field Trains/LOC		AA Red/PA 1		Move to PA 37 when Bn clear PL Bow					
Ammo/POL						R3): Btry 1 Class I, V, IX vic CP 56		R3P: Btry K Class I, V, IX vic CP 56	
BAS		Colocated with Field Trains/LOC ——————————————————————————————→							

Page number

CLASSIFICATION

CLASSIFICATION

ENCLOSURE 3 (Artillery Target Overlay) to TAB B (Artillery Fire Plan) to APPEN-DIX 19 (Fire Support) to ANNEX C (Operations) to Operation Order (Number)

(U) REFERENCE: Map

(The overlay contains artillery targets, fire support coordinating measures, and unit boundaries.)

ENCLOSURE 4 (Schedules of Fire) to TAB B (Artillery Fire Plan) to APPENDIX 19 (Fire Support) to ANNEX C (Operations) to Operation Order (Number)

(This enclosure contains schedules of fire for artillery units for the operation. Scheduling worksheets may be used. Successive tables are numbered as follows: 4-1, 4-2, etc.)

ENCLOSURE 5 (Observation/Target Acquisition Plan) to TAB B (Artillery Fire Plan) to APPENDIX 19 (Fire Support) to ANNEX C (Operations) to Operation Order (Number)

(This enclosure contains information concerning observation. The plan is prepared as a supplement to the collection plan of the supported unit and higher headquarters. The plan outlines mission statements for the collection of specific information, reporting requirements (e.g., as acquired, on a time schedule), positioning, and sectors of coverage of the various assets employed by the artillery; e.g., FOs, artillery OPs, radars, and aerial observers employed under artillery control. The plan may associate a specific firing unit to a means of observation. Instructions for the exchange of information, requirements for visibility diagrams, and cueing of weapons locating radars are examples of information applicable to this enclosure.)

ENCLOSURE 6 (Survey/Metro Plan) to TAB B (Artillery Fire Plan) to APPENDIX 19 (Fire Support) to ANNEX C (Operations) to Operation Order (U)

(This enclosure provides information concerning survey and meteorology operations. Requirements and methods of dissemination are addressed. Support requirements to other units/agencies are identified.)

CLASSIFICATION

Sample Format of Tab C to Fire Support Appendix

CLASSIFICATION

> Copy no. _ of _copies
> ISSUING HEADQUARTERS
> PLACE OF ISSUE
> Date/time group

TAB C (Naval Surface Fires Plan) to APPENDIX 19 (Fire Support) to ANNEX C (Operations) to Operation Order—(U)

(U) REFERENCE:

(U) TIME ZONE:

(U) TASK ORGANIZATION

The task organization for naval surface fire support is presented in the form of tactical arrangements of fire support groups, units and elements, according to tasks assigned.

1. (U)   Situation

    Provide details of the situation, particularly on naval surface fire support.

2. (U)   Mission

    State the missions to be accomplished by the fire support groups.

3. (U)   Execution

    This subparagraph provides information needed by the supported unit for the employment of NSFS. Examples: tactical mission assignments, relief of ships, firing procedures (e.g., massing of fires, counter-mechanized fires, SEAD fires, restrictions, calls for fire, etc. as required), procedures for requesting additional NSFS, employment of SFCPs/AOs. An example follows:

    a. (U)   At BMNT, D Day, take FSS as assigned in Enclosure 1 and conduct destruction and neutralization gunfire in Naples sector in accordance with Enclosure 2.

    b. (U)   Ship assignments

SHIP	MISSION	SUPPORTED UNIT
DD-945	General Support	6th Marines
DD-970	Direct Support	1/6
DDG-23	Direct Support	3/6

Page number

CLASSIFICATION

CLASSIFICATION

c. (U) <u>Coordinating Instructions</u>. Information that is applicable to two or more subordinate elements, usually based on SOP. Important information to be addressed includes:

- Fire support coordinating measures/procedures. Air space coordination.
- Restrictions. Such as safety limits and restrictions of munitions.
- Standard FFE salvos.
- Massing criteria.

4. (U) <u>Administration and Logistics</u>

  Provide information concerning allowance of ammunition to ships. Identify ammunition replenishment plan.

5. (U) <u>Command and Signal</u>

  Provide information concerning communications or make reference to an enclosure or other document containing this information.

ACKNOWLEDGE RECEIPT

/s/

ENCLOSURES:
1 Naval Surface Fire Support Operations Overlay
2 NSFS Schedule of Fires
3 NSFS Reports
4 Radar Beacon Plan

CLASSIFICATION

CLASSIFICATION

Copy no. _ of _copies
ISSUING HEADQUARTERS
PLACE OF ISSUE
Date/time group

ENCLOSURE 1 (Naval Surface Fire Support Operations Overlay) to TAB C (Naval Surface Fire Plan) to APPENDIX 19 (Fire Support) to ANNEX C (Operations) to Operation Order (Number) (U)

(U) REFERENCE: Map

(This overlay contains unit boundaries, designated boat lanes, zones of fire, fire support areas and stations, naval surface fires targets, target areas, marginal data, helicopter lanes, and landing force objectives.)

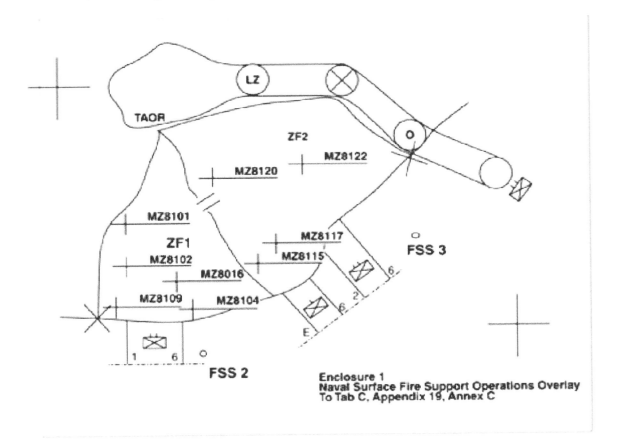

Enclosure 1
Naval Surface Fire Support Operations Overlay
To Tab C, Appendix 19, Annex C

Page number

CLASSIFICATION

CLASSIFICATION

ENCLOSURE 2 (NSFS Schedule of Fires) to TAB C (Naval Surface Fire Plan) to AP-PENDIX 19 (Fire Support) to ANNEX C (Operations) to Operation Order (Number) (U)

(The schedule of fire presents information and instructions necessary for executing pre-arranged naval surface fire support. The schedule identifies the ships, radio frequencies, armament, targets to be engaged, ammunition allowance, time periods, restrictions on fires, and remarks/notes.)

TGT OR AREA #	DESCRIPTION	COORD	Alt FT	SIZE YDS	BEARING GRIND NO.	CAL&AMT 5"	AMMO Other	REMARKS
NZ1001	Wpns Revet	571450	50	10x15		42		Sched Dest
NZ1002	Trench Line	582473	135	200x600		110		Sched Neut
NZ1003	Plt Position	635505	65	200x600	45	70		On-call Neut

ENCLOSURE 3 (NSFS Reports) to TAB C (Naval Surface Fire Plan) to APPENDIX 19 (Fire Support) to ANNEX C (Operations) to Operation Order (Number) (U)

(This enclosure prescribes reports to be made by fire support ships during the operation. Report flow will be based on command relationships. The reports provide information on the status of fire support ships. The enclosure gives direction for the flow of infor-mation to command ships, code names, methods, time, originator, addresses, and cir-cuits to be used in making reports, and instructions for maintaining naval surface fires support logs.)

ENCLOSURE 4 (Radar Beacon Plan) to TAB C (Naval Surface Fire Plan) to APPEN-DIX 12 (Fire Support) to ANNEX C (Operations) to Operation Order (Number) (U)

1. (U) General

    (This enclosure contains instructions for the employment of the radar beacon.)

2. (U) Mission

    The mission of radar beacon teams is to provide fire support ships with an electronic aid to navigation.

3. (U) Employment

    (This subparagraph provides information concerning the employment of the radar beacons. Examples: plan for establishment ashore, initial positions, an-tenna azimuths, range errors, codes, security requirements, and communica-tions links are addressed.)

Page number

CLASSIFICATION

Sample Format for Tab E to Fire Support Appendix

CLASSIFICATION

Copy no. _ of _copies
ISSUING HEADQUARTERS
PLACE OF ISSUE
Date/time group

<u>TAB E (Targeting) to APPENDIX 19 (Fire Support) to ANNEX C (Operations) to Operation Order (Number) (U)</u>

(U) REFERENCE:

(U) TIME ZONE:

1. (U)   <u>General</u>

This paragraph provides information concerning targeting. Targeting priorities and guidance, target precedence, target classification (in amphibious operations), target processing, assignment of priority targets, target number allocations, etc., are addressed. The information is recorded in separate lettered subparagraphs. The tab may include targeting tools, a target list and/or a list of targets. Reference is made to Annex B (Intelligence).

2. (U)   <u>Targeting Boards</u>

This paragraph provides coordinating instructions for targeting boards. This can include board composition and targeting cycle timelines.

ENCLOSURES: (2-4 Omitted. See MCWP 3-16, chapter 4 or MCRP 3-16A, *TTP for the Targeting Process.*)
1 Target List
2 High Payoff Target List
3 Attack Guidance Matrix
4 Target Selection Standards

Page number

CLASSIFICATION

CLASSIFICATION

Enclosure 1, Tab E, Appendix 19, of Annex C to OPORD _____

Target List Worksheet

1st Mar, 1st MARDIV OPORD 070620ZFEB00

For use of this form see FM 6-20-40; Proponent agency is TRADOC

DATUM: WGS-84

SHEET ___ of ___

Line No	Target No a	Description b	Location c	Altitude d	Attitude e	Size Length f	Size Width g	Source/ Accuracy h	Remarks i
1	AC0001	120 mm Mortar Plt	499377						
2	AC0002	Rifle Company	516325						DPICM
3	AC0003	Rifle Platoon	554296						
4	AC0004	OP	570281						VT 50%, WP 50%
5	AC0005	MG Position	566260						
6	AC0006	Trail Intersection	572247						CP 11
7	AC0007	Comm Site	489254			Radius 400			
8	AC0008	Road Intersection	493250		2400	400			
9	AC0009	AOA	512245						
10	AC0010	Trail Intersection	525231						CP 28
11									
12									
13									
14									
15									

Page number

CLASSIFICATION

Sample Format for Tab F to Fire Support Appendix

CLASSIFICATION

Copy no. _ of _copies
ISSUING HEADQUARTERS
PLACE OF ISSUE
Date/time group

TAB F (Fire Support Coordination Plan) to APPENDIX 19 (Fire Support) to ANNEX C (Operations) to Operation Order (Number) (U)

(U) REFERENCE:

(U) TIME ZONE:

1. (U)   <u>Situation</u>

   Provide appropriate details of the general situation bearing particularly on fire support coordination.

2. (U)   <u>Execution</u>

   In separate lettered subparagraphs, the fire support coordination plan is stated. Coordination measures, firing restrictions, fire plan processing, and coordination of fires are addressed. Procedures are identified when existing procedures are inadequate. Fire support coordination tasks are designated. In amphibious operations, procedures for the passage of control and coordination responsibilities to the MAGTF commander are identified/referenced.

3. (U)   <u>Command and Signal</u>

   Provide instructions necessary for the conduct of fire support coordination. When required, fire support communications information may be disseminated in a separate tab (TAB G).

   a. (U)   <u>Command Relationships</u>. (As required.)

   b. (U)   <u>Signal</u>.

   c. (U)   <u>Command Posts</u>. (Location of MAGTF FFCC.)

   ACKNOWLEDGE RECEIPT

                                        /s/

ENCLOSURES:
1. Fire Support Coordination Overlay
*Other enclosures as required
                          Page number

CLASSIFICATION

CLASSIFICATION

Copy no. _ of _ copies
ISSUING HEADQUARTERS
PLACE OF ISSUE
Date/time group

ENCLOSURE 1 (Fire Support Coordination Overlay) to TAB F (Fire Support Coordination) to APPENDIX 19 (Fire Support) to ANNEX C (Operations) to Operation Order (Number) (U)

(U) REFERENCE: Map

(This overlay depicts information applicable to fire support coordination. It contains fire support coordination measures, unit boundaries, etc.)

Page number

CLASSIFICATION

Sample Format of Tab G to Fire Support Appendix

CLASSIFICATION

Copy no. _ of _ copies
ISSUING HEADQUARTERS
PLACE OF ISSUE
Date/time group

TAB G (Fire Support Communications Plan/MCFSS) to Appendix 19 (Fire Support) to
Annex C (Operations) to Operation Order (Number) (U)

(U) REFERENCES:

    a. (U) Map

    b. (U) UNIT SOP

(U) TIME ZONE:

1. (U) <u>Situation</u>. Refer to paragraph 1 of this order.

    <u>Organization for Combat</u>

FIRE SUPPORT	MISSION	SUPPORTED
_/_/_/11/MR_ (11M)	DS	FS/C/1_/MD_
_/_/A/6_/27_ (627)	GS	F/S/C/1_/MD_
_/_/_/1_/11_ (111)	DS	F/S/C/1_/MR_
_/_/_/2_/11_ (211)	DS	F/S/C/5_/MR_
_/_/_/3_/11_ (311)	DS O/O GS	F/S/C/7_/MR_ F/S/C/1_/MD_
_/_/_/5_/11_ (511)	R O/O GS	_/_/_/5_/11_ F/S/C/1_/MD_
F/D/C/1_/37_ (137)	GS	F/S/C/1_/MD_

2. (U) <u>Execution</u>

    a. (U) In separate lettered paragraphs, the fire support communications plan/
MCFSS is stated. This tab focuses on the additions to or differences with Annex K,
Command, Control, Communications Systems. These paragraphs should address automated systems, specifically: TCO, IOW, AFATDS, and CTAPS/TBMCS. The enclosures will cover the detailed information such as geometries, subscriber tables,

CLASSIFICATION

CLASSIFICATION

communications tables, and initial database construction and desired guidances to be used by automated systems. Prioritization of automated assets, such as the comm OPFAC vs plans OPFAC if one is not mission capable, must be discussed. In conjunction with the G/S-6's plan in Annex K, net prioritization must be established to ensure the most valuable nets maintain connectivity.

    b. (U) <u>AFATDS</u>

    c. (U) <u>TCO/IAS/IOW/C2PC</u>

    d. (U) <u>CTAPS/TBMCS</u>

    e. (U) <u>Other automated systems</u>

3. (U) <u>Communications</u>

    a. (U) Communications will be conducted in accordance with Annex K.

    b. (U) Subscriber table and digital nets guard chart are provided in enclosure 2 and 3 of this TAB.

    c. (U) <u>Reports</u>. Battery BCS submit an AFU;UPDATE with OUTTIL immediately prior to displacement and a corrected AFU;UPDATE with READY when in place and guns are up. All BCS will report ammo to their controlling AFATDS.

ENCLOSURES:
1 Initial Geometry
2 Digital Communications Guard Chart
3 Subscriber Table
4 Initial Database and Guidances for Automated Systems

ACKNOWLEDGE RECEIPT

J. A. LEJEUNE
General, U. S. Marine Corps
Commanding

OFFICIAL:

S. D. BUTLER
Col   USMC
G-3

Page number

CLASSIFICATION

CLASSIFICATION

<u>ENCLOSURE 1 (Initial Geometry) to TAB G (Fire Support Communications Plan/
MCFSS) to Appendix 19 (Fire Support) to Annex C (Operations) to Operations Order
(Number) (U)</u>

All geometry is effective at the start of operations unless otherwise indicated by an on-call time.

1. (U) <u>Zones</u>

   a. (U) <u>ZO11MR</u>

PT#	GRID/ALT	GZ	PT#	GRID/ALT	GZ	PT#	GRID/ALT	GZ
1	558 550/110	34	2	555 489/170	34	3	556 427/180	34
4	557 377/165	34	5	561 345/110	34	6	599 285/140	34
7	718 358/160	34	8	712 482/155	34	9	710 525/50	34
10	665 530/85	34	11	656 528/90	34	12	617 548/70	34
13	609 549/90	34	14	598 547/90				

   b. (U) <u>ZO11A1</u>

PT#	GRID/ALT	GZ	PT#	GRID/ALT	GZ	PT#	GRID/ALT	GZ
1	558 550/110	34	2	555 489/170	34	3	556 427/180	34
4	557 377/165	34	5	617 382/170	34	6	617 548/70	34
7	609 549/90	34	8	598 547/90				

   c. (U) <u>ZO12A1</u>

PT#	GRID/ALT	GZ	PT#	GRID/ALT	GZ	PT#	GRID/ALT	GZ
1	617 548/70	34	2	617 382/170	34	3	718 358/160	34
4	665 530/85	34	5	656 528/90	34			

   d. (U) <u>ZO13A1</u>

PT#	GRID/ALT	GZ	PT#	GRID/ALT	GZ	PT#	GRID/ALT	GZ
1	665 530/85	34	2	666 368/175	34	3	718 358/160	34
4	712 482/155	34	5	710 525/50	34			

CLASSIFICATION

CLASSIFICATION

2. (U) <u>Objectives</u>

    a. (U) <u>OB31MF</u>

      GRID/ALT GZ RADIUS
      750 290/160 34 2500m

    b. (U) <u>OB11MR</u>

      GRID/ALT GZ RADIUS
      616 435/190 34 800m

    c. (U) <u>OB21MR</u>

      GRID/ALT GZ RADIUS
      620 330/150 34 1000m

3. (U) <u>FLOTs</u>. FL11MR.

PT#	GRID/ALT	GZ	PT#	GRID/ALT	GZ	PT#	GRID/ALT	GZ
1	707 487/150	34	2	666 497/160	34	3	632 511/155	34
4	598 519/120	34	5	555 518/100	34			

4. (U) <u>Phase Lines</u>

    a. (U) <u>PL11M</u>

PT#	GRID/ALT	GZ	PT#	GRID/ALT	GZ
1	709 481/130	34	2	556 482/150	34

    b. (U) <u>PL21MR</u>

PT#	GRID/ALT	GZ	PT#	GRID/ALT	GZ
1	712 446/170	34	2	556 455/180	34

5. (U) <u>Battle Areas</u>

    a. (U) <u>Close</u>

PT#	GRID/ALT	GZ	PT#	GRID/ALT	GZ	PT#	GRID/ALT	GZ
1	427 573	34	2	437 568	34	3	480 565	34
4	558 550	34	5	598 547	34	6	609 549	34
7	617 548	34	8	656 528	34	9	665 530	34
10	710 525	34	11	765 528	34	12	777 500	34
13	780 420	34	14	773 331	34	15	718 358	34
16	599 285	34	17	436 278	34	18	431 360	34
19	435 455	34						

Page number

CLASSIFICATION

CLASSIFICATION

b. (U)   <u>Rear</u>

PT#	GRID/ALT	GZ	PT#	GRID/ALT	GZ	PT#	GRID/ALT	GZ
1	423 626	34	2	427 573	34	3	437 568	34
4	480 565	34	5	558 550	34	6	598 547	34
7	609 549	34	8	617 548	34	9	656 528	34
10	665 530	34	11	710 525	34	12	765 528	34
13	773 567	34	14	597 625	34	15	514 636	34

c. (U)   <u>Deep</u>

PT#	GRID/ALT	GZ	PT#	GRID/ALT	GZ	PT#	GRID/ALT	GZ
1	718 358	34	2	599 285	34	3	436 278	34
4	451 245	34	5	482 220	34	6	560 165	34
7	642 148	34	8	719 150	34	9	780 168	34
10	780 241	34	11	773 331	34			

6. (U)   <u>CFLs</u>. CL11MR.

PT#	GRID/ALT	GZ	PT#	GRID/ALT	GZ	PT#	GRID/ALT	GZ
1	712 470/155	34	2	609 498/180	34	3	555 498/170	34

7. (U)   <u>FSCLs</u>. FS11MD.

PT#	GRID/ALT	GZ	PT#	GRID/ALT	GZ	PT#	GRID/ALT	GZ
1	367 391	34	2	773 331/140	34	3	718 358/90	34
4	599 285	34	5	436 278/125	34			

8. (U)   <u>RFLs</u>. RL11MR.

PT#	GRID/ALT	GZ	PT#	GRID/ALT	GZ	PT#	GRID/ALT	GZ
1	620 405/170	34	2	599 418/175	34	3	586 436/180	34

CLASSIFICATION

CLASSIFICATION

9. (U)   RFAs. RF31MF (ONCALL, Effective from H+10 to H+480) Restriction: No AIR or FA delivered FASCAM.

PT#	GRID/ALT	GZ	RADIUS
1	516 416/80	34	1300

10. (U) NFAs. NF11MF.

GRID/ALT	GZ	RADIUS
715 535/90	34	1200m

11. (U) FFAs. FF11MF (ONCALL from H+10 to H+480).

PT#	GRID/ALT	GZ	PT#	GRID/ALT	GZ	WIDTH
1	709 206/180	34	2	680 225/225	34	

ENCLOSURE 2 (Digital Communications Guard Chart) to TAB G (Marine Corps Fire Support Communications Plan/MCFSS) to Appendix 19 (Fire Support) to Annex C (Operations) to Operation Order (Number) (U)

Enclosure 2 shows a sample digital communications guard chart.

CLASSIFICATION

CLASSIFICATION

A=As Req C=Net Ctrl R=Relay W=When Dir X=Guard Y=Yes	1MF MFFC	1MD DFSC	1MR RFSC	5MR RFSC	7MR RFSC	11M RFD2	TPC	RDMET	1/1 COF	2/1 COF	3/1 COF	1/11 FD	1/5 COF	2/5 COF	3/5 COF	2/11 FD	1/7 COF	2/7 COF	3/7 COF	3/11 FD	TAR/HR
PROTOCOL L=LAN T=TACFIRE V=VMF 1=188-220	L	V	V	V	V	V	L	1	T	T	T	1	T	T	T	1	T	T	T	1	V
KEYTIME		0.7	0.7	0.7	0.7	0.7		0.7	2.1	2.1	2.1	0.7	2.1	2.1	2.1	2.1	2.1	2.1	2.1	0.7	0.7
FSK 1=12/24 2=13/21 3=NRZ 4=CDP		3	3	3	3	3		3	1	1	1	3	1	1	1	3	1	1	1	3	3
BLK MODE									1	1	1		1	1	1		1	1	1		
DATA RATE (bps)	16k	16k	16k	16k	16k	16k		16k	1.2k	1.2k	1.2k	16k	1.2k	1.2k	1.2k	16k	1.2k	1.2k	1.2k	16k	16k
CARRIER DROP OUT TIME		0.5	0.5	0.5	0.5	0.5															0.5
COMSEC		Y	Y	Y	Y	Y		Y	Y	Y	Y	Y	Y	Y	Y	Y	Y	Y	Y	Y	Y
1MF FFCC	C																				X
3AW TACC	X																				
1MD FSCC	X	C																			X
3AW DASC	X	X																			C
1MR FSCC		X	C																		X
1al FSCC		X							C												X
1al FOs									X												
2al FSCC		X								C											X
2as FOs										X											
3al FSCC		X									C				X						X
3al FOs											X										
5MR FSCC		X		C																	X
1a5 FSCC			X						C				C								X
1a5 FOs									X				X								
2A5 FSCC			X							C				C							X
2a5 FOs										X				X							
3A5 FSCC			X								C				C						X
3a5 FOs											X				X						

CLASSIFICATION

CLASSIFICATION

A=As Req C=Net Ctrl R=Relay W=When Dir X=Guard Y=Yes	1 MF MFFC	1 MD DFSC	1 MR RFSC	5 MR RFSC	7 MR RFSC	11M RFD2	TPC	RDMET	1/1 COF	2/1 COF	3/1 COF	1/11 FD	1/5 COF	2/5 COF	3/5 COF	2/11 FD	1/7 COF	2/7 COF	3/7 COF	3/11 FD	TAR/HR
7MR FSCC		X			C																X
1a7 FSCC					X												C				X
1a7 FOs																	X				
2a7 FSCC					X													C			X
2a7 FOs																		X			
3a7 FSCC					X														C		X
3a7 FOs																			X		
11M FDC		X				C	X														
11M TPC							C	C													
11M MET								X													
11M RADAR								X													
UAV	X																				
111 FDC		X			X					X		C									
A11 FDC												X									
B11 FDC												X									
C11 FDC												X									
211 FDC			X		X											C					
E11 FDC																X					
F11 FDC																X					
G11 FDC																X					
311 FDC				X		X							C	C						C	
I11 FDC													X							X	
K11 FDC													X							X	
L11 FDC														X						X	
511 FDC					X									C	C						
R11 FDC														X							
S11 FDC															X						
A27 FDC					X																

Page number

CLASSIFICATION

CLASSIFICATION

ENCLOSURE 3 (Subscriber Table) to TAB G (Marine Corps Fire Support Communications Plan/MCFSS) to Appendix 19 (Fire Support) to Annex C (Operations) to Operations Order (Number) (U)

Enclosure 3 details the subscriber table in communications net order (MEF FSC Net, then Div FSC net, etc.)

Line #	Own Name	Host-Name	Net	Protocol	Net Access	Add	IP Address	Subnet Mask	Router Add	Rank
1	FSCC 1MR		DFSC	VMF	Adaptive	16				4/11
2	FSCC 1MR		RFSC	VMF	Adaptive	02				1/10

Line #	Station Name	Host Name	Add	IP Address	FO#	Route
1	FSCC 1MD		12			PD via DFSC net
2	FSCC FWD 1MD		13			PD via DFSC net
3	DASC 3AW		14			PD via DFSC net
4	DASC FWD 3AW		15			PD via DFSC net
5	FSCC 5MR		18			PD via DFSC net
6	FSCC FWD 5MR		19			PD via DFSC net
7	FSCC 7MR		20			PD via DFSC net
8	FSCC FWD 7MR		21			PD via DFSC net
9	FDC 11MR		22			PD via DFSC net
10	FDC FWD 11MR		23			PD via DFSC net
11	FSCC FWD 1MR		03			PD via DFSC net
12	FSCC 1/1		04			PD via DFSC net
13	FSCC FWD 1/1		05			PD via DFSC net
14	FSCC 2/1		06			PD via DFSC net
15	FSCC FWD 2/1		07			PD via DFSC net
16	FSCC 3/1	08				PD via DFSC net
17	FSCC FWD 3/1	09				PD via DFSC net
18	FDC MAIN 1/11	10				PD via DFSC net
19	FDC FWD 1/11	11				PD via DFSC net

Page number

CLASSIFICATION

CLASSIFICATION

Line #	Own Name	Host Name	Net	Protocol	Net Access	Add	IP Address	Subnet Mask	Router Add	Rank
1	FSCC 1/1		RFSC	VMF	Adaptive	04				1/10
2	FSCC 1/1		COF	TACFIRE	1/3/3/5	C				

Line #	Station Name	Host Name	Add	IP Address	FO#	Route
1	FSCC 1MR		02			PD via RFSC net
2	FSCC FWD 1MR		03			PD via RFSC net
3	FSCC FWD 1/1		05			PD via RFSC net
4	FSCC 2/1		06			PD via RFSC net
5	FSCC FWD 2/1		07			PD via RFSC net
6	FSCC 3/1		08			PD via RFSC net
7	FSCC FWD 3/1		09			PD via RFSC net
8	FDC 1/11		10			PD via RFSC net
9			A			SD via COF A
10	FDC FWD 1/11		11			PD via RFSC net
11			B			SD via COF A
12	FO 11 A CO__			E	11	PD via COF A
13						SI via FDC MAIN
14	FO 12 B CO__			F	12	PD via COF A
15						SI via FDC MAIN
16	FO 13 C CO__			G	13	PD via COF A
17						SI via FDC MAIN

CLASSIFICATION

Line #	Own Name	Net	Net Access	Phy Add
1	F/O/A/11/___	COFA	4	E

Line #	Net	Logical Name	Comptr	Phy Add
1	COFA	_/_/_/1_11_	Y	A
2		F/W/D/1_/11_	Y	B
3		F/S/C/1_/1_	Y	C
4		F/W/D/1_/1_	Y	D
5		/ /A/1_/11_	Y	I
6		F/O/B/12/__	N	F
7		F/O/C/13/__	N	G

Line #	Own Name	Net	Net Access	Phy Add
1	F/O/B/12/___	COFA	4	F

Line #	Net	Logical Name	Comptr	Phy Add
1	COFA	_/_/_/1_11_	Y	A
2		F/W/D/1_/11_	Y	B
3		F/S/C/1_/1_	Y	C
4		F/W/D/1_/1_	Y	D
5		/ /A/1_/11_	Y	I
6		F/O/A/11/__	N	E
7		F/O/B/12/__	N	F

Page number

CLASSIFICATION

CLASSIFICATION

ENCLOSURE 4 (Initial Database and Guidances for Automated Systems) to TAB G
(Marine Corps Fire Support Communications Plan/MCFSS) to Appendix 19 (Fire Support) to Annex C (Operations) to Operations Order (Number) (U)

1. (U)   Observer and Radar Assignments

Unit	Assigned Observer/ Radar	FLOT Points
F/S/C/1_/1__(1A1)	F/O/A/11/___	01-02
	F/O/B/12/___	03-04
	F/O/C/13/___	05-06
F/S/C/2_/1__(2A4)	F/O/E/14/___	07-08
	F/O/F/15/___	09-10
	F/O/G/16/___	11-12
F/S/C/3_/1__(3A4)	F/O/I/14/___	13-14
	F/O/L/15/___	15-16
	F/O/K/16/___	17-18
_/_/1/11/MR_(11M)	C/M/R/01/___	

2. (U)   Map Mod

   a. (U)   Center coordinates:776000 03537000

   b. (U)   Grid zone:+34

   c. (U)   Datum:WGS 84

3. (U)   Target Number Assignments

STATION	TARGET BLOCK	ASR NUMBER BLOCK
D/A/S/3_/AW_(DAS3AW)	AL4500-4999	ALD0000-ALD0999
F/S/C/1_/MR_(1MR)	AA0000-0499	AAA0000-AAA0499
F/S/C/1_/1_(1A1)	AA1000-1499	AAB0000-AAB0199
F/S/C/2_/1__(2A1)	AA2000-2499	AAC0000-AAC0199
F/S/C/3_/1_(3A1)	AA3000-3499	AAD0000-AAD0199
_/_/1_/11__(111)	AG4000-4999	
_/_/A/1_/11__(A11)	AG5000-5199	
_/_/B/1_/11__(B11)	AG5200-5399	
_/_/C/1_/11__(C11)	AG5400-5599	

Page number

CLASSIFICATION

CLASSIFICATION

4. (U)   Commander's Criteria

a. (U)   Target Selection Standards and Decay Times

TARGET	MAX TLE(m)	MAX REP AGE (min)	DECAY TIME
CP, Regiment	300	60	4 hours
CP, Battalion	300	45	4 hours
CP, Division	300	240	4 hours
CP, Small	250	30	4 hours
ARTY, Towed	200	45	1 hour
ARTY, Unknown	200	45	1 hour
MSL, Medium	400	60	30 minutes
APC	200	30	30 minutes
Armored, Vehicle	200	30	30 minutes
AA, Troops	400	60	30 minutes
AA, Trps and Armor	400	45	30 minutes
AA, Troops and Vehicle	400	45	30 minutes
ADA, MSL	100	90	30 minutes
Bunker	100	300	30 minutes
Patrol	100	30	10 minutes

Note: *Fire requests will not be checked against TSS.*

CLASSIFICATION

CLASSIFICATION

b. (U) HVT List.

TARGET CATEGORY	RELATIVE VALUE								
C3									
Fire Support									
Maneuver									
ADA									
Engineer									
RSTA									
REC									
NUC/CHEM									
POL									
Ammunition									
Maintenance									
Lift									
LOC									

c. (U) HPT List.

HPT MATRIX												
Target	Effects	When	Relative Value									
CP, Regiment	Destroy	I										
Arty, Towed	Neutralized	I										
Tank, Med	Neutralize	A										
AA, Trps & Armor	Suppress	P										

Key: I=Immediate
       A=As acquired
       P=Planned

CLASSIFICATION

CLASSIFICATION

d. (U) <u>Attack Guidance</u>

ATTACK GUIDANCE MATRIX		
TARGET	EFFECTS	WHEN
C3	Destroy	I
Fire Support	15%	I
Maneuver	Neutralize	A
ADA	Suppress	P
Engineer	Suppress	A
RSTA	10%	A
REC	Neutralize	A
NUC/CHEM	Destroy	I
POL	15%	P
Ammunition	20%	P
Maintenance	Neutralize	A
Lift	Suppress	P
LOC	Suppress	P

e. (U) <u>Target and Fire Support System Exclusions</u>. Railroad targets will not be attacked due to the need to maintain the infrastructure of the country.

f. (U) <u>Mission Prioritization</u>

TARGET TYPE: Weight 30
PRIORITY OF FIRES: Weight 50
ON-CALL TGTS: Weight 5
TAI: Weight 15

g. (U) <u>Mission Cutoff Values</u>

FA: 20
AIR: 30
MORTAR: 10
NGF: 10
Rkt/Msl   30
Aviation 20

Page number

CLASSIFICATION

CLASSIFICATION

h. (U) Priority of Fire

UNIT	RANK
1/1	(1)
3/1	(2)
2/1	(3)

i. (U) Target Area of Interest Rank. TA11MD.

j. (U) System Attack Parameters

    FA: FDC 1BN 11MAR 1MARDIV
    NGF: FSCC 1MD
    AIR: FSCC 1MD

k. (U) Immediate missions will be routed to the FDC 3BN 11MAR 1MARDIV.

l. (U) Air Attack Methods

TARGET CATEGORY/TYPE PREFERENCE
C3/CP Regiment   6 GP bombs, 4 Napalm

m. (U) NSFS Attack Methods

TARGET CATEGORY/TYPE PREFERENCE
FS/Missile, Med   20 rds, 5"54 HE, 20 rds WP

n. (U) FA Restrictions. Maximum volleys for FA is 3, (This has to be entered at each OPFAC under the FUs as the units with restrictions, using DETAILED attack analysis) and maximum fire units per target for Div. FSCC/Regt. FDC is 7. Maximum fire units per target for Regt. FSCC/BN. FDC is 3. Concrete piercing fuzes are restricted from use. (This data is entered for each FSCC UNIT ID that the unit is supported by).

o. (U) FA Attack Methods

TARGET CATEGORY/TYPE PREFERENCE
FS/Arty, Towed   Battery 2 volleys DPICM, 4 volleys HE/VT
MAN/AA, Troops & Armor Bn, 1 volley DPICM, 3 volleys HE/PD

p. (U) FA Immediate Attack Methods

Immediate Suppression: Platoon, 1 volley, DPICM
Immediate Smoke: Platoon, 1 volley WP/PD, 1 volley WP2/TI
                        Page number

CLASSIFICATION

CLASSIFICATION

q. (U) Target Duplication

TARGET SEPARATION DISTANCE
ANY TARGETS: 100 meters
SIMILAR TARGETS: 400 meters

r. (U) Fire Support System Buffers

FA:	600 meters	NSFS:	750 meters
Mortar:	400 meters	Air:	1000 meters
Aviation:	500 meters	Rkt/Msl:	1000 meters

s. (U) Artillery Target Intelligence (ATI)

(1) (U) Suspect Target Maximum Overlay. 30%

(2) (U) ATI Reporting. The following will be reported in ATI message formats:

t. (U) Battlefield Geometry. Current support data. Initial support data is provided in enclosure 1 of this TAB.

u. (U) Ammunition and Firing Units

(1) (U) Controlled Supply Rate for 155MM

AMMUNITION	D-DAY	S-DAY
HE	80	100
RAP	60	100
DPICM	120	160
Copperhead	0	8

(2) (U) Critical Ammunition Levels for 155MM

AMMUNITION	DEGRADED	CRITICAL	NO-GO
HE	60%	40%	10%
RAP	50%	30%	10%
DPICM	65%	40%	15%
Copperhead	50%	25%	20%

CLASSIFICATION

APPENDIX F. ADVANCED FIELD ARTILLERY TACTICAL DATA SYSTEM

This appendix, used with MCWP 3-16.2, *Tactics, Techniques, and Procedures for Marine Corps Fire Support System (TTP for MCFSS)*, and MCRP 3-16.2A, *Tactics, Techniques, and Procedures for Advanced Field Artillery Tactical Data System (AFATDS)*, sets forth guidelines for operating in automated environments.

The Marine Corps Fire Support System (MCFSS) is employed at fire and air control agencies including fire direction centers (FDCs) and fire support coordination centers (FSCCs) from battalion through the MEF force fires coordination center (FFCC), the direct air support center (DASC), the tactical air control center (TACC), the supporting arms coordination center (SACC), and the rear area operations center (RAOC) of the CSSE command element. The system allows these agencies to operate with first generation digital input/output devices that have entered the Marine Corps inventory. The Advanced Field Artillery Tactical Data System (AFATDS) allows these stations to transition to a single software system that will eventually replace the Initial Fire Support Automated System (IFSAS), Battery Computer System (BCS), and Multiple Launched Rocket System (MLRS) Fire Direction System (FDS).

DEVELOPMENT

AFATDS is one of five systems that compose the Army Tactical Command and Control System (ATCCS). AFATDS, the only jointly developed system, provides fire support planning and execution software. AFATDS will be developed through three software versions. Version two (A98) was used as a test bed in I MEF. Version three (A99) will be fielded in FY2001. With further software development, currently fielded devices will be compatible with AFATDS via VMF protocol. Upon the completion of fielding, all IFSAS/TACFIRE devices will be replaced by AFATDS. In addition, all artillery technical fire direction for cannon and rocket systems will be computed by AFATDS.

SOFTWARE PREMISE

AFATDS software is developed as a fire support tool. The computer is provided with detailed guidance derived from the staff planning process and the decide-detect-deliver-assess (D3A) targeting methodology. This guidance provides AFATDS with "rules" to use during processing of fire support missions. Through this process, the commander and staff determine the appropriate responses during the period of staff planning. These decisions are executed rapidly by AFATDS during the periods of intense activity that characterize modern maneuver warfighting. Failure to provide adequate preplanned guidance will prevent the system from executing according to commander's intent.

GUIDANCE MANAGEMENT

Incoming fire missions and fire plan targets are validated by guidance entered at each fire support and fire direction echelon. For rapid and efficient attack of targets and fire plan scheduling, this guidance data must be managed.

Several guidance windows must be maintained to manage the fire support system, such as—

- Target Selection Standards (TSS).
- HVT List.
- Target Management Matrix.
- Mission Prioritization.
- System Tasks.
- Fire Support Attack Parameters.
- Munitions Restrictions.

The responsibility for creating and disseminating guidance is an intrinsic element of command and thus resides with the force commander.

Prior to establishing the landing force ashore, the MAGTF FFC receives guidance from the AF commander. This guidance is transmitted to the SACC and subordinate FSCCs and fire support assets controlled by the MAGTF FFCC.

After establishing the landing force ashore, the GCE FSCC modifies guidance in accordance with the CLF and GCE commander's intent, orders, and verbal direction. This guidance is transmitted to the SACC (afloat) and subordinate FSCCs, FDCs, and fire support assets. Changes to guidance should not be disseminated between echelons as each echelon optimizes their guidance based on their mission and role. AFATDS performs functions based on its established echelon (regiment or battalion) and role (FSCC, FDC, or other).

FIRE MISSION PROCESSING

Fire mission processing is a key function of the fire support system. AFATDS uses guidance's, task organization, and received mission information to select the appropriate fire support asset, and to route the fire mission to the appropriate operational facility (OPFACS). Processing through multiple OPFACS is usually required to move the mission from the requester to the shooter. The processing and route may be transparent to some of the OPFACS depending on intervention criteria.

INTERVENTION CRITERIA

AFATDS can use database information to automatically process, coordinate, and possibly deny fire missions without operator intervention. Intervention points allow operators to stop automatic processing under given conditions to review and alter. Intervention criteria are comprised of a set of rules that govern the interruption of the automatic fire mission process. An almost endless number of intervention rules can be established, however, development and use of intervention points can significantly decrease responsiveness. Each rule is built around the following categories of mission information:

- Battle Area.
- Attack Option.
- Mission Precedence.
- Target Type.
- Filters.
- Analysis Result.

These six criteria may be set in any combination to create a single rule. Multiple rules may be constructed.

Default Setup

When the database is initially constructed, a single default rule is incorporated that causes all fire missions to be subject to intervention. Deleting this rule causes all fire missions to process automatically. Missions assigned for attack by ATACMS are automatically displayed for operator intervention without regard to operator established intervention criteria.

Tracking Fire Missions

When a fire mission is processed without any intervention, each OPFAC can maintain situational awareness of active missions as described below.

Active fire missions can be displayed on an overlay. This will cause any received fire mission, regardless of intervention criteria, to appear on the screen of the SHRD as a bold target symbol. The operator can ascertain information about the target by clicking the symbol that appears.

All fire missions received are placed in the active target list until the mission is ended by receipt of a mission fired report. At any time the operator can display mission information for any target.

Each method allows the operator to display the target status window. The status window displays all fire mission messages received or transmitted for the mission in question. The status of the mission can also be requested or traced to obtain the status of the mission at every station involved.

Fire requests and fire orders may be printed when they are received and/or transmitted. This is accomplished by making entries in the configure printing setup. This function is accessed by selecting alerts and messages, messages, and configure printing setup.

Intervention by OPFAC

The following are recommended for employment of intervention criteria.

Battalion FSCC

- Denied missions.
- Air and NSFS missions if these assets are available to the battalion FSCC.

Regiment FSCC

- Denied missions.
- Any other rules dictated by the FSC.
- Air and NSFS missions if these assets are available to the regiment FSCC.

Division FSCC

- Denied missions.
- All fire missions in the rear operations area.
- All fire missions in the deep operations area.
- All air missions.

Battalion FDC

All fire missions.

Regiment FDC

All fire missions.

ATTACK ANALYSIS

During attack analysis, AFATDS considers various parameters of a given fire mission; e.g., mission type, observer request or target location; the guidance that is in effect; the allocated attack units available; FSCMs; and attack option ranking criteria to develop attack options to achieve defeat criteria of the target. The three levels of attack analysis in AFATDS are FS system, unit, and detailed.

FS System Attack Analysis

System attack analysis allows an FSCC to perform attack analysis only to the level of detail needed to select an FS system and transmit the mission to the appropriate agency for further processing. When performing FS system attack analysis, no detailed information (locations of firing units, munitions status, etc.) is required. To use FS system attack analysis correctly, the FS attack parameters window must be filled out. Generally, this level of attack analysis will be used only at the higher level FSCCs, such as the MAGTF FFCC.

Unit Attack Analysis

Unit attack analysis allows an OPFAC to conduct more detailed attack analysis using "rollup" unit information. This level of attack analysis would normally be used in higher level artillery FDCs/FA CPs. Fire units directly supporting or commanded by the OPFAC performing the analysis are analyzed using unit data (location, munitions capabilities, operational status, etc.) to determine if they can attack the target. Firing units with an intermediate FDC between them and the OPFAC are not analyzed in detail. They are analyzed using the "rollup" data contained in the unit subordinate information window. For unit attack analysis to be used correctly, the status for subordinate units must have been transmitted to the OPFAC.

Detailed Attack Analysis

Detailed attack analysis allows an OPFAC to determine and evaluate all individual fire units (as well as collective groupings of fire units for massing) against a given target. It uses all unit data (munitions, operational status, location, etc.) to determine a solution for the target. This method is available for all OPFACs, but is generally used at the lower echelon; e.g., regiment and below, FDCs, and FSCCs.

FIRE MISSION ROUTING

Fire missions are routed through OPFACS to select the optimum fire support asset, provide a conduit for coordination, and to increase situational awareness. Routing of the mission depends on the source, however the central hub of fire support is the FSCC.

Options

AFATDS classifies if a selected fire support asset is a capable option to engage a target into four categories:

- Green—the asset is a capable option and no coordination is required.
- Yellow—the asset is a capable option but coordination is required.
- Red—attack options exist but there are restrictions that prevent that asset from being capable of firing the mission.
- Black—no attack options exist for that FS system; i.e., the unit does not have any firing units in support.

To determine the restrictions of a RED option, open the attack options window from the menu bar of the mission window. A series of icons (ammunition, range, achievable effects, etc.) will display illustrating whether or not each of these passed or failed.

Battalion FSCC

Fire missions requested by an artillery or mortar observer are transmitted to the battalion FSCC. The observer unit information must indicate that the battalion FSCC that the observer reports to is both the command and supported unit (command unit ID and supported unit ID in the general unit information window for the observer). The battalion FSCC normally possesses only organic mortars with which to engage the target. Regardless, the battalion FSCC computer will consider only those fire support assets that are commanded by or support the battalion FSCC. If the mission is recommended for denial or processing to an air or NSFS asset, the mission appears in the intervention window and remains there until the operator takes action. If the battalion's organic mortars cannot adequately service the target, artillery, air, and NSFS (when air and NSFS

are held at a higher FSCC) may be selected. These missions are transmitted to the regiment FSCC because the battalion FSCC has entered the regiment FSCC name in the fields of the system attack parameters window as the agency to route missions. The mission may be resolved in many ways.

Coordination Requests

These requests are transmitted to the agencies responsible for violated boundaries or FSCMs. The transmitting computer will wait until the mission is approved to transmit the fire request to the regimental FSCC.

Mission Denied

The mission may be denied either by failures of guidance or denial from an agency from which coordination was requested. The operator at the battalion FSCC may reprocess the mission.

Missions Not Requiring Coordination

Missions are transmitted to the regiment FSCC.

Missions Requiring Coordination with Electronic Warfare Assets

Missions requiring coordination with electronic warfare assets (as indicated by guidance) will transmit a request for coordination to the IEW agency listed in the mission routing info window. Denial or approval will cause the mission to process as if coordination from another FSCC was required.

No Solution

AFATDS may not be able to determine a solution. In this event the AFATDS recommends "Denied, no capable option." The operator can select unsupportable causing the mission to be transmitted to the regimental FSCC (the battalion's support unit ID) for reevaluation of fire support engagement.

Override

The operator can override AFATDS' solution and transmit any solution to any station. Overriding and transmitting a RED option does not allow the automatic routing of FO commands.

Regiment FSCC

The regiment FSCC processes the mission and intervenes only on denied missions. The mission may not be assigned to the same asset as predicted by the battalion FSCC if the guidance at the regiment differs from those at the battalion. The mission may be—

- Transmitted to any fire support asset that the regiment FSCC commands. If additional coordination is required, requests are routed before transmitting the mission to the fire support asset.

- Determined unsupportable. The operator can then transmit the mission, due to supported unit ID, to the division FSCC.

- Overridden. The operator can override the computer solution and transmit any solution to any station.

Battalion FDC

The battalion FDC processes the mission to subordinate battery FDCs. The battalion FDC always performs detailed attack analysis due to software default. Fire missions will never be denied at battalion FDC. Though several options may be available to the battalion FDC, one of three possible solutions will be selected by the battalion FDC:

- The fire mission can be passed to the firing unit(s) selected by AFATDS.

- The fire mission can be transmitted to any subordinate or reinforcing unit regardless of the option AFATDS selected.

- The mission can be returned to the regiment FSCC as unsupportable. This option should not be required if the regiment FSCC is in detailed attack analysis. However, if unsupportable is selected, the mission is returned to the regiment FSCC, reprocessed, and most likely transmitted to the division FSCC as unsupportable. This is AFTADS' method of "request for reinforcing fires." Since the fire mission may be received again by the battalion FDC as part of a massed fire mission solution from

the regiment FDC, any mission that is returned to the regiment FDC as unsupportable is immediately manually deleted from the active fire target list by the battalion FDC.

Division FSCC

The division FSCC processes fire missions received but seldom intervenes. NSFS missions are printed and handed off to the representative of this asset (unless automated communications are available to these units). Artillery missions are passed to the regiment FDC for processing. Air missions are transmitted to the DASC.

Regiment FDC

The regiment FDC processes received fire missions using detailed attack analysis. Fire Orders are passed to subordinate battalion FDCs. If the mission is unsupportable, it is returned as an unsupportable mission to the division FSCC. The regiment FDC does not deny the mission.

RADAR FIRE MISSION AND THE TPC

Radars held in GS are controlled by the TPC. The TPC will process all fire missions to the regiment FDC by clicking unsupportable. Since TPC is commanded by the regiment FDC, missions are automatically passed to them.

All radar fire missions require coordination since they will plot in the zone of a maneuver unit. Coordination is normally effected by coordination requests automatically generated at the regiment FDC, not at the TPC. Unsupportable missions do not require coordination until an attack option is determined.

Radars in DS of a battalion are directly linked to that FDC. Command and support relationships of these radars are changed to reflect this and the fire missions transmitted are processed by the battalion FDC in the same fashion as fire missions received by an FO.

APPENDIX G. ESTIMATES OF SUPPORTABILITY

Estimates of supportability are performed in detailed planning and fragmentary order planning. They analyze the supporting arms' current capabilities; the current area of operations, enemy capabilities, and each course of action proposed; and cite advantages and disadvantages of each course of action. The extent of the estimate varies with the time available. The following formats for formal written estimates cover artillery, aviation, and naval surface fires.

Sample Format of Artillery Estimate of Supportability

CLASSIFICATION

Copy no. _ of _copies
ISSUING HEADQUARTERS
PLACE OF ISSUE
Date/time group

ARTILLERY ESTIMATE OF SUPPORTABILITY (U)
TITLE (U)

(U) REFERENCES: (List applicable references; e.g., maps, operation plans, doctrinal publications, SOPs, etc.)

1. (U) Mission

    (State the mission of the command.)

    a. (U) Artillery Concept. (State the artillery concept to support the mission.)

    b. (U) Previous Decisions. (State any previous decisions by the maneuver commander.)

2. (U) Situation and Considerations

    a. (U) Characteristics of the Area of Operations. (Refer to the Intelligence Estimate.)

    b. (U) Enemy Capabilities and Most Probable Course of Action. (Refer to the Intelligence Estimate.)

    c. (U) Friendly Forces. (State the friendly artillery forces available for the operation or refer to the planning document or other document setting forth available forces.)

    d. (U) Courses of Action. (The proposed courses of action are stated in full.)

Page number

CLASSIFICATION

CLASSIFICATION

e. (U) <u>Assumptions</u>. (State any assumptions on which the estimate is based, including assumptions regarding anticipated enemy action.)

3. (U) <u>Artillery Analysis</u>

a. (U) <u>Considerations Having Equal Effect</u>. (State all considerations of the analysis that have equal effect on all proposed courses of action.)

b. (U) <u>Courses of Action</u>. Each course of action is discussed from a strictly artillery point of view. All influencing factors are considered. Considerations include but are not limited to the ability of artillery to cover the area of operation of the supported unit; ammunition availability (total or CSR, munition types, desired packages); positioning and displacement requirements (rate of movement, counterfire threat); ability to mass fires; ability to provide CSS (external transportation assets if required, artillery culminating points); security of artillery (ground, indirect fire threat); troops available; effects of terrain and weather (operations, observation, ammunition effectiveness, and communications).

4. (U) <u>Evaluation</u>

(Each course of action is evaluated in turn. Advantages and disadvantages of each course of action are enumerated.)

5. (U) <u>Conclusions</u>

a. (U) <u>Best Course</u>. (This is a statement of which course of action can best be supported from an artillery point of view.)

b. (U) <u>Other Courses</u>. (Other courses of action are listed in their order of supportability, and a statement is made of their salient disadvantages.)

c. (U) <u>Significant Problems</u>. (This is a statement of significant problems to be solved and limitations to be taken into account. Measures required to solve the problems should be included.)

/s/_____

_____

Page number

CLASSIFICATION

Sample Format of Aviation Estimate of Supportability

CLASSIFICATION

Copy no. _ of _ copies
ISSUING HEADQUARTERS
PLACE OF ISSUE
Date/time group

AVIATION ESTIMATE OF SUPPORTABILITY (U)
TITLE (U)

(U) REFERENCES: (List applicable references; e.g., maps, operation plans, doctrinal publications, SOPs, etc.)

1. (U)   Mission

    a. (U)   Basic Mission. (State the mission of the command.)

    b. (U)   Previous Decisions. (State any previous decisions by the commander.)

2. (U)   Situation and Considerations

    a. (U)   Enemy

        (1) (U) Present disposition of major elements. (Refer to the Intelligence Estimate.)

        (2) (U) Capabilities. (Refer to the Intelligence Estimate.)

    b. (U)   Friendly

        (1) (U) Present disposition of major elements.

        (2) (U) Probable tactical developments.

    c. (U)   Courses of Action. (The proposed courses of action are stated in full.)

    d. (U)   Characteristics of the Area. (Refer to the Intelligence Estimate.)

    e. (U)   Assumptions. (State any assumptions on which the estimate is based, including assumptions regarding anticipated enemy action.)

3. (U)   Air Support Analysis

    a. (U)   Mission of the Force. (Restate the mission with emphasis on aviation support and participation required.)

    b. (U)   Concept of Employment. (State the concept of employment of aviation elements.)

Page number

CLASSIFICATION

CLASSIFICATION

c. (U) <u>Enemy Situation and Capabilities</u>. (State the enemy capabilities with respect to air support to the force.)

d. (U) <u>Requirement for Aviation Support</u>. (A general statement as to which course of action will require the most aviation support.)

e. (U) <u>Topography</u>. (A general statement of the potential sites and landing zones for use in the operation.)

f. (U) <u>Weather</u>. (A general statement of the impact of weather on aviation support of the operation.)

g. (U) <u>Observation and Surveillance</u>. (A general statement regarding observation and surveillance as they concern aviation support of the operation.)

h. (U) <u>Communication Requirements</u>. (A general statement regarding communications requirements for aviation support of the operation.)

i. (U) <u>Logistics Support</u>. (A general statement regarding logistics support for aviation support of the operation.)

j. (U) <u>Hydrographic Conditions</u>. (A general statement regarding the impact hydrography will have on aviation support.)

4. (U) <u>Evaluation</u>

(Each course of action is evaluated in turn. Advantages are enumerated, and then disadvantages enumerated.)

5. (U) <u>Conclusions</u>

a. (U) <u>Best Course</u>. (This is a statement of which course of action can best be supported from an aviation support point of view.)

b. (U) <u>Other Courses</u>. (Other courses of action are listed in their order of supportability, and a statement is made of their salient disadvantages.)

c. (U) <u>Significant Problems</u>. (This is a statement of significant problems to be solved and limitations to be taken into account. Measures required to solve the problems should be included.)

/s/_____

_____

Page number

CLASSIFICATION

Sample Format of Naval Surface Fires Estimate of Supportability

CLASSIFICATION

> Copy no. _ of _copies
> ISSUING HEADQUARTERS
> PLACE OF ISSUE
> Date/time group

NAVAL SURFACE FIRES ESTIMATE OF SUPPORTABILITY (U)
TITLE (U)

(U) REFERENCE:

1. (U) Mission

    a. (U) Basic Mission. (Of the command as a whole.)

    b. (U) Previous Decisions. (If any.)

    c. (U) Purpose of This Estimate. (To determine the course of action that can best be supported by naval surface fires.)

2. (U) Situation and Considerations. (Omit subparagraphs not applicable.)

    a. (U) Enemy

        (1) (U) Present Disposition of Major Elements. (Reference may be made to Intelligence Estimate.)

        (2) (U) Major Capabilities.(Enemy tactical capabilities likely to affect naval surface fires matters.)

        (3) (U) Other Capabilities. (Those of a nontactical nature which are likely to affect the naval surface fires situation.)

    b. (U) Own Forces

        (1) (U) Own Courses of Action. (A statement of the tactical courses of action under consideration.)

        (2) (U) Naval Surface Fire Support Means. (A breakdown of the number and types of ships that will be available for the operation. At this stage of the operation, this may be purely an estimate from the NAVY AMPHIBIOUS COMMANDER.)

        (3) (U) Training. (A statement of the state of training of SFCPs and the ships that will be supporting the operation, if known.)

Page number

CLASSIFICATION

CLASSIFICATION

c. (U) Characteristics of the Area. (Those affecting the naval surface fires situation such as weather, terrain, and hydrography. Reference may be made, in part, to the Intelligence Estimate.)

d. (U) Assumptions. (If any.)

e. (U) Special Factors. (Items not covered elsewhere which may have a bearing on the naval surface fires situation.)

3. (U) Naval Surface Fires Analysis

(Under each of the following subheadings, each course of action under consideration is analyzed in the light of all significant factors to determine problems which will be encountered, measures required to solve such problems, and any limiting features which will exist.)

a. (U) Hydrography

b. (U) Terrain

c. (U) Weather

d. (U) Means Required

e. (U) Training

f. (U) Intelligence

g. (U) Helicopter Support Requirements

h. (U) Electronic Warfare

i. (U) Miscellaneous

4. (U) Considerations Having Equal Effects

(Discuss those factors that will affect all courses of action equally.)

5. (U) Evaluation

(Based on the foregoing analysis, the advantages and disadvantages of each course of action under consideration are summarized and compared from a naval surface fires viewpoint.)

CLASSIFICATION

CLASSIFICATION

6. (U) <u>Conclusions</u>

(Omit subparagraphs not applicable.)

a. (U) (A statement as to which course of action under consideration can best be supported from a naval surface fires viewpoint.)

b. (U) (A statement of the salient disadvantages which render the other courses of action less desirable from a naval surface fires viewpoint.)

c. (U) (A statement of significant naval surface fires problems to be solved and limitations to be taken into account.)

d. (U) (A statement of measures required to solve naval surface fires problems involved.)

/s/ _____

_____

Page number

CLASSIFICATION

Appendix H. Example of FRAG Order Fire Support Plan With Quick Fire Support Planning

1. <u>Commander's Guidance for Fire Support</u>

The main effort is 1/6 and they will have priority of fires during their assault. Disrupt enemy fires during our movement forward. Plan fires to limit possible enemy mech attack on our left flank. Disrupt enemy positions on the objective by neutralizing the armored vehicles and suppressing his direct fires during the assault. Maximize CAS against tanks and artillery while the air threat remains low. Limit reinforcing enemy tanks. Disrupt the enemy's indirect fires, particularly while 1/6 moves through the pass. Ensure our artillery's displacement plan can keep up with our movement.

2. <u>Concept of Fires</u>

    a. (U) <u>Pre-Assault Phase</u>

        (1) (U) <u>Task</u>. Disrupt the enemy's indirect fire capabilities.

        (2) (U) <u>Purpose</u>. To enable 6th Mar freedom of maneuver to objective A.

        (3) (U) <u>Method</u>. 6th Mar has priority of fires for counterfire prior to crossing the line of departure. Target acquisition (TA) allocate 6th Mar 1 radar CFZ per battalion assembly area. Artillery POF to 1/6. FAC (A) neutralize all radar acquisitions, 2 sorties fixed-wing on-call. Recon Tm 2 (primary) and 1/6 (alternate) controls 2 sections of rotary-wing to locate/destroy OPs in vicinity of the pass. 1/6 fires AJ 2005/06/14/15, 50 salvos NSFS (DD 987 & DD 980) to neutralize all EW-located artillery and ADA targets. EW identify artillery COF/ADA nets, identify/locate artillery/ADA units, and on order jam ADA nets. Pri Tgts are ADA assets, C3, artillery. FSCL 1 is in effect and 6th Mar CFL is established at PL Gold.

        (4) (U) <u>Effect.</u> Enemy indirect fires into assembly areas limited. Active artillery and ADA units destroyed (3 of 6 batteries) and (4 of 8 launchers). COF nets identified for Movement and Assault phase. No CAS losses to ADA.

    b. (U) <u>Movement Phase</u>

        (1) (U) <u>Task.</u> Disrupt enemy indirect fires from LD until 1/6 is in attack position.

        (2) (U) <u>Purpose</u>. Enable freedom of maneuver to the objective. Preserve combat power.

        (3) (U) <u>Method</u>. Artillery POF and NGF to 1/6. TA allocate 1/6 radar CFZ along route of march. FAC(A) will be used for time critical targets and radar acquisitions, 2 sorties fixed-wing on-call and NSFS (DD 980) is alternate to neutralize additional radar acquisitions. EW on order jam ADA; be prepared to jam artillery COF.

CLASSIFICATION

(4) (U) Effect. Enemy indirect fires ineffective. Active artillery units neutralized or forced to displace.

(5) (U) Task. Limit possible enemy attack to left flank.

(6) (U) Purpose. Protect regiment left flank and maintain momentum of the attack.

(7) (U) Method. 2/6 allocated quick fire plan (QFP) TURTLE (4 NSFS, 2 Arty TGTs- counter-mech program). On order, 2/6 has priority of rotary-wing CAS and NSFS (DD 987); on order FAC (A) locate/neutralize mech battalion in named area of interest (NAI) 1 with 2 sections F/A-18; suppress dismounted troops in NAI 1 -2 sect rotary-wing. HA Mamba in effect. NSFS (DD 987) and Artillery on order neutralize mech unit in NAI 1 (QFP TURTLE-TGTs TBD). Artillery be prepared to provide suppression along route of march.

(8) (U) Effect. Enemy attack disrupted without regiment committing ground units.

(9) (U) Task. Neutralize the motorized rifle battalion on objective A.

(10) (U) Purpose. Neutralize enemy direct fires prior to assault and begin destruction of forces on the objective.

(11) (U) Method. Priority of all Fires to 1/6 at PL RED. 1/6 allocated QFP TADPOLE (4 NSFS, 2 Arty TGTs- prep fires). NSFS (DD 987) neutralize motorized rifle battalion QFP TADPOLE (TGTs TBD). Artillery destroy neutralize rifle battalion QFP TADPOLE (TGTs TBD). On-call, 2 TGTs (AJ 2008, 2009). CAS neutralize MRB on OBJ A -2 sections of rotary wing, -1 sortie fixed-wing. BP BLACK, ACA SKUNK in effect.

(12) (U) Effect. Enemy long range direct fires neutralized. Motorized rifle companies neutralized.

c. (U) Assault Phase

(1) (U) Task. Disrupt enemy indirect fires during assault.

(2) (U) Purpose. Prevent suppression of attacking units.

(3) (U) Method. EW jam artillery COF.

(4) (U) Effect. Enemy COF required to jump.

(5) (U) Task. Limit enemy tank company's on OBJ B ability to reinforce OBJ A.

(6) (U) Purpose. Isolate OBJ A.

Page number

CLASSIFICATION

CLASSIFICATION

(7) (U) <u>Method</u>. 1/6 has POF for CAS. 1/6, through FAC(A), controls CAS to neutralize tank co. in TAI 1 -2 sorties fixed-wing, 2 sections rotary CAS. BP GREEN, ACA POSSUM in effect. 1/6 emplaces 1 400x400, medium density, short duration, RAAMS minefield (AJ 2010). 1/6 neutralizes tank co with NSFS (DD 980) (Series PERCH- AJ 2011, 2012, 2013, 2014). CFL 2 in effect, CFL 3 on order.

(8) (U) <u>Effect</u>. Tank company neutralized.

d. (U) <u>Consolidation Phase</u>

(1) (U) <u>Task</u>. Limit the enemy's counterattack.

(2) (U) <u>Purpose</u>. Allow consolidation of combat power.

(3) (U) <u>Method</u>. Priorities of fire to 6th Mar. TA establish 1 CFZ per battalion. 1/6 receives 1 Artillery battery FPF. 6th Mar FSCC controls CAS to locate/destroy enemy in NAI 2 -1 section rotary CAS. EW identify/locate command net.

(4) (U) <u>Effect</u>. Enemy counterattack detected, disrupted.

CLASSIFICATION

CLASSIFICATION

3. (U) Fire Support Execution Matrix

	AA	LOD	PL RED	OBJ A/B	CONSOLID
6TH MAR	CF POF from Div		QUICK FIRE PLAN TADPOLE	O/O AJ 2010	POF-All
1/6	POF - Arty		POF - All	O/C AJ 2008, 2009	Arty 1 Btry FPF
2/6		O/O POF - RCAS, NSFS, QFP TURTLE			POF - NSFS
NSFS	N - Counterfire	N - Counterfire O/O QFP TURTLE	QFP TADPOLE	O/O Series PERCH	
2/10		O/O QFP TURTLE	QFP TADPOLE	O/C AJ 2008, 2009 O/O AJ 2010	1 Btry FPF
CAS (Rotary)	2 Sect, L/D OPs	2 Sect O/O N/S NAI 1	2 Sect, D OBJ A	2 Sect, N OBJ B	1 Sect, Scout NAI 2
CAS (Fixed)	2 Sorties N - Counterfire	2 Sorties N- Counterfire	1 Sortie, D OBJ A	2 Sorties, N OBJ B	
EW	ID - COF/ADA Locate ATRY/ADA O/O - Jam ADA	O/O JAM ADA BPT JAM COF	JAM COF	JAM ADA	ID/L CMD
FSCMs	FSCL 1	CFL 3	BP BLACK ACA SKUNK	BP GREEN ACA POSSUM	

4. (U) Coordinating Instructions

a. (U) CFL #3 in effect effective 050600 OCT at grid 433644 through 503644.

b. (U) Target nominations, Quick fire plans, due NLT 050000 OCT. Updated list of targets will be transmitted NLT 050200 OCT.

Target allocation.
Regt: 20
1/6: 10
2/6: 10

c. (U) Recon team RFAs will be transmitted NLT 042300 OCT.

Page number

CLASSIFICATION

CLASSIFICATION

5. (U) Critical Information

    a. Artillery

       (1)   # of BN 1 round missions available: 30.

       (2)   # of FASCAM (MED DEN 400 x 400) available: 2.

       (3)   # of minutes of M825 smoke for 300M screen: 20.

       (4)   RAP reserved for counterfire missions unless approved by this HQ.

    b. CAS

       (1)   Rotary-wing CAS sections (2 on station) from 050500 through 051600 OCT. FARP grid 422610.

       (2)   Fixed-wing CAS sorties from 050200 through 050400 OCT available from CVBG in AOA; from 050400 through 051600 OCT available from 2d MAW, LAGGER POINT RENO, grid 350500.

    c. NSFS

    d. USS O'Bannon, DD 987, DS to 6th Mar from FSA 1 effective 050000 OCT. Off station 051200 through 051400 OCT for UNREP.

    e. USS Moosbrugger, DD 980, GS to 6th Mar from FSA 2 effective 050600 OCT.

Page number

CLASSIFICATION

APPENDIX I. TARGETING AND EXECUTION TOOLS

Targeting and execution tools are incorporated into the fire support annex of the OPORD and are used to task subordinate elements.

Although not normally developed on the battalion level, FSCCs at lower echelons may use the high-payoff target list (HPTL) and adjust the higher headquarters AGM according to their scheme of maneuver to determine their own AGM, subordinate taskings, targets, and fire support execution matrix (FSEM). The FSC can modify and apply each of the following examples (or combinations) to meet his needs and the current tactical situation. See MCRP 3-16A/FM 6-20-10, *Targeting*, for a detailed discussion of targeting and execution tools.

HIGH-PAYOFF TARGET LIST

The HPTL is a prioritized list of high-payoff targets (HPTs). Define HPTs as accurately as possible.

In table I-1, combat outpost (COP) targets have been further defined to only those in the zone of the main attack. Priority #2 could pose problems. Are both of these systems the same priority throughout this phase? If non-Firefinder assets are allocated to detect them, which system is allocated for first? (Get clarifying guidance from the regimental FSC.) ADA systems in #3 can cause a lack of focus. Are all systems, regardless of location, an HPT? Consider only those that can affect the battalion's airspace.

Table I-1. HPTL.

Phase/Event: Security Zone	
PRIORITY	TARGET
1	COPs in main attack zone
2	2S1 and 2S19
3	2S6, SA9, SA13
4	Mortars in main attack zone
5	Regimental CP

TARGET SELECTION STANDARDS MATRIX

TSS are criteria established to evaluate potential target information considering its source, accuracy, reliability, and timeliness. Knowledge of the enemy's use of deceptive techniques or decoys and changes in tactics in an attempt to counter friendly action or deceive targeting sources will affect TSS.

HPTs identified from the collection effort must be reported to the delivery system within the designated timeliness criteria and meet the target location error goal under accuracy in order to be attacked. Commanders can override this criteria at any time, but this gives the targeting team guidance to execute in the absence of further orders. See table I-2.

Table I-2. TSS Matrix.

HPT	TIMELINESS	ACCURACY
COPS in main attack zone	3 hr	100 m
2S1 and 2S19	30 min	150 m
2S6, SA9, SA13	1 hr	200 m
Mortars in main attack zone	30 min	150 m
Regiment CP	4 hr	500 m

ATTACK GUIDANCE MATRIX

Knowing target vulnerabilities and the effect an attack will have on enemy operations allows the targeting team to propose the most efficient available attack option. Key guidance is the type of effects the commander wishes to inflict on the target. After commander's approval, attack guidance is summarized in the AGM. See table I-3. The AGM consists of—

- The HPTL—a prioritized list of HPTs by phase of the operation.

- When—the time the target should be engaged.

Table I-3. Attack Guidance Matrix.

HPT	WHEN	HOW	EFFECT	REMARKS
COPs	P	Arty	N	Plan in initial Prep
RSTA and OPs	P	Arty	N	Plan in initial Prep
2S1 and 2S3	I	CAS (FIXED)	N	Plan in initial Prep
2S6, SA-9, SA-13	P	Arty	S	SEAD for CAS
Regt CP	A	EW/Arty	EW/N	Coord with ECM prior to Neutralizing
Reserve Bn	P	CAS (fixed)	D	Intent to attack reserve Bn in EA HOT
LEGEND	I = IMMEDIATE A = AS ACQUIRED P = PLANNED		S = SUPPRESS N = NEUTRALIZE D = DESTROY EW = JAMMING OR OTHER OFFENSIVE EW	

- How—the attack system that will engage the target.
- Effect—desired effects on target or target system.
- Remarks—remarks on if BDA is required, whether coordination must take place, etc.

Guidance for when an asset is to be attacked is described as immediate, as acquired, and planned.

- Immediate—the commander wants this target attacked as soon as acquired, before any others.
- As acquired—these targets will be attacked in the order they are acquired and received by the fire support asset. Immediate takes precedence over as acquired.
- Planned—targets are not to be attacked but are to be planned for a later time to be attacked as part of a preparation, program or schedule of fires.

MCRP 3-16A/FM 6-20-10 has additional information on the AGM.

HPTL/TSS/AGM

The FSC can combine one or more tools to meet his requirements. Table I-4 shows the most common at-tack systems used. Table I-5, on page I-4, shows an HPTL with an AGM.

In table I-4, across the top portion of the matrix (prioritized from left to right) are the HPTs by category. Below each category, specific target types can be listed for clarification.

Along the left-hand column are the attack systems that can be used to attack the HPTs. At the intersection of the HPT's column and the attack system row is a box that contains the asset prioritization, TSS, and damage criteria. (See graphic at the bottom of the page.) In the top right hand corner of the box is a small number—the asset prioritization. It helps the FSC or watch officer determine which asset to use to attack the target. Artillery is the second choice to attack indirect fire assets. The TSS displays target location error, engagement criteria (how big the target must be to engage), what the target is doing, and the target decay time. The location given by the observer must be within 100m of the target's location. The target must be larger than platoon size, stationary, and should not have been reported longer than 30 minutes ago. Should the request for fire for the identified target meet the TSS and the asset determined to be first choice to attack the target is unavailable, then artillery would be used to attack an indirect fire asset.

Table I-4. HPTL/TSS/AGM.

PHASE: 1-				DTG:	

		HIGH-PAYOFF TARGETS				
PRI		1	2	3	4	REMARKS
DESCRIPTION		INDIRECT FIRE	ADA SYSTEMS	MANEUVER	RSTA	
ATTACK SYSTEMS	Arty	1 100M / 2 Platoon> / 3 Stationary / 4 30 Min — box 2, N	1 100MM / 2 PLT(-) / 3 Stationary / 4 45 Min — box 1, N	1 100MM / 2 Platoon> / 3 Stationary / 4 <45 Min — box 3, S	1 100M / 2 CoHq / 3 Stationary / 4 <45 Min — box 1, N	
	81 MM	1 100M / 2 Platoon / 3 Stationary / 4 30 Min — box 5, S	1 100M / 2 PLT(-) / 3 Stationary / 4 45 Min — box 3, S	1 100M / 2 Platoon> / 3 Stationary / 4 <45 Min — box 5, S	1 100M / 2 CoHq / 3 Stationary / 4 <45 Min — box 5, S	
	RWCAS	1 500M / 2 Battery / 3 Stationary / 4 <1 Hour — box 3, D	1 500M / 2 PLT(-) / 3 Stat/Moving / 4 <1 Hour — box 4, D	1 500M / 2 Platoon> / 3 Stat/Moving / 4 <1 Hour — box 2, D	1 500M / 2 CoHq> / 3 Stat/Moving / 4 <1 Hour — box 3, N	
	NSFS	1 100M / 2 Platoon> / 3 Stationary / 4 30 Min — box 4, S	1 100M / 2 PLT(-) / 3 Stat/Moving / 4 45 Min — box 2, S	1 100M / 2 Platoon> / 3 Stat/Moving / 4 <45 Min — box 4, S	1 100M / 2 CoHq> / 3 Stat/Moving / 4 <45 Min — box 2, N	
	FWCAS	1 1KM / 2 >Battery / 3 Stationary / 4 45 Min — box 1, D	1 1KM / 2 PLT(-) / 3 Stat/Moving / 4 <1 Hour — box 5, D	1 1KM / 2 Platoon> / 3 Stat/Moving / 4 <1 Hour — box 1, D	1 1KM / 2 CoHq> / 3 Stat/Moving / 4 <1 Hour — box 4, D	

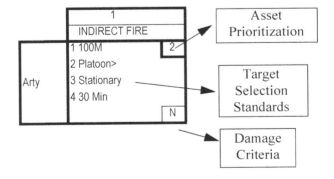

Table I-5. High-Payoff Target List/Attack Guidance Matrix.

EVENT OR PHASE: Attack to Objective C					
PRI	CATEGORY	HPTs	WHEN	HOW	COMMENTS
1	ADA	SA-8, SA-11, SA-15	A/P	N	
2	FIRE SPT	Arty CP MRL, C/B Wpns	I	N/EW	Coord with ECM
3	ENGINEER	Bridging Units, pontoons	A	N	
4	C³	MRR, MRD CP	A	N/EW	Coord with ECM
5	MANEUVER	1st Ech/lead division	A	N	
6	RSTA	Fwd intercept DF nodes	I	N	
-	NUKE/CHEM		I	D	Need BDA
-	REC		A	N	Not HPT
-	CLASS III POL		A	N	Not Hpt
-	CLASS V AMMO		A	N	Not HPT
-	CLASS IX MAINT		A	N	Not HPT
-	LIFT		A	N	Not HPT
-	LOC		A	N	Not HPT

LEGEND
I = IMMEDIATE
A = AS ACQUIRED
P = PLANNED

Arty = Artillery
C/B = Counterbattery
Ech = Echelon
ECM = Electronic countermeasures. (ECM is used only in NATO. Electronic attack and electronic protection are used in DOD.)

S = SUPPRESS
N = NEUTRALIZE
D = DESTROY
EW = JAMMING OR OTHER OFFENSIVE EW

MRD = Motorized rifle division
MRL = Multiple rocket launcher
MRR = Motorized rifle regiment

REACTIVE ATTACK GUIDANCE MATRIX

The reactive attack guidance matrix (RAGM) provides a quick means to determine whether an emerging target should be struck, possibly diverting fire support assets from a planned target. The RAGM prioritizes reactive target sets, specific targets within those target sets, and targeting objectives within specific geographic locations. It can be used to determine reallocation of fires assets, and quickly identify specific target sets and targets within those target sets to engage quickly. The RAGM must be updated every 6-12 hours. Within table I-6, if a planned target is being engaged and an enemy MRL appears in the Port City area, necessary fire support assets would be employed to engage the reactive target. This tool is used primarily by the MEF, but division FSCs should be aware of this product.

Table I-6. Reactive Attack Guidance Matrix.

	1	2	3	4
AREA	Port City	Northwest Mountains MSR	Eastern Approach to Port City	Capital to Port City MSR
TARGET CATEGORY PRIORITY	FS-MRL/LR/COASTAL C3I-Corps/DIV DEFENSE MMR-MECH/ARM	C3I-CORPS/DIV FS-MRL/LR MOB/CM MVR-MECH/ARV/AVIATION	C3I-CORPS/DIV FS-MRL/LR MVR-MECH/ARM	FM-MRL/LR MVR-MECH/ARM
UNIT PRIORITY	20th Arty BDE 15th Corps HQ	5th Div HQ 22 Arty BDE	3d Army CE 4th BDE	42d BDE
INTENT	Defeat ground force in vicinity of Port City to set conditions for force entry operations	Prevent LR Arty from interdicting 1 MEF forces	Prevent remnant forces, special op & bypassed units from interfering with 1 MEF rear area operations	Prevent forces from disrupting planned 1 MEF river crossings

DAMAGE CRITERIA MATRIX

See table I-7. The damage criteria matrix is a deliberate targeting tool FSCs can use to evaluate the effectiveness of targeting objectives against enemy strengths/capabilities and the desired targeting effects. It can also help anticipate future fire support requirements and reallocate fire support assets. This matrix is designed to be a "big picture" guide and will change periodically (probably between phases of the battle). This tool is used primarily by the MEF, but could be used within the GCE.

Note: "50% CE" means physical damage to the unit of 50% of the notional T/O and T/E.

Table I-7. Damage Criteria Matrix - Example from MEF.

	Destroy		Neutralize	
	Endstate	MOE	Endstate	MOE
Maneuver				
Armor/Mech	Unable to operate above company level	Reg: 30% CE Res: 40% CE	Unable to perform mission 24-48 hrs	Reduce 10% current T/O-T/E
Motorized/Foot	Unable to operate above battalion level	Reg: 40% CE Res: 30% CE		
Fire Support				
MRL/Arty	Unable to operate at battery level	50% CE	Unable to mass fires at BN and abv 24-48 hrs	Essential system components soft kill
Radar	Physically destroy		Unable to emit 24-48 hrs	Essential system components soft kill
C2			Unable cmd/coord 24-48 hrs	
Air Defense				
IADs	Unable to integrate multiple air defense sites	C2 nodes destroyed	Unable to coordinate air defense for 24-48 hrs	Comm, power, TA assets damaged
AAA	Unable to significantly interfere with friendly air ops	0% CE	Forced into autonomous ops for 24-48 hrs	Reduce units 10%
SAM		Crew served SAMs inop		Reduce units 10%

TARGETING SYNCHRONIZATION MATRIX

See table I-8. The TSM synchronizes targets with acquisition assets and firing assets by assigning responsibilities to detect, deliver, and assess attacks on specific HPTs. HPTs are listed in priority by category (decide column). Units and agencies are listed under the detect, deliver, and assess columns across from the specific HPTs for which they are responsible. As responsibilities are fixed, the asset envisioned to be used is indicated. This provides the targeting team a check to ensure all assets are used and that assets or agencies are not overtaxed. TSMs could also be prepared for a specific event or for each phase of the battle.

Table I-8. TSM.

DECIDE			DETECT		DELIVER		ASSESS	
Pri	Category	HPTs	Agency	Asset	Agency	Asset	Agency	Asset
1	Fire Support	M46	Arty Regt	Q-36	1-Arty Regt	1-Arty, MLRS	ACE	Debriefs
		Astros/BM-21	G-2	UAVs	2-ACE		G-2	Analysis/ UAVs
		FROG 2S5	Rad Bn	MEWSS, TPCS				
		D-20, D-30	Arty Regt	Q-36	Arty Regt	Arty, MLRS		
		Atk Helo	ACE	Organic	ACE, Arty Regt	Organic Arty MLRS		
2	ADA	Skyguard	ACE	EA-6B,	Arty Regt	Arty, MLRS	ACE	Analysis,
		Crotale		A/C RHAW				Debriefs,
		SA-6, SA-8, 2S6		Debriefs	MEF G-3 ACE	EA-6B (EA) F-18 (Strike)		EA-6B
3	RSTA	Rasas/Cymb	ACE	EA-6B	Arty Regt	Arty, MLRS	ACE	Debriefs
		Giraffe	G-2	Recon Patrols	ACE	F-18, AV-8B	G-2	Recon Debriefs
		Patrols, Ops	Regt	Organic	Regt	Organic	Regt	Organic
4	MVR	3-47 AR,	2d LAR	Organic	Rad Bn	TPCS	G-2	UAVs, LAR/
		15th Mech Bde	G-2	JSTARS SLAR	Arty Regt	Arty, MLRS		8th MAR
		14th Mech Bde	8th MAR	Organic	ACE	CAS, DAS		SPOTREPS
		3d Recon Bn	Rad Bn			(R/F)	ACE	Debriefs
LEGEND		Atk Helo = attack helicopter EA = electronic attack			mech = mechanized SPOTREPS = spot reports			

FIRE SUPPORT EXECUTION MATRIX

See figure I-1 on page I-8. The FSEM is a concise planning and execution tool that graphically displays the fire support plan to facilitate execution. It assists the FSCs, observers, supporting assets, and the maneuver commander in understanding how the fire support plan supports the commander's intent. It is a valuable planning and execution tool for both offense and defense. The matrix explains the portions of the fire support plan that each FSC, FO, and maneuver commander is responsible for executing. When approved by the maneuver commander, the matrix becomes the primary execution tool for the FSC and maneuver commanders. It is particularly useful in fixing responsibility for execution. It can use maneuver control measures such as TRPs or checkpoints to help integrate maneuver and fire. The FSEM must be event-driven, not based on time (this amplifies the importance of close cooperation between the FSC and the maneuver and artillery S-2s). IPB reveals possible and likely enemy locations, avenues of approach, and provides the initial framework for developing the fire support plan. Information that should be included on the FSEM follows:

- Phases or breakdown of how the commander plans to execute (should be same as scheme of maneuver).

- Maneuver units (including reconnaissance, STA, and LAR). Maneuver units are responsible for executing targets.

- Supporting assets. Position areas and scheduled movements should be displayed to give executors situational awareness.

- FSCMs. FSCMs facilitate the fire support execution.

- Priorities of Fire (POF). POF tells whose requests for fire will be answered first, as long as a higher ranked HPT is requested at same time. POF does not mean that other units will not have requests answered.

- Primary and alternate executors of targets. Always plan a back-up executor, especially for Copperhead (CPHD) and laser guided PGMs.

DD FORM 1972, JOINT TACTICAL AIR STRIKE REQUEST

See figure I-2 on page I-9. All U.S. Armed Forces use the JTAR to request CAS. Using this form is mandatory unless otherwise authorized by a higher authority.

ASSAULT SUPPORT REQUEST

See figure I-3 on page I-10. The ACE executes assault support missions as preplanned or immediate. The ACE executes both types of support in response to specific requests. The type of request determines the type of support.

Phase/ Unit	Phase I Pre H-Hr	Phase IA LD-PL Red	Phase IB Occupy Asslt Pos	Phase II Occupy Spt Pos	Phase III Lane Reduction	Phase IIIA Assault	Phase IV Exploit
FSCC							
Co I - Support			POF Arty & NGF AA4008/9/10 A2A —————		Kelly Toucan AA4007		⟶
Co K - Breach % Exploit			POF Mtr —————————		Kelly (a) Toucan (a) AA4007 (a) ⟶		POF NGF, Arty. & Mtr Jane
Co L - Assault						POF Mtr —————	⟶
STA 1	POF Arty AA4001 Parrot	AA4003/04 Macaw AA4008/09/10 (a) ⟶					
STA 2	POF Mtr AA4001 (a) Parrot (a)	AA4003/04 (a) Macaw (a) AA4008/09/10 (p) ⟶					
81mm Mortar	1st Sect MA1 POF to STA 2	2nd Sect O/M to MA 2 AA4008/09/10 ⟶	1st Sect O/M to MA 2 ———————		Kelly AA4007		2nd Sect DS to Co K, MA 3 1st Sect POF to Co K
Artillery	PA 1/2/3 POF to STA 1 AA 4001 Parrot	⟶	POF to Co I AA4008/9 A2A —————		Kelly Toucan Battery O/M to PA 4	⟶	POF to Co K Jane
NSFS/NGF	POF to RW FAC (A) Lisa	⟶	POF to CoI AA4008/9 A2A —————		Kelly Toucan	⟶	Jane
RW FAC(A)	POF NFG Lisa JTAR 18-6/7 1 Sect —————	JTAR 18-10/11 1 Sect					
FW FAC(A)	Parrot (a) JTAR 18-4/5	Macaw (a) JTAR 18-8/9					
RW/CAS	BP Boa PGMs —————	⟶			BP Habu 20mm/Rkt JTAR 18-14/15 1 Sect	⟶	BP Asp PGMs JTAR 18-1 1 Sect
FW/CAS	Mk-20 JTAR 18-4/5	Mk-20 JTAR 18-8/9			Mk 83/84 JTAR 18-12/13 1 Sect	⟶	Mk 82 JTAR 18- 2/3 1 Sect
EW	ID ADA/COF/C2 % EA		EA ADA/COF ————————————			EA C2	
Radar	CFFZ 1 CFFZ 2 —————	⟶	CFZ 2			⟶	CFZ 3
FSCMs	FSCL 1 FFA CFL 1 —————				%CFL 2 ⟶		⟶

ARTY ORG FOR CMBT 3/11 (155, T): DS 7th Mar 5/11 (155, T): GSR 3/11	MORTARS MA 1: ND 267456 AOF: 4700 MA 2: ND 299428 AOF: 5100 MA 3: ND 350418 AOF: 5100	CAS 3X AV-8B Sorties (AGM-65B) 2X AH-1Z Sorties (FAC[A]) 3X AH-1Z Sorties (Rockets/PGMs) 2X F/A-18 Sorties (FAC(A)/PGMs)	FSC LOC W/ BN CDR AFSC-FSCC
FSCMS CFL: PL Bullet O/O PL Shotgun NFA: 300 M RAD over STA O/O ACA RED: No fires west of 24 Northing	**HIGH-PAYOFF TGTS** PHI: ACRVs, OPs, C3 PHII: C3, BMP TK PLT, ENG PHIII: Same as PH2 PHIV: C3, BMP PLT, TK PLT	**ATTACK GUIDANCE** D: C3, ACRV, ENG (Breach) N: BMP, Tank Platoons S: ADA, FS (Battery)	**REFINEMENT CUT-OFF TIME** 031600 MAR 96
AMMO RESTRICTIONS Clear SMK Missions through REGT	**ENGAGEMENT CRITERIA** BMPs, Tanks: Platoon C3, ENG, RECON, ADA: 1 VEH	**AMMO AVAILABLE** DPICM: 15 Volleys (BN 3) SMK-FA: 25 MINX500MX50M SMK-M: 10 MINX500MX50M FASC: 1X400 x 400 SD-MD-R&A FASC: (REFT Planned)	**FS REHEARSAL TIME** 032100 MAR 96

Figure I-1. FSEM.

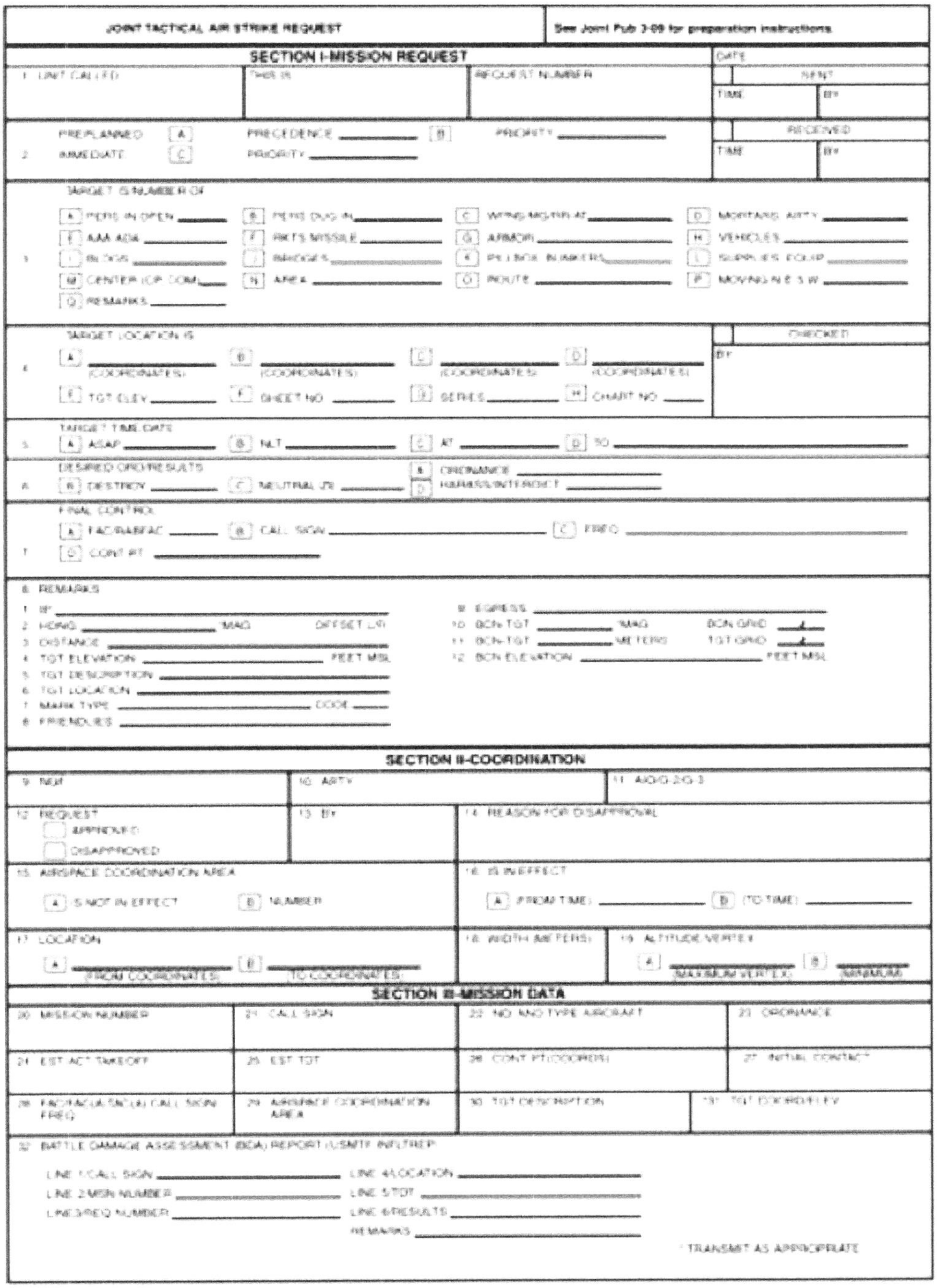

JOINT TACTICAL AIR STRIKE REQUEST — See Joint Pub 3-09 for preparation instructions.

SECTION I-MISSION REQUEST

1. UNIT CALLED — THIS IS — REQUEST NUMBER — DATE — SENT — TIME — BY

2. PREPLANNED [A] PRECEDENCE ____ [B] PRIORITY ____ ; IMMEDIATE [C] PRIORITY ____ — RECEIVED — TIME — BY

3. TARGET IS/NUMBER OF: [A] PERS IN OPEN [B] PERS DUG IN [C] WPNS/MG/RR/AT [D] MORTARS, ARTY [E] AAA ADA [F] RKTS MISSILE [G] ARMOR [H] VEHICLES [I] BLDGS [J] BRIDGES [K] PILLBOX, BUNKERS [L] SUPPLIES, EQUIP [M] CENTER (CP, COM) [N] AREA [O] ROUTE [P] MOVING N E S W [Q] REMARKS

4. TARGET LOCATION IS: [A] (COORDINATES) [B] (COORDINATES) [C] (COORDINATES) [D] (COORDINATES) [E] TGT ELEV [F] SHEET NO [G] SERIES [H] CHART NO — CHECKED — BY

5. TARGET TIME/DATE: [A] ASAP [B] NLT [C] AT [D] TO

6. DESIRED ORD/RESULTS: [A] DESTROY [C] NEUTRALIZE [E] ORDNANCE [D] HARASS/INTERDICT

7. FINAL CONTROL: [A] FAC/RABFAC [B] CALL SIGN [C] FREQ [D] CONT PT

8. REMARKS
1 IP
2 HDG ____ MAG OFFSET L/R
3 DISTANCE
4 TGT ELEVATION ____ FEET MSL
5 TGT DESCRIPTION
6 TGT LOCATION
7 MARK TYPE ____ CODE
8 FRIENDLIES
9 EGRESS
10 BCN-TGT ____ MAG BCN GRID
11 BCN-TGT ____ METERS TGT GRID
12 BCN ELEVATION ____ FEET MSL

SECTION II-COORDINATION

9. NGF — 10. ARTY — 11. AIO/G-2/G-3
12. REQUEST: APPROVED / DISAPPROVED — 13. BY — 14. REASON FOR DISAPPROVAL
15. AIRSPACE COORDINATION AREA: [A] IS NOT IN EFFECT [B] NUMBER — 16. IS IN EFFECT: [A] (FROM TIME) [B] (TO TIME)
17. LOCATION: [A] (FROM COORDINATES) [B] (TO COORDINATES) — 18. WIDTH (METERS) — 19. ALTITUDE/VERTEX: [A] (MAXIMUM VERTEX) [B] (MINIMUM)

SECTION III-MISSION DATA

20. MISSION NUMBER — 21. CALL SIGN — 22. NO. AND TYPE AIRCRAFT — 23. ORDNANCE
24. EST/ACT TAKEOFF — 25. EST TOT — 26. CONT PT (COORDS) — 27. INITIAL CONTACT
28. FAC/TAC(A)/ASC(A) CALL SIGN FREQ — 29. AIRSPACE COORDINATION AREA — 30. TGT DESCRIPTION — 31. TGT COORD/ELEV
32. BATTLE DAMAGE ASSESSMENT (BDA) REPORT (USMTF INFLTREP)
LINE 1/CALL SIGN — LINE 4/LOCATION
LINE 2/MSN NUMBER — LINE 5/TOT
LINE 3/REQ NUMBER — LINE 6/RESULTS
REMARKS
*TRANSMIT AS APPROPRIATE

DD Form 1972, (REVISED) 15 NOV 1994, Supersedes DD Form 1972, Apr 1975

Figure I-2. DD Form 1972, JTAR.

ASSAULT SUPPORT REQUEST FORM		

SECTION I — MISSION REQUEST

		DATE
1. UNIT CALLED	THIS IS	REQUEST NUMBER	SENT

2. REQUEST FOR	3. MISSION CATEGORIES	4. TYPE MISSION	TIME BY
A. q HELICOPTER	A. q PREPLANNED: PRECEDENCE _____	A. q TACTICAL	
B. q FIXED-WING	B. q PRIORITY _____	B. q ADMINISTRATIVE	
	C. q IMMEDIATE: PRIORITY _____		

5. MISSION IS	6. PAYLOAD IS
A. q ASSAULT TRANSPORT G. q TRAP	A. q TROOPS _____
B. q LOGISTICAL SUPPORT H. q SAR	
C. q AIR EVACUATION I. q ILLUMINATION	B. q EXTERNAL CARGO (WT) _____
D. q MEDEVAC J. q SPECIAL OPS	C. q INTERNAL CARGO (WT/CU) _____
E. q AERIAL DELIVERY K. q OTHER _____	
F. q C2	LARGEST ITEM (LxWxH) _____

7. INSTRUCTIONS

	PICKUP TIME	COORDINATES	LZ TIME	COORDINATES
A.	_____	_____	_____	_____
B.	_____	_____	_____	_____
C.	_____	_____	_____	_____
D.	_____	_____	_____	_____

8. LZ DESCRIPTION

A. WIND DIRECTION/VELOCITY _____   B. ELEVATION _____ (FT MSL)
C. SIZE _____   D. OBSTACLES _____
E. FRIENDLY POS _____   DIR/DIST _____/_____
F. ENEMY POS _____   DIR/DIST _____/_____
G. LAST FIRE RECEIVED TIME/TYPE _____/_____   DIR/DIST _____/_____

9. LZ WILL BE A. q UNMARKED	10. LZ MARKED WITH A. q PANELS B. q SMOKE C. q FLARES
B. q MARKED WITH COLOR _____	D. q MIRROR E. q LIGHTS F. q NAVAID G. q OTHER

11. COMMUNICATIONS   A. PICKUP ZONE CALL SIGN _____ /FREQUENCY (COLOR CODE) _____
                            B. LZ CALL SIGN _____ /FREQUENCY (COLOR CODE) _____

12. REMARKS	ACKNOWLEDGED
	BN/REGT
	DIVISION
	OTHER

SECTION II — COORDINATION

13. MSFS

16. ESCORT/AERIAL REFUELING   A. q REQUESTED   B. q ASSIGNED
C. NO/TYPE A/C _____   D. CALL SIGN _____
E. COMMUNICATIONS _____   F. ARMAMENT _____

17. REQUEST	19. REASON FOR DISAPPROVAL
q APPROVED q DISAPPROVED	

20. RESTRICTIVE FIRE/AIR PLAN	21. IS IN EFFECT
A. q IS NOT B. q NUMBER _____	A. q (FROM TIME) _____ B. q (TO TIME) _____

22. LOCATION	23. WIDTH (METERS)	24. ALTITUDE/VERTEX
A. q _____ (FROM COORDINATES) B. q _____ (TO COORDINATES)		A. q _____ MAX/VERTEX B. q _____ MINIMUM

SECTION III — MISSION DATA

25. MISSION NUMBER	26. CALL SIGN	27. NO/TYPE AIRCRAFT
28. EST/ACT TAKEOFF	29. ETA/ATA	

30. MISSION CANCELLED/DIVERTED   A. q CANCELLED   B. q DIVERTED   BY: _____
31. TERMINATE REQUEST   A. q GO/NO GO DTG _____   B. q WHEN COMPLETED _____

32. MISSION RESULTS	ACKNOWLEDGE
A. q COMPLETE	
B. q INCOMPLETE	
C. q OTHER _____	

Figure I-3. ASR.

APPENDIX J. RADAR ZONE MANAGEMENT

ZONE PLANNING SEQUENCE

Tactical Employment

Prioritize the unit's sector for zone planning that meets the maneuver commander's planning guidance (FSCC). The FSC must allocate and approve the zones that support the scheme of maneuver, meet the commander's guidance for force protection, and facilitate the engagement of HPTs (commander, targeting team, FSCC). The fire support staff must incorporate the zones into the appropriate synch matrixes and intelligence collection plans (FSCC, Arty S2/S3). Refine the zones during COA development and war-gaming process (FSCC, Arty S2/S3).

Technical Employment

Rehearse the cueing and use of zones during combined arms and FS rehearsals (FSCs, Arty S3/S2 and radar section). As the IPB improves and scheme of maneuver changes during execution, radar zones must be refined. Radar positions must be selected that optimize the probability of acquisition and support the coverage of planned zones (Bn S2/S3, Radar Plt Cdr or section chief).

RESPONSIBILITIES

The key to successful planning and execution of radar employment is the active involvement of FSCs and the maneuver staff in developing and executing the plan. The FSC, S2, S3, targeting officer, and observer-liaison chief must assist the controlling artillery S2 in triggering and refining radar zones for effective force protection and delivery of responsible counterfire. To ensure the Firefinder radar employment plan is effective, all leaders and planners must understand the capabilities, limitations, and products of the system. Plans that do not manage the high volume of digital fire missions and artillery intelligence data generated by the radar negate the system's influence on the battlefield. Plans that do not clarify clearance of fires for counterfire missions will limit the artillery's ability to provide responsive counterfire.

Targeting Team

The targeting team is made up of the unit XO, unit FSCC, targeting officer (if assigned), AO, Arty Bn S2/S3, FDO, NGLO, and the Mortar Rep (if assigned).

Coordinate and integrate all target acquisition asset employment and radar zone allocation.

Ensure planned zones are prioritized to support the HPTL and the concept of operations.

Assign cueing agents to trigger the radar, which activates planned zones that correspond to NAI and IRs.

FSC/Arty LNO

Translate the maneuver commander's guidance for force protection and engagement of enemy indirect fire weapons.

Give guidance to subordinate FSCCs and solicit CFZs from each.

Recommend zones to the commander during the planning process.

Ensure the radar employment plan is incorporated into the R&S plan.

Ensure the ground scheme of maneuver is coordinated with the radar movement plan.

Ensure priorities and triggers are developed for the activation and inactivation of each planned zone.

Integrate the planned triggers for radar movement and zones into the appropriate synch matrix.

Incorporate zone management into the combined arms and FS rehearsals.

Ensure zones are sent to the DS Bn S2 for inclusion in the radar deployment order (RDO).

Subordinate FSCs/Arty LNO

Develop zones to support the unit's plan, breach sites, battle positions, and others.

Nominate zones to the senior commander for approval and priority.

Develop precise triggers for zone activation and inactivation. Ensure that the developed triggers for approved zones are incorporated into the supported unit's Synch Matrix.

Establish ownership and responsibility for the zones.

Ensure any changes to the scheme of maneuver are balanced against planned zones.

Ensure refinement is completed and sent to the artillery S2 for transmission to the radar.

Artillery S2

Develop CFFZs based on the templated enemy artillery positions and confirmed intelligence data.

Develop CFZs for FA units.

Nominate zones to FSCC for approval.

Ensure the radar employment plan is integrated into the R&S plan.

Receive approved zones from the FSCC for inclusion into the RDO.

Construct the RDO and brief the radar platoon commander or section chief.

Refine zones as IPB improves or the scheme of maneuver changes.

Artillery S3

Incorporate zone management and radar positioning into the Synch Matrix.

Ensure TA enclosure to the artillery fire plan includes coordination measures for zone development and radar positioning.

Ensure land management for the radar is coordinated with the maneuver COC.

Ensure clearance of fires and attack guidance for counterfire missions within the unit's sector are coordinated and understood by all members of the COC.

Radar Platoon Commander Section Chief

Ensure the capabilities and limitations of the radar system are considered during the planning process.

Select radar positions that support the search sector requirements of planned zones, optimize the probabilities of acquisition and facilitate required moves to support the scheme of maneuver.

Identify zone restrictions violated during the planning and rehearsal process.

Participate in all appropriate rehearsals.

APPENDIX K. LASER EMPLOYMENT

Laser weapons systems consists of ground and airborne designators used with surface or air delivered guided munitions. Systems include laser designators/rangefinders, laser acquisition/spot trackers or seekers, laser guided weapons, and delivery platforms. Laser systems are used by artillery FOs, NSF spotters, FACs, reconnaissance personnel, and fixed-and rotary-wing pilots. Several references for laser employment and procedures exist. Joint Pub 3-09.1, *JTTP for Laser Target Designation Operations*, provides detailed information on all Service laser systems and munitions. MCWP 3-16.6, *Supporting Arms Observer, Spotter, and Controller*, provides detailed information on ground laser systems.

BASIC REQUIREMENTS

The five basic requirements to use laser designators with laser seekers or laser guided munitions follow.

A pulse repetition frequency (PRF) code is used for the laser designator, the laser spot tracker (LST), and the laser guided weapon (LGW). Each must use the same code when operating together.

An agreed upon direction of attack is necessary. The LST or LGW must be able to acquire the energy reflected from the target.

The laser designator must be lasing/designating the target at the correct time and for the proper duration.

The delivery system must release the munition within the specific munition delivery envelope.

Line of sight must exist between the designator and the target, as well as between the target and the tracker or LGW. The LGW can have LOS before or after launch, depending upon the system capabilities.

LASER TARGET DESIGNATION, RANGING, AND POINTING SYSTEMS

Laser designators provide the energy source that is reflected from a designated target to provide terminal guidance for LGWs. These systems emit discrete pulses of infrared energy, invisible to the naked eye. Characteristics of these pulses are determined by a PRF code of the laser energy that can be set by a series of switches on the equipment. Laser target ranging systems provide accurate range direction and elevation information for use in locating enemy targets or other positions but are not capable of designating for laser guided munitions. IR pointers simply provide visual identification of targets. Systems vary from handheld to aircraft-mounted devices. The laser designator/rangefinder inventory within the Marine Corps follows.

Modular Universal Lasing Equipment

The modular universal laser equipment (MULE) (AN/PAQ-3) is a laser designator/rangefinder capable of designating moving targets to a range of 2,000 meters or stationary targets to 3,500 meters. Maximum rangefinding capability is 10,000 meters. The MULE system has a north-seeking capability that allows self-orientation for direction and a readout of both grid and true azimuths. It is capable of detecting multitarget reflections. The MULE can be operated during periods of darkness or reduced visibility at slightly reduced ranges by use of a night vision device. It is interoperable with the digital message system (DMS), and indirectly, through the DMS, with the battery computer system (BCS). When used in conjunction with the precision lightweight GPS receiver (PLGR), it provides accurate observer and target location. The MULE is powered by vehicle for sustained operations or battery for a shorter duration.

Target Location Designation and Hand-off System

The TLDHS is a modular, man-portable (43 pounds for LLDR and THS), automated target acquisition, location, and designation system that can digitally hand-off target data to fire support platforms. It has the capability of designating moving targets to 3,000 meters and stationary targets to 5,000 meters. Maximum rangefinding capability is 10,000 meters. TLDHS is comprised of two independent subsystems. The lightweight laser designator-rangefinder (LLDR) provides the target location and designation capability through the integration of day and thermal optics, eye-safe laser rangefinder, angle and vertical angle, GPS receiver, and a laser designator for LGWs and spot trackers. The second subsystem is the target hand-off system (THS). THS provides the capability to compose, transmit, and receive digital fire support messages.

Laser Infrared Observation Set (AN/GVS-5)

The AN/GVS-5 is a hand held, battery operated laser rangefinder. It has no ability to designate targets or determine direction. It has a 7 x 50 monocular sighting system and an accuracy of plus/minus 10 meters for distances from 200 to 9,990 meters. It can provide a maximum of 100 range readouts per battery charge.

Laser Target Designator/Rangefinder Pod

The F/A-18 C/D is capable of carrying AN/AAS-38 LTD/R pod which provides two functions. Its laser designator provides terminal weapons guidance for all LGWs, as well as designating targets for airborne coded laser acquisition/spot trackers (LSTs).

Night Targeting System

The AH-1W attack helicopter contains the NTS, which provides laser target designator/rangefinder capability, as well as forward looking infrared (FLIR) visual capability and video capture. It performs the same functions as the LTD/R pod for fixed-wing platforms.

Illumination Devices

Handheld lasers emit infrared (IR) light for compatibility with NVGs. These devices can either "flood" IR light within 1,000 meters to enhance general NVG performance, or focus a small beam up to 4 kilometers to pinpoint a specific target or mark friendly positions with an IR light beam for any unit or weapon system employing NVGs. Examples include IZLID and GCB-1B.

LASER ACQUISITION DEVICES

Laser acquisition devices are systems that allow visual acquisition of a coded laser designated target. They must be set to the same PRF code as the laser designator for the user to see the target being lased. There are two types of laser acquisition devices. Note that the AH-1W has the capability to use onboard Hellfire munitions as an improvised LST prior to firing.

Laser Acquisition/Spot Tracker Pod

The coded laser acquisition/spot tracker (LST) can be carried on the F/A-18 A/C/D. Once it acquires the laser spot (target), it passes necessary ballistic information to allow FLIR or radar acquisition of target and visual display. Desired PRF codes are in-flight selectable. It then employs LGWs or executes visual deliveries of non-laser ordnance.

Angle Rate Bombing System

The ARBS is used on the AV-8B. It consists of a 3-axis gimballed television/LST, enabling view of the laser spot. It provides day or night attack and reattack information for either LGW or non-guided bombs. The system allows in-flight selection of PRF codes but is affected by smoke or obscurants.

WARNING

Care must be taken to remain oriented on the target, ensuring that the LST has acquired and locked onto target reflected laser energy. There are instances when LSTs have acquired and locked onto the laser signature caused by atmospheric attenuation around the laser designator device.

LASER GUIDED WEAPONS

These munitions hone in on reflected laser energy during the terminal portion of the attack. Such munitions are part of the precision guided munition (PGM) family.

Copperhead

The Copperhead (M732 CLGP) is a 155 millimeter cannon-launched, laser-guided projectile used to defeat high-payoff targets. It has a maximum range of 16,800 meters and a minimum range of 3,000 meters. Copperhead targets can be designated by ground or airborne designators. Multiple targets in large target arrays or widely separated targets may be engaged. The projectile follows one of two trajectories depending on visibility conditions. Upon reaching a point on its descending trajectory, the laser designator operator lases the target. The projectile acquires the reflected laser energy and maneuvers to the designated target. Its payload consists of a 15-pound-shaped charge.

Maverick

The Maverick AGM-65E is an air launched, laser guided air to ground missile employed on the AV-8B, and F/A-18 aircraft. It can be used against armored vehicles, field fortifications, or surface combatants. The missile requires lock on before launch. Once, the Maverick is launched, the aircraft can break away or launch another missile. It employs a 125 pound or 300 pound warhead. If Maverick loses the spot, the missile goes ballistic over the target and does not explode. The PRF code is cockpit selectable.

Hellfire

The Hellfire (AGM-114) is a laser-guided, anti-armor missile launched from the AH-1W/Z Super Cobra aircraft. It can be employed in indirect (lock on after launch) or direct (lock on before launch) fire methods. Hellfire can be launched in four firing modes: one missile (single), two or more missiles on the same code (rapid), two or more missiles launched on different codes using multiple laser designators (ripple), or multiple codes and designators used in combination of rapid and ripple fire. The PRF code is cockpit selectable.

Laser-Guided Bombs

The MK-82, -83, and -84 are Marine Corps designations for the 500, 1,000, and 2,000 pound bombs that can be converted to the GBU-12, GBU-16, and GBU-10 laser-guided bombs, respectively. These bombs use common laser guidance and control subassemblies, with only the aerodynamic surfaces changed to match the particular size of warhead.

Paveway I and II LGBs require ballistically accurate delivery (release within an envelope) and continuous laser energy during the last 10 seconds of flight. When delivered from a low-altitude loft maneuver, lasing is restricted to the last 10 seconds of flight to prevent bombs missing short. They can be employed in a standoff capacity. The PRF codes are set before aircraft launch.

LASER-GUIDED WEAPONS PLANNING

Due to the enhanced complexity of laser weapon systems and their specific requirements for employment, prior planning and coordination is required for optimal performance in battle.

Integration

Optimum use of PGMs is on preplanned targets or engagement areas outside or at the maximum range of maneuver direct fire weapons (typically 3,000 meters). This allows for early engagement of high-payoff targets and reduces the effects of an obscured battlefield. However, integration into the overall battle plan is necessary. Integration with direct fire weapons creates a combined arms effect as well as ensures mutual support.

Environmental Conditions

LGWs require line of sight with both the designator and the target, and the LGW and the target. Irregular terrain and vegetation must be considered in the location of EAs, LTDs, and LGWs. Rain, snow, fog, and low clouds can reduce the effectiveness of laser-guided munitions ability to acquire radiation. Laser designators line of sight can be reduced. Snow on the ground produces a negative effect on laser-guided munition accuracy or cause spillover. Extreme temperatures (below

32 degrees) can affect MULE battery life. Obscuration of the battlefield can also reduce the effectiveness of LGWs. When possible, employ techniques such as attacking downwind targets first.

Munition Employment Characteristics

The specific engagement requirements for each LGW varies and must be considered in planning. Considerations include minimum and maximum ranges, minimum visibility and required designation times, and maximum angle of acquisition.

For example, Copperhead has engagement templates, a 13 second designation requirement, and a maximum acquisition angle of 800 mils (45 degrees) between the observer and GTL. The minimum visibility to effectively use Copperhead is 5,000 meters. The Maverick has a maximum range of 24 kilometers, requires continual lasing, and has a 60 degree maximum acquisition angle. The Hellfire has an 8 kilometer maximum range, a 60 degree maximum acquisition angle, and also requires continual lasing.

Designator Location and Characteristics

Whether airborne or ground designator, the location of the laser designator must ensure line of sight to the target while allowing the LGW to acquire the target within the parameters of its attack angle, 1067 mils (60 degrees) in most cases. Blocking line of sight between the LGW and the laser designator produces false lockon. Airborne designators should remain behind delivery platforms while ground designators use terrain or vegetation to break line of sight when possible. The short lifespan of battery powered designators should be considered in extended operations.

PRF Codes

Laser coding permits the simultaneous use of multiple laser designators and laser guided weapons/seekers. Laser designators and seekers use a PRF coding system to ensure that a specific seeker and designator combination work in harmony. By setting the same code in both the designator and the seeker, the seeker tracks only the target that is designated with that code.

Code Description

The system uses either a three-digit or four-digit numeral system, depending on the type of laser equipment. Three digit settings range from 111 to 788, while four digit settings range from 1,111 to 1,788. All three and four digit designator/seekers are compatible. Lower numbered PRF codes provide higher quality designation due to faster pulse repetition.

Code Allocation and Assignment

Laser guided weapons system codes must be controlled and coordinated. At the MAGTF level, different blocks of codes are assigned to artillery, air, and NGF to prevent interference between supporting arms activities.

Each supporting arm then assigns codes to its subordinate units for individual missions and changes codes periodically as the situation requires. Subordinate FSCCs provide positive coordination of the code settings through the various fire support representatives. Normally codes are given to individual observers, however observers are able to use the same codes as long as it is coordinated; e.g., observers use the same code when one is a back-up.

Each MULE/TLDHS operator normally uses his own PRF code unless employing LGBs or for preplanned missions with distinct PRFs. His PRF code is confirmed before mission execution of aerial delivered LGWs. LGBs PRF codes cannot be changed in flight.

For preplanned CAS, codes are ultimately assigned to each flight. The LTD must match the preset LGB codes, while Maverick, Hellfire, and Copperhead can be set to match the designators PRF code.

Security

The PRF codes are handled in the same manner as other classified material. Secure means should be used, if available, when codes are passed between laser designators and the munition delivery unit/aircraft. However, the absence of compatible secure means should not normally dictate the termination of a laser guided munition attack. In certain situations, codes may have to be prebriefed.

Safety

There are two hazards associated with laser systems applicable in both combat and peacetime training. The first is the ability of the LST or LGW to acquire and guide in on spillover laser energy rather than the target; i.e., the laser designator. This is known as false lock-on. The second is the laser beam's intense infrared radiation that can cause serious eye damage and blindness.

False Lock-on

A seeker may detect scattered radiation that is caused by suspended matter in the atmosphere. It is called atmospheric scatter/attenuation or backscatter.

To mitigate the effects of atmospheric scatter, 20-degree angle with its origin at the target and bisecting the laser designator establishes a safety exclusion zone for air delivered munitions (excluding Copperhead) and LSTs.

Aerial platforms must avoid this zone during designation to reduce the likelihood of an LST or LGW acquiring the designator vice the target. The exclusion zone is not an absolute safety measure as some LSTs have acquired the atmospheric scatter in front of the ground laser designator even though the LSTs were outside the safety zone.

In combat, attack headings should avoid this zone if possible. Peacetime employment follows training safety requirements.

Eye Hazard

During combat, take care to avoid friendly casualties from indiscriminate laser designation. Be cautious in designating highly reflective targets that can cause dangerous reflected beams. The policy of the United States Armed Forces prohibits employing laser weapons that are specifically designed to, or have a combat function of, causing permanent blindness. Peacetime use of lasers imposes strict safety requirements during training exercises. Range and unit safety SOPs must be adhered to in their employment.

EMPLOYMENT

Key factors must be considered when employing laser systems. Adverse effects of these factors can often be overcome by planning and skillful employment of the laser designators.

Ground Mode

Ground laser designators identify targets for artillery, NSFS, and aircraft delivered munitions. MULE equipped teams can designate for laser-guided munitions as well as conventional ordnance delivered by LST. Standard calls for fire are used except that the laser code must be exchanged between the ground designator and the firing unit or the aircraft.

Airborne Mode

Airborne laser target designators identify targets for all types of aircraft delivered munitions. Airborne designator systems operating in support of ground maneuver forces can employ all types of laser guided munitions. Standard calls for fire or request for air support are used, except that the code being used must be exchanged.

Communications

Positive communications between the designator operator and the munition delivery means is required to coordinate the proper PRF code, the seeker/laser designator alignment, and target designation timing.

Enemy Countermeasures (NATO)

Judicious use of laser target designators limit the enemy's countermeasure capability. Designator vulnerability must be considered when designating point targets such as tanks, BMPs, and guns that can detect radiation and suppress designators. Offset aim points reduce a target's ability to react.

Aim Points

The nature of the target surface affects the aim point as it varies the amount and direction of reflected radiation. Concave or poorly defined targets; e.g., caves and tunnels, may absorb the laser spots. Horizontal flat surfaces can refract or cause enough spillover to cause misses.

Battlefield Obscuration

Smoke, dust, and debris can impair the use of laser guided munitions. Reflective scattering of laser light by smoke particles may present false targets. The night sight, alternate positions on higher ground, and alternate designators can be useful in reducing smoke and dust effects.

Darkness

Targets are more difficult to locate, range, and designate during low illumination. The night sight on the designator will overcome the effects of darkness and can assist during periods of poor visibility and inclement weather.

APPENDIX L. TARGETING, SYMBOLOGY, AND SCHEDULING

TYPES OF TARGETS

Target of Opportunity

A target visible to a surface or air sensor or observer, which is within range of available weapons and against which fire has not been scheduled or requested. (JP 1-02)

Planned Target

In artillery and naval surface fire support, a target on which fire is prearranged. The degree of prearrangement varies, but some prior coordination/action has been done to facilitate its engagement. Planned targets may be further subdivided into scheduled or on-call targets. Some planned targets may be designated as priority targets and FPFs.

Scheduled Target

In artillery and naval surface fire support, a planned target on which fire is to be delivered at a specific time. Fires are prearranged as to location and time of firing. This time may be related to an H-hour or another time reference.

On-Call Target

In artillery and naval surface fire support, a planned target other than a scheduled target on which fire is delivered when requested. The on-call target is prearranged as to location and is fired on request or on signal. The on-call target requires less reaction time than a target of opportunity.

Priority Target

A target which when requested for attack takes precedence over all the fires for the designated firing unit or element. Priority targets are designated by the maneuver commander that controls the firing asset, who also provides specific guidance as to when the targets will become priority, munitions to use, accuracy, and de-

sired effects. When not engaged in fire missions, firing units will lay on priority targets. Do not assign more priority targets than can be supported. A rule of thumb is no more than three priority targets to a 6-gun battery. If the priority target is an FPF only one is assigned to a battery (see next paragraph). Two priority targets may be assigned to an 81mm mortar platoon. Designation of priority targets may be planned to shift as the supported unit moves forward; e.g., crossing phase lines.

Final Protective Fires

An immediately available prearranged barrier of fire designed to impede enemy movement across defensive lines or areas. (JP 1-02) An FPF is a priority target placed on a likely enemy avenue of approach. FPFs consist of final protective lines (FPLs), principal direction of fires (PDFs), and barrages. FPLs and PDFs apply to small arms and crew served weapons, while artillery and mortars fire continuous barrages. A barrage is a prearranged barrier of fire, except that delivered by small arms, designed to protect friendly troops and installations by impeding enemy movements across defensive lines or areas. (excerpt from JP 1-02) The location of the FPF is any distance from the friendly position that supports the current tactical situation within range of organic direct fire weapons, normally 200 to 400 meters (within danger close). Artillery FPFs are fired by an entire battery (6 guns). In mortars, an FPF may be assigned to each squad, section or the platoon. FPF size depends on the type and number of weapons. See table L-1.

Table L-1. Size of FPF.

Weapon	Size (meters)
60mm mortar Section (3 tubes)	90 x 30

81mm mortar
  Platoon (8 tubes)
  Section (4 tubes)
  Squad (1 tube)
	280 x 35
	140 x 35
	35 x 35

120mm mortar
  Platoon (6 tubes)
  Squad (1 tube)
	360 x 60
	60 x 60

155mm howitzer Battery (6 guns)	300 x 50

Target Numbering System

To designate targets for fire support operations, the Marine Corps adheres to the provisions of A-Arty P-1 and QSTAG 221. Provisions to the target numbering system are specified in the fire support plan.

The Target Number

The target number consists of six characters, comprising two letters and four numerals; e.g., AB1234. The two letter group may be used to indicate the originator of the target number and/or the level controlling the target data.

First Letter

The CINC, joint, or the common commander to Army and Marine forces assigns the first letter of the target number to Army Corps and the MEF/MAGTF. The national identifying letters for NATO and ABCA armies are American, British, Canadian, and Australian. Nations with corresponding first letters follow:

- Belgium/Luxembourg, B.
- Canada, C, Z.
- Denmark, D.
- France, F.
- Greece, E.
- Germany, G.
- Italy, I.
- Netherlands, H.
- Norway, N.
- Portugal, P.
- Spain, S.
- Turkey I,O,T.
- United Kingdom, J,U, X.
- United States, A, K,Y,W.
- Others, V.

Second Letter

The second letter designates units within the MAGTF. See table L-2.

Table L-2. Letter Assignments—Marine Units.

I MARINE EXPEDITIONARY FORCE	A
1ST MARINE DIVISION	B
1st Marine Infantry Regiment	C
5th Marine Infantry Regiment	D
7th Marine Infantry Regiment	E
11th Marine Artillery Regiment	F
II MARINE EXPEDITIONARY FORCE	G
2D MARINE DIVISION	H
2d Marine Infantry Regiment	I
6th Marine Infantry Regiment	J
8th Marine Infantry Regiment	K
10th Marine Artillery Regiment	L
III MARINE EXPEDITIONARY FORCE	M
3D MARINE DIVISION	N
3d Marine Infantry Regiment	O
4th Marine Infantry Regiment	P
12th Marine Artillery Regiment	Q
MARINE FORCES RESERVE	R
4TH MARINE DIVISION	S
23d Marine Infantry Regiment	T
24th Marine Infantry Regiment	U
25th Marine Infantry Regiment	V
14th Marine Artillery Regiment	W
UNASSIGNED	X,Y, Z

Numbers

Numbers further designate units. See table L-3.

Table L-3. Number Assignments—MEF Command Elements.

0000-0999	MEF FFCC
1000-1999	MEB Command Element
2000-2999	Lowest Numbered MEU Command Element
3000-3999	Second Lowest Numbered MEU Command Element
4000-4999	Third Lowest Numbered MEU Command Elements
5000-5999	MAW
6000-6999	FSSG/RAOC
7000-7999	Force Reconnaissance Company
8000-8999	Unassigned
9000-9999	Weapons of Mass Destruction

I MEF will assign MEB and MEU(SOC) numbers to 1st MEB, 11th, 13th, and 15th MEU's. II MEF will assign MEB and MEU(SOC) numbers to 2d MEB, 22nd, 24th, and 26th MEUs. III MEF will assign MEB and MEU(SOC) numbers to 3d MEB, 31st MEU(SOC).

Units assigned to the MEB and MEU(SOC) use their block of numbers assigned under the division to which they belong. See tables L-4 through L-7.

Table L-4. Number Assignments—Marine Divisions.

0000-0999	Division FSCC
1000-1999	Tank Battalion
2000-2999	LAR Battalion
3000-3999	Reconnaissance Battalion
4000-9999	Unassigned

Table L-5. Number Assignments—Marine Infantry Regiments.

0000-1999	Infantry Regiment FSCC
2000-2999	Lowest Numbered Infantry Battalion
3000-3999	Second Lowest Numbered Infantry Battalion
4000-4999	Third Lowest Numbered Infantry Battalion
5000-5999	Attached Battalion
6000-6999	Attached Battalion
7000-9999	Unassigned

Table L-6. Number Assignments—Marine Artillery Regiments.

0000-0999	Regimental Fire Direction Center
1000-1999	Lowest Numbered Artillery Battalion
2000-2999	Second Lowest Numbered Artillery Battalion
3000-3999	Third Lowest Numbered Artillery Battalion
4000-4999	Attached Artillery Battalion
5000-5999	Attached Artillery Battalion
6000-6999	Counterfire
7000-9999	Unassigned

Table L-7. Number Assignments—Marine Infantry Battalions.

0000-0199	Infantry Battalion FSCC
0200-0299	Lowest Lettered Infantry Company
0300-0399	Second Lowest Lettered Infantry Company
0400-0499	Third Lowest Lettered Infantry Company
0500-0599	Weapons Company
0600-0699	Scout Sniper Platoon
0700-0799	81mm MTR Platoon
0800-0899	Attachment
0900-0999	Attachment

Each Infantry battalion block of numbers assigned will be different based on whether they are the lowest numbered battalion, second lowest numbered battalion, or the third lowest numbered battalion.

Forward observers and naval gunfire spotters will use target numbers assigned to them from the Infantry company they are supporting. Table L-8 provides number blocks for artillery battalion FDCs. Table L-9 provides examples as discussed in tables L-2 through L-8.

Table L-8. Number Assignments—Marine Artillery Battalions.

0000-0199	Artillery Battalion FDC
0200-0299	Lowest Lettered Artillery Battery
0300-0399	Second Lowest Lettered Artillery Battery
0400-0499	Third Lowest Lettered Artillery Battery
0500-0599	Attachment
0600-0699	Attachment

Target Symbols

Standard symbols are used to prepare maps, charts, and overlays to identify targets by type.

Point Target

A target of such small dimension that it requires the accurate placement of ordnance in order to neutralize or destroy it. (JP 1-02). It is generally a target that is 200 meters or less in length and width. The symbol shows the proper placement of the target number. See figure L-1.

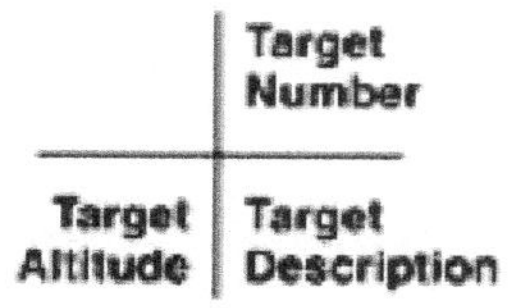

Figure L-1. Point Target.

Table L-9. Examples of Marine Corps Target Numbering System.

MEF	
I MEF FFCC	AA 0000-0999
11th MEU FFCC	AA 2000-2999
3D MEB FFCC	AM 1000-1999

DIVISION	
3D MARDIV FSCC	AN 0000-0999
10th MARINES FDC	AL 0000-0999
1ST TANK BATTALION	AB 1000-1999

INFANTRY REGIMENT	
8TH MARINES FSCC	AK 0001-0999
2/3 FSCC	AO 3000-3199
1/7 FSCC	AE 2000-2199

ARTILLERY REGIMENT	
B BTRY 1/10	AL 1300-1399
F BTRY 2/11	AF 2300-2399
A BTRY 1/12	AQ 1100-1199

INFANTRY BATTALION	
B CO. 1/6 FO	AJ 1300-1399
SCOUT SNIPER 2/3	AO 3600-3699
*BLT 3/1 (CHOPPED TO 11TH MEU)	AC 4000-4999
SPOT TM C/1/7	AE 2400-2499

*BLT 3/1 Supports 11th MEU. BLT 3/1 will use 1st Marines target numbers.

Linear Target

A target that is more than 200 meters but less than 600 meters long. Targets longer than 600 meters may be subdivided into multiple targets for attack with indirect fire. A linear target is designated on the target list or list of targets by two grids or a center grid, length, and attitude. Automated systems define linear targets by a ratio of at least 5:1, length to width, respectively. See figure L-2.

Figure L-2. Linear Target.

Rectangular Target

A target wider and longer than 200 meters. It is designated on the target list or list of targets by a center grid, length, width, and attitude. Automated systems define rectangular targets by a ratio of less than 5:1, length to width, respectively. See figure L-3.

Figure L-3. Rectangular Target.

Circular Target

A target that is circular in nature or is vague as to its exact shape. It is designated by a center grid and a radius on the target list or list of targets. See figure L-4.

Figure L-4. Circular Target.

Final Protective Fire

The FPF is normally drawn as a linear target. For a mortar, FPFs assigned to individual weapons may be depicted as a circular target. The symbol used includes the target number, the designation of FPF, and the system/unit to deliver the fires. The FPF symbol is drawn to scale. See figure L-5.

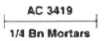

Figure L-5. FPF.

Target Reference Point (TRP)

Maneuver elements use an easily identifiable TRP to orient direct fire weapons systems. TRPs should only be identified in terms of the direct fire system, not the target numbering system. The symbol is the same as that for a standard target with a TRP letter. Only TRPs used as triggers for fire support events are integrated into the scheme of fires. Essential TRPs are included on internal lists of targets and identified in the remarks section as TRP. This provides observers direct interface with direct fire systems. See figure L-6.

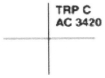

Figure L-6. TRP.

AFATDS Geometries

Figure L-7 on page L-6 shows how AFATDS displays target symbols. See MCRP 3-16.2A for specific instructions for AFATDS.

Geometry	Situation: Friendly (F) Enemy (E)	Border Color: Friendly (F) Enemy (E)	Current Symbol	Planned Symbol
Target Area of Interest	F	F-Blue	TAI Name	TAI Name
Point Target	F	F-Black	number altitude|description	number altitude|description
Rectangular Target	F	F-Black	number	number
Circular Target	F	F-Black	Number	Number
Linear Target	F	F-Black	number	number
Target Reference Point	F	F-Black	number	number

Figure L-7. AFATDS Targeting Geometries.

Target List Worksheet

The target list worksheet is a document that facilitates fire planning by the FSC (see fig. L-8) for a sample. It is a preliminary listing of all targets and their descriptions from which the FSC can select and plan. The U.S. Army publishes the worksheet as DA Form 4655R. The information contained on target list worksheets can be maintained and transmitted digitally as well. Instructions to prepare the DA Form 4655-R follow.

Heading

On the left hand side, place the unit that filled out the target list worksheet, the OPORD, and the DTG. On the right side, fill in the number of target list pages. Place the DATUM that the targets were described from. This may not always be WGS-84.

Line Number

This is an administrative control measure for internal use. Assign each target a line number.

Target Number

Assign each target a target number from the block of numbers given to the planning source.

Description

Enter a concise target description that is adequate for a decision on how the target should be attacked.

Location

Enter grid coordinates for point, rectangular, and circular targets. For linear targets, enter coordinates of the center point. If writing in the endpoints use two lines.

Altitude

Show the altitude of the target in meters, unless otherwise specified.

Attitude

Enter the attitude of linear and rectangular targets in grid azimuths.

Size (Length and Width)

Enter no dimensions for a point target, one dimension (length) for a linear target, two dimensions (length and width) for a rectangular target, or the radius of a circular target (width).

Source and/or Accuracy

The information in this column aids in determining how to attack the target. When known, enter the source and accuracy of the target data.

Remarks

Enter any special considerations for attack of the target such as requested munitions or method of attack.

1st Mar, 1st MARDIV OPORD _____ 070620ZFEB00	Target List Worksheet For use of this form see FM 6-20-40; Proponent agency is TRADOC								DATUM: WGS-84 SHEET____ of ____					
LINE NO	TARGET NO	DESCRIPTION	LOCATION	ALTITUDE	ATTITUDE	SIZE		SOURCE/ ACCURACY	REMARKS					
						LENGTH	WIDTH							
	a	b	c	d	e	f	g	h	i					
1	AC0001	120 mm Mortar Plt	499377											
2	AC0002	Rifle Company	516325						DPICM					
3	AC0003	Rifle Platoon	554296											
4	AC0004	OP	570281						VT 50%, WP 50%					
5	AC0005	MG Position	566260											
6	AC0006	Trail Intersection	572247						CP 11					

Figure L-8. Sample Target List Worksheet.

Target List Worksheet

For use of this form see FM 6-20-40; Proponent agency is TRADOC

DATUM: WGS-84

SHEET ___ of ___

| LINE NO | TARGET NO a | DESCRIPTION b | LOCATION c | ALTITUDE d | ATTITUDE e | SIZE | | SOURCE/ ACCURACY h | REMARKS i |
						LENGTH f	WIDTH g		

Figure L-9. Blank Target List Worksheet.

Work Columns

These columns are used to indicate targets that are to be included in a particular fire support schedule. Enter one diagonal line (/) under the appropriate column to show the target is to be included in a particular schedule. When the target has been scheduled, enter an opposing diagonal line, forming an X to show the action is complete.

Figure L-9 is a blank target list worksheet.

Automated Target List

Automated systems, such as AFATDS, will have the means to store, execute, and refine lists of targets. See figure L-10. Because of their storage capability, these automated systems can maintain several target lists at

once. These target lists include active, inactive, on-call, suspect, planned, and any named target lists.

TYPES OF PLANNED FIRES

Group of Targets

A group is two or more targets on which fire is desired simultaneously. A group of targets is designated by a letter/number/letter combination. It is graphically displayed by circling the targets. The first letter is that of the country (as assigned by the MAGTF or senior headquarters). The number is assigned sequentially as it is used. The last letter is the letter assigned to the unit planning the group. When planning groups of targets, consideration must be

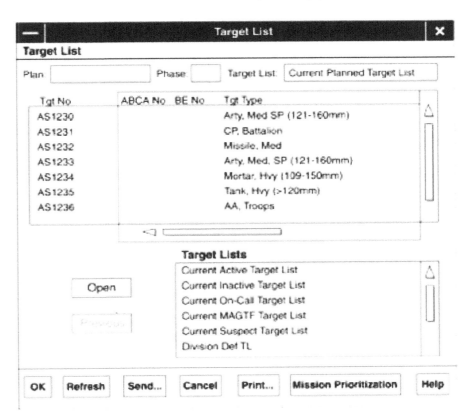

Figure L-10. Example of an AFATDS.

given to the number of firing units (artillery units [battery/battalion], mortar platoon, or NSFS) available. For NSFS, multiple targets may be assigned to a ship if the ship is equipped with multiple gun mounts and a surface fires control system which can accommodate the missions; e.g., MK-86 GFCS. Targets included in a group may be engaged individually if required. Groups are executed at a predetermined time, on-call, or when a certain event occurs. Figure L-11 illustrates the graphic designation of a group.

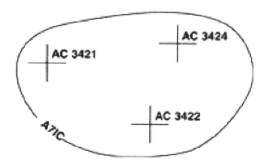

Figure L-11. Group of Targets.

Series of Targets

In artillery and NSFS, a number of targets and/or groups(s) of targets planned to support a maneuver phase. The targets in a series are fired in accordance with a time sequence. A series is given a nickname by the unit planning the series. A series may include mortars and CAS also. A series may be fired at a predetermined time, on-call, or when a certain event occurs. See figure L-12 for a graphic illustration of a series.

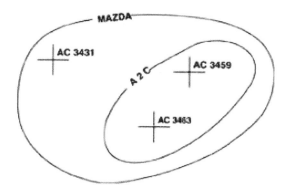

Figure L-12. Series of Targets.

Program of Targets

A program is the predetermined sequential attack of targets of a similar nature. It may be executed on-call, at a specific time, or when a particular event occurs. Targets are designated by their nature and based upon the commander's guidance. For example, in a counterfire program, all the targets are artillery system related OPs, artillery batteries, mortar platoon, CPs. Programs may be planned for various purposes; e.g., counterfire, SEAD, counter-OP, countermechanized. Programs are not graphically displayed.

Preparation Fire

Fire delivered on a target preparatory to an assault. (JP 1-02). It is an intense volume of fire delivered in accordance with a time schedule. The fires normally commence prior to H-hour and may extend beyond it. They may start at a prescribed time or be held on-call. The duration of the preparation is influenced by factors such as the fire support needs of the entire force, numbers of targets, and firing assets and ammunition available.

Preparation fires may not always be warranted. Factors influencing the commander's decision of whether or not to plan/execute a prep include availability of accurate targets, fire support and ammunition available, whether the benefits produced by the prep will offset the loss of surprise, and the time available. The timing and the execution of the prep should take into account the enemies ability to recover. The prep may include all supporting arms.

Critical targets may be identified for damage assessment. Observation on these targets can be achieved by various sources; e.g., reconnaissance teams, weapons locating radars of the artillery regiment. If desired effects have not been achieved, reattack may be required.

Generally, adjustments cannot be made during the preparation. Therefore, observers must refine target locations for all scheduled fires, and firing units must emphasize proper gunnery procedures to promote accurate fires. Procedures must be established to engage priority targets during the prep if necessary. These targets may be identified as on-call targets on the schedule. This may require a firing unit to be temporarily removed from the prep, engage the priority target, and then resume firing the prep. Firing units will notify the

FSCC of any assigned targets that were not engaged or that were only partially engaged.

Counterpreparation Fire

Intensive prearranged fire delivered when the imminence of the enemy attack is discovered. It is designed to: break up enemy formations; disorganize the enemy's systems of command, communications, and observation; decrease the effectiveness of artillery preparation; and impair the enemy's offensive spirit. (JP 1-02).

Barrage Fire

Fire which is designed to fill a volume of space or area rather than aimed specifically at a given target. (JP 1-02) Barrage fire is a prearranged technique for the engagement of targets of opportunity or planned targets. The target area is configured to effect the desired results. The target area may be defined to restrict the enemy's movement; e.g., avenue of approach or to isolate an enemy unit (prevent reinforcement or withdrawal). The volume and duration of fire is based on its intended effect and tactical situation. The fires may be delivered in a prearranged target configuration; e.g., a horseshoe pattern around the friendly position or in a random, sweeping manner throughout the target area.

Program Names in Automated Systems

AFATDS names programs and schedules of fire in accordance with the above paragraphs. However due to its fixed message formats, IFSAS can only name geometries and fireplans using six characters. Refer to FMFM 6-18-1/MCWP 3-16.2, *MCFSS*, appendix C, for the naming convention required by IFSAS. Below are some IFSAS naming convention examples:

SE21A6	2d Series established by 1st Bn, 6th Mar
CF1T10	1st Counterfire Program established by 10th Mar TPC
SA12MD	1st SEAD Program established by 2d MARDIV

SCHEDULING OF FIRE

The procedures provided in this paragraph are used in scheduling fires. The quick fire support plan form or the scheduling worksheet form may be used.

General Procedures for All Schedules

Worksheet

A separate worksheet is used for each schedule planned to support an operation. Groups may be recorded on the same worksheet.

Heading of Worksheet

The worksheet heading includes type/name of the schedule and the supported unit for which it is prepared.

Timing Block

To the right of the block labeled firing unit is the timing block. The fire planner writes the appropriate minute each hash mark is to indicate in the schedule; e.g., -6 through +4.

Firing Unit Line Number

Each firing unit is assigned its own line number in the schedule. Record the unit; e.g., 2/10, the caliber of weapon; e.g., 155, the type of weapon; e.g., T for towed or SP for self-propelled, and the firing unit; e.g., D.

Dots and Lines

For each target to be engaged by a single volley, indicate the TOT by a dot on the worksheet at the appropriate time. For each target to be fired with more than one volley, indicate the duration of the fires by drawing a horizontal line between the appropriate time lines. The first rounds will impact at the time corresponding with the beginning of the line, and the last rounds will impact at the time corresponding with the end of the line. The number of rounds fired depends on the rate of fire for scheduling. Figure L-13 on page L-12 illustrates the use of dots and lines on the worksheet.

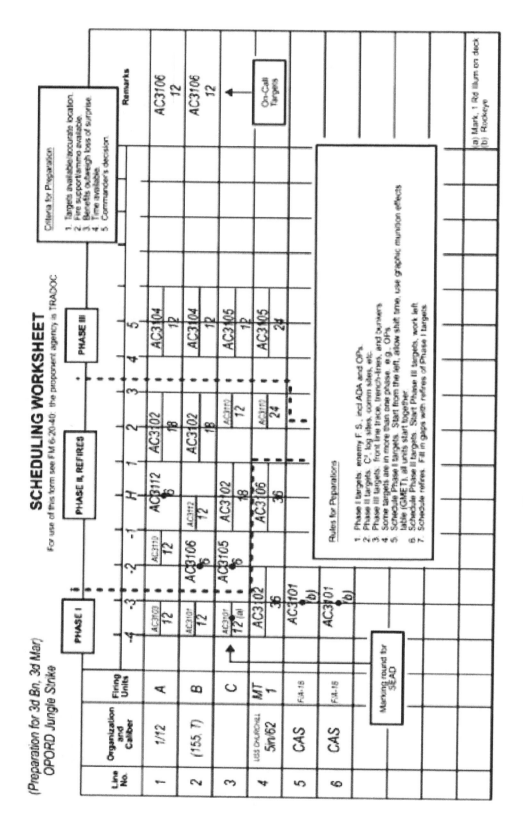

Figure L-13. Preparation Fires.

Damage Criteria

See chapter 3, section II.

Target Number and Ammunition

The target number is shown above the line/dot with the amount of ammunition to be fired below the line/dot. If the munition is other than standard, this is indicated by use of a subscript with specific instructions recorded in the remarks column. Remarks should be recorded one line beneath the last scheduled line.

Shift Times and Rates of Fire for Scheduling

Shift time is the length of time needed for the firing unit to cease firing on one target and commence firing on its next scheduled target. When scheduling fires, shift times must be allowed. Gaps (2 or more shift times) should be avoided, except in a series of targets. The number of rounds fired by a weapon in a specific duration (designated by length of line on scheduling worksheet) is based on the rates of fire in table L-10.

Table L-10. Rates of Fire.

Weapon	Rates of Fire For Scheduling	Shift Time
60mm mortar	20 rpm	1min
81mm mortar (M-252)	15 rpm	1min
155mm howitzer	1 rpm	1min
5"/62 naval gun	12 rpm	1min
5"/54 naval gun	20 rpm	1min

On-Call Targets

On-call targets for a particular schedule are indicated by recording the target number in the remarks column on the line of the assigned firing unit. Below the target number, show the number of rounds to be fired. Do not use a line or dot and ammunition entry. If a unit is ordered to fire on its on-call target while they are firing the schedule, the unit will leave the schedule, fire the on-call target at the maximum rate of fire, rejoin the schedule at the real time, and report those targets that were not engaged to the appropriate headquarters.

Instructions for Specific Schedules

Preparation Fires

Targets are divided into three categories. Phase I targets include hostile fire units; e.g., batteries, OPs, radars, anti-air defenses. Phase II targets include command and control; e.g., CPs, supply/logistics areas, communications sites. Phase III targets include front line elements; e.g., trench lines, dug in positions. If a target fits more than one category, categorize it where it poses the greatest threat.

Phase I targets are scheduled first, beginning from the left on the appropriate line(s) of the worksheet. (See fig. L-13 on page L-12.) All units must start firing at the same time. Phase III targets are scheduled next, beginning from the right. All units finish firing at the same time. Phase II targets are scheduled between phase I and III targets. Gaps are filled with re-fires of phase I targets. Units should, when possible, have commenced firing on the last targets in one phase before or at the same time that they begin firing on targets in the next phase.

Counterpreparation

Counterprep is fired in two phases with firing beginning and ending with all units participating and no gaps permitted. Phase I and phase III targets are scheduled together as one phase; then phase II targets are scheduled. Counterpreparation fires are always on-call and scheduled starting at 0 in the timing block.

Groups of Targets

The group schedule is normally on-call and is not scheduled for a time sequence. It is scheduled so that fires will strike the targets at the same time. The group number is shown in the timing block space. Below the group number, list the targets of the group opposite the firing unit assigned the target. Below each target number, show the number of rounds to be fired. No line or dot is drawn. More than one group for a given operation may be scheduled on the same scheduling worksheet. See figure L-14, on page L-14.

(Groups for 3d Mar)
OPORD Jungle Strike

SCHEDULING WORKSHEET

For use of this form see FM 6-20-40; the proponent agency is TRADOC.

DTM: WGS-84

SHEET 1 OF 1

Line No.	Organization and Caliber	Firing Units	(A1C)	(A2C)								Remarks
1	1/12	A	AC4403 18 (b)	AC3106 6								
2	(155, T)	B	AC3101 18 (b)									
3		C	AC3101 18 (b)	AC3106 6								
4	USS CHURCHILL 5in/62	MT 1	AC3102 36									a) HE/VT

Figure L-14. Groups.

Series of Targets

The series of targets are normally fired on-call and are scheduled starting at 0 on the timing line. Units are not required to commence and end firing together. There may be gaps in the schedule. Targets are not scheduled by category. The commander will normally indicate the sequence in which he wants the targets attacked. See figure L-15, on page L-16.

Programs of Targets

Programs of targets are fired on-call at the commander's request. Each type program is scheduled starting at 0 on the timing line and extended as long as needed. Instructions for completing the program are the same as those for the series of targets.

Countermechanized Programs

These fires must be scheduled to impact at the time intervals corresponding to the rate of march speed of the various echelons of the enemy formation. Table L-11 will assist the fire planner in scheduling countermechanized fires.

This table provides the time required to travel 1 kilometer (or 1 mile) while using specified march speeds. Travel times are calculated based on rates of march (miles/kilometers in 1 hour) and includes time for scheduled short halts and time lost due to road and traffic conditions. The time for long halts must be added to the total time traveled (miles or kilometers) by the travel time factor for 1 mile or 1 kilometer for the designator speed.

Table L-11. Time Distance Table.

Speed Miles/ Kilometers per hour	Rate of March Miles/ Kilometers In 1 Hour	Minutes to Travel 1 Kilometer/ 1 Mile
10 mph 16 kph	8 mph 12 kph	5/7.5
15 mph 24 kph	12 mph 20 kph	3/5
20 mph 32 kph	16 mph 25 kph	2.4/3.75
25 mph 40 kph	20 mph 32 kph	1.84/3
30 mph 48 kph	25 mph 40 kph	1.5/2.4
35 mph 56 kph	30 mph 46 kph	1.3/2
40 mi/h 64 km/h	35 mi/h 53 km/h	1.13/1.5

(Series Dog for 3d Bn, 3d Mar)
OPORD Jungle Strike

SCHEDULING WORKSHEET

For use of this form see FM 6-20-40; the proponent agency is TRADOC.

DTM WGS-84

SHEET 1 OF 1

Line No.	Organization and Caliber	Firing Units	1	2	3	4	5	6	7	Remarks
1	1/12	A	AC3403 18(a)		AC3106 6					
2	(155, T)	B	AC3101 18(a)			AC3102 18(a)				
3		C	AC3101 18(a)		AC3106 6(b)					
4	USS CHURCHILL 5in/62	MT 1		AC3102 36						(a) HE/VT (b) Provide WP Mark

Figure L-15. Series.

APPENDIX M. REPORTS

A decisionmaker needs good information to make good decisions. A report system provides essential information at a preestablished time or when the event occurs. Standardizing report formats facilitates passing information.

Figure M-1 shows report requirements for fire support coordination agencies, supporting arms representatives assigned to combat companies, and supporting arms units. See figures M-2 through M-8 for formats.

REPORT	FIG	SUBMITTING/FORWARDING AGENCY							
		FO	FAC	NGF SPOT	BN FSCC	REGT FSCC	DIV FSCC	ARTY FDC	NSFS SHIP
Firing Capabilities (FIRECAP)	X-2							HS	
Displacement Report (DISREP)	X-3							HS	
Shelling Report (SHELREP)	X-4	HA	HA	HA	HA	HA	S		
Guns Up Ready to Fire (GURF)	X-5								S
FLASHREP/SPOTREP/TAREP	X-6	H	H	H	H	H	A	S	
Naval Gunfire Support (NGFS)	X-7								S
Command Post Report (CPREP)	X-8							HS	
KEY:									
H - To higher headquarters S - To supported headquarters HS - To higher and supported headquarters				A - To supporting arms unit HA - To higher headquarters and supporting arms					

Figure M-1. Fire Support Coordination Reports.

Title: Fire Capabilities (FIRECAP) Report.
Purpose: To report artillery battery in position and ready to fire or to report a change in the number of weapons available.
Occasion: When the battery is ready to fire or when a change occurs in the number of weapons functioning.

ELEMENT	INFORMATION
Type of Report	FIRECAP
Line A	Unit (call sign)
Line B	Grid (encoded)
Line C	Azimuth of fire (in mils and encoded)
Line D	Number of weapons (encoded)
EXAMPLE:	
FIRECAP	To report battery ready to fire with 4 guns
Line A	A7W (call sign of battery)
Line B	714 438 (encoded)
Line C	0800 (encoded)
Line D	4 (encoded)
FIRECAP	To report change in number of guns able to fire
Line A	A7W (call sign of battery)
Line D	6 (encoded)
NOTE: Use only applicable lines.	

Figure M-2. FIRECAP.

Title: Displacement Report (DISREP).
Purpose: To report displacement of artillery battery.
Occasion: When unit displaces; i.e., can no longer fire.

ELEMENT	INFORMATION
Type of Report	DISREP
Line A	Unit
Line B	Time
Line C	Destination
Line D	Number of weapons
EXAMPLE	
DISREP	To report 4 guns displacing to new position
Line A	A7W (call sign of battery)
Line B	0710Z
Line C	714 438 (encoded)
Line D	4 (encoded)
NOTE: Use only applicable lines.	

Figure M-3. DISREP.

Title: Shelling Report (SHELREP).
Purpose:To report bombing, shelling or mortaring by the enemy.
Occasion: Submitted as soon as possible after incident.

ELEMENT	INFORMATION
Line A	Unit of origin
Line B	Position of observer
Line C	Direction in mils
Line D	Time from
Line E	Time to
Line F	Area bombed, shelled or mortared
Line G	Number and nature of guns; i.e., mortars, rockets
Line H	Nature of fire
Line I	Number, type, and caliber of weapons
Line J	Time of flash to bang
Line K	Damage
EXAMPLE:	
Line A	Current call sign, address, group, or code name
Line B	Encode if headquarters or important OP or column F gives information on location
Line C	Measured clockwise from grid North in degrees or mils (state which) of flash, sound or groove of shell (state which) Omit for aircraft
Line D	Time from
Line E	Time to
Line F	Grid reference in clear or direction to impact in degrees or mils, distance in meters
Line G	Mortar, rocket launchers, aircraft, or other methods of delivery
Line H	Registration, bombardment, harassing, etc.
Line I	State whether measured or assumed of shells, rockets, missiles, or bombs
Line J	Omit for aircraft
Line K	Encode if required

NOTE: Use only applicable lines.

Figure M-4. SHELREP.

Title: Guns up Ready to Fire (GURF) Report.
Purpose:To report NGF ship capabilities.
Occasion: When ship comes on station.

ELEMENT	INFORMATION
Type of Report	GURF Report
Line A	Call sign of ship and DTG of message assigning ship to the NGF mission
Line B	"On station and ready" and DTG (local) end of NGF ship's assignment
Line C	Planned firing location (grid coordinates). If the ship will be firing from a track, enter the approximate center of the track
Line D	Significant reduction in capability, including mount casualties and/or ammunition shortages
Line E	Ammunition aboard, by type, available for NGF
Line F	Any other information of value
EXAMPLE:	
GURF	
Line A	A2W, 012100Z NOV 00
Line B	On station and ready, 022200P NOV 00
Line C	LB 614 212
Line D	High explosive 60, white phosphorus 15
Line E	High explosive 140, white phosphorus 60
Line F	Starting 021700P AUG 00, off station for 60 minutes for ammo resupply

NOTE: Use only applicable lines.

Figure M-5. GURF Report.

Title: FLASHREP/SPOTREP/TAREP and Follow-Up Reports.	
Purpose: Target reports (TAREPs) are used to pass target data.	
Occasion. When potential target is discovered or after attack of significant target or target on target list.	
ELEMENT	**INFORMATION**
Type of Report	
Line A	Precedence: Flash/Immediate/Priority/Routine
Line B	Reporting Unit
Line C	Time: DTG of Report DTG of Incident
Line D	Reference: Original SPOTREP DTG or Target Number
Line E	Location: Enemy Friendly
Line F	Incident Description: Target Description Vulnerability Accuracy of Location (In Meters) Size, Shape, and Orientation (In Meters and Mils) Associated/Equipment or Units
Line G	Action Taken:
Line H	Friendly Casualties: KIA WIA MIA
Line I	Enemy Casualties: KIA EPW
Line J	Enemy Weapons/Equipment/Documents Captured:
Line K	Friendly Weapons/Equipment Damaged/Destroyed/Lost:
Line L	Remarks:

NOTE: Use only applicable lines. The group of digits must always be preceded by the block of two capitals designating the 100km square; e.g., LB6448 (STANAG No. 2029). *(*See FM 6-121, Field Artillery Target Acquisition.)When reporting attack or target or result of attack, include lines C2 (DTG of incident) and E1 (location of enemy). Intelligence agencies need this information.

Figure M-6. FLASHREP/SPOTREP/TAREP.

NGFS REPORT		
Firing Ship Call Sign		Date-Time Group
REPORT (CHECK ONE)	**INCLUDE ITEMS**	**TYPE OF REPORT**
[ ] CANDY	ALFA, BRAVO, CHARLIE, DELTA, ECHO, & FOXTROT	MISSION BEGINS
[ ] HONEY	ALFA, BRAVO, CHARLIE, & INDIA	NEW TARGET SIGHTED
[ ] PICKLE	BRAVO, CHARLIE, & GOLF	TARGET NOT FIRED
[ ] PEPPER	HOTEL	CURRENT AMMO SUMMARY
ALFA	Type of Mission	
BRAVO	Target Number and Grid Coordinates	
CHARLIE	Target Description	
DELTA	Agency Controlling Fire - Voice Call	
ECHO	Target Assessment - Destroyed, Neutralized, Details	
FOXTROT	Ammunition Expended - Code, Number, type, & Caliber	
GOLF	Reason Target Not Fired On	
HOTEL	Enter Using Code, Amount, Type, & Caliber of Each Type of Bombardment Ammunition Remaining	
INDIA	Action Taken or Contemplated	

NOTE: Use only applicable lines.

Figure M-7. NGFS REPORT.

Title: Command Post Report (CPREP).	
Purpose: To report the time of opening and closing of the CP and the location of the new CP.	
Occasion: When a CP is opened and closed.	
ELEMENT	**INFORMATION**
Type of Report	CPREP
Line A	Unit (call sign)
Line B	Location (encoded)
Line C	Date-time group CP established
EXAMPLE:	
CPREP	CPREP
Line A	W1P
Line B	742 210 (encoded)
Line C	160800Z AUG 00

NOTE: Use only applicable lines.

Figure M-8. CPREP.

APPENDIX N. SAMPLE FSCC STATUS BOARD AND SHEET FORMATS

Available Fire
Support Agencies

	Mortars			CAS		DTG	Time Ammo Status Updated
	Field Artillery			TA			
	NSFS			Other			

Unit	Location	Call Sign	Frequency	Tactical Mission/ Weapons Status	Type	Amount (Number of Guns)	Remarks

Figure N-1. FSCC Status Board.

Priority Targets/FPF					Fire Support Coordinating Measures			
Supported Unit	Unit to Fire	Target Number	Shell/Fuze Combination	DTG Effective	FSCM	Establishing Unit	DTG Effective	Location
Remarks:								

Figure N-2. FSCC Status Sheet.

APPENDIX O. FIRE SUPPORT REFERENCE DATA

Tactical Missions	INHERENT RESPONSIBILITIES						
Arty Unit with Mission of	Answers Calls for Fire in Priority From	Has As Its Zone of Fire	Furnishes Forward Observers	Establishes Liaison With	Establishes Comm With	Is Positioned By	Has Its Fires Planned By
DIRECT SUPPORT	1. Supported unit. 2. Own observers. 3. Higher artillery headquarters.	Zone of supported unit.	To each company sized maneuver element of supported unit.	Supported unit (down to battalion level).	Supported unit.	Unit commander as deemed necessary or ordered by higher artillery headquarters.	Develops own fire plan.
REINFORCING	1. Reinforced unit. 2. Own observers. 3. Higher artillery headquarters.	Zone of fire of reinforced unit.	No requirement.	Reinforced unit.	Reinforced unit.	Reinforced unit or ordered by higher artillery headquarters.	Reinforced unit.
GENERAL SUPPORT-REINFORCING	1. Higher artillery headquarters. 2. Reinforced unit. 3. Own observers.	Zone of supported unit to include zone of fire of reinforced unit.	No requirement.	Reinforced unit.	Reinforced unit.	Higher artillery head-quarters or reinforced unit subject to prior approval by higher artillery headquarters.	Higher artillery headquarters.
GENERAL SUPPORT	1. Higher artillery headquarters.	Zone of supported unit.	No inherent responsibility.	No inherent responsibility.	No inherent responsibility.	Higher artillery head-quarters.	Higher artillery headquarters.

Figure O-1. Artillery Tactical Missions.

Written in operation orders or plans as follows:	2/10 (155, T): DS 6th Mar 5/10 (155, T): GS		
Artillery Unit	**Caliber/T:Towed,SP: Self-Prop**	**Mission Assigned**	**Supported unit; not req for GS**
2nd Bn, 10th Mar	(155: T);	DS	6th Mar
5th Bn, 10th Mar	(155,T)	GS	Highest maneuver HQ through senior artillery HQ
On-order missions are written as follows: 1st Bn, 14th Mar (155, T): GSR 2d Bn, 14th Mar, O/O DS 24th Mar			
Nonstandard missions are written as follows: 1st Bn, 10th Mar (155, T): GS 2d MarDiv, 2d PCFF 2d LAR Bn until 131600R NOV* * 1st Bn is GS to the division, but 2d priority in calls for fire (PCFF) is to 2d LAR Bn.			

Figure O-2. Formats for Assigning Artillery Units Tactical Missions.

Ship with a Mission of	Normally Assigned in Support of	Has Its Fires Planned by	Positioned by
DIRECT SUPPORT	Committed Battalions	SFCP	Navy Amphib Commander
GENERAL SUPPORT	Regiment and/or Division	Supported Unit	Navy Amphib Commander

Figure O-3. Naval Gunfire Tactical Missions.

Mortar Platoon or Element with a Mission of	Normally Assigned in Support of	Has Its Fires Planned by	Positioned by
DIRECT SUPPORT	Company	Supported Unit	Mortar Platoon Commander
GENERAL SUPPORT	Battalion	Battalion	Mortar Platoon Commander

Figure O-4. Mortar Tactical Missions.

Weapon	Max Range (m) Full Charge	RAP	Max Range (m) Reduced Charge	Rate of Fire Per Tube (MAX/SUST)	Ammo	Fuzes
5"/54	23,100	29,181	12,200	20/20	HE, HC, ILLUM, WP, RAP, ICM (Mk 172)	Q, MT, CVT, VT, DEL
5"/62	82,000 (ERGM) 40,000 (Mk 172 ICM) 23,100 (Conv)	29,181	12,200	10/3-5 (ERGM) 20/10-12 (Conv)	HE, HC, ILLUM, WP, RAP, ERGM, ICM (Mk172)	Q, MT, CVT, VT, DEL, GPS
LASM	300,000	N/A	N/A	N/A	HE, Blast fragmentation	
LEGEND:	CVT–controlled variable time DEL–delay HC–high capacity		HE–high explosive ILLUM–illumination MT–mechanical time GPS–global positioning system		Q–quick RAP–rocket assisted projectile VT–variable time WP–white phosphorus	

Figure O-5. Naval Gunfire Weapon Systems.

Hull #	Name	Armament	GFCS	Hull #	Name	Armament	GFCS
Ticonderoga Class (CG), 27 Ships, Active As Of Oct 2001							
CG 47	Ticonderoga	2 - 5"/54	MK-86	CG 61	Monterey	2 - 5"/54	MK-86
CG 48	Yorktown	2 - 5"/54	MK-86	CG 62	Chancellorsville	2 - 5"/54	MK-86
CG 49	Vincennes	2 - 5"/54	MK-86	CG 63	Cowpens	2 - 5"/54	MK-86
CG 50	Valley Forge	2 - 5"/54	MK-86	CG 64	Gettysburg	2 - 5"/54	MK-86
CG 51	Thomas S. Gates	2 - 5"/54	MK-86	CG 65	Chosin	2 - 5"/54	MK-86
CG 52	Bunker Hill	2 - 5"/54	MK-86	CG 66	Hue City	2 - 5"/54	MK-86
CG 53	Mobile Bay	2 - 5"/54	MK-86	CG 67	Shiloh	2 - 5"/54	MK-86
CG 54	Antietam	2 - 5"/54	MK-86	CG 68	Anzio	2 - 5"/54	MK-86
CG 55	Leyte Gulf	2 - 5"/54	MK-86	CG 69	Vicksburg	2 - 5"/54	MK-86
CG 56	San Jacinto	2 - 5"/54	MK-86	CG 70	Lake Erie	2 - 5"/54	MK-86
CG 57	Lake Champlain	2 - 5"/54	MK-86	CG 71	Cape St George	2 - 5"/54	MK-86
CG 58	Philippine Sea	2 - 5"/54	MK-86	CG 72	Vella Gulf	2 - 5"/54	MK-86
CG 59	Princeton	2 - 5"/54	MK-86	CG 73	Port Royal	2 - 5"/54	MK-86
CG 60	Normandy	2 - 5"/54	MK-86				
Arleigh Burke Class (DDG), 32 Ships Active, 19 Under Construction As Of Oct 2001							
DDG 51	Arleigh Burke	1 - 5"/54	MK-34	DDG 67	Cole	1 - 5"/54	MK-34
DDG 52	Barry	1 - 5"/54	MK-34	DDG 68	The Sullivans	1 - 5"/54	MK-34
DDG 53	John Paul Jones	1 - 5"/54	MK-34	DDG 69	Milius	1 - 5"/54	MK-34
DDG 54	Curtis Wilbur	1 - 5"/54	MK-34	DDG 70	Hopper	1 - 5"/54	MK-34
DDG 55	Stout	1 - 5"/54	MK-34	DDG 71	Ross	1 - 5"/54	MK-34
DDG 56	John S. McCain	1 - 5"/54	MK-34	DDG 72	Mahan	1 - 5"/54	MK-34
DDG 57	Mitscher	1 - 5"/54	MK-34	DDG 73	Decatur	1 - 5"/54	MK-34
DDG 58	Laboon	1 - 5"/54	MK-34	DDG 74	McFaul	1 - 5"/54	MK-34
DDG 59	Russell	1 - 5"/54	MK-34	DDG 75	Donald Cook	1 - 5"/54	MK-34
DDG 60	Paul Hamilton	1 - 5"/54	MK-34	DDG 76	Higgins	1 - 5"/54	MK-34
DDG 61	Ramage	1 - 5"/54	MK-34	DDG 77	O'Kane	1 - 5"/54	MK-34
DDG 62	Fitzgerald	1 - 5"/54	MK-34	DDG 78	Porter	1 - 5"/54	MK-34
DDG 63	Stethem	1 - 5"/54	MK-34	DDG 79	Oscar Austin	1 - 5"/54	MK-34
DDG 64	Carney	1 - 5"/54	MK-34	DDG 80	Roosevelt	1 - 5"/54	MK-34
DDG 65	Benfold	1 - 5"/54	MK-34	DDG 81	Winston S. Churchill	1 - 5"/54	MK-34
DDG 66	Gonzalez	1 - 5"/54	MK-34	DDG 82	Lassen	1 - 5"/54	MK-34
Spruance Class (DD), 28 Ships, Active As Of Oct 2001							
DD 963	Spruance	2 - 5"/54	MK-86	DD 977	Briscoe	2 - 5"/54	MK-86
DD 964	Paul F Foster	2 - 5"/54	MK-86	DD 978	Stump	2 - 5"/54	MK-86
DD 965	Kinkaid	2 - 5"/54	MK-86	DD 982	Nicholson	2 - 5"/54	MK-86
DD 967	Elliot	2 - 5"/54	MK-86	DD 985	Cushing	2 - 5"/54	MK-86
DD 968	Arthur W Radford	2 - 5"/54	MK-86	DD 987	O'Bannon	2 - 5"/54	MK-86
DD 969	Peterson	2 - 5"/54	MK-86	DD 988	Thorn	2 - 5"/54	MK-86
DD 970	Caron	2 - 5"/54	MK-86	DD 989	Deyo	2 - 5"/54	MK-86
DD 971	David R Ray	2 - 5"/54	MK-86	DD 991	Fife	2 - 5"/54	MK-86
DD 972	Oldendorf	2 - 5"/54	MK-86	DD 992	Fletcher	2 - 5"/54	MK-86
DD 973	John Young	2 - 5"/54	MK-86	DD 997	Hayler	2 - 5"/54	MK-86
DD 975	OBrien	2 - 5"/54	MK-86				
LEGEND:	CG - guided missile cruiser DDG - guided missile destroyer DD - destroyer						

Figure O-6. Naval Gunfire Platforms.

Caliber	105mm[1]	105mm[1]	155mm	155mm[1]	227mm[1]	607mm[1]
Model	M102	M119A1	M198	M109A5/A6	MLRS	ATACMS
Ammunition	HE, HC, WP, ILLUM, APICM	HE, HC, WP, ILLUM, APICM, DPICM	HE, HC, WP, ILLUM, APICM, DPICM, M825 SMK, FASCAM CPHD	HE, HC, WP, ILLUM, APICM, DPICM, M825 SMK, FASCAM CPHD	DPICM	APAM
Fuzes	PD, VE, MT, MTSQ, CP, DELAY	PD, VT, MT, MTSQ, CP, DELAY	PD, VT, MT, MTSQ, DELAY	PD, VT, MT, MTSQ, DELAY	ET	ET
Maximum Range (meters)	11,400	11,500	18,300 22,000[4]	18,200 21,700[4]	32,000[1] 45,000[5] 60,000[6]	165,000[1] 300,000[7]
Range of RAP (meters)	15,300	19,500	30,100	30,000		
Range of DPICM (meters)	10,500	14,100	18,000 28,200[8]	17,900 28,100[8]		
Minimum Range (meters)					10,000 13,000	25,000 70,000
Maximum Rate of Fire (rounds per minute)	10	10	4	4	12/40 sec	2/20 sec
Sustained Rate of Fire (rounds per minute)	3	3	2	1	N/A	N/A
Illum Time (Seconds)	75	75	120	120		
HE Burst Width (1 round)	35	35	50	50	100	
FPF	210 6 guns	210 6 guns	300 6 guns	300 6 guns 150 3 guns	N/A	N/A

Figure O-7. Characteristics of U.S. Mortars, Artillery, and Rockets.

Caliber	60mm	81mm	120mm
Model	M224	M252	M285
Ammunition	HE, WP, ILLUM	HE, WP, RP, ILLUM	HE, WP, ILLUM
Fuzes	MO	MO	MO
Maximum Range (meters)	3,500[2]	5,600[3]	7,200[1]
Minimum Range (meters)	75	70	200
Maximum Rate of Fire (rounds per minute)	30	35	15
Sustained Rate of Fire (rounds per minute)	20	15	5
Illum Time (seconds)	25	60	70
HE Burst Width (1 round)	28	35	60
FPF	90 3 tubes	35 1 tube	60 1 tube

NOTES: 1. USMC units do not have these weapon systems. USMC units may operate with Army units equipped with these weapons.
2. With M720 ammunition.
3. With M821 ammunition.
4. With M795 HE, M825 Smk ammunition.
5. Extended Range MLRS was fielded in FY 99.
6. Guided MLRS to be fielded in FY 02.
7. Block 1A ATACMS was fielded in FY 98.
8. Base Burn DPICM M864.

LEGEND: APICM–antipersonnel improved conventional munitions.
BB–base burn
CPHD–copperhead
DPICM–dual-purpose improved conventional munitions.
ET–electronic time
HE–high explosive
ILLUM–illumination

MO–multi-option fuze, VT, PD, Delay
MT–mechanical time
MTSQ–mechanical time superquick
PD–point detonating
RAP–rocket assisted projectile
RP–red phosphorus
SMK–smoke
VT–variable time
WP–white phosphorus

Figure O-7. Characteristics of U.S. Mortars, Artillery, and Rockets (Continued).

Type of Aircraft	Comm Package	Navigation	Guns	Conventional Ordnance		Laser Equipment	
				External	Max Load	Tracker	Designator
AV-8B	2 UHF	TACAN INS Radar **	25mm 300 rounds	LGBs AGM-65 Maverick General-purpose bombs CBUs Napalm 2.75" rockets 5.00" rockets LUU-2 flares 25-mm cannon AGM-122 Sidearm	8,000 lbs	Yes (ARBS) No (Radar)	No
AH-1W	2 UHF * 2 VHF-AM * 2 VHF-FM *	TACAN ADF FM Homer Radar Beacon	20mm 750 rounds or 20mm Pod 300 rounds	2.75 Rockets 5.0 Rockets TOW missile Hellfire SIDEARM	2,500 lbs	No	Yes
F/A-18C	2 UHF * 2 VHF-AM * 2 VHF-FM *	TACAN ADF INS Radar FLIR	20mm 580 rounds	All	13,700 lbs	Yes (Pod)	Yes
F/A-18D	2 UHF * 2 VHF-AM * 2 VHF-FM *	TACAN ADF INS Radar FLIR	20mm 515 rounds	All	13,500 lbs	Yes (Pod)	Yes
A-10	UHF VHF-AM VHF-FM	TACAN INS	30mm 1,100 rounds	All	16,000 lbs	Yes (Pod)	No
AH-64	UHF VHF-AM VHF-FM	TACAN ADF Doppler	30mm 1,200 rounds	70 mm rocket Hellfire	3,000 lbs	Yes	Yes
F-16	UHF * VHF-AM * VHF-FM *	TACAN ADF INS Radar ILS	20mm 515 rounds	All	12,000 lbs	No	Yes ***
F-15E	UHF	TACAN ADF INS Radar ILS	20mm 512 rounds	All	13,220 lbs	No	Yes ***

* Can only monitor two frequencies at a time.
** AV-8B "Plus" is equipped with radar.
*** F-16C/D and F-15E can designate if equipped with a LANTRN pod.

LEGEND: ADF–automatic direction finder
        ARBS–angle rate bombing system
        FAE–fuel air explosive
        FLIR–forward looking infrared
        ILS–instrument landing system

INS–inertial navigation system
TACAN–tactical air navigation system
TOW–tube launched, optically tracked, wire command link, guided missile system

Figure O-8. U.S. Aircraft Capabilities Guide.

Weapon	Effective Range (m)	Maximum Load (rounds)
2.75RX, 10-lb	7,500	76
2.75RX, 17-lb	6,000	76
2.75 MK 66/M151 22.95-lb	6,900	38
7.62mm minigun	1,000	5,000
.50 Cal machine gun	1,830	500
20mm cannon	1,500	750
30mm cannon	3,000	1,200
40mm grenade launcher	1,600	265
TOW	3750	8

Figure O-9. Aviation Direct Fire Weapons Systems Ranges.

Type Munitions	Remarks
General Purpose (GP) Bombs	
MK-82, LD, 500 lb.; MK-83, LD, 1000 lb.; MK84, LD, 2000 lb.	All are similar in construction and vary only in size and weight. Streamlined cylindrical body with conical fins designed for low drag. Effects: Blast, fragmentation and deep cratering (with a delayed fuze).
MK-82 HDGP (SNAKE-EYE)	MK-82 with four MK-15 retarding fins. Selectable high (HD) or low drag (LD). Effects: Blast, fragmentation and deep cratering (with a delayed fuze).
MK-82 Air Inflatable Retarder (Air) HDGP	General purpose bombs with AIR tail assembly.
MK-84 (AIR) HDGP	Uses a ballute as a retarding device. Selectable HD/LD. Effects: Blast and fragmentation.
MK-36 (Destructor)	MK-82 snake-eye with a MK-75 arming kit which converts the bomb into a land or water mine. HD only. Timed self-destruct or magnetic fuzing.
BLU-109/B (I-2000) Penetrator Bomb	2000 lb. improved GP bomb. Effects: Cratering and hard target penetration.
M-1 17, 750 lb. GP Bomb	Effects: Blast, fragmentation and deep cratering (with a delayed fuze).
M-1 17R	Selectable HD/LD by means of a retarding tail assembly.
M-1 17D (Destructor)	Equipped with a MK-75 arming kit for ground implant and shallow water mining. HD only.
M-118 3000 lb. Demolition Bomb	Effects: Blast, fragmentation and cratering. Not good for penetration.
Guided Bombs	
GBU-10/GBU-12	Laser-guided, maneuverable, free-falling weapons. GBU-10 is a MK-84 and the GBU-12 is a MK-82. Effects: Blast, fragmentation and deep cratering (with a delayed fuze).
GBU-16	Laser-guided, maneuverable, free-falling weapons. Effects: Blast, fragmentation and deep cratering (with a delayed fuze).
GBU-24/B LLLGB	Low level, laser-guided, maneuverable free-fall weapon. MK-84 body. Can be released at very low altitudes. Bomb bumps up approx. 450 ft above release altitude. Effects: Blast and fragmentation.
GBU-24A/B LLLGB	Same as GBU-24/B but uses BL-109/B bomb body. Used for hard target penetration.
GBU-15	TV or IR guided, automatically or manually by the WSO. MK-84 or MK-109 body. Effects: Blast, fragmentation, cratering and hard target penetration.
Missiles	
AGM-65 (Maverick)	A and B models are guided based o visual contrast. D and G models use IR guidance. The Marine Corps E model is laser guided. Designed for standoff acquisition and destruction of point targets. Effects: Shaped charge produces a good penetration of hard targets such as tanks and bunkers.
AGM-130	Rocket powered version of GBU-15. Standoff range out to 15 nautical miles (NM).

Figure O-10. Munitions Description.

Type Munitions	Remarks
AGM-114B (Hellfire)	Solid propellant laser/radar guided antiarmor missile. Max range in excess of 8000 meters.
Guns	
20mm	750 to 850 rounds per minute. AP, HE and incendiary.
20mm Gattling	2500 to 6000 rounds per minute. TP, HEI, API, TPI, HEIT.
Cluster Bombs	
GAU-8, 30mm Gattling	42000 rounds per minute. 1.5 lb. projectile TP, HEI, API on the A/OA-10 only.
CBU-24	SUU-30 LOADED WITH 665 BLU-26 BOMBLETS. The BLU-26 submunition is baseball sized, spins to arm and detonates on impact. Dispersion pattern is torus or donut shaped.
CBU-30	SUU-13 with 40 canisters containing 32 CS bomblets each. Bomblets will start dispensing CS gas 5 to 6 seconds after release and will dispense for 10 to 15 seconds. Dispersion is linear.
CBU-38	SUU-13 containing 40 BLU-49 antimaterial HE bomblets that will penetrate jungle canopies. Dispersion is linear.
CBU-49	Same as CBU-24 except bomblets have delay timers to detonate at random times after impact. Dispersion pattern is torus or donut shaped.
CBU-52	SUU-30 loaded with 220 BLU-61 softball sized bomblets with an incendiary lining and a scored steel casing for fragmentation. Dispersion pattern is torus or donut shaped.
CBU-55	Slow sped Fuel Air Explosive (FAE). Used against blast sensitive targets. Kills by overpressure.
CBU-58	SUU-30 loaded with 650 BLU-63 baseball sized bomblets with incendiary pellets and scored casing for fragmentation. Dispersion pattern is torus or donut shaped.
CBU-71	Same as CBU-58 except submunitions have delay fuzes that detonate at random times after impact. Dispersion pattern is torus or donut shaped.
CBU-87 (Combined Effects Munitions [CEM])	SUU-65 loaded with 202 BLU-97 bomblets. BLU-97 has a shaped charge for armor; steel scored liner for fragmentation and incendiary ring. Dispersion is rectangular.
CBU-89 (GATOR)	SUU-64 loaded with a mix of 72 BLU-91/B antiarmor and 22 BLU-92/B antipersonnel mines with preset self-destruct time. Dispersion pattern varies from circular at high angles to linear at low angles.
CBU-97/B (Sensor Fused Weapons)	SUU-64 with an airbag dispensing system and 10 BLU-108/B submunitions designed to provide multiple kills per pass capability against tanks, armored vehicles, artillery, APC's and support vehicles.
MK-20 (Rockeye)	MK-7 loaded with 247 MK-118 antiarmor submunitions with antipersonnel capabilities. Dispersion pattern varies from circular at high angles to linear at low angles.
BL-755	European munitions loaded with 147 antiarmor submunitions. Designed for low altitude low angle deliveries against armor but produces more fragmentation than the MK-20 Rockeye. Dispersion pattern is rectangular.
GBU-55/72	High speed FAE. Used against blast sensitive targets. Kills by overpressure.

Figure O-10. Munitions Description (Continued).

Risk-Estimate Distances

See figures O-11 and O-12. The term "danger close" is used when there are friendly troops or positions within a prescribed distance of the target, specifically 600 meters for cannon artillery. This is simply a warning and not a restriction to both the maneuver commander and the fire direction center to take proper precautions. Risk-estimate distances are defined as the distance in meters from the intended center of impact at which a specific degree of risk and vulnerability will not be exceeded. The casualty criterion is the 5-minute assault criterion for a prone soldier in winter clothing and helmet. The probability of incapacitation (PI) means that a soldier is physically unable to function in an assault within a 5-minute period after an attack. The 0.1 percent PI value can be interpreted as being less than or equal to one chance in a thousand. The ground commander must accept risk when targets are inside 0.1 percent PI. These distances in figures O-11 and O-12 are designed for wartime and should not be applied for peace-time training.

Item/ System	Description	Risk Estimate Distances (Meters)					
		10% PI			0.1% PI		
		1/3	2/3	Max range	1/3	2/3	Max range
M102/M119	105mm Howitzer	85	85	90	175	200	275
M109/M198	155mm Howitzer	100	100	125	200	280	450
M109/M198	155mm DPICM	150	180	200	280	300	475
M270A1	MLRS	TBD	TBD	TBD	TBD	TBD	2 km
M270A1	ATACMS	TBD	TBD	TBD	TBD	TBD	5 km
M224	60mm mortar	60	65	65	100	150	175
M29/M29A	81mm mortar	75	80	80	165	185	230
M30	107mm (4.2in) mortar	TBD	TBD	TBD	TBD	TBD	TBD
M120	120mm mortar	TBD	TBD	TBD	TBD	TBD	TBD
NSFS MK-45	5"/54 gun	210	225	250	450	450	600

Figure O-11. Risk Estimates Distances for Indirect Fire Assets.

Item	Description	Distance (meters)	
		10% PI	0.1% PI
MK-82 LD	500 lb bomb	250	425
MK-82 HD	500 lb bomb (retarded)	100	375
MK-82 LGB	500 lb bomb (GBU-12)	250*	425*
MK-83 HD	1,000 lb bomb	275	475
MK-83 LD	1,000 lb bomb	275	475
MK-83 LGB	1,000 lb bomb (GBU-16)	275*	475*
MK-84 HD/LD	2,000 lb bomb	325	500
MK-84 LGB	2,000 lb bomb (GBU-10/24)	225*	500*
MK-20**	Rockeye	150	225
MK-77	500 lb Napalm	100	150
CBU-55/77**	Fuel-air explosive	*	*
CBU-52**	CBU (all types)	275	450
CBU-58/71** ***	CBU (all types)	350	525
CBU-87**	CBU (all types)	175	275
CBU-89/78**	CBU (all types)	175	275
2.75" FFAR	Rocket with various warheads	160	200
SUU-11	7.62mm minigun	*	*
M-4, M-12, SUU-23, M-61	20mm Gattling gun	100	150
CAU-12	25mm gun	100	150
GPU-5a, GAU-8	30mm Gattling gun	100	150
AGM-65*****	Maverick (TV, IIR, laser-guided)	25	100
MK-1/MK-21	Walleye II (1,000 lb. TV-guided bomb)	275	500
MK-5/MK-23	Walleye II (2,400 lb. TV-guided bomb)	*	*
AC-130	105mm canon 40/25/20mm	80**** 35	200** 125

* Risk-estimate distances are to be determined. For LGBs, the values shown are for weapons that do not guide and that follow a ballistic trajectory similar to GP bombs. This does not apply to GBU-24 bombs, because GBU-4s do not follow a ballistic trajectory.

** Not recommended for use near troops in contact.

*** CBU-71/CBU84 bombs contain time-delay fuzes, which detonate at random times after impact. CBU-89 bombs are antitank and antipersonnel mines and are not recommended for use near troops in contact.

**** AC-130 estimates are based on worse case scenarios. The 105mm round described is the M-1 HE round with M-731 proximity fuze. Other fuzing would result in smaller distances. These figures are accurate throughout the firing orbit. The use of no-fire headings has no benefits for reducing risk-estimate distances and should not be used in contingency situations.

***** The data listed applies only AGM-65 A, B, C and D models. AGM-65 E and G models contain a larger warhead and risk-estimate distances are not currently available.

Figure O-12. Risk Estimate Distances for Aviation Munitions.

Manufacturer/ Weapon	Basic Range (meters)	BB/RAP Range (meters)	Rate of Fire		Countries Possessing	Remarks
			Max	Sust		
AUSTRIA						
GHN-45, 155mm Towed	30,300	39,600	7/min	2/min	Iran, Iraq, Thailand	None
BRAZIL						
ASTROS II, MRL	---	30,000 60,000	32/min 4/min	Reload Reload	Saudi Arabia, Iran, Qatar	None
CHINA						
WS-1, 320mm MRL	---	80,000	4/min	Reload	None	None
Type 83, 273mm MRL Type 71,	---	40,000	4/min	Reload	None	None
180mm MRL	---	20,000	10/min	Reload	None	None
WA 021, 155mm Towed Type 83,	30,000	39,000	5/min	2/min	None	None
152mm Towed Type 82/85,	30,400	38,000	4/min	2/min	Iraq	None
130mm MRL Type 59-1, 130mm	---	15,000	60/5min	Reload	Thailand	None
Towed	27,500	38,000	10/min	10/min	Iran, Iraq, Oman, N Korea, Egypt, Lebanon	None
FRANCE						
GCT, 155mm SP	23,000	29,000	6/min	2/min	Iraq, Kuwait, Saudi Arabia	None
GCT, 155 Towed	24,000	32,000	3/18sec	6/min	Cyprus	None
MkF3, 155mm SP	20,000	25,000	3/min	1/min	Iraq, Kuwait, UAE	None
GERMANY						
PzH 2000, 155mm SP	30,000	40,000	3/10sec	9/min	None	None
IRAN						
N10, 450mm MRL	---	150,000	1/min	2/hour	None	None
IRAQ						
ABABEL 100, 400mm MRL	---	100,000	4/min	Reload	None	None
ABABEL 50, 262mm MRL	---	50,000	12/min	Reload	Frmr Yugoslavia, Bosnia Serb Army, Croatia	None
ISRAEL						
845, 155mm Towed	24,000	39,000	5/min	2/min	None	None
M71, 155mm Towed	23,500	30,000	5/min	2/min	Singapore, Thailand, South Africa	None
ITALY						
PALMARIA, 155mm SP	24,700	30,000	3/20sec	4/min	Libya, Nigeria	None
LEGEND:	BB–base burn CHEM–chemical munitions capable INA–information not available LGM–laser-guided munitions capable		MRL–multiple rocket launcher NUKE–nuclear munitions capable SP–self-propelled			

Figure O-13. World Artillery, Mortars, and Rocket Launchers.

Manufacturer/ Weapon	Basic Range (meters)	BB/RAP Range (meters)	Rate of Fire Max	Rate of Fire Sust	Countries Possessing	Remarks
North Korea						
M1985, 240mm MRL	---	43,000	12/min	Reload	Iran	CHEM
M1987, 170mm SP	40,000	---	INA	INA	Iran, Iraq	None
M46, 130mm SP	27,500	---	6/min	1.1/mm	None	None
BM 11, 122mm MRL	---	20,500	30/min	Reload	PLO, Syria, Iran, Iraq, Uganda	None
M1981, 122mm SP	23,900	---	INA	INA	None	None
M1992, 120mm SP Mortar	8,700	---	INA	INA	None	None
Russia/CIS						
FROG-7, MRL	---	70,000	1/min	1/hour	Frmr Warsaw Pact, Afghan, Algeria, Cuba, Egypt, Iraq, North Korea, Libya, Syria, Yemen Kuwait, UAE	NUKE, CHEM
SMERCH, 30mm MRL	---	70,000	12/min	Reload	Iraq, Czech Republic	None
2S4, 240mm, SP Mortar	9,600	18,000	1/min	40/hour	IRA, Iraq, North Korea, Egypt, Oman, Lebanon	NUKE, LGM
M240, 240mm, Towed Mortar	9,700	18,000	1/min	38/hour	Afghanistan, Syria	NUKE, LGM
BM 27, 220mm MRL	---	35,000	16/min	Reload	Czech Republic, Poland, Slovakia	CHEM, MINES
2S7, 203mm SP	37,500	47,000	2/min	2/min	India, Iraq, Egypt, Syria	None
2S3, 180mm Towed	30,400	43,800	1/min	1/2min	Hungary, Iraq, Libya, Syria	None
2S3, 152mm SP	20,600	24,000	4/min	1/min	None	None
2S19, 152mm SP	24,700	30,000	8/min	8/min	None	LGM
2S5, 152mm SP	28,400	37,000	5/min	5/min	Finland	None
2A36, 152mm Towed	28,400	37,000	5/min	1/min	Algeria, China, Cuba, Egypt, Vietnam, Frmr Yugoslavia	None
D-20, 152mm Towed	17,230	30,000	5/min	1/min	Algeria, Afghanistan, Cambodia, China, Egypt, Syria, North Korea, Vietnam	None
BM 14, 122mm MRL	---	9,800	16/min	Reload	China, Egypt, India, Iran, Iraq, North Korea, others	CHEM
BM 21, 140mm, MRL	---	20,400	40/min	Reload	None	CHEM, MINES
2S1, 122mm SP	15,300	22,000	8/min	1.1/min	China	None
D-30, 122mm Towed	15,300	22,000	8/min	1.1/min	Afghanistan	None
2S9, 120mm SP Mortar	8,900	13,000	6/min	6/min	None	LGM
2S23, 120mm SP Mortar	8,900	12,900	10/min	10/min	Hungary	LGM
2B9, 82mm SP/T Mortar	4,300	---	120/min		None	
SOUTH AFRICA						
G-6, 155mm SP	30,800	39,600	3/21sec	4/min	UAE, Oman	None
G-5, 155mm Towed	30,200	39,000	3/min	3/min	None	None
UNITED KINGDOM						
FH 70, 155mm Towed	24,700	31,500	3/13sec	2/min	Germany, Italy, Japan, Saudi Arabia	None
FORMER YUGOSLAVIA						
M-77, 128mm MRL	---	20,600	32/min	Reload	Bosnia, Bosnian Serb Army, Croatia, Iraq, Serbia, Monte Negro	None

NOTE: A complete listing of all world artillery systems and their characteristics is available in the classified National Government Intelligence Center series Field Artillery Worldwide. Reference DST 1130S-115-94, Cannon and Mortars; DST 1130S-94 Vol 2 Sup 1; and NGIC 1143-200D-95, Multiple Rocket Launcher Systems.

LEGEND: BB–base burn
CHEM–chemical munitions capable
INA–information not available
LGM–laser guided munitions capable

MRL–multiple rocket launcher
NUKE–nuclear munitions capable
SP–self-propelled

Figure O-13. World Artillery, Mortars, and Rocket Launchers (Continued).

APPENDIX P. ENVIRONMENTAL AND TERRAIN CONSIDERATIONS

MOUNTAIN OPERATIONS

FM 90-6, *Mountain Operations,* provides more detailed information.

Munitions

IPB helps determine where and what munitions are most effective. Consideration of munitions employment and effect follow.

Snow

Mechanical time fuzes are the most effective air burst. VT demonstrates fuze sensitivity.

HE/PD (point detonating) or DELAY, CBUs, and ICM are less effective due to fragmentation absorption by the snow.

FASCAM may settle into snow. This may cause anti-handling devices to prematurely detonate the munitions.

Laser designated munitions may be ineffective (specular activity).

WP can burn undetected in snow for up to 4 days.

Smoke effectiveness is reduced.

Snow slides can be started.

Rocky Terrain

HE/PD is very effective. It produces fragmentation from splintering rocks.

VT and time fuzes are effective.

ICM is effective; however, it has reduced efficiency on greater than 60 degree slopes.

FASCAM can be used to deny the enemy the use of narrow defiles, valleys, roads, and usable terrain.

Laser-guided weapons can be effective on canalized targets.

Swirling winds and slopes will make smoke employment difficult.

Changing atmospheric conditions make unobserved fires less accurate and require more meteorological support for artillery and mortars.

Rockslides can start.

Target Acquisition and Observation

Forward Observers

Surface observation is compartmentalized due to multiple terrain crests.

FOs may require airlift or mountaineering support to overcome terrain masks and compartments.

Heavy fogs and low clouds may obscure observation.

Observers tend to underestimate range when looking upward; overestimate range when looking down.

Aircrews

Aircrews can effectively observe areas not visible by ground means; e.g., in deep defilade, on reverse slopes, deep targets. They are vulnerable to enemy air defenses when compartmentalized. Aircrews may be confined to valleys and lower elevations because of atmospheric conditions for flight.

Radars

Terrain masks can degrade the effective range of radar. Enemy high angle, indirect fires are easily detected. Additional use of ground surveillance radars and remote sensors may be required. More extensive use of SHELREPs is required.

Targeting

IPB should identify—

- Routes that can be used by the enemy to attack, withdraw, and resupply.
- Likely position areas for indirect fire assets, command and control elements, CSS assets, and observation posts.
- Any terrain that is subject to snowslides, rockslides, or avalanches.

Considerations

High angle fires (artillery and mortars) are often required to clear the intervening crests and to attack the reverse slopes.

VT fuze employment requires additional intervening crest considerations.

CAS can effectively attack canalized targets and reverse slope targets.

Naval gunfire must fire reduced charge for intervening crests which reduces range.

Position areas for artillery and mortars are limited, have limited access, and are likely to be targeted by enemy counterfire actions.

Limited ingress/egress routes allow effective enemy employment of ADA.

JUNGLE OPERATIONS

See FM 90-5, *Jungle Operations*, for more information. Contact with the enemy will often be at extremely close ranges. Fire support must be responsive enough to support troops in close contact, quickly and decisively. Depending on the size of enemy elements, supporting arms employment may be decentralized to accomplish responsive fires.

Munitions

Munitions used will vary with the type vegetation and terrain. Knowledge and employment of the type of munitions best suited for the terrain is vital. Vary-ing terrain includes triple canopy jungle, heavy ground vegetation, swamps, and small clearings. In triple canopy jungle—

- HE/VT, HE/Time, and ICM and other payload-submunitions (CBUs, FASCAM) are ineffective or less effective.
- HE/delay will penetrate treetops and create additional fragmentation from splintering.
- Heavy CAS ordnance with fuze extenders can clear away jungle canopy.
- M825 smoke has limited effectiveness unless fired graze burst.
- White phosphorous is effective as a marking round and in initial adjustments.

Target Acquisition and Observation

Triple canopy jungle makes observation beyond 25 to 50 meters very difficult. Target location, self-location, and friendly unit location is difficult.

Forward Observers

FOs often cannot see rounds and must be able to adjust fire by sound. This requires experience (see MCWP 3-16.6 for additional information).

Marking rounds can be fired to assist in self-location. Marking rounds are usually fired center of sector or at least 400 meters forward of friendly units. After the round is fired, the FDC sends the grid of the impact.

GPS is essential for quick target and self-location. Night vision devices are essential for low light observation.

Aircrews

Aircrews can see exposed movements and positions that the ground observer cannot. They can assist in relay of fire support communications and mark targets for CAS. Aircrews are ineffective in triple canopy jungle.

Radars

Radars are very effective. Proactive counterfire that is based on IPB must be rehearsed and fully integrated into the fire support plan to be effective.

Ground surveillance radars and remote sensors are effective. SHELREPs may only be usable for intelligence collection versus reactive counterfire.

Targeting

Isolated units prepare 360 degree defenses with appropriate fire plans including FPFs. Consider planning munitions specific required supply rates (RSR) to support operations.

Considerations

Artillery positions are limited and often inaccessible by road. Static positions require 6400 mil firing capability and defensive fire planning.

Units employing CAS need positive identification of friendly troops; e.g., prearranged signals, procedures.

Increased requirements on helicopter support results in increased SEAD support.

Communications in triple canopy are severely degraded. Proper use of antennas, relays, and re-transmission stations helps offset this limitation.

DESERT OPERATIONS

FM 90-3, *Desert Operations*, will provide more detailed information.

The three types of desert terrain are mountainous, rocky plateau and sandy dunes. Fire support planning considerations will vary significantly between operations in each type of desert terrain. Typical engagements are at extended and maximum ranges with greater dispersion and mobility of units. Continuous fire support for highly mobile maneuver forces requires considerable planning.

Munitions

Mountain and Rocky Plateau Deserts

Munitions effectiveness for mountain deserts is the same as for any mountainous region except that the considerations of snow are not usually applicable.

Sandy or Dune Deserts

HE/delay, ICM, and CBUs are ineffective in deep sands. Laser-guided munitions can be employed at max ranges. Smoke and illumination can be used effectively to obscure or silhouette enemy.

Target Acquisition and Observation

Forward Observers

Laser range finders and global positioning systems are essential for accurate and timely target location.

Targets can be detected by observing dust signatures.

Training in vehicle ID at extended ranges is required.

Equipment maintenance increases due to heat, sand, and dust.

Aircrews

Aerial navigation/target location is difficult in featureless terrain. Aircraft are vulnerable to enemy air defenses at maximum ranges. Positive identification of friendly troops is more difficult; use prearranged signals and procedures.

Radars

Radars are effective to maximum ranges. Effective integration into counterfire programs is essential.

Targeting

Identify trafficable terrain for wheeled and tracked vehicles and likely mortar and artillery positions. Assess the impact of wadis, gulches, wet lakebeds, and other significant terrain to compartmentalize or canalize friendly and enemy units. Identify likely enemy forward observation positions.

Considerations

Mobility may affect supporting arms ability to maintain fire support for maneuver.

Aircraft are vulnerable to the maximum ranges of enemy ADA.

CAS can employ standoff ranges in target engagement.

Target marking requirements increase.

LOCs for sustainment increase.

Volumes of fire for simple munitions increase with dispersion of target elements (target size increases).

Helicopter operations are difficult to execute due to dusty conditions.

COLD WEATHER OPERATIONS

FM 90-11, *Cold Weather Operations*, contains additional information on aspects of operating in a cold weather environment.

Fire planning for cold weather operations is similar to that for more temperate regions. However, limited ground mobility of artillery weapons and ammunition supply and increased time of operation must be considered by the fire support planner.

Munitions

Munitions effectiveness in snow is the same as those listed under mountain operations. Low temperatures may cause illuminating rounds to malfunction.

Target Acquisition and Observation

Forward Observers

Visibility diagrams require constant update due to drifting snow. Ground burst may be difficult to observe in deep snow.

Aircrews

Aircrews are not as prone to disorientation as are ground observers. Weather conditions may reduce the availability of aircraft.

Radars

Extreme cold weather may degrade radar's operations. Ground surveillance radars are effective. Deep snow may reduce remote sensors effectiveness.

Targeting

Visual target detection may be limited. Heavy precipitation may reduce LOCs to predictable routes. Ice fogs and snow clouds created by moving enemy formations reveal targets. Tracks in the snow may indicate enemy positions.

Considerations

Extreme cold weather will reduce a weapon's range.

Mobility of maneuver and indirect fire assets is often extremely limited.

Frequent poor weather reduces availability of CAS.

Target marking and friendly unit self-marking requirements increase.

Effective communications are hampered by electronic interference, weakened batteries.

Routes and firing positions may be limited due to frozen terrain. May require explosives to emplace howitzers.

MILITARY OPERATIONS ON URBANIZED TERRAIN

MCWP 3-35.3, *Military Operations on Urbanized Terrain*, contains additional information on aspects of operating in a MOUT environment. FMFM 4-7C-3/ FM 101-61-10, *MOUT JMEMS*, provides specific information on munitions effects.

Characteristics of the MOUT environment include high concentrations of populace and infrastructure and the consideration of collateral damage to both. Intensity of conflict and ROE have an exponential effect on the employment of fire support in the MOUT environment. The effective employment of fires in what can be a constraining environment is essential to success.

Munitions

HE/VT and time fuzes can effectively clear rooftops of enemy troops. *Varying heights of buildings can cause VT to prematurely function.*

HE/PD is effective on masonry targets only in PD mode. HE/Delay may only penetrate the first wall or the roof.

Only concrete piercing (CP) fuzes can penetrate multiple-layer masonry structures.

Calculated minimum safe distances are not accurate in cities since buildings give added protection.

NSFS effectiveness is decreased by the height of the buildings. Try to position so GTL is parallel with "urban canyon."

Dead-space beyond buildings is 5 times the height of the building for low-angle fire and 3 times the height of the building for high-angle fire.

Laser-guided munitions are effective against hardened targets. Have to be wary of specular reflectivity.

Heavy CAS ordnance, artillery, and NSFS can quickly and effectively create rubble and demolish structures. Rubblization, however, can often create problems for friendly forces, especially during clearing operations.

Smoke, WP, and illumination are effective and can create incendiary effects but tend to help the enemy defenders since they plan and lay their defensive fires for limited visibility.

Target Acquisition and Observation

Forward Observers

OPs can be established in high structures. However, survivability conditions may preclude the occupation of rooftops.

Buildings may limit or compartmentalize ground observation. Ground obstacles will limit or impede movement. Build observer plan with observers inside and outside the built-up area to lessen gaps in coverage.

GPS functioning may be degraded since buildings may mask satellite signals.

Aircrews

Aircrews can quickly locate exposed or moving targets; however, they have to be aware of dead space and air defense ambushes in contained urban areas.

Aircrews often cannot locate origin of fires from within buildings.

FAC(A)s can facilitate CAS employment, especially masked targets.

FAC(A)s and observers must be wary of laser employment. Specular reflectivity off the various reflective surfaces will demand detailed planning for the successful use of laser designators and IR pointers.

The multitude of light from a city can decrease a FAC(A) or observers ability to identify targets. Lights will degrade NVG effectiveness.

Radars

Employment can be degraded due to masking by buildings. Emplacement outside of built up areas may provide more effective employment.

Targeting

Identify mobility corridors, resupply routes, and applicable choke points.

Identify civil infrastructure points (communications, utilities or government).

Identify likely enemy artillery and mortar positions.

Plan fires to accompany penetrations, unless the enemy is withdrawing.

Identify ROE restricted targets.

Be aware of "shoot and scoot" tactics within any built-up areas.

Considerations

Determine what is acceptable collateral damage to populace and infrastructure.

Interdict and canalize by creating rubble and obstacles.

Use fires to prevent enemy movement on streets and occupation of rooftops for observation.

Employment of howitzers in direct fire may be required (possible attachment to maneuver units). Howitzers can be used to create breaches in walls or be set on PDFs. "Killer junior" will be the munition of choice. 155 millimeter towed howitzers may often have difficulty maneuvering through city streets or "digging in" on pavement or concrete.

High angle indirect fires may be required due to masking by buildings. In many cases, high-angle fire on a howitzer may still not be able to prosecute the targeted area. As a result, mortars may become the indirect fire weapon of choice.

NSFS engagements may be limited due to masking.

IPs and BPs for CAS aircraft must be thoroughly planned. Prominent buildings, structures, and parks may be used. Must be easily identifiable.

CAS is effective, especially against masked targets, but may have to increase dive angle.

CAS is vulnerable to enemy air defenses, especially when compartmentalized.

Positioning for artillery and mortars includes masking, dispersion, and trafficability.

Radio communications are degraded; consider wire or existing civil communication lines. Build a comm relay plan.

Current military mapping does not provide the detail to move, target, and observe fires in MOUT. Smaller scale maps such as tourist maps may be required to operate effectively; 8-digit grids will be required within cities.

Meteorological conditions in the city are different than those outside the city. Atmospheric changes in the city (ambient heat radiated from buildings, industrial smog, and deviation in winds) may increase the frequency of meteorological measurements.

Survey datums in most underdeveloped countries are at best unreliable. Survey must be extended into the town. Compasses and magnetic equipment may be adversely affected by the structures.

Plan and secure resupply routes. Ammunition expenditure (class V[w]) increases during MOUT.

Create Molotov cocktail and RPG screens on vehicles and howitzers to defeat or decrease effectiveness of these weapons.

The release of toxic industrial chemicals due to fires must be planned for. Place RFA or NFAs on likely locations of industrial chemicals. Have NBCD officer determine effects of chemicals if released (down wind hazard area and time viable).

Plan and disseminate how friendlies will mark occupied buildings. Aircraft must be able to identify.

Hold CAS aircraft over nonhostile terrain to allow aircrew to build SA without overly worrying about threat. Fixed-wing aircraft generally need 16 kilometers (4X4) area to hold effectively.

Parks, fields, school yards, and other obvious positions are obvious to the enemy and will be targeted.

Stabilize mortar base plates on concrete with sandbags.

MLRS/HIMARS should not be positioned in built up areas due to the low trajectory of the weapon.

APPENDIX Q. GLOSSARY

SECTION I. ABBREVIATIONS AND ACRONYMS

A . . . . as required
AA . . . . antiaircraft
AAA . . . . antiaircraft artillery
AAV . . . . assault amphibious vehicle
AAW . . . . antiair warfare
ABCA . . . . . American, British, Canadian, Australian
ACA . . . . airspace coordination area
ACE . . . . aviation combat element
ADAM . . . . area denial artillery munition
AF . . . . amphibious force
AFSC . . . . assistant fire support coordinator
AGL . . . . above ground level
AGM . . . . attack guidance matrix
AirO . . . . air officer
A/NGF . . . . air/naval gunfire
AO . . . . area of operations
AOA . . . . amphibious objective area
AoF . . . . azimuth of fire
AP . . . . antipersonnel; attack position
APICM . . . . antipersonnel improved
conventional munition
arty . . . . artillery
ASC . . . . air support controller/coordinator
ASC (A) . . . . . assault support coordinator (airborne)
ASE . . . . air support element
ASL . . . . air support list
ASLT . . . . air support liaison team
ASR . . . . assault support request
ATCCS . . . . Army Tactical Command
and Control System
ATF . . . . amphibious task force
ATFIC . . . . . amphibious task force intelligence center
ATGM . . . . antitank guided missile
ATIZ . . . . artillery target intelligence zone
ATO . . . . air tasking order

BA . . . . basic allowance

BAT . . . . brilliant antitank
BBDPICM . . . . base burn dual purpose
improved conventional munition
BCS . . . . battery computer system
BDA . . . . battle damage assessment
BE . . . . basic encyclopedia
Bn . . . . battalion

C2 . . . . command and control
CA . . . . combat assessment
CAS . . . . close air support
CATF . . . . commander, amphibious task force
CBAE . . . . . commander's battlespace area evaluation
CBU . . . . cluster bomb unit
CCIR . . . . commander's critical information
requirements
CE . . . . command element
CEP . . . . circular error probable
CFF . . . . calls for fire
CFL . . . . coordinated fire line
CFZ . . . . critical friendly zones
CI . . . . counterintelligence
CINC . . . . commander in chief
CIS . . . . . . communications and information systems
CLF . . . . commander, landing force
cmd . . . . command
COA . . . . course of action
COC . . . . combat operations center
COF . . . . conduct of fire
COG . . . . center of gravity
CONPLAN . . . . contingency plan
COP . . . . combat outpost
CP . . . . checkpoint; contact point;
command post
CPHD . . . . Copperhead
CPREP . . . . command post report
CSB . . . . common sensor boundary

CSR . . . . controlled supply rate
CSS . . . . combat service support
CSSE . . . . combat service support element
CV . . . . critical vulnerability
CVT . . . . controlled vehicle time
CZ . . . . censor zone

D3A . . . . decide-detect-deliver-assess
DA . . . . Department of the Army
DACT . . . . data automated communications terminal
DAS . . . . direct air support
DASC . . . . direct air support center
DCT . . . . digital communications terminal
DF . . . . direction finding
DIA . . . . Defense Intelligence Agency
DISN . . . . Defense Information System Network
DISREP . . . . displacement report
DMS . . . . digital message system
DOCC . . . . deep operations coordination center
DP . . . . dual purpose
DPICM . . . . dual purpose improved
conventional munition
DS . . . . direct support
DST . . . . decision support template

EA . . . . electronic attack
EFST . . . . essential fire support tasks
EMC . . . . Execution Management Control
EP . . . . electronic protection
EPLRS . . . . enhanced position location
reporting system
ES . . . . electronic warfare support
EW . . . . electronic warfare
EWCC . . . . electronic warfare coordination center
EWO . . . . electronic warfare officer

FAC . . . . forward air controller
FAC(A) . . . . forward air controller (airborne)
FAE . . . . fuel air explosive
FAHQ . . . . force artillery headquarters
FARP . . . . forward arming and refueling point
FASCAM . . . . family of scatterable mines
FCL . . . . final coordination line

FD . . . . fire direction
FDA . . . . functional damage assessment
FDC . . . . fire direction center
FDO . . . . fire direction officer
FEBA . . . . forward edge of the battle area
FFA . . . . free-fire area
FFC . . . . force fires coordinator
FFCC . . . . force fires coordination center
FFE . . . . fire for effect
FIRECAP . . . . firing capabilities
FLASHREP . . . . flash report
FLIR . . . . forward looking infrared
FLOT . . . . forward line of own troops
FMF . . . . Fleet Marine Force
FMFM . . . . Fleet Marine Force manual
FO . . . . forward observer
FOB . . . . forward operating base
FPF . . . . final protective fire
FPL . . . . final protective line
frag . . . . fragmentary
FRAGO . . . . fragmentary order
FS . . . . fire support
FSA . . . . fire support area
FSC . . . . fire support coordinator
FSCC . . . . fire support coordination center
FSCL . . . . fire support coordination line
FSCM . . . . fire support coordinating measure
FSEM . . . . fire support execution matrix
FSS . . . . fire support station

GCE . . . . ground combat element
GCU . . . . guidance control unit
GFCS . . . . gunfire control system
GPS . . . . global positioning system
GS . . . . general support
GS-R . . . . general support-reinforcing
GTL . . . . gun-target line
GURF . . . . guns up ready to fire

HA . . . . holding area
HARM . . . . high-speed antiradiation missile
HC . . . . hexachloroethane (artillery smoke)
HD . . . . helicopter direction

HDC . . . . helicopter direction center
HE . . . . high explosive
HERA . . . . .HE rocket-assisted
HF . . . . .high frequency
HIMARS . . . . . high mobility artillery rocket system
HPT . . . . high-payoff target
HPTL . . . . high-payoff target list
HQ . . . . headquarters
HR . . . . helicopter request
HUMINT . . . . human intelligence
HVT . . . . high-value target

I . . . . immediate
IADS . . . . integrated air defense system
ICM . . . . .improved conventional munitions
IFSAS . . . . . . .Initial Fire Support Automated System
INTSUM . . . . intelligence summary
IOC . . . . intelligence operations center
IP . . . . initial point
IPB . . . . .intelligence preparation of the
battlefield/battlespace
IR . . . . .infrared radiation

JAAT . . . . .joint air attack team
JDAM . . . . joint direct attack munitions
JFC . . . . joint force commander
JIC . . . . .joint intelligence center
JMEM . . . . joint munitions effectiveness manual
JP . . . . joint publication
JTAR . . . . .joint tactical air strike request
JTCB . . . . .joint targeting coordination board
JTF . . . . .joint task force
JTL . . . . joint target list

kbps . . . . .kilobits per second
KOCOA . . . . key terrain, observation and
fields of fire, cover and concealment,
obstacles, and avenues of approach

LAAD . . . . low altitude air defense
LAN . . . . local area network
LAR . . . . light armored reconnaissance
LASM . . . . land attack standard missile

LF . . . . landing force
LFOC . . . . landing force operations center
LGW . . . . laser guided weapon
LLDR . . . . . .lightweight laser designator rangefinder
LNO . . . . .liaison officer
LOI . . . . letter of instruction
LOS . . . . line of sight
LST . . . . laser spot tracker
LTC . . . . low altitude air defense team control
LWC . . . . . . low altitude air defense weapons control

m . . . . meter
MACCS . . . . Marine air command and control system
MACS . . . . modular artillery charge system
MAGTF . . . . .Marine air-ground task force
MarDiv . . . . Marine division
MASS . . . . Marine air support squadron
MAW . . . . Marine aircraft wing
MBA . . . . .main battle area
Mbps . . . . megabites per second
MC . . . . mobility corridors
MCCRES . . . . Marine Corps Combat Readiness
Evaluation System
MCDP . . . . .Marine Corps doctrinal publication
MCPP . . . . Marine Corps Planning Process
MCR . . . . .multi-channel radio
MCRP . . . . Marine Corps reference publication
MCWP . . . . . . Marine Corps warfighting publication
MEA . . . . munitions effect assessment
MEDEVAC . . . . medical evacuation
MEF . . . . .Marine expeditionary force
met . . . . .meteorological
METT-T . . . . . . mission, enemy, terrain and weather,
troops and support available-time available
MEU . . . . Marine expeditionary unit
MEU(SOC) . . . . .Marine expeditionary unit
(special operations capable)
MFR . . . . .mission-fired report
MHz . . . . megahertz
MIDB . . . . .modernized integrated data base
MILSTD . . . . military standard
MLRS . . . . .multiple launch rocket system
mm . . . . millimeter

MOE . . . . measure of effectiveness
MOI . . . . message of interest
MOS . . . . military occupational specialty
MOUT . . . . . . military operations on urbanized terrain
MPI . . . . mean point of impact
MSC. . . . . .major subordinate command
MSL. . . . . mean sea level
MULE . . . . .modular universal laser equipment
NAI . . . . .named area of interest
NATO . . . . North Atlantic Treaty Organization
NBCD . . . . nuclear, biological, and chemical defense
NCO. . . . . noncommissioned officer
NFA. . . . . no-fire area
NGF. . . . . naval gunfire
NGFSO . . . . naval gunfire officer
NGLO . . . . naval gunfire liaison officer
NSFS . . . . naval surface fire support
NTS . . . . naval telecommunications system
NVG . . . . night vision goggles

OAS. . . . . offensive air support
obj . . . . objective
OIC . . . . officer in charge
OMFTS . . . . .operational maneuver from the sea
OOB. . . . . order of battle
OP . . . . observation post
OPFACS . . . . operational facility
OPLAN . . . . operation plan
OPORD . . . . operation order
OTH. . . . . over-the-horizon

P. . . . . planned
P&A. . . . . production and analysis
PA . . . . position area
PAH. . . . . .platoon area hazard
PCFF . . . . priority in calls for fire
PCP . . . . .penetration control point
PD . . . . .point detonating (fuze action)
PDF . . . . principal direction of fire
PGM . . . . precision-guided munition
PI . . . . .probability of incapacitation
PIFAS . . . . portable inductive artillery fuze setter

PIR/IR . . . . priority intelligence requirement/
intelligence requirement
PLGR. . . . . precision lightweight GPS receiver
PLI. . . . . position location information
PLRS . . . . position location reporting system
POF . . . . priority of fires
PRF . . . . .pulse repetition frequency
PZ . . . . .pickup zone

QSTAG . . . . . quadripartite standardization agreement

RAAMS. . . . . remote antiarmor mine system
RABFAC. . . . . . .radar beacon forward air controller
RAGM. . . . . reactive attack guidance matrix
RAOC . . . . rear area operations center
RAP. . . . . .rocket assisted projectile
RAS. . . . . rear area security
RDO . . . . .radar deployment order
RFA. . . . . restricted fire area
RFL. . . . . .restrictive fire line
ROE. rules of engagement
RR . . . . reattack recommendations
R&S. . . . . reconnaissance and surveillance
RSR . . . . required supply rate
RSTA. . . . . reconnaissance, surveillance,
and target acquisition
RV . . . . report values

SAC. . . . . supporting arms coordinator
SACC . . . . .supporting arms coordination center
SADARM . . . . sense and destroy armor munition
SAM . . . . .surface-to-air missile
SARC . . . . surveillance and reconnaissance cell
SCAMP . . . . .sensor control and management platoon
SCR . . . . single-channel radio
SEAD . . . . suppression of enemy air defenses
S/EWCC . . . . .signals intelligence/electronic
warfare coordination center
SFCP . . . . shore fire control party
SHELREP . . . . shelling report
SINCGARS . . . . .single channel ground
and airborne radio system
sit. . . . . situational

SOP . . . . standard operating procedure
SPOTREP . . . . spotting report
STA . . . . surveillance and target acquisition
STANAG . . . . .standardization agreement
SYSCON . . . . .systems control center

TA . . . . target acquisition
TAC . . . . .tactical air command
TAC(A) . . . . tactical air coordinator (airborne)
TACC . . . . .Marine tactical air command center;
      Navy tactical air control center
TACGRU . . . . .tactical air control group
TACP . . . . tactical air control party
TACRON . . . . tactical air control squadron
TAD .tactical air direction
TADC . . . . tactical air direction center
TAH . . . . target area hazard
TAI . . . . .targeted area of interest
TAR . . . . tactical air request
TARBUL . . . . target bulletin
TAREP . . . . .target report
TATC . . . . tactical air traffic control(ler)
TBMCS . . . .Theater Battle Management Core System
TCIM . . . . . tactical communications interface module
TCO . . . . .tactical combat operations
TDA . . . . target damage assessment
TDN . . . . tactical data network
TGTINFOREP . . . . .target information report
TGTINTELO . . . . target intelligence officer
THS . . . . target handoff system
TIC . . . . .target information center
TIO . . . . target information officer
TIS . . . . target information section

TLDHS . . . . target location designation
          hands-off system
TLE . . . . target location error
T/O . . . . table of organization
TOT . . . . .time on target
TOW . . . . .tube launched, optically tracked,
    wire command link, guided missile system
TPC .target processing center
TPL . . . . time-phase line
TPME . . . . task, purpose, method, and effect
T&R . . . . training and readiness
TRI-TAC . . . . .Tri-Service Tactical
        Communications System
TRP . . . . .target reference point
TSM . . . . target synchronization matrix
TSS . . . . target selection standards
TTT . . . . time to target
TVA . . . . target value analysis

UAV . . . . unmanned aerial vehicle
UHF . . . . ultra-high frequency
ULCS . . . . unit-level circuit switches
USMC . . . . United States Marine Corps

VHF . . . . .very high frequency
VMAQ . . Marine tactical electronic warfare squadron
VMF . . . . variable message format
VT . . . . .variable time (fuze)

WEO . . . . weapons employment officer
WP . . . . .white phosphorus

XO . . . . executive officer

SECTION II. DEFINITIONS

advance force—(DOD, NATO) A temporary organization within the amphibious task force which precedes the main body to the objective area. Its function is to participate in preparing the objective for the main assault by conducting such operations as reconnaissance, seizure of supporting positions, minesweeping, preliminary bombardment, underwater demolitions, and air support. (JP 1-02)

airborne alert—(DOD, NATO) A state of aircraft readiness wherein combat-equipped aircraft are airborne and ready for immediate action. (DOD) It is designed to reduce reaction time and to increase the survivability factor. (JP 1-02)

air defense—(DOD) All defensive measures designed to destroy attacking enemy aircraft or missiles in the Earth's envelope of atmosphere, or to nullify or reduce the effectiveness of such attack. (JP 1-02)

air liaison officer—(DOD) An officer (aviator/ pilot) attached to a ground unit who functions as the primary advisor to the ground commander on air operation matters. (JP 1-02)

allocation—(DOD) In a general sense, distribution of limited resources among competing requirements for employment. Specific allocations (e.g., air sorties, nuclear weapons, forces, and transportation) are described as allocation of air sorties, nuclear weapons, etc. (JP 1-02)

amphibious force—An amphibious task force and a landing force together with other forces that are trained, organized, and equipped for amphibious operations. (JP 3-02)

amphibious objective area—(NATO) A geographical area (delineated for command and control purposes in the order initiating the amphibious operation) within which is located the objective(s) to be secured by the amphibious force. This area must be of sufficient size to ensure accomplishment of the amphibious force's mission and must provide sufficient area for conducting necessary sea, air, and land operations. (JP 3-02)

apportionment (air)—(DOD) The determination and assignment of the total expected air effort by percentage and/or by priority that should be devoted to the various air operations and/or geographic areas for a given period of time. Also called **air apportionment**. (JP 1-02)

area of influence—(DOD, NATO) A geographical area wherein a commander is directly capable of influencing operations by maneuver or fire support systems normally under the commander's command or control. (JP 1-02)

area of interest—(DOD, NATO) That area of concern to the commander, including the area of influence, areas adjacent thereto, and extending into enemy territory to the objectives of current or planned operations. This area also includes areas occupied by enemy forces who could jeopardize the accomplishment of the mission. (JP 1-02)

attack position—Maneuver area used by attack helicopters which contain firing points laterally and in depth. When activated, attack positions may be airspace coordination areas.

barrage—(DOD) A prearranged barrier of fire, except that delivered by small arms, designed to protect friendly troops and installations by impeding enemy movements across defensive lines or areas. (JP 1-02)

battle damage assessment—An estimate of damage or degradation resulting from the application of military force, either lethal or nonlethal, against a target. This estimate should be timely and accurate. Battle damage assessment can be applied to the employment of all types of weapon systems (air, ground, naval, and special forces weapons systems) throughout the range of military operations. Battle damage assessment is primarily an intelligence responsibility with required inputs and coordination from the operators. Battle damage assessment is composed of physical damage assessment, functional damage assessment, and target system assessment. Also called BDA. (Proposed by JP 3-60 for inclusion in JP 1-02.)

battlespace—(DOD) The environment, factors, and conditions which must be understood to successfully apply combat power, protect the force, or complete the mission. This includes the air, land, sea, space, and the included enemy and friendly forces, facilities, weather, terrain, the electromagnetic spectrum, and information environment within the operational areas and areas of interest. See also joint intelligence preparation of the battlespace. (JP 1-02). All aspects of air, surface, subsurface, land, space, and electromagnetic spectrum which encompass the area of influence and area of interest. (MCRP 5-12C)

barrage fire—(DOD, NATO) Fire which is designed to fill a volume of space or area rather than aimed specifically at a given target. (JP 1-02)

battlefield surveillance—(DOD, NATO) Systematic observation of the battle area for the purpose of providing timely information and combat intelligence. (JP 1-02)

centers of gravity—Those characteristics, capabilities, or localities from which a military force derives its freedom of action, physical strength, or will to fight. Also called COG. (JP 1-02) A key source of strength without which an enemy cannot function. (MCDP 1-2)

close air support—(DOD) Air action by fixed- and rotary-wing aircraft against hostile targets which are in close proximity to friendly forces and which require detailed integration of each air mission with the fire and movement of those forces. (JP 1-02)

close operations—Military actions conducted to project power against enemy forces which pose an immediate or near term threat to the success of current battles and engagements. These military actions are conducted by committed forces and their readily available tactical reserves using maneuver and combined arms (MCRP 5-12C).

close support—That action of the supporting force against targets or objectives which are sufficiently near the supported force as to require detailed integration or coordination of the supporting action with the fire, movement, or other actions of the supported force (JP 1-02).

close supporting fires—Fire placed on enemy troops, weapons, or positions, which, because of their proximity, present the most immediate and serious threat to the supported unit (JP 1-02).

combat assessment—The determination of the overall effectiveness of force employment during military operations. Combat assessment is composed of three major components, (a) battle damage assessment (BDA), (b) munitions effects assessment (MEA), and (c) reattack recommendation. Also called CA. (Proposed by JP 3-60 for inclusion in JP 1-02.)

combat power—(DOD, NATO) The total means of destructive and/or disruptive force which a Military unit/formation can apply against the opponent at a given time. (JP 1-02)

combined arms—The full integration of combat arms in such a way that to counteract one, the enemy must become more vulnerable to another. (MCRP 5-12C)

constraint(s)—Something which must be done that limits freedom of action. See also restraint(s). (MCRP 5-12C)

control point—(DOD, NATO) A position marked by a buoy, boat, aircraft, electronic device, conspicuous terrain feature, or other identifiable object which is given a name or number and used as an aid to navigation or control of ships, boats, or aircraft. (JP 1-02)

counterattack—(DOD, NATO) Attack by part or all of a defending force against an enemy attacking force, for such specific purposes as regaining ground lost or cutting off or destroying enemy advance units, and with the general objective of denying to the enemy the attainment of his purpose in attacking. In sustained defensive operations, it is undertaken to restore the battle position and is directed at limited objectives. (JP 1-02)

counterfire—(DOD, NATO) Fire intended to destroy or neutralize enemy weapons. (DOD) Includes counterbattery, counterbombardment, and countermortar fire. (JP 1-02)

countermechanized defensive fire—The fire of targets planned on routes of approach which logically would be used by enemy mechanized forces. Normally, it is scheduled for delivery on call of the supported landing force. (NWP 3-09.11M (Rev C)/FMFM 1-7)

counterpreparation fire—(DOD, NATO) Intensive prearranged fire delivered when the imminence of the enemy attack is discovered. (DOD) It is designed to: break up enemy formations; disorganize the enemy's systems of command, communications, and observation; decrease the effectiveness of artillery preparation; and impair the enemy's offensive spirit. (JP 1-02)

course of action—(DOD) 1. A plan that would accomplish, or is related to, the accomplishment of a mission. Also called COA. (JP 1-02)

covering force—(DOD, NATO) 1. A force operating apart from the main force for the purpose of intercepting, engaging, delaying, disorganizing, and deceiving the enemy before he can attack the force covered. 2. Any body or detachment of troops which provides security for a larger force by observation, reconnaissance, attack, or defense, or by any combination of these methods. (JP 1-02)

covering force area—(DOD) The area forward of the forward edge of the battle area out to the forward positions initially assigned to the covering forces. It is here that the covering forces execute assigned tasks. (JP 1-02)

critical point—(DOD) A key geographical point or position important to the success of an operation. (JP 1-02)

critical vulnerability—An aspect of a center of gravity that if exploited will do the most significant damage to an adversary's ability to resist. A vulnerability cannot be critical unless it undermines a key strength. Also called CV. (MCRP 5-12 C)

damage assessment—(DOD, NATO) The determination of the effect of attacks on targets. (JP 1-02)

deep operations—Military actions conducted against enemy capabilities which pose a potential threat to friendly forces. These military actions are designed to isolate, shape, and dominate the battlespace and influence future operations (MCRP 5-12C).

deep supporting fires—Fire directed on objectives not in the immediate vicinity of our forces, for neutralizing and destroying enemy reserves and weapons, and interfering with enemy command, supply, communications, and observations (JP 1-02).

delaying operation—(DOD, NATO) An operation in which a force under pressure trades space for time by slowing down the enemy's momentum and inflicting maximum damage on the enemy without, in principle, becoming decisively engaged. (JP 1-02)

deliberate attack—(DOD, NATO) A type of offensive action characterized by preplanned coordinated employment of firepower and maneuver to close with and destroy or capture the enemy. (JP 1-02)

deliberate targeting—The methodical identification, compilation, and analysis of potential fixed or semi-fixed targets followed by the decision of which potential targets will be attacked, when, and/or by what weapon and ordnance. It is practiced primarily during the planning phase of an operation, when planning for an attack, or when the tempo of combat is slow. (MCRP 5-12C)

destruction fire—(DOD) Fire delivered for the sole purpose of destroying material objects. (JP 1-02)

direct air support center—(DOD) The principal air control agency of the US Marine air command and control system responsible for the direction and control of air operations directly supporting the ground combat element. It processes and coordinates requests for immediate air support and coordinates air missions requiring integration with ground forces and other supporting arms. It normally collocates with the senior fire support coordination center within the ground combat element and is subordinate to the tactical air command center. (JP 1-02)

direct support—(DOD) A mission requiring a force to support another specific force and authorizing it to answer directly the supported force's request for assistance. (JP 1-02)

exploitation—(DOD, NATO) An offensive operation that usually follows a successful attack and is designed to disorganize the enemy in depth. (JP 1-02)

fathom—A unit of length equal to 6 feet used especially for measuring the depth of water. Used when planning desirable depths of water for fire support areas/fire support stations.

final protective fire—(DOD, NATO) An immediately available prearranged barrier of fire designed to impede enemy movement across defensive lines or areas. (JP 1-02)

fire plan—(DOD, NATO) A tactical plan for using the weapons of a unit or formation so that their fire will be coordinated. (JP 1-02) Fire plans are developed by supporting arm agencies and incorporated into the fire support plan.

firepower—(DOD, NATO) 1. The amount of fire which may be delivered by a position, unit, or weapon system. 2. Ability to deliver fire. (JP 1-02)

fire support—Fires that directly support land, maritime, amphibious, and special operations forces to engage enemy forces, combat formations, and facilities in pursuit of tactical and operational objectives. (JP 1-02)

fire support area—(DOD) An appropriate maneuver area assigned to fire support ships by the naval force commander from which they can deliver gunfire support to an amphibious operation. (JP 1-02) A fire support area is assigned to each fire support unit or, in certain cases, each individual fire support ship executing fire support missions. Fire support areas are assigned by CATF, in consideration of recommendations of the NGFO on the landing force staff. Fire support areas are located for minimum interference with any waterborne and airborne ship-to-shore movement. The size, shape, and location of the fire support area are dependent upon several factors, such as ship maneuvering room, hydrographic conditions (e.g., sand bars, reefs, shoals, shallow water), obstacles (including minefields), antiaircraft, and antisubmarine disposition; and the best position in respect to range, gun-target line, and observation for potential employment targets. Fire support areas are delineated on an overlay with a dot-dash line representing a boundary, annotated in degrees true north; and labeled with the letters FSA and a Roman numeral (e.g., FSA I). The boundary is a straight line to a recognizable point on the beach or a navigational aid to assist the ships in remaining within their respective FSAs.

fire support coordination—(DOD, NATO) The planning and executing of fire so that targets are adequately covered by a suitable weapon or group of weapons. (JP 1-02)

fire support coordination center—(DOD, NATO) A single location in which are centralized communications facilities and personnel incident to the coordination of all forms of fire support. (JP 1-02)

fire support coordinator—The officer in charge of the fire support coordination center. He is the direct representative of the landing force commander for the planning and coordination of all available fire support. (MCRP 5-12C)

fire support plan—A plan on how indirect fires and target acquisition will be used to support an operation. It should include a portion for each means of fire support involved. (MCRP 5-12A)

fire support station—(DOD) An exact location at sea within a fire support area from which a fire support ship delivers fire. (JP 1-02) Fire support stations are more restrictive than an FSA. Fire support stations are useful where maneuvering room is restricted, and usu-

ally afford increased accuracy, firing at shorter ranges, and optimum gun-target line. However, a disadvantage of the FSS is the loss of the mobility of the ship. Fire support stations are delineated on an overlay by the letters FSS and an Arabic numeral (e.g., FSS 1).

forward air controller—(DOD) An officer (aviator/pilot) member of the tactical air control party who, from a forward ground or airborne position, controls aircraft in close air support of ground troops. (JP 1-02)

forward air controller (airborne)—(DOD) A specifically trained and qualified aviation officer who exercises control from the air of aircraft engaged in close air support of ground troops. The forward air controller (airborne) is normally an airborne extension of the tactical air control party. (JP 1-02)

forward arming and refueling point—(DOD) A temporary facility, organized, equipped, and deployed by an aviation commander, and normally located in the main battle area closer to the area of operation than the aviation unit's combat service area, to provide fuel and ammunition necessary for the employment of aviation maneuver units in combat. The forward arming and refueling point permits combat aircraft to rapidly refuel and rearm simultaneously. (JP 1-02)

forward edge of the battle area—(DOD, NATO) The foremost limits of a series of areas in which ground combat units are deployed, excluding the areas in which the covering or screening forces are operating, designated to coordinate fire support, the positioning of forces, or the maneuver of units. (JP 1-02)

forward line of own troops—(DOD) A line which indicates the most forward positions of friendly forces in any kind of military operation at a specific time. The forward line of own troops normally identifies the forward location of covering and screening forces. (JP 1-02)

functional damage assessment—The estimate of the effect of military force to degrade/destroy the functional or operational capability of the target to perform its intended mission and on the level of success in achieving operational objectives established against the target. This assessment is based upon all-source information, and includes an estimation of the time required for recuperation or replacement of the target function. (Proposed by JP 3-60 for inclusion in JP 1-02.)

general support—(DOD, NATO) That support which is given to the supported force as a whole and not to any particular subdivision thereof. (JP 1-02)

ground alert—(DOD, NATO) That status in which aircraft on the ground/deck are fully serviced and armed, with combat crews in readiness to take off within a specified short period of time (usually 15 minutes) after receipt of a mission order. (JP 1-02) The readiness time may be at other intervals, and is usually specified in the operation order.

group of targets—(DOD, NATO) Two or more targets on which fire is desired simultaneously. A group of targets is designated by a letter/number combination or a nickname. (JP 1-02)

harassing fire—(DOD, NATO) Fire designed to disturb the rest of the enemy troops, to curtail movement and, by threat of losses, to lower morale. (JP 1-02)

hasty attack—(DOD, NATO) In land operations, an attack in which preparation time is traded for speed in order to exploit an opportunity. (JP 1-02)

helicopter direction center—(DOD, NATO) In amphibious operations, the primary direct control agency for the helicopter group/unit commander operating under the overall control of the tactical air control center. (JP 1-02)

high-payoff target—(DOD) A target whose loss to the enemy will significantly contribute to the success of the friendly course of action. High-payoff targets are those high-value targets, identified through wargaming, which must be acquired and successfully attacked for the success of the friendly commander's mission. Also called HPT. (JP 1-02)

high-payoff target list—A list identifying the high-payoff targets for a phase of the battle in the order of their priority. (MCRP 3-1.6.14)

high-value target—(DOD) A target the enemy commander requires for the successful completion of the mission. The loss of high-value targets would be expected to seriously degrade important enemy functions

throughout the friendly commander's area of interest. Also called HVT. (JP 1-02)

holding area—An area where attack helicopter aircrews await targets or mission. Holding areas should provide cover, concealment, and space for dispersion. The area(s) is positioned to enhance responsiveness.

immediate air support—(DOD, NATO) Air support to meet specific requests which arise during the course of a battle and which by their nature cannot be planned in advance. (JP 1-02)

initial point—(DOD) A well-defined point, easily distinguishable visually and/or electronically, used as a starting point for the bomb run to the target. (JP 1-02)

intelligence preparation of the battlespace—(DOD) An analytical methodology employed to reduce uncertainties concerning the enemy, environment, and terrain for all types of operations. Intelligence preparation of the battlespace builds an extensive data base for each potential area in which a unit may be required to operate. The data base is then analyzed in detail to determine the impact of the enemy, environment, and terrain on operations and presents it in graphic form. Intelligence preparation of the battlespace is a continuing process. Also called IPB. (JP 1-02). In Marine Corps usage, the systematic, continuous process of analyzing the threat and environment in a specific geographic area. (MCRP 5-12C)

interdiction fire—(NATO) Fire placed on an area or point to prevent the enemy from using the area or point. (JP 1-02)

joint intelligence center—(DOD) The intelligence center of the joint force headquarters. The joint intelligence center is responsible for providing and producing the intelligence required to support the joint force commander and staff, components, task forces and elements, and the national intelligence community. (JP 1-02)

killing zone—(DOD) An area in which a commander plans to force the enemy to concentrate so as to destroy him with conventional weapons or the tactical employment of nuclear weapons. (JP 1-02)

linkup—A meeting of friendly ground forces (such as when an advancing force reaches an objective area previously seized by an airborne or air assault force, when an encircled element breaks out to rejoin friendly forces, or when converging maneuver forces meet). (MCRP 5-12A)

list of targets—(DOD) A tabulation of confirmed or suspect targets maintained by any echelon for informational and fire support planning purposes. (JP 1-02)

MAGTF rear area—That area extending rearward from the rear boundary of the ground combat element to the MAGTF rear boundary. (FMFM 2-6)

main effort—The designated subordinate unit whose mission at a given point in time is most critical to overall mission success. It is usually weighted with the preponderance of combat power and is directed against a center of gravity through a critical vulnerability. (MCRP 5-12C)

maneuver—(DOD, NATO) Employment of forces on the battlefield through movement in combination with fire, or fire potential, to achieve a position of advantage in respect to the enemy in order to accomplish the mission. (JP 1-02)

Marine Corps Planning Process—A six-step methodology which helps organize the thought processes of the commander and staff throughout the planning and execution of military operations. It focuses on the threat and is based on the Marine Corps philosophy of maneuver warfare. It capitalizes on the principle of unity of command and supports the establishment and maintenance of tempo. The six steps consist of mission analysis, course of action development, course of action analysis, comparison/decision, orders development, and transition. Also called MCPP. NOTE: Tenets of the MCPP include top down planning, single battle concept, and integrated planning. (MCRP 5-12C)

mark—(DOD) In artillery and naval gunfire support, to call for fire on a specified location in order to orient the observer/spotter or to indicate targets. (excerpt from JP 1-02)

marking fire—(DOD, NATO) Fire placed on a target for the purpose of identification. (JP 1-02)

massed fire—(DOD). The fire of the batteries of two or more ships directed against a single target. 2. Fire from a number of weapons directed at a single point or small area. (JP 1-02)

maximum effective range—(DOD, NATO) The maximum distance at which a weapon may be expected to be accurate and achieve the desired result. (JP 1-02)

maximum ordinate—(DOD, NATO) In artillery and naval gunfire support, the height of the highest point in the trajectory of a projectile above the horizontal plane passing through its origin. (JP 1-02)

maximum range—(DOD, NATO) The greatest distance a weapon can fire without consideration of dispersion. (JP 1-02)

mean point of impact—(DOD, NATO) The point whose coordinates are the arithmetic means of the coordinates of the separate points of impact/burst of a finite number of projectiles fired or released at the same aiming point under a given set of conditions. (JP 1-02)

mean sea level—(DOD) The average height of the surface of the sea for all stages of the tide, used as a reference for elevations. (JP 1-02)

minimum range—(DOD) 1. Least range setting of a gun at which the projectile will clear an obstacle or friendly troops between the gun and the target. 2. Shortest distance to which a gun can fire from a given position. (JP 1-02)

mission precedence—The determination of the relative order of attacking multiple targets confronting the unit simultaneously. The sequence for attack may be prearranged, and is based on the commander's guidance, commander's intent, and the tactical situation.

MK-86—A gun fire control system employed on naval ships. MK-86-equipped ships can store up to eight prearranged target locations, and can conduct simultaneous fire missions.

movement to contact—An offensive operation designed to gain or reestablish contact with the enemy. (OH 6-1)

named area of interest—A point or area along a particular avenue of approach through which enemy activity is expected to occur. Activity or lack of activity within an NAI will help to confirm or deny a particular enemy course of action. Also called NAI. (MCRP 5-12C)

neutralization fire—(DOD) Fire which is delivered to render the target ineffective or unusable. (NATO) Fire which is delivered to hamper and interrupt movement and/or the firing of weapons. (JP 1-02)

obscuration fire—Fire delivered to suppress the enemy by obscuring his view of the battlefield.

on-call—(DOD, NATO) A term used to signify that a prearranged concentration, air strike, or final protective fire may be called for. (JP 1-02)

on-call target—(DOD, NATO) In artillery and naval gunfire support, a planned target other than a scheduled target on which fire is delivered when requested. (JP 1-02)

passage of lines—(DOD, NATO) An operation in which a force moves forward or rearward through another force's combat positions with the intention of moving into or out of contact with the enemy. (JP 1-02)

planned targets—Targets that are known to exist in an operational area and which effects are scheduled in advance or are on-call. Examples range from targets on joint target lists (JTLs) in applicable campaign plans, to targets detected in sufficient time to list in the air tasking order (ATO), mission-type orders, or fire support plans. Planned targets have two subcategories: scheduled or on-call. (Proposed by JP 3-60 for inclusion in JP 1-02.)

prearranged fire—(DOD, NATO) Fire that is formally planned and executed against targets or target areas of known location. Such fire is usually planned well in advance and is executed at a predetermined time or during a predetermined period of time. (JP 1-02)

preliminary weaponeering—A preliminary analysis of the target to determine what, if any, weapons will be effective against the target and the degree of damage it is possible to achieve with various types and quantities of ammunition.

preparation fire—(DOD, NATO) Fire delivered on a target preparatory to an assault. (JP 1-02)

preplanned air support—(DOD, NATO) Air support in accordance with a program, planned in advance of operations. (JP 1-02) Preplanned air support is either scheduled or on-call.

preplanned on-call air support mission—Air missions in which aircraft are preloaded for a particular target and placed in an appropriate ground/airborne alert readiness condition. In requesting on-call missions, the supported unit specifies the period the support is required. Detailed mission planning and briefing is normally not possible before launch. (FMFM 5-41)

preplanned scheduled air support mission—Air missions which are executed at a specific time. Aircrews are assigned a time on target. Scheduled missions provide effective coordination and economical use of aircraft and ordnance. (FMFM 5-41)

priority of fires—The organization and employment of fire support means according to the importance of the supported unit's missions. (MCRP 5-12A)

priority target—A target on which the delivery of fires takes precedence over all the fires for the designated firing unit or element. The firing unit or element will prepare, to the extent possible, for the engagement of such targets. A firing unit or element may be assigned only one priority target. The designation may be based on either time or importance. (MCRP 5-12A)

program of targets—A number of planned targets of a similar nature. A program of targets identified by a code name may be initiated on-call, at a specified time, or when a particular event occurs. Targets are fired in a predetermined sequence. (MCRP 5-12A)

pursuit—(DOD, NATO) An offensive operation designed to catch or cut off a hostile force attempting to escape, with the aim of destroying it. (JP 1-02)

radar beacon—(DOD) A receiver-transmitter combination which sends out a coded signal when triggered by the proper type of pulse, enabling determination of range and bearing information by the interrogating station or aircraft. (JP 1-02)

rate of fire—(DOD, NATO) The number of rounds fired per weapon per minute. (JP 1-02)

reactive target—The method used for targeting targets of opportunity. It is used when time and situation do not allow for targeting; i.e., during deliberate targeting, during an attack, when defending against an attack, or upon discovery of the location of a target such as a radio jammer, tank, or antiaircraft weapon. (MCRP 5-12C)

rear area operations center—A command and control facility that serves as an area/subarea commander's planning, coordinating, monitoring, advising, and directing agency for area security operations. (JP 1-02)

rear area security—The measures taken before, during, and/or after an enemy airborne attack, sabotage action, infiltration, guerrilla action, and/or initiation of psychological or propaganda warfare to minimize the effects thereof. (MCRP 5-12 C)

rear operations—Military actions conducted to support and permit force sustainment and to provide security for such actions (MCRP 5-12C).

reinforcing—(DOD, NATO) In artillery usage, tactical mission in which one artillery unit augments the fire of another artillery unit. (JP 1-02)

relief in place—(DOD, NATO) An operation in which, by direction of higher authority, all or part of a unit is replaced in an area by the incoming unit. The responsibilities of the replaced elements for the mission and the assigned zone of operations are transferred to the incoming unit. The incoming unit continues the operation as ordered. (JP 1-02)

restraint(s)—Something which is prohibited that limits freedom of action. See also constraint(s). (MCRP 5-12C)

retirement—(DOD, NATO) An operation in which a force out of contact moves away from the enemy. (JP 1-02)

retrograde movement—(DOD) Any movement of a command to the rear, or away from the enemy. It may be forced by the enemy or may be made voluntarily. Such movements may be classified as withdrawal, retirement, or delaying action. (JP 1-02)

scheduled fire—(DOD, NATO) A type of prearranged fire executed at a predetermined time. (JP 1-02)

scheduled targets—Planned targets on which fire is to be delivered at a specific time. (Proposed by JP 3-60 for inclusion in JP 1-02.)

screening smoke—Smoke used to conceal friendly forces, positions, and activities from enemy ground or air observation. Screening smoke is normally placed between friendly and enemy forces. (FMFM 6-8)

security area—Area that begins at the forward area of the battlefield and extends as far to the front and flanks as security forces are deployed. Forces in the security area furnish information on the enemy and delay, deceive, and disrupt the enemy and conduct counter-reconnaissance. (MCRP 5-12A)

series of targets—(NATO) In artillery and naval gunfire support, a number of targets and/or group(s) of targets planned to support a maneuver phase. A series of targets may be indicated by a nickname. (JP 1-02)

shore fire control party—(DOD) A specially trained unit for control of naval gunfire in support of troops ashore. It consists of a spotting team to adjust fire and a naval gunfire liaison team to perform liaison functions for the supported battalion commander. (JP 1-02)

summit—(DOD) The highest altitude above mean sea level that a projectile reaches in its flight from the gun to the target; the algebraic sum of the maximum ordinate and the altitude of the gun. (JP 1-02)

supporting arms—(DOD) Air, sea, and land weapons of all types employed to support ground units. (JP 1-02)

supporting arms coordination center—(DOD) A single location on board an amphibious command ship in which all communication facilities incident to the coordination of fire support of the artillery, air, and naval gunfire are centralized. This is the naval counterpart to the fire support coordination center utilized by the landing force. (JP 1-02)

supporting fire—(DOD, NATO) Fire delivered by supporting units to assist or protect a unit in combat. (JP 1-02)

suppression of enemy air defenses—(DOD) That activity which neutralizes, destroys or temporarily degrades surface-based enemy air defenses by destructive and/or disruptive means. (JP 1-02)

suppressive fire—(DOD) Fires on or about a weapons system to degrade its performance below the level needed to fulfill its mission objectives, during the conduct of the fire mission. (JP 1-02)

sustained rate of fire—(DOD, NATO) Actual rate of fire that a weapon can continue to deliver for an indefinite length of time without seriously overheating. (JP 1-02)

tactical air command center—(DOD) The principal US Marine Corps air command and control agency from which air operations and air defense warning functions are directed. It is the senior agency of the US Marine air command and control system which serves as the operational command post of the aviation combat element commander. It provides the facility from which the aviation combat element commander and his battle staff plan, supervise, coordinate, and execute all current and future air operations in support of the Marine air-ground task force. The tactical air command center can provide integration, coordination, and direction of joint and combined air operations. (JP 1-02)

tactical air control center—(DOD) The principal air operations installation (ship-based) from which all aircraft and air warning functions of tactical air operations are controlled. Also called Navy TACC. (JP 1-02)

tactical air control party—(DOD, NATO) A subordinate operational component of a tactical air control system designed to provide air liaison to land forces and for the control of aircraft. (JP 1-02)

tactical air direction center—(DOD) An air operations installation under the overall control of the tactical air control center (afloat)/tactical air command center, from which aircraft and air warning service functions of tactical air operations in an area of responsibility are directed. (JP 1-02)

tactical fire direction—The control of one or more units in the selection of targets to attack, designation of the unit or units to fire, selection of the method of attack, and selection of the most suitable ammunition for the mission. (MCWP 3-16.1)

tactical mission—Defines the fire support responsibility of an artillery, naval gunfire, or mortar unit to a supported unit.

target—A geographical area, complex, or installation planned for capture or destruction by military forces. (JP 1-02)

target acquisition—(DOD, NATO) The detection, identification, and location of a target in sufficient detail to permit the effective employment of weapons. (JP 1-02)

target analysis—(DOD, NATO) An examination of potential targets to determine military importance, priority of attack, and weapons required to obtain a desired level of damage or casualties. (JP 1-02)

targeted area of interest—The geographical area or point along a mobility corridor where successful interdiction will cause the enemy to either abandon a particular course of action or require him to use specialized engineer support to continue, where he can be acquired and engaged by friendly forces. Not all TAIs will form part of the friendly course of action; only TAIs associated with high-payoff targets are of interest to the staff. These are identified during staff planning and wargaming. TAIs differ from engagement areas in degree. Engagement areas plan for the use of all available weapons. TAIs might be engaged by a single weapon. (MCRP 5-12A)

target bulletin—An information message, used by the commander responsible for maintaining the target list, to keep interested commanders informed of all changes to the list. (FMFM 1-7)

target information—Unevaluated data of every description concerning targets that, when processed, may produce target intelligence. (FM 6-121)

target intelligence—(DOD, NATO) Intelligence which portrays and locates the components of a target or target complex and indicates its vulnerability and relative importance. (JP 1-02)

target list—(DOD) The listing of targets maintained and promulgated by the senior echelon of command; it contains those targets that are to be engaged by supporting arms, as distinguished from a "list of targets" that may be maintained by any echelon as confirmed, suspected, or possible targets for informational and planning purposes. (JP 1-02)

target number—(NATO) The reference number given to the target by the fire control unit. (JP 1-02)

target overlay—(DOD, NATO) A transparent sheet which, when superimposed on a particular chart, map, drawing, tracing or other representation, depicts target locations and designations. The target overlay may also show boundaries between maneuver elements, objectives, and friendly forward dispositions. (JP 1-02)

target precedence list—The commander's list of types of mobile potential targets arranged in the order in which they are to be attacked.

target reference point—An easily recognizable point on the ground (either natural or manmade) used for identifying enemy targets or controlling direct fires. Target reference points are usually designated by company commanders or platoon leaders for company teams, platoons, sections, or individual weapons. They can also designate the center of an area where the commander plans to distribute or converge the fires of all his weapons rapidly. Target reference points are designated by using the standard target symbol, a target number, and a target reference point letter. Essential target reference points may be included in lists of targets during fire planning.

target value analysis—A method for providing a systematic determination of which targets out of the entire target array should be attacked for the greatest tactical benefit.

targeting—(DOD) The process to detect, select, and prioritize targets, match the appropriate action, and assess the resulting effects based on the commander's objective, guidance, and intent. (Proposed by JP 3-60 for inclusion in JP 1-02.)

time on target—(DOD) 1. Time at which aircraft are scheduled to attack/photograph the target. 2. The actual time at which aircraft attack/photograph the target. 3. The time at which a nuclear detonation is planned at a specified desired ground zero. (NATO) In other than air operations, the time of the first weapons effect on the target or target groups.

time-sensitive targets—Those targets requiring immediate response because they pose (or will soon pose) a clear and present danger to friendly forces or are highly lucrative, fleeting targets of opportunity. (JP 1-02)

time to target—(DOD) The number of minutes and seconds to elapse before aircraft ordnance impacts on target. (JP 1-02)

trigger point—An identifiable point on the ground used to time the delivery of fire with a moving target. A firing unit is given a command to fire as the target passes over or near the trigger point. The trigger point is selected in consideration of reaction time of the firing unit, time of flight of the projectile, and the rate of march of the enemy.

Universal Time—A measure of time that conforms within a close approximation, to the mean diurnal rotation of the Earth and serves as the basis of civil timekeeping. Universal Time (UT1) is determined from observations of the stars, radio sources, and also from ranging observations of the moon and artificial Earth satellites. The scale determined directly from such observations is designated Universal Time Observed (UTO); it is slightly dependent on the place of observation. When UTO is corrected for the shift in longitude of the observing station caused by polar motion, the time scale UT1 is obtained. When an accuracy better than one second is not required, Universal Time can be used to mean Coordinated Universal Time (UTC). Also called ZULU time. Formerly called Greenwich Mean Time. (JP 1-02)

visibility diagram—A sketch that is drawn to scale by the observer of the area of observation. It shows those portions of the terrain which cannot be observed from a given observation post. The visibility diagram is dispatched to infantry and artillery S-2 officers for evaluation of target area coverage so gaps can be covered. (FMFM 6-8)

weapons free—(DOD, NATO) In air defense, a weapon control order imposing a status whereby weapons systems may be fired at any target not positively recognized as friendly. (JP 1-02)

weapons hold—(DOD, NATO) In air defense, a weapon control order imposing a status whereby weapons systems may only be fired in self-defense or in response to a formal order. (JP 1-02)

weapons tight—(DOD, NATO) In air defense, a weapon control order imposing a status whereby weapons systems may be fired only at targets recognized as hostile. (JP 1-02)

withdrawal operation—(DOD, NATO) A planned operation in which a force in contact disengages from an enemy force. (JP 1-02)

zone of action—(DOD, NATO) A tactical subdivision of a larger area, the responsibility for which is assigned to a tactical unit; generally applied to offensive action. (JP 1-02)

zone of fire—(DOD) An area into which a designated ground unit or fire support ship delivers, or is prepared to deliver, fire support. Fire may or may not be observed. (JP 1-02).

Appendix R. References

Joint Publications (JPs)

1-02	DOD Dictionary of Military and Associated Terms
3-02	Joint Doctrine for Amphibious Operations
3-09	Doctrine for Joint Fire Support
3-09.1	Joint Tactics, Techniques, and Procedures for Laser Designation Operations
3-09.3	TTP for Close Air Support (CAS)

Marine Corps Doctrinal Publication (MCDP)

1-0	Marine Corps Operations

Marine Corps Warfighting Publications (MCWPs)

2-1	Intelligence Operations
2-12	MAGTF Intelligence Production and Analysis
3-1	Ground Combat Operations
3-15.1	Machine Guns and Machine Gun Gunnery
3-15.2	Tactical Employment of Mortars
3-16.4	Field Artillery Manual Cannon Gunnery
3-16.6	Supporting Arms Observer, Spotter, and Controller
3-2	Aviation Operations
3-22.2	Suppression of Enemy Air Defenses
3-23	Offensive Air Support
3-23.1	Close Air Support
3-24	Assault Support
3-25	Control of Aircraft and Missiles
3-25.5	Direct Air Support Handbook
3-31.1	Supporting Arms in Amphibious Operations (NWP 3-09.11M (Rev.C))
3-35.3	Military Operations on Urbanized Terrain (MOUT)
3-37.1	Chemical Operations Principles and Fundamentals
3-41.1	MAGTF Rear Area Operations
5-1	Marine Corps Planning Process
6-2	MAGTF Command and Control

Marine Corps Reference Publications (MCRPs)

2-12A	Intelligence Preparation of the Battlefield (IPB) (FM 34-130)
3-16A	Tactics, Techniques, and Procedures for the Targeting Process
3-16B	The Joint Targeting Process and Procedures for Targeting Time-Critical Targets
3-16C	Fire Support for Combined Arms Commander
3-16.1	Field Artillery Survey
3-16.1C	Tactics, Techniques and Procedures for Multiple Launch Rocket System (MLRS) Operations
3-23A	Multiservice Procedures for Joint Air Attack Team Operations
5-12A	Operational Terms and Graphics

Fleet Marine Force Manual (FMFMs)

1-7	Supporting Arms in Amphibious Operations
6-9	Marine Artillery Support
6-18-1	MCFSS Techniques and Procedures

Fleet Marine Force Reference Publication (FMFRP)

5-71	MAGTF Aviation Planning

Marine Corps Order (MCO)

3501.26	Artillery Unit Training and Readiness Manual

Allied Tactical Publication (ATP)

37	Supporting Arms in Amphibious Operations

U. S. Army Field Manuals (FMs)

6-20-30	Tactics, Techniques, and Procedures for Fire Support for Corps and Division Operations
6-20-40	Tactics, Techniques, and Procedures for Fire Support for Brigade Operations
34-1	Intelligence and Electronic Warfare Operations
90-3	Desert Operations
90-5	Jungle Operations
100-5	Operations

Joint Munitions Effectiveness Manuals (JMEMs)

JMEMs are in the FMFM 4-7 series and are classified. FSCs should have ready access to the JMEMs for the weapons used.

Standardization Agreements (STANAGs)

1181	Supporting Arms in Amphibious Operations (ATP-37)
2103	Reporting Nuclear Detonations, Biological and Chemical Attacks, and Predicting and Warning of Associated Hazards and Hazard Areas ATP 45(A)
2104	Friendly Nuclear Strike Warning
2111	Target Analysis-Nuclear Weapons
3736	Air Interdiction and Close Air Support - ATP-27(C)
QSTAG 221	Target Numbering System

Allied Publication

AArty P1	Artillery Procedures

Made in the USA
Middletown, DE
30 August 2023

37671891R00150